FROMMER'S

SOUTHERN ATLANTIC STATES

SUSAN POOLE

1990–1991

Published by Prentice Hall Trade Division
A Division of Simon & Schuster Inc.
15 Columbus Circle
New York, NY 10023

ISBN 0-13-332644-6
ISSN 1044-2316

Manufactured in the United States of America

CONTENTS

MAPS

To my mother and father,
who gave me my southern heritage.

A DISCLAIMER

Although every effort was made to ensure the accuracy of the prices and travel information appearing in this book, it should be kept in mind that prices do fluctuate in the course of time, and that information does change under the impact of the varied and volatile factors that affect the travel industry. Thus, in the lifetime of this edition —particularly in its second year (1991)—the wise traveler will add 15% to 20% to the prices quoted throughout these pages.

Readers should also note that the establishments described under Readers' Selections or Suggestions have not in many cases been inspected by the author, and that the opinions expressed there are those of the individual reader(s) only. They do not in any way represent the opinions of the publisher or author of this guide.

INTRODUCING THE SOUTHERN ATLANTIC STATES

Ask almost anybody about to set out on a visit south of the Mason-Dixon Line what they expect to find and you'll get an amazingly muddled reply. Margaret Mitchell's *Gone with the Wind* antebellum South; William Faulkner's Mississippi Deep South; Tennessee Williams's aging New Orleans southern belles or would-be belles; Atlanta's shiny, cosmopolitan image of the "new South"; tales of notorious speedtraps for out-of-state cars—all come together in a confused preconception of the region.

My own expectations were somewhat different. I was born and raised in the Southern Atlantic region, and my travels to research this book have been somewhat in the nature of a return pilgrimage. Having lived "up North" for some years now, I headed for the southern states that line this country's Atlantic coast with a little apprehension and the awareness that I would be seeing them from a new perspective. Periodic trips back home to visit relatives were different. This time I would be looking at *my* part of the country with the eyes of an "outsider." I would try to see it from the viewpoint of someone who hadn't grown up with tales of colonial heroes who lived and fought and argued over constitutional phrases right in the neighborhood—to see with fresh vision the sandy beaches and unspoiled, almost wild, Outer Banks of North Carolina, the softer beauty of South Carolina's Hilton Head, and Georgia's Golden Isles. The Blue Ridge Mountains and Atlanta's intriguing mix of old and new must be seen as if for the first time. It would be my task to wander through the orderly, historic streets of Alexandria, Williamsburg, Savannah, and Charleston to find their unique charm all over again.

To my delight, I found that being a "tourist" in my home region is fun—the very things that made growing up there rather special have been those that added zest and flavor to this odyssey. Expectations? They hadn't been high enough. Preconceptions? They were confirmed and refuted in varying degrees as I went from place to place, meeting people and places that hadn't changed in years and others that were completely different from my memories. As a visitor, I came away with the firm conviction that the Southern Atlantic region is one of the most interesting and enjoyable sections of this country for the tourist. And above all, I came back with a renewed appreciation for its people.

Meeting people is, in my book, one of the primary joys of travel. Certainly that is true in these Southern Atlantic states. There is an unfailing courtesy and native friendliness that marks everyone you meet. I was not, of course, totally unprepared for that, having been taught from childhood that rudeness is an unforgivable sin (my grandmother once told me that a lady could tell anyone to "go to hell" if she did it politely!). But courtesy to the tourist seems to extend far beyond mere politeness to a real concern for comfort and convenience. Hospitality, that much-advertised attribute of Southerners, extends to today's paying guests as much as it ever did to house guests. Pride, another much-portrayed southern characteristic, extends to the South as a whole, one's native state, one's own part of that state, and especially to a hometown, all of which Southerners are eager to share with visitors. "I'll be proud to show you around" comes naturally to Southerners. They are equally proud of history, of which there is plenty, and progress, evident everywhere you turn. They'll point with regional pride to a relic of the Civil War (which most now consider valiantly fought and fortunately lost), then direct your attention to a new industry or cultural center that makes it plain the South has a future as well as a past.

The Old South? The New South? They're both here in these four states. Whatever your preconceptions, come with an open mind, come prepared to relax and enjoy, and come secure in the knowledge that nowhere will you be more welcomed or go away more satisfied.

1. About this Book

These four Southern Atlantic states—Virginia, North and South Carolina, and Georgia—have a total area of some 181,369 square miles. That's a lot of ground to cover, and if you head south with no definite idea of what you want most to see and do, where to stay and eat, you can waste time, money, and temper getting around. It is to help in making your plans before you start out that this book has been written.

The hotels, restaurants, sightseeing attractions, and nightspots you'll read about have been carefully checked out, not within any specified maximum or minimum in price, but with the notion that you should get the *most* for your money whether you go luxury, moderate, or budget class. Because, however, most of today's travelers are in the medium-income group, you will find the emphasis throughout the book on prices that are neither in the highest nor lowest range. My own experience has taught me that there are times when price has little to do with quality: a "luxury" restaurant may serve mediocre, or even poor food, and a budget establishment can be so loaded with charm that it would be a good buy at *any* price. The evaluations in this book were made with an eye on cost (of course an expensive hotel or restaurant may, indeed, give you your money's worth but be well above the reach of most of us), but primarily with an eye on quality, and if you find a rave about an inexpensive place to stay or eat, it's because I found it exceptional as well as inexpensive. My judgments are, admittedly, entirely personal, and if the charm of a small hotel or restaurant means less to you than the sometimes colorless conveniences of large chains, the choice is yours to make (my choice is for the former). I hope that with these necessarily brief descriptions of what is available all along the way you'll be able to make that choice knowledgeably.

A WORD ABOUT PRICES QUOTED

Inflation, even with its occasional fluctuations, has become a part of the American scene. Thus the prices shown here are *only those in effect at the time of writing.* Nowhere did I run into an establishment that promised to keep its prices stabilized or to give readers of this book any sort of price guarantee. Even if there is a variation in price by the time you reach a particular destination, however, the price *range* is likely to be the same—a medium-range hotel today will probably still be medium-priced for the area even with a hike in charges, although "medium" may be somewhat higher than at the time of this writing. In this sense, this is a *guide,* as the name says, to finding low-, medium-, and top-priced facilities.

HOSTELS

American Youth Hostels offers, for a small membership fee, hostel accommodations in many Southern Atlantic states. For membership information and a directory, write American Youth Hostels, Dept. 860, Box 37613, Washington, D.C. 20013 (tel. 202/783-6161).

HOTELS IN THE SOUTHERN ATLANTIC STATES

Most of the medium-priced hotel and motel chains have branches in the states written about in this book. Some of the luxury chains, such as Hilton and Hyatt, are also represented in larger cities. In *all* of these, you will find air conditioning, color TV, and two double beds (unless noted otherwise in a description). Holiday Inns, Howard Johnson's, and other like chains tend to be pretty standard, and if a particular member is outstanding or differs in any respect, I've noted that for you. The higher-priced, luxury hotels will have additional features in rooms, such as separate dressing rooms, extra washbasins, etc.

The prices quoted throughout this book are for double-occupancy *rooms,* not per person. A money-saving technique when more than two people travel together is room-sharing. Instead of paying for two double rooms, three or more people may rent one double room and pay a small extra fee for each additional *person,* which usually runs about $15 per night, much less than the cost of an extra room. If as many as five or six share a room, which will normally have two double beds, most motels will install rollaway cots for a small extra charge. Families, of course, often get a real price break when motels permit children under a certain age to occupy the same room as their parents at no additional charge. The age limit varies from 6 all the way up to 18, and unless you really can't stand having the kids underfoot at night, it will pay to look for these "family plan" establishments.

One further note about hotel accommodations: regardless of when you plan to travel—even if *you* consider it "off-season"—it's foolhardy to go without reservations. If your itinerary is not set and you cannot book for the entire trip before leaving home, it pays to call ahead just as soon as you know your next stopping point. Americans are on the road in increasing numbers and there is *always* the possibility of being stranded without a room. Many motel chains have toll-free telephone numbers and some will teletype ahead for you if you'll be staying in another chain member in the next city.

Two Dependable Budget Motel Chains

The Marriott Hotel chain has long been a leader in upmarket, luxury accommodations, and, in 1987, they tapped into the budget-priced market with a chain of economy motels named **Fairfield Inn by Marriott.** The chain will have grown to more than 100 inns by the early 1990s. Already, the inns have been selected as the "best economy chain" by professional travel planners polled by *Business Travel News.*

Architecture is the same at all locations, a three-story building with outdoor pool. The attractively furnished guest rooms provide either a king-size bed or two doubles, upholstered chair with ottoman, a well-lit work desk, separate vanity area adjacent to the bathroom, alarm clock, individual temperature control, and a card-key security system. No-smoking rooms and those with facilities for the handicapped are available, and local telephone calls are free. Other amenities include complimentary morning coffee and tea in the lobby, a meeting room to accommodate up to 10, and a checkout computerized "scorecard" system that lets you rate both inn features and staff performance.

Rates in this first-class chain run between $30 and $40 single occupancy; children under 18 stay free in the same room with an adult, and there's a senior citizen discount. A money-saving feature of the rate structure is the policy of giving a free night's stay at any Fairfield Inn when you have accumulated 12 paid nights (they do not have to be consecutive or at the same inn), and there's no time limit within which to have stayed at the inns for 12 nights.

If you sign up for their INNsiders Club (no fee), your spouse stays free; you'll have a complimentary morning newspaper; there's a reservation guarantee that pays your bill at comparable accommodations, plus a $100 penalty if they fail to hold your room; and you'll have personal check-cashing privileges and express check in.

Fairfield Inns are located in all four Southern Atlantic states, with more on the drawing board. You'll find them listed under specific destinations in the pages ahead, and for a full directory or reservations, call 800/228-2800. Highly recommended.

For travelers with families, as well as those who prefer to spend their hard-earned dollars for things other than a place to sleep, the dependable economy/limited-service **Motel 6** chain maintains unusually high standards despite a price range of $18 to $30 (children under 18 stay free in same room with parents). The more than 500 motels in some 41 states have swimming pools, and guests enjoy free color TV with two free in-room feature films each day, and free local phone calls. Rooms are an adequate size and comfortably, though not luxuriously, furnished—the motto here is, "Don't pay for what you don't choose to use," a philosophy that has great appeal to those of us who must keep a close watch on the budget. For a free copy of the current Motel 6 nationwide directory, write Motel 6, Dept. D., 14651 Dallas Parkway, Dallas, TX, or pick one up at any Motel 6.

Bed and Breakfast

Even though bed-and-breakfast accommodations are becoming more and more popular across the country, it is sometimes difficult to know just how to go about finding one at your destination. There are, of course, several guidebooks now in bookshops, but not all are appropriate for all regions of the country. You can eliminate a lot of bookshop browsing by picking up a copy of *The South: Country Inns, Lodges and Historic Hotels,* by Anthony Hitchcock and Jean Lindgren (published by Burt Franklin and Co., Inc.). It covers some 11 states, with illustrations, photos, and maps for each inn or guesthouse described.

Also try *Frommer's Bed & Breakfast North America,* by Hal Gieseking (published by Prentice Hall Travel, $11.95), which covers all 50 states and several Canadian provinces.

Two Dependable Luxury Chains

Actually, this heading is a bit misleading for the elegant **Guest Quarters Hotels.** Luxury, they certainly are, yet prices are in many instances on a par with or lower than luxury hotels that offer only a room. At each Guest Quarters location, what you'll get for those prices is: a designer-furnished living room with dining area, completely equipped kitchen, one or two bedrooms, spacious closets and bath, and all the services of a fine hotel. All those in the areas covered by this book have outdoor swimming pools, and each has a guest library, a notary public, and secretarial services for business travelers. Those completely equipped kitchens include (complimentary) coffee and tea for your first day, and there's a grocery-shopping service if you decide to make full use of the facilities. Not only is this an ideal way for families to take a break from the constant eat-out routine, but for executives, it offers an opportunity to entertain important clients (catering can be arranged through the excellent restaurants at each hotel). Extras that are available include 24-hour full-menu suite service at many locations, membership privileges at sports clubs, courtesy transportation to airports or inter-city destinations, a self-service guest laundry, and babysitting services. In the Southeast, you'll find Guest Quarters in Alexandria, Virginia; Greensboro and Charlotte, North Carolina; and Atlanta, Georgia. Rates range from $95 for a one-bedroom suite to $180 for two bedrooms (rates vary from location to location, with some two-bedrooms as low as $110). I'll list addresses and rates for those along the way, but for a complete listing of Guest Quarters in other locations, write: Guest Quarters, 30 Rowes Wharf, Boston, MA 02211 (tel. 617/330-1440).

Residence Inns by Marriott also offer all-suite hotels, with penthouse and studio suites in town-house clusters set in landscaped grounds that include swimming pool with heated whirlpool spa and a fitness court for basketball, volleyball, etc. The feeling of a residential neighborhood is enhanced by the complimentary hospitality hour held weekday evenings and a weekly manager's bar-becue. All suites have exceptionally spacious floor plans, and many have a wood-burning fireplace. All feature nicely appointed living areas and fully equipped kitchens. Penthouse suites are on two levels, with two bedrooms, two full baths, and even two TVs. There's a complimentary breakfast buffet daily, as well as a free grocery-shopping service.

A unique feature of the Residence Inns is the rate scale, which is geared to length of stay—daily charges decrease for stays of more than 6 nights, and even more drastically for stays of more than 29 nights. Even if your stay is a short one, however, you'll find rates in the moderate range and very good value for the money, which is what this book is all about. Specific locations are listed in all four states, and you can expect to pay anywhere from $72 to $115 for studio suites, $91 to $140 for penthouse suites. For a directory, call 800/331-3131, or contact Residence Inn by Marriott, Mariott Drive, Washington, DC 20058.

A WORD ABOUT NIGHTLIFE

Nightlife in the Southern Atlantic states, except for larger cities like Atlan-ta, tends to be concentrated in hotel lounges or to center around home enter-taining. Where there are outstanding nightspots, you'll find them listed; otherwise, a friendly conversation or two with people who live in the locality will point you to the best current after-dark action.

. . . AND SHOPPING

Not being an avid shopper myself, I tend to overlook what may well be one of your primary interests. In the larger cities, I'll list major shopping centers for you, but all along the way, keep your eyes open for small, local shops—there are outstanding bargains to be found in small towns, where a little window-shopping during a lunch break may turn up a treasure. Look especially for lo-cally made crafts, which will let you take a little of the regional charm home in your suitcase. In areas where such craft shops have been long established, I will tell you about them, but because they are sometimes transitory in nature and might have moved on while this book is still in print, a great many true artisans are no doubt omitted from these pages.

AN INVITATION TO READERS

Like all Frommer Guides, *Frommer's Southern Atlantic States* is my best ef-fort to clue you in on how to get the most for your money. If, as a dollarwise traveler, you find I've missed an establishment that you find to be a particularly good value (or even one that's just fun and other readers ought to know about), I'd like to hear about it, and I invite you to write so it may be included in the next edition of this book. If, on the other hand, by the time you get to a particu-lar destination you find a restaurant or hotel is *not* up to my description (chefs *do* change and hotels *do* deteriorate!), please write me about that, as well—the last thing I want in this book is misleading or untimely information. Any additional travel tips you may come up with (off days to visit attractions when they're less crowded, etc.) will also be appreciated. And, oh yes, if you find this guide to be especially helpful, do drop me a line about *that*. Send whatever you have to say to me at Prentice Hall Travel, 15 Columbus Circle, New York, NY 10023.

2. Frommer's Dollarwise® Travel Club—How to Save Money on All Your Travels

In this book we'll be looking at how to get your money's worth in the Southern Atlantic region, but there is a "device" for saving money and determining value on *all* your trips. It's the popular, international Frommer's Dollarwise Travel Club, now in its 29th successful year of operation. The club was formed at the urging of numerous readers of the $-A-Day and Frommer Guides, who felt that such an organization could provide continuing travel information and a sense of community to value-minded travelers in all parts of the world. And so it does!

In keeping with the budget concept, the annual membership fee is low and is immediately exceeded by the value of your benefits. Upon receipt of $18 (U.S. residents), or $20 U.S. by check drawn on a U.S. bank or via international-postal money order in U.S. funds (Canadian, Mexican, and other foreign residents) to cover one year's membership, we will send all new members the following items.

(1) Any two of the following books

Please designate in your letter which two you wish to receive:

Frommer $-A-Day® Guides
Europe on $40 a Day
Australia on $30 a Day
Eastern Europe on $25 a Day
England on $50 a Day
Greece on $30 a Day
Hawaii on $60 a Day
India on $25 a Day
Ireland on $35 a Day
Israel on $40 a Day
Mexico (plus Belize and Guatemala) on $30 a Day
New York on $50 a Day
New Zealand on $40 a Day
Scandinavia on $60 a Day
Scotland and Wales on $40 a Day
South America on $35 a Day
Spain and Morocco (plus the Canary Is.) on $40 a Day
Turkey on $30 a Day
Washington, D.C. & Historic Virginia on $40 a Day

($-A-Day Guides document hundreds of budget accommodations and facilities, helping you get the most for your travel dollars.)

Frommer Guides
   Alaska
   Australia
   Austria and Hungary
   Belgium, Holland & Luxembourg
   Bermuda and The Bahamas
   Brazil
   California and Las Vegas
   Canada
   Caribbean
   Egypt
   England and Scotland
   Florida
   France
   Germany
   Italy
   Japan and Hong Kong
   Mid-Atlantic States
   New England
   New York State
   Northwest
   Portugal, Madeira & the Azores
   Skiing USA—East
   Skiing USA—West
   South Pacific
   Southeast Asia
   Southern Atlantic States
   Southwest
   Switzerland and Liechtenstein
   Texas
   USA
(Frommer Guides discuss accommodations and facilities in all price ranges, with emphasis on the medium-priced.)

Frommer Touring Guides
   Australia
   Egypt
   Florence
   London
   Paris
   Scotland
   Thailand
   Venice
(These new, color-illustrated guides include walking tours, cultural and historic sites, and other vital travel information.)

Gault Millau
   Chicago

France
Italy
London
Los Angeles
New England
New York
San Francisco
Washington, D.C.

(Irreverent, savvy, and comprehensive, each of these renowned guides candidly reviews over 1,000 restaurants, hotels, shops, nightspots, museums, and sights.)

Serious Shopper's Guides

Italy
London
Los Angeles
Paris

(Practical and comprehensive, each of these handsomely illustrated guides lists hundreds of stores, selling everything from antiques to wine, conveniently organized alphabetically by category.)

A Shopper's Guide to the Caribbean

(Two experienced Caribbean hands guide you through this shopper's paradise, offering witty insights and helpful tips on the wares and emporia of more than 25 islands.)

Beat the High Cost of Travel

(This practical guide details how to save money on absolutely all travel items—accommodations, transportation, dining, sightseeing, shopping, taxes, and more. Includes special budget information for seniors, students, singles, and families.)

Bed & Breakfast—North America

(This guide contains a directory of over 150 organizations that offer bed & breakfast referrals and reservations throughout North America. The scenic attractions, and major schools and universities near the homes of each are also listed.)

California with Kids

(A must for parents traveling in California, providing key information on selecting the best accommodations, restaurants, and sightseeing attractions for the particular needs of the family, whether the kids are toddlers, school-age, preteens, or teens.)

Frommer's Belgium

(Arthur Frommer unlocks the treasures of a country overlooked by most travelers to Europe. Discover the medieval charm, modern sophistication, and natural beauty of this quintessentially European country.)

Frommer's Cruises
(This complete guide covers all the basics of cruising—ports of call, costs, fly-cruise package bargains, cabin selection booking, embarkation and debarkation and describes in detail over 60 or so ships cruising the waters of Alaska, the Caribbean, Mexico, Hawaii, Panama, Canada, and the United States.)

Frommer's Skiing Europe
(Describes top ski resorts in Austria, France, Italy, and Switzerland. Illustrated with maps of each resort area. Includes supplement on Argentinian resorts.)

Guide to Honeymoon Destinations
(A special guide for that most romantic trip of your life, with full details on planning and choosing the destination that will be just right in the U.S. [California, New England, Hawaii, Florida, New York, South Carolina, etc.], Canada, Mexico, and the Caribbean.)

Marilyn Wood's Wonderful Weekends
(This very selective guide covers the best mini-vacation destinations within a 200-mile radius of New York City. It describes special country inns and other accommodations, restaurants, picnic spots, sights, and activities—all the information needed for a two- or three-day stay.)

Manhattan's Outdoor Sculpture
(A total guide, fully illustrated with black and white photos, to more than 300 sculptures and monuments that grace Manhattan's plazas, parks, and other public spaces.)

Motorist's Phrase Book
(A practical phrase book in French, German, and Spanish designed specifically for the English-speaking motorist touring abroad.)

Paris Rendez-Vous
(An amusing and *au courant* guide to the best meeting places in Paris, organized for hour-to-hour use: from power breakfasts and fun brunches, through tea at four or cocktails at five, to romantic dinners and dancing 'til dawn.)

Swap and Go—Home Exchanging Made Easy
(Two veteran home exchangers explain in detail all the money-saving benefits of a home exchange, and then describe precisely how to do it. Also includes information on home rentals and many tips on low-cost travel.)

The Candy Apple: New York for Kids
(A spirited guide to the wonders of the Big Apple by a savvy New York grandmother with a kid's-eye view to fun. Indispensable for visitors and residents alike.)

The New World of Travel
(From America's #1 travel expert, Arthur Frommer, an annual sourcebook with the hottest news and latest trends that's guaranteed to change the way you travel

—and save you hundreds of dollars. Jam-packed with alternative new modes of travel that will lead you to vacations that cater to the mind, the spirit, and a sense of thrift.)

Travel Diary and Record Book
(A 96-page diary for personal travel notes plus a section for such vital data as passport and traveler's check numbers, itinerary, postcard list, special people and places to visit, and a reference section with temperature and conversion charts, and world maps with distance zones.)

Where to Stay USA
(By the Council on International Educational Exchange, this extraordinary guide is the first to list accommodations in all 50 states that cost anywhere from $3 to $30 per night.)

(2) Any one of the Frommer City Guides
Amsterdam and Holland
Athens
Atlantic City and Cape May
Boston
Cancun, Cozumel, and the Yucatán
Chicago
Dublin and Ireland
Hawaii
Las Vegas
Lisbon, Madrid, and Costa del Sol
London
Los Angeles
Mexico City and Acapulco
Minneapolis and St. Paul
Montréal and Québec City
New Orleans
New York
Orlando, Disney World, and EPCOT
Paris
Philadelphia
Rio
Rome
San Francisco
Santa Fe, Taos, and Albuquerque
Sydney
Washington, D.C.

(Pocket-size guides to hotels, restaurants, nightspots, and sightseeing attractions covering all price ranges.)

(3) A one-year subscription to *The Dollarwise Traveler*
This quarterly eight-page tabloid newspaper keeps you up to date on fastbreaking developments in low-cost travel in all parts of the world bringing you the latest money-saving information—the kind of information you'd have to pay $35 a year to obtain elsewhere. This consumer-conscious publication also

features columns of special interest to readers: **Hospitality Exchange** (members all over the world who are willing to provide hospitality to other members as they pass through their home cities); **Share-a-Trip** (offers and requests from members for travel companions who can share costs and help avoid the burdensome single supplement); and **Readers Ask . . . Readers Reply** (travel questions from members to which other members reply with authentic firsthand information).

(4) Your personal membership card

Membership entitles you to purchase through the club all Frommer publications for a third to a half off their regular retail prices during the term of your membership.

So why not join this hardy band of international budgeteers and participate in its exchange of travel information and hospitality? Simply send your name and address, together with your annual membership fee of $18 (U.S. residents) or $20 U.S. (Canadian, Mexican, and other foreign residents), by check drawn on a U.S. bank or via international postal money order in U.S. funds to: Frommer's Dollarwise Travel Club, Inc., 15 Columbus Circle, New York, NY 10023. And please remember to specify which *two* of the books in section (1) and which *one* in section (2) you wish to receive in your initial package of members' benefits. Or, if you prefer, use the order form at the end of the book and enclose $18 or $20 in U.S. currency.

Once you are a member, there is no obligation to buy additional books. No books will be mailed to you without your specific order.

---

3. Getting There

Many factors will determine how you get to the Southern Atlantic region—budget, first of all; the amount of time you'll have for the trip; and just *where* you're headed in the region. If your time is limited and you're coming from a long way off, say, the West Coast, it would make sense to fly cross country, then either rent a car or travel by public ground transportation. If your home is on the East Coast, you may be no more than a day or two of driving from your destination—or a train or bus ride of short duration. You'll find pertinent information about the public conveyances that reach each state in the introductory chapters for each. I'll let you in on some of my personal preferences (none of them based on solicitations or special considerations); however, remember that airlines, railroads, and bus companies *all offer frequent special fares, with substantial discounts and of limited duration,* that can save you considerable money. The fares shown are for regular, economy-class travel, but you should be *sure* to check on current details, schedules, and rates for all public carriers before figuring your costs. Remember, too, that public transportation can often turn out to be cheaper than driving, as well as letting you travel with the freedom to enjoy the scenery instead of constant map reading.

BY AIR

Flying is, of course, the fastest way to get where you're going. Figuring all costs, it may be no more expensive than some others, even cheaper than still others. And the smart traveler will consider buying such standard, always-in-effect, money-saving tickets as excursion plans and the limited-time promotional fares seen so often these days. These usually entail such inconveniences as traveling on certain days of the week, staying a specified length of time, or other limiting conditions. However, it is possible to travel much less expensively just by planning your trip to meet those conditions.

The sample average fares for air travel to major points in these four states that are shown here are for economy-class, round-trip tickets *at the time of writing* (subject to almost certain change):

To	From New York	From Chicago	From Los Angeles
Alexandria, Va. (Washington, D.C.)	$188	$203	$238
Raleigh, N.C.	$198	$218	$338
Charleston, S.C.	$218	$238	$338
Atlanta, Ga.	$258	$198	$318

Delta and **USAir (Piedmont)** blanket the Southern Atlantic region with frequent flights, and attractive fly-drive packages are available to many destination cities. You can save as much as 25% on air fare, have the convenience of a rental car (which will be waiting for you at the airport), and hotel arrangements are usually quite satisfactory, allowing enough flexibility in schedule and itinerary to permit comfortable travel. The airlines or your travel agent will have details and be able to make reservations.

In short, depending on your needs, the times you must fly, etc., you will find a sort of airline supermarket that will require some astute shopping on your part.

BY TRAIN

Amtrak serves the Southern Atlantic region well. Of all modes of public transportation, rail represents the most economical use of fuel (Amtrak yields twice as many passenger miles per gallon as the next most economical, bus, and astonishingly higher percentages when compared to automobile and plane), and many travelers find it a transportation method which becomes positively addictive. I am, personally, so enamored of the "romance of the rails" that not even the convenience of my own automobile sways me when a journey of any distance looms.

Amtrak has also come up with rail/car packages to many destinations that will provide a rental car to be picked up and returned to train depots, thus combining the best features of both.

In addition, there's a good variety of package-tour programs for major southern cities. In 1989, a three-day tour of Jamestown, Williamsburg, and Monticello cost $209 plus rail fare, and covered hotels, sightseeing and round-trip transfers to hotel. Virginia Beach, Charleston, and several other regional destinations had similar bargains. The six-day "Antebellum Era" tour covered Savannah and Charleston for $262. For information on current offerings, consult your local Amtrak tour desk or call toll free 800/USA-RAIL (that's 800/872-7245) and request "Amtrak's America."

On the whole, Amtrak has very good coverage along the eastern seaboard, rather spotty when you get away from the coast. My personal love of train travel is based both on economy and the fact that it, unlike plane travel or automobile travel along our superhighways, not only gives you a good look at the countryside, but some interesting backyards as well. In addition, today's trains are a pleasure to ride, with much more leg room than there used to be, wider seats, bar and restaurant (or snackbar) cars, and slumber coaches, roomettes, or compartments for longer trips. Diner-car meals suffered a bit during cost cutbacks but have now come almost up to the high standards they've always met in the past.

Booking train travel is now much more convenient than it once was, when Amtrak stations were the only ticket dispensers. Not only do more than 10,000 travel agents now issue tickets, but you can also call a computerized service (tel. toll free 800/USA-RAIL) for train, hotel, and rental-car reservations.

As economical as regular coach fares are on Amtrak, there are frequent special excursion rates that save as much as 35% to 40%. Also, there are periodic unlimited-travel passes available for specified time limits. In 1989 there were three Special All Aboard America fares that divided the country into three regions: Eastern, Central, and Western. There was no advance-purchase requirement, and the regular All Aboard America fares, which allow one stopover in each direction, were $189, $269, and $309. The alert train traveler will keep abreast of Amtrak's latest offerings and try to schedule trips to take advantage of them. Incidentally, the popular U.S.A. Rail Pass is sold only outside the U.S. to residents of other countries—foreign visitors will also find available less expensive regional unlimited-travel passes, such as the Southern Region pass, which is good for two weeks. Those, too, must be bought before coming to the U.S.

The sample rail fares shown below to major points in the Southern Atlantic region are, with only one exception, All Aboard America round-trip coach costs at the time of writing. Be sure to check for excursion and other one-destination fares, which may be lower if you meet the required conditions.

To	From New York	From Chicago	From Los Angeles
Alexandria, Va.	$108	$189	$309
Raleigh, N.C.	$189	$189	$309
Charleston, S.C.	$189	$189	$309
Atlanta, Ga.	$189	$189	$309

In addition to excellent package deals available through its tour desk service, Amtrak can arrange discount car rentals at almost all destinations.

BY BUS

That cover-the-country giant, **Greyhound,** will get you to the Southern Atlantic states from almost any starting point. Furthermore, although its standard fares are the cheapest way to travel, it offers even greater bargains. It offers a "Go Anywhere" fare of $68 one way, $136 round trip, to cover travel between any two points within the country, with a 30-day advance purchase and some day-of-the-week restrictions. At the time of writing, there are no plans to discontinue these amazingly low fares, so unless you are traveling a very short distance when the regular one-way fare falls below $68, you can count on a $136 ceiling.

BY CAR

Although there was a time when automobile travel to the Southern Atlantic region could be hazardous if you wandered down the eastern coast via U.S. 1, there are now Interstate highways leading into the region from every direction, connecting with well-planned, beautifully maintained state and federal roadways within the states, with roadside rest areas at frequent intervals. Welcome centers are at many state borders, providing special assistance to motorists as well as tons of tourist information. From a purely "easy to get around" point of view, driving is the most convenient way to come, particularly if you don't plan to stay in one of the metropolitan centers once you get there.

A Word About Car Rentals

You'll find all major car-rental companies throughout the region. However, my own experience with most of them leads to this personal recommendation. You'll find **Thrifty Car Rentals** throughout the region, and best of all, you'll find rates that are usually far below those of the major firms, primarily because of their very realistic policy of not paying for high airport-rental space, but offering instead an airport pickup service (the same is true of your hotel or motel if you wish). Most locations can furnish a wide range of car sizes (all the way up to a nine-passenger station wagon), and there are real money-saving specials offered from time to time at all locations. Thrifty also features cars for nonsmokers and special rates for luxury cars. I'll list the locations in each state introductory chapter, but for a Thrifty worldwide directory and rate schedule, call 800/367-2277.

BY YACHT

No, this section is *not* devoted to yacht owners—it's meant to tell you about a delightful way to get to and around the region as a quasi-private guest aboard a luxurious, yet intimate, cruise ship. The Intracoastal Waterway, which runs all along the Atlantic seaboard from Norfolk, Virginia, to Fort Lauderdale, Florida is the pathway for three deluxe yachts operated by **Clipper Cruise Line,** 7711 Bonhomme Ave., St. Louis, MO 63105 (tel. toll free 800/325-0010). The *Newport Clipper, Yorktown Clipper,* and the *Nantucket Clipper* carry between 102 and 138 passengers, each in accommodations that are likely to meet your fondest fantasies of sailing with the very rich. Decks are hand-laid of teakwood; public rooms are circled by glass to give panoramic views; staterooms are beautifully done up and have wide picture windows; and crew members do indeed treat each passenger as an invited guest. Meals are served in one seating, with a cuisine featuring the freshest ingredients (many bought the same day) prepared to perfection. Low-key, high-caliber entertainment is provided in the evenings for those passengers who stay aboard rather than search out onshore events, and while there's plenty to keep you occupied (library, card games, etc.), there's never any pressure to join in group activities as is so often the case on more structured, large-ship cruises. Shore excursions are easy-going, with docking many times in marinas close to the center of land attractions. All in all, if you can't own a yacht of your own, this is the next best thing and will pamper you within an inch of your life!

Itineraries through the Southern Atlantic region include a seven-day Colonial South cruise that drops anchor in Savannah, St. Simons Island, Beaufort, Charleston, and Hilton Head. There's also a Chesapeake Bay itinerary that includes Baltimore, Annapolis, St. Michaels, Yorktown (for Williamsburg excursions), St. Marys City, and Washington, D.C. (Outside our territory, but an intriguing possibility, is the seven-day Virgin Islands cruise to St. Thomas, Tortola, Norman Island, Virgin Gorda, Jost Van Dyke, and St. John—just thought I'd let you know about it.) Of course, the ultimate yachting experience would be the 29-day Great American Odyssey cruise that travels from Boston to Fort Lauderdale. Prices for all seven-day cruises in 1989 range from $1,498 to $2,298, double occupancy (slightly higher for singles). For full particulars, schedules, and booking, contact Clipper Cruise Line at the address above, or see your travel agent.

READER'S TRANSPORTATION TIP: "In planning and executing a trip to several places on the East Coast, all by air, we found that in many locations renting a car for the days we were there was no more expensive for the four of us than simple transit back and forth to the airport would have been. In other locations, such as Washington, D.C., only because we had lived there did we know that the sensible choice was to avoid Dulles and Baltimore/Friendship airports, fly into National, and get ourselves into the city via the Metro for a few cents each. It pays to gather information on the relative convenience and cost of traveling via public transportation between tourist attractions in a particular location" (M. Aldrich, Minneapolis, Minn.).

---

4. Getting Around

BY AIR

There are several local airlines that fly within the region, and Delta and USAir (Piedmont) have rather frequent air service to major points. I'll supply names of the most prominent local airlines as we go along.

BY TRAIN

Introductory chapters for each state have Amtrak stops listed, but it would pay to investigate thoroughly schedules between interstate points. Connections are not always easy to plan and time can be lost between trains. The railroads offer very good access to the Southern Atlantic area, not so good movement around it.

BY BUS

Greyhound makes it easy to get around and between states, and equipment is modern and quite comfortable.

BY CAR

As I said, highways in every Southern Atlantic state are in good shape, and it is seldom, if ever, that you'll run into a badly paved roadway. The infamous speedtraps that visitors once feared in Georgia and South Carolina have been virtually eliminated, although most state patrolmen keep a close eye on motorists to see that the speed limit is not exceeded on state highways. There are frequent roadside picnic tables, some with outdoor grills, along both state and federal roads in this region, and picnicking can be a delightful way to save money, as well as a welcome break to enjoy the outdoors while you lunch or have a light supper. I have always found, too, that it's much easier when traveling by car to pack a small "hot pot" and cups for late-night or early-morning coffee. In fact, my family very often cuts down on eating costs by breakfasting in our room on sweet rolls or doughnuts bought the night before and served with instant coffee or hot chocolate, courtesy of the hot pot. Possible, of course, when you're traveling by other means, but most convenient when you can simply tuck a small box of eating supplies in the car.

II

INTRODUCTION TO VIRGINIA

1. BY WAY OF BACKGROUND
2. TRAVELING TO VIRGINIA
3. TRAVELING WITHIN VIRGINIA

The Commonwealth of Virginia, sometimes called "The Gateway to the South," is very much a part of my own growing up. I finished high school there, married, and began my family on its coast, and somewhere along the line absorbed a love for its rich history that seems to imbue every native and is quick to hook most visitors. Virginia rightly claims "More America to the Mile" than any other part of the country (although New England states just might quarrel with that claim), and only the most complete dullard could travel the state and come away without a very real sense of this nation's beginnings.

1. By Way of Background

VIRGINIA PAST AND PRESENT

The Old Dominion, and this country, had its start in the London Company's small expeditionary force that settled at Jamestown on May 13, 1607. It was to become the first permanent English settlement, but for those first few years it almost didn't make it. Ill suited to deal with the primitive conditions in which they found themselves, those first colonists fell prey to dysentery, plague, fire, hunger that amounted to near starvation in 1609, and much internal bickering. Things picked up in 1610 when new settlers and fresh supplies arrived from England. Then, when John Rolfe (who married the Indian princess Pocahontas) managed to convince enough farmers of the wisdom of growing tobacco as a "cash crop," and the first harvest was exported in 1614, they were off and running toward a sound economy. Two things happened in 1619 that would cast long shadows into the future: a representative legislative assem-

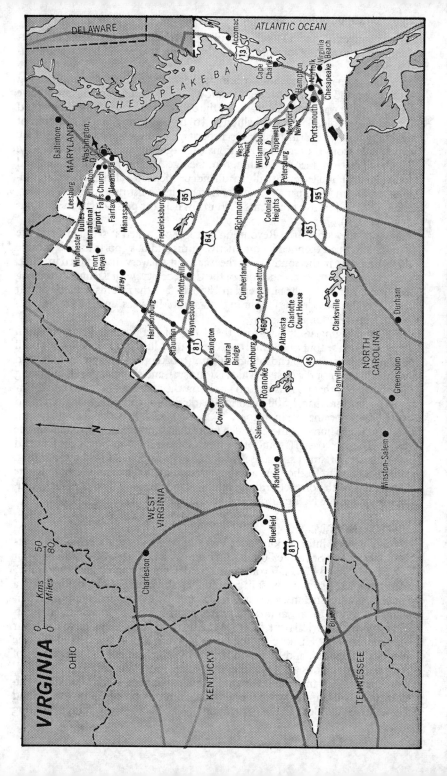

bly was convened, and a Dutch man-of-war arrived carrying the first black indentured servants, the forerunner of a slave traffic that would later tear the nation apart.

Thus from its base of tobacco farming that spawned huge plantations along broad rivers and bays, an early democratic-governing forum, and the use of slave labor, Virginia was a natural theater for the drama of history in which she would play a leading role. Bacon's Rebellion in 1676 was the first overt expression of dissatisfaction with British rule; it set the stage for events in the next century that sprang from the words and actions of Virginians such as Patrick Henry, Thomas Jefferson, George Washington, George Mason, James Madison, and John Marshall, and led eventually to full independence for all the American colonies. And from Virginians the new nation got its Constitution, Bill of Rights, and four of its first five presidents (Virginians held the presidency for 32 of our first 36 years!).

From the end of the Revolution until 1861, when it seceded from the Union, Virginia expanded its productive farms and busy ports until it became the richest state in the South. With the war against slavery that erupted in 1861, she became the very heart and soul of the Confederacy, with Richmond serving as its capital almost to the bitter end in 1865. In fact, the first major battle of that long, bloody struggle was fought in the state at Manassas, and the final act was played out at Appomattox.

After digging itself out from the debris of the postwar Reconstruction years, Virginia set out once more on a course of industrial growth. Today you'll find it a harmonious blend of agriculture (tobacco, wheat, apples, corn, and hay), industry (not the least of which is tourism), and shipping. And, following the philosophy that people who do not know their past can have no future, Virginia posts more than 1,500 historical markers throughout the state to remind you of its important role in history.

You'll also find that there's much more than simple history to entertain the visitor. The east coast has some of the most popular beach resorts in the East and is a virtual sportsman's paradise, with excellent fishing, surf-riding, hunting, tennis, and golf. To the west are the Shenandoah Valley and the Blue Ridge Mountains, with horseback riding, hunting, and camping, as well as such natural wonders as the Natural Bridge and the Luray Caverns.

VISITOR INFORMATION

For general information about Virginia, write: **Virginia Division of Tourism,** 202 N. 9th St., Suite 500, Richmond, VA 23219 (tel. 804/786-4484 or toll free 800/548-9797). If you're interested in golf, ask for "Golf in Virginia," their complete list of courses; in fishing, "Fresh Water Fishing in Virginia," a list of freshwater streams, lakes, and rivers, and "Salt Water Sport Fishing in Virginia," a guide to the annual saltwater sport-fishing tournament; in sightseeing with a historical bent, "Civil War Battlefield Parks," a guide to Civil War attractions, and "Historic Homes of Virginia," listing nearly 100 historic plantations, estates, and homes in the Old Dominion. For the full picture of Virginia's attractions and annual events, ask for the "Virginia Travel Guide." Gardeners will want to ask for the "Virginia Garden Week" booklet. Outdoorsmen will want to write the **Virginia Commission of Game and Inland Fisheries,** P.O. Box 11104, Richmond, VA 23220, for Virginia hunting and fishing information, or call the Game Commission at 804/257-1000. New Yorkers will find a **Travel Service** office at 11 Rockefeller Plaza (tel. 212/245-3080).

VIRGINIA TELEPHONE AREA CODES

Alexandria, 804; Williamsburg, 804; Virginia Beach, 804; Charlottesville, 804; Roanoke, 703.

HOTEL ACCOMMODATIONS

Virginia has a generous supply of hotels, motels, campgrounds, and a few guesthouses in some locations. As for prices, they cover everything from super-deluxe to budget. The accommodations you'll find listed in this book have been selected purely on the basis of a personal inspection and evaluation, and the prices, it must be said again, are those in effect *at the time of writing*—and in these uncertain days of rising costs, are very much subject to change.

As a rule, reservations will be less tight in fall, winter, and early spring, since Virginia draws its largest crowds during the summer months. The one exception is the Blue Ridge section, where thousands throng the parkway in October and early November for a last look at fall foliage.

BED AND BREAKFAST

For those who prefer going the bed-and-breakfast, small-guesthouse, and charming-inn route, one of the most comprehensive aids to finding these establishments in Virginia is the pictoral guidebook *Bed and Breakfast and Unique Inns of Virginia,* by Muncy, Muncy, and Davis. There are descriptions of some 55 accommodations, including history and personality, as well as color photographs and an index of more than 350 such inns in the state. To order, send check for $15.95 plus $2 for shipping to Crystal Springs Publishing, P.O. Box 8814, Roanoke, VA 24014, or order with Visa or MasterCard by calling 703/982-2029.

CAMPING

You'll find some campgrounds listed for each Virginia location, but very helpful publications are available if you're planning to sleep via tent, camper, or trailer and want to take advantage of the 17 state parks that offer camping facilities. For detailed information, write the Virginia Division of Parks and Recreation, 1201 Washington Bldg., Capitol Square, Richmond, VA 23219 (tel. 804/786-2134). The Virginia Division of Tourism, Bell Tower, Capitol Square, 101 N. 9th St., Richmond, VA 23219 (tel. 804/786-4484), can furnish a campground directory.

VIRGINIA RESTAURANTS

One thing you can always do—and always do well—in Virginia is eat. From the strictly southern-cured (or "Virginia") ham, fried chicken, and black-eyed peas to seafood you can count on to be deliciously fresh, you'll be fed well in restaurants that rival New York or San Francisco establishments, colonial taverns that have been serving food for centuries, plenty of medium-priced modern restaurants staffed by chefs steeped in regional cooking, or sometimes—if you're lucky—in very small, plain restaurants of the old-time, small-town-café home-cooking tradition. A reassuring thing to know is that compared to big-city prices, those in most restaurants in Virginia are modest.

As for alcoholic beverages, you must be 21 or older to buy beer in state stores and licensed restaurants and food stores or to be served wine or mixed drinks. The licensing of restaurants and lounges to serve alcohol by the drink is on a local-option basis; you may run into a "dry" locality, but don't get upset—in most you can buy mixers and bring your own.

CRAFTS

Virginia is chockablock with artisans of virtually every persuasion. In the northern part of the state look for: the **Torpedo Factory Art Center** in Alexandria, a concentration of craft studios; outstanding hand-hammered pewter and hand-spun items by the **Helbles** of Leesburg; handmade quilts and hand-carved wooden items at the **Apple Pie** shop in McLean; and handmade baskets in **Sterling,** in Fairfax County. Along the Eastern Shore, Chincoteague Island is a central shopping point for hand-carved wooden duck decoys, and near the southern tip of the shore, Virginia birds and waterfowl are depicted by potter Jose Dovis in the little town of Exmore. Central Virginia is home to such craft centers as the **General Store** at Michie Tavern, near Charlottesville (with a strong emphasis on toys), and **Cudahy's Gallery** in Richmond, which features pottery, stoneware, and a wide variety of other crafts. In the eastern part of the state, Williamsburg is a mecca for 18th-century craft artisans, with more than 20 shops covering a broad crafts spectrum, from basket-making to pottery to pewter to glass blowing. On the coast, Norfolk's **d'Art Center** shelters some 35 artisans, and to the west, native crafts abound at the **Alleghany Highlands Arts and Crafts** in Clifton Forge; the **Cave House Craft Shop** in Abingdon; the **Faith Mountain Company** in Sperryville; and **Rooftop of Virginia** in Galax.

For a directory of Virginia's craft outlets and a calendar of the many craft festivals held throughout the year, contact the Virginia Division of Tourism, 202 N. 9th St., Suite 500, Richmond, VA 23219 (tel. 804/786-4484).

CLIMATE

As you can see, mean temperatures in Virginia are pretty much in the moderate range, falling slightly lower in fall and winter in Alexandria in the northern part of the state and Roanoke in the west than along the coast.

	High	Low
Alexandria	87	29
Norfolk	88	32
Roanoke	88	29

2. Traveling to Virginia

BY AIR

American, Delta, Continental, Pan Am, Northwest, TWA, USAir (Piedmont), United, and other domestic and international carriers fly into Washington National Airport and Dulles International, both of which are in Virginia and close to Alexandria. USAir (Piedmont) serves Washington National Airport and also goes to Norfolk, Newport News, Charlottesville, Danville, Lynchburg, Roanoke, and Richmond.

BY TRAIN
Amtrak has stops in Alexandria, Manassas, Culpepper, Quantico, Fredericksburg, Ashland, Richmond, Charlottesville, Monroe, Williamsburg, Newport News, Petersburg, Lynchburg, and Danville. Bear in mind that Amtrak excursion and special discount fares are considerably lower than regular coach fares. Also, your nearest Amtrak tour desk can furnish details on such bargains as "Williamsburg Close Up" and "Jamestown, Williamsburg and Monticello" package tours.

BY BUS
Greyhound will take you to almost any destination in the Old Dominion. As with Amtrak, check specials in effect when you plan your trip.

BY CAR
Several Interstate highways cross Virginia: I-64 runs east and west; I-66 runs east and west in the northern part of the state; I-77, north and south in the southwestern corner of the state; I-81, north and south the entire length of the western part of the state; I-95, north and south in the eastern part of the state. **Virginia Information Stations,** in attractive, colonial-style buildings, are located within a mile or two of major entry points.

---

3. Traveling Within Virginia

BY AIR
Within the state, United, TWA, and USAir (Piedmont) have service between Washington's two airports (both in Virginia) and Norfolk. American has service between Washington's two airports and Richmond. USAir (Piedmont) has frequent service to Charlottesville, Danville, Lynchburg, Newport News, Norfolk, Richmond, and Roanoke.

BY TRAIN
You *can* travel around the state via Amtrak, although be forewarned that it takes some doing, with a good deal of planning for connections between major and spur lines, and it will almost certainly involve considerable waits. Nevertheless, Amtrak has stops at Alexandria, Fredericksburg, Richmond, Williamsburg, Newport News, and Petersburg (with a bus connection to Norfolk and Virginia Beach) in the east. In other parts of the state, it's possible to go

by train to Culpeper, Charlottesville, Monroe, Lynchburg, Danville, Staunton, Clifton Forge, Quantico, Ashland, and Lee Hall.

BY BUS

Greyhound will take you almost anywhere.

BY CAR

Virginia has more than 54,000 miles of paved roads, so driving is a pleasure. My best advice is not to leave home without the official state-highway map, issued free by the Virginia Department of Transportation, 1401 E. Broad St., Richmond, VA 23219. A letter will bring it to you, and besides road information, it's loaded with sightseeing information. It's also available at welcome centers at all major entry points.

All major car-rental firms have offices in key cities, and there are Thrifty offices in Alexandria, Falls Church, Fredericksburg, Leesburg, Manassas, Newport News, Norfolk, Richmond, Roanoke, and Woodbridge.

III

ALONG THE VIRGINIA COAST

1. ALEXANDRIA
2. WILLIAMSBURG
3. RICHMOND
4. TIDEWATER VIRGINIA AND THE EASTERN SHORE

For sheer density of tourist attractions and excursions into Virginia's history, its east coast takes top honors. It was here, after all, that the earliest arrivals set up shop at sites which provided port access for those all-important ships that linked them to England and which would later serve as jumping-off points for the push westward.

1. Alexandria

Alexandria is one of Virginia's 40 independent cities; that is, it's not a part of any county, but a separate entity. A sister city to Georgetown, just across the Potomac River, it was literally put on the map by George Washington, who helped lay out the streets and drew its first map as a 17-year-old surveyor's apprentice in the 1750s. As a matter of fact, our first president had many close ties to the town: he drilled his first troops in Market Square in 1754, held a pew at Christ Episcopal Church, and in later years quite often came up to Alexandria to transact business as well as to find diversion in its busy social life. A little later, Robert E. Lee spent much of his childhood and prepared for West Point in Alexandria.

GETTING THERE
If you're driving, Alexandria can be reached on I-95 from the north and west, I-495 from the south, U.S. 1 from north or south, and Va. 7 from the west. Washington National Airport is just 10 minutes north on the George

Washington Memorial Parkway, and Dulles International is 30 minutes to the northwest. Both the Greyhound bus terminal and the Southern Railroad train station are just minutes from the historic area of Old Town.

A FIRST STOP

A fantastic restoration and preservation of more than a thousand 18th- and 19th-century buildings in **Old Town** makes it easy for today's visitor to see how this historic port city went about its business in those far-off days. It is even easier if that visitor heads for the historic Ramsay House Visitors Center that dates from 1724 and now houses the **Alexandria Convention and Visitors Bureau** at 221 King St. (tel. 703/838-4200). Their services far exceed those of many agencies of this kind. Here are just some of the ways in which they'll make your stop in their town most interesting: they will give you a free brochure for a self-guided walking tour; make hotel and restaurant reservations; provide foreign-language guides if you give them enough notice; arm you with more than 40 area-attraction brochures, as well as lists of art galleries, specialty shops, antique shops, restaurants, hotels, and special events; and will even pass out free-parking passes for out-of-town cars in the metered parking zones! And if you should need anything beyond all this, the friendly, efficient staff will almost certainly be able to help you out.

WHERE TO STAY

Guest Quarters–Alexandria, 100 S. Reynolds St., Alexandria, VA 22304 (tel. 703/370-9600, or toll free 800/424-2900), gives you the luxury of one- or two-bedroom suites in a peaceful setting combined with convenience to historic Old Town, shopping, corporate centers, and downtown Washington (which is just about 10 minutes away). You'll find their usual high standards of decor and service, and the lovely Quarters Court restaurant. Rates are $120 to $140 double in a one-bedroom suite and $175 for two bedrooms. Each additional person pays $15, children under 18 stay free, and there are special weekend and package rates.

At the rather special **Alexandria Compri Hotel,** 2700 Eisenhower Ave., Alexandria, VA 22314 (tel. 703/329-2323 or toll free 800/426-6774), guest rooms are spacious and luxuriously furnished, with an exceptionally large work space and desk, comfortable seating, and two telephones. What sets the hotel apart, however, is the Compri Club, a large living room with a cocktail area, eating space, library, and big-screen TV. Social gatherings here are encouraged, a decided boon at those times when you're beginning to feel a bit isolated and lonely from being "on the road," whether for pleasure or business. This is the setting for a hosted reception in the evening and late-night snacks, as well as impromptu gatherings throughout the day. There is also a health club and whirlpool; and a full, cooked-to-order breakfast is included in the rates. Rooms for the handicapped and nonsmoking rooms are available. Rates range from $91 to $170, and there's no charge for children under 12 sharing a room with adults.

The **Morrison House,** 116 S. Alfred St., Alexandria, VA 22314 (tel. 703/838-8000 or toll free 800/533-1808 in Virginia, 800/367-0800 rest of U.S.), is an elegant, European-style small inn (47 rooms) right in the heart of Old Town. Its marble foyer, parlor complete with fireplace, and mahogany-paneled library feature Federalist furnishings. Guest rooms are individually decorated, and many come with poster beds and fireplaces. Facilities for the handicapped are available, and the staff is multilingual. Though small, Morrison House is a full-service hotel, with an excellent restaurant, **Le Chardon D'or,** serving all three meals, a convivial bar, and 24-hour room service. There's also valet parking (additional charge) and afternoon tea served by English butlers. Rates are in the $120 to $180 range; children under 12 stay free with parents, and there are weekend and honeymoon rates available.

For convenience as well as comfort, there is no better place to stay than the **Old Town Holiday Inn,** 480 King St., Alexandria, VA 22314 (tel. 703/549-6080). The Robert E. Lee home is just a half mile away, Mount Vernon an easy eight-mile drive, and Washington's National Airport just three miles (they furnish free transportation to and from). And all of Old Town is just outside the door. The inn's brick exterior even looks like part of the restoration, and that illusion is reinforced when you walk into its lobby furnished with period reproductions. The Independence Restaurant has the same colonial decor and specializes in American dishes, with roast beef high on the list, as is fresh seafood. The Tavern, just down the hall from the restaurant, is all low lights, dark wood, and pewter, and there's entertainment most of the year. An indoor pool provides year-round swimming. Rooms are spacious and comfortable, and far from budget priced ($108 to $130 double; children under 18 stay free in the room with their parents), but as a close-at-hand refuge after a day of foot-weary touristing, it can't be beat. Weekend package plans offer attractive savings.

On the north side of town, the **Ramada Hotel–Old Town,** 901 N. Fairfax St., Alexandria, VA 22314 (tel. 703/683-6000), is an attractive high-rise with a pool, restaurant, and entertainment in the lounge. Rooms are a comfortable size and attractively decorated in bright colors. If you're arriving or departing at nearby airports, there's free shuttle service. Rates are in the $78 to $105 range for doubles, but children under 18 stay free in the room with their parents, and there are lower weekend rates available.

The **Best Western Old Colony Inn,** 625 1st St., Alexandria, VA 22314 (tel. 703/548-6300 or toll free 800/528-1234), is a complex of 11 brick buildings laid out in the style of a colonial estate. Located on the George Washington Memorial Parkway (which is Washington Street when it passes through Alexandria), the Old Colony is only five minutes away from Washington's National Airport (with free airport and Metro shuttle service every half hour) and especially convenient to Washington sightseeing. The desk clerk here is happy to arrange Gray Line tours, which begin and end at the motel. All 223 rooms are attractively decorated, some with canopied double beds, and most are furnished in a modified colonial decor. There's a pool, screened from traffic by a serpentine brick wall and landscaping. Also, a restaurant is on the premises as well as a cocktail lounge and free HBO in every room, and there are excellent dining facilities within walking distance. Small pets are accepted, children under 18 stay free when sharing a room with their parents, and weekend rates are available. Doubles are in the $85 to $106 range, and kitchenette units, double occupancy, are $105.

The **Days Inn Alexandria,** 110 S. Bragg St., Alexandria, VA 22312 (tel. 703/354-4950), is just one block off the I-395/Duke Street intersection, with the top-quality accommodations typical of this chain. There's a pool, playground, and restaurant, and you can bring your pets along if you like (there's a small additional fee). This location is a good one if you plan much Washington sightseeing, since the Metro bus is just one block away. Rates are seasonal, with doubles running $50 to $54. Children under 18 pay $1.

The **Econo Lodge,** 700 N. Washington St., Alexandria, VA 22314 (tel. 703/836-5100 or toll free 800/446-6900), is conveniently located to restaurants, shops, and sightseeing. Its attractive guest rooms are comfortably furnished, children under 18 stay free with parents, cribs are furnished at no charge, rooms for the handicapped and nonsmokers are available, and there are senior-citizen and military-personnel discounts. Rates are in the $39.95 to $49.95 range.

The **Red Roof Inn,** 5975 Richmond Hwy., Alexandria, VA 22303 (tel. 703/960-5200), is south of downtown at the intersection of I-95 and U.S. 1 South (Exit 1A). Its comfortable guest rooms have extra-long double beds and free sports and movie TV. There's free morning coffee and a daily newspaper in the lobby, and restaurants and shopping are close at hand. Children under 18 share room with parents at no charge, and there's a discount for seniors. Rates run from $39.95 to $52.95.

Though not in Alexandria itself, two of the excellent **Fairfield Inns by Marriott** (see Introduction) are in the vicinity. Very close to Dulles International Airport, Residence Inn, 315 Elden St., Herndon, VA 22090 (tel. 703/0044 or toll free 800/331-3131), is within easy reach of Alexandria, Washington, and Tysons Corner shopping center and Wolf Trap (see below). Even handier for avid shoppers is the Residence Inn, 8616 Westwood Center Dr., Tysons Corner, VA 22180 (tel. 703/893-0120 or toll free 800/331-3131). Rates at both run $95 to $115 for studios, $130 to $150 for penthouse suites.

Guesthouses

Alexandria has a very good bed-and-breakfast program, with accommodations available in over 30 guesthouses in Old Town and surrounding areas. Contact E. J. Mansmann, 819 Prince St., Alexandria, VA 22314 (tel. 703/683-2159). Rates range from $65 to $90 for doubles, and there's a two-day minimum stay.

Camping

If you're traveling the camper route, where you stay will depend on which direction you come from or are headed. Closest camping toward the west and the Blue Ridge Mountains is the **Yogi Bear Jellystone Park,** at 14004 Shelter Lane in Haymarket (tel. 703/754-7944, or 754-8877 if no answer), about 40 miles away on Va. 234, eight miles northwest of I-66. Most of the 150 sites have water and electric hookups; there's a recreation building, pool, laundry, store, and LP gas service. Rates are $13 to $17, depending on full or no hookups.

From Williamsburg, the **Aquia Pines Campground,** 3071 Jefferson Davis Hwy., Stafford, VA 22554 (tel. 703/659-3447), is about 25 miles south of the Washington Beltway (or 20 miles south of Alexandria) off I-95 at Exit 48 (Aquia Interchange). Follow the signs about half a mile to the park. There are 121 sites for full hookups and tents, and a store, pool, laundry, mini-golf, and LP gas. Rates are $15 to $19 for no to full hookup, respectively.

FOR COUNTRY-MUSIC LOVERS

One of the nation's leading centers for country, bluegrass, folk, and traditional Celtic music is located in Alexandria, drawing top artists who often cross the country for the opportunity to appear here, and audiences from up and down the East Coast. The **Birchmere,** 3901 Mt. Vernon Ave. (tel. 703/549-5919), is a large place (holding about 500 people) that manages to exude a cozy, "family" ambience for its devoted patrons. It says a lot for the quality of entertainment here that owner/managers Gary and Linda Oetze feel it unnecessary to serve libations any stronger than beer and soft drinks. Snacks (onion rings, french fries, burgers, crab cakes, etc.) suffice in the food department (for a highly recommended full-meal restaurant nearby, see below).

It is, indeed, for the performances and the friendly staff that people flock to the Birchmere. The sound system is well nigh perfect, and sightlines good—not a bad seat in the house. Audiences, which often include young children, singles, couples, parents, and even grandparents, show great respect for the talent on stage, maintaining near silence during each number. And small wonder, when that talent could well be Waylon Jennings, Willie Nelson, or others of the same stature. Rapport between performer and audience is extraordinary, and artists very often stay around after the show to hobnob with patrons.

The Birchmere sometimes closes one night a week, so it pays to telephone before coming. Also, the cover charge (no minimum) varies with the artists, from about $7.50 to as much as $25 for top headliners. So popular is this place that you may have to join the waiting line that forms before doors open, around 6:30 p.m. for shows that begin at 8:30 p.m. If this kind of music is your first love, you won't want to miss the Birchmere.

Note: For those who need more than fast-food snacks to see them through a night at the Birchmere, there's an excellent full-service restaurant close by. **R.T.'s,** 3804 Mt. Vernon Ave. (tel. 684-6110), specializes in fresh seafood at moderate prices.

FOR SHOPPERS

This part of northern Virginia has developed, over the past few years, into a shopping mecca for the entire metropolitan Washington area. In Alexandria, the summer of 1989 saw the opening of the gigantic **Landmark Shopping Center,** Duke Street and I-395 (Shirley Hwy.). In addition to some 160 retail outlets, there are scores of restaurants and an open-air center. In nearby Tyson's Corner shopping center (north of Alexandria, just off I-495, the Capital Beltway), and the Galleria Mall at Tysons II constitute one of the largest retail-shopping complexes on the East Coast, with branches of leading national stores such as Macy's, Saks Fifth Ave., Neiman-Marcus, etc.

OTHER HISTORIC SITES NEARBY

Mount Vernon (c/o Mount Vernon Ladies' Association; tel. 703/780-2000), George Washington's home from 1754 until he died in 1799, is nine miles south of Alexandria on the George Washington Memorial Parkway, and nobody in his or her right mind would want to miss it. If our first president has always seemed cool and aloof, he'll become a living presence as you walk through this home he loved above all and where he spent his happiest years. Stand on the wide, two-story, columned porch and you'll see the same peaceful view, with the long, green lawn sweeping down to the river. And inside, those responsible for restoration of the mansion have been careful to preserve the sense of "home" that warmed Washington's heart. Although only 500 of the 8,000 acres that made up the estate in its prime are still intact (outlying farms were willed by the president and his wife to various descendants), they have been maintained just as he planned them, with a small group of service buildings close by the mansion. You can visit about a dozen of these "dependencies" for a vivid picture of plantation life. And both George and Martha lie at rest in the tomb "at the foot of the vineyard enclosure," as he directed. Don't plan to hurry around Mount Vernon—allow yourself well over an hour to absorb this lovely memorial to our first president. It's open every day of the year, and it's usually jammed during the summer months, particularly on weekends and holidays. But go, even if you have to join the throngs during those times. Hours are 9 a.m. to 5 p.m., except for November through February when the gates close at 4 p.m. Admission is $4.50 for adults, $4 for those 62 and over, $2 for children 6 to 11; and there's a free open house held the third Monday in February to celebrate Washington's birthday.

The **Mount Vernon Inn,** located at the gate entrance to the Mount Vernon estate, serves moderate-priced lunches (from $5) and dinners (from $12) in a colonial atmosphere. There's also a gift shop and snackbar.

Three miles west of Mount Vernon is **Woodlawn Plantation** (tel. 703/557-7880), the home built on property that Washington gave Nelly Custis (Martha's granddaughter) and her husband. Visiting hours are 9:30 a.m. to 4:30 p.m. every day except major holidays. Admission is $4 for adults, $3 for senior citizens and students.

Still farther south of Alexandria (19 miles on the G. W. Parkway and U.S. 1) is **Gunston Hall,** Mason Neck, Worton, Va 22079 (tel. 703/550-9220), one of the most elegant of the historic houses in this area. Built between 1755 and 1759, the brick house was the residence of George Mason, who was often called the "Pen of the Revolution" for his work on the Fairfax Resolves, the first constitution of Virginia, and the Virginia Declaration of Rights (which formed the basis of the Federal Bill of Rights). He was one of the most active framers of the Constitution 200 years ago. Its formal interior is noted for its Palladian style and Chinese Chippendale woodwork. The gardens, built around a boxwood allee planted by George Mason, are a delight. It's open from 9:30 a.m. to 5 p.m. daily except Thanksgiving, Christmas, and New Year's Day; admission is $4 for adults, $3.25 for those over 60, $1 for students age 6 to 15.

The entire town of **Fredericksburg** (49 miles south of Alexandria on I-95 or U.S. 1) could qualify as a historic site, for since 1728 it has been witness to events momentous in the birth and development of the United States. James Monroe, Lafayette, and John Paul Jones all lived or visited here, and the **Rising Sun Tavern** was the scene of fiery political rallies before the Revolution. George Washington grew to manhood here, and it was here he chopped down that famous cherry tree. This is also the site of a major Civil War battle. An afternoon's stroll through the town with its many restored homes and public buildings (pick up self-guided walking tour information and the "Walk in Washington's Footsteps" brochure at the **Fredericksburg Visitor Center** at 706 Caroline St.; tel. 703/373-1776) will leave you feeling you should climb into a carriage or onto a horse to end it rather than into a 20th-century automobile! Aside from

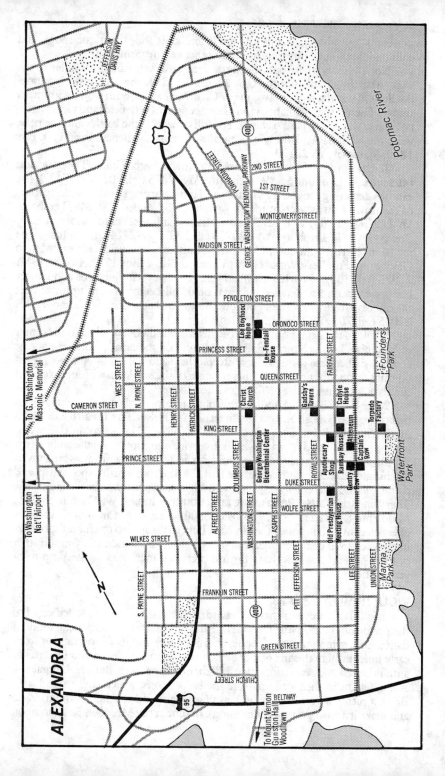

museums and historic buildings, you'll find craft shops, antique shops, and colonial-style restaurants to sustain that other-century atmosphere.

Not all history lies south of Alexandria, however. About 20 miles to the west, near the intersection of U.S. 29 and Va. 234, the **Manassas National Battlefield** was the scene of two major Civil War battles, both won by Southern troops. There's an informative visitors center on the battlefield, and picnic facilities if you want to make a day of it. For full details on the battles and the park, write the National Park Service, Manassas National Battlefield Park, P.O. Box 1830, Manassas, VA 22110.

To the north of Alexandria, Leesburg attracts history buffs. The **Loudoun Museum,** 16 Loudoun St. SW, Leesburg, VA 22075 (tel. 703/777-7427), has exhibits depicting the county's history and is the starting point of walking tours of the town; **Retrospect-Loudoun Artisans,** 15 Loudoun St. SW, Leesburg, VA 22075 (tel. 703/777-8277), is a crafts and antiques center; **Morven Park,** Rte. 3, Box 50, Leesburg, VA 22075 (tel. 703/777-2414), has tours of the mansion, carriage museum, fox-hunting museum, and gardens from May to October; and the **Willowcroft Farm** Vineyards, Rt. 2, Box 174A, Leesburg, VA 22075 (tel. 703/777-8161), will arrange tours of their vineyards and winery by appointment. For detailed information on all Leesburg attractions, contact the Office of Tourism, County of Loudoun, 108-D South St., SE, Leesburg, VA 22075 (tel. 703/777-0519).

While in the neighborhood, go by nearby **Middleburg,** which is the center of Virginia's horse country. Each spring and fall, thousands from around the country gather here for traditional steeplechase and point-to-point races. Periodically throughout the year, tours of some of the stables can be arranged; for details, contact the Office of Tourism listed above.

Note: If you land in Middleburg around mealtime, there are two small inns that offer superb meals and overnight facilities. The **Red Fox Tavern,** 2 E. Washington St., Middleburg, VA 22117 (tel. 703/687-6301), is a colonial gem dating from 1728. Food is award-winning, service is gracious, and the ambience is the ultimate in time travel. Many residents in the locality, from as far away as Washington and Alexandria, feel the Red Fox Tavern is worth a special trip, and if you fall under its spell, there are charming guest rooms for an overnight stay. The **Windsor House Restaurant and Country Inn,** 2 W. Washington St., Middleburg, VA 22117 (tel. 703/687-6800), is an 1824 townhouse that now offers elegant guest rooms, the Unicorn Pub, and a superb restaurant specializing in such local dishes as pheasant, quail, squab, and standing rib roast. Either of these hostelries will serve to furnish cherished memories of the Virginia of years gone by.

WOLF TRAP FARM PARK

Just 20 minutes away from Alexandria, the first national park dedicated to the performing arts, **Wolf Trap Farm Park,** has exciting ballet, opera, modern dance, jazz, symphony, and popular music concerts in its **Filene Center** from early June through the first part of September. Performances are in a Douglas-fir amphitheater, and seats run $10 to $30 for evening shows. But a real bargain— and a delight in nice weather—are the lawn tickets, which cost around $10. Bring a picnic if you like (many Washingtonians and northern Virginians do and make it a lawn-party–type evening), or dine at the Meadows Restaurant on the grounds. To find out about current schedules, and program information, call 703/255-1900. Wolf Trap is in Vienna, just off I-495 (Capital Beltway at exit 10, then 2½ miles west on Va. 7). There's also an intimate year-round theater, The Barns of Wolf Trap, which presents drama, films, and music from jazz to opera. For current schedules, write 1624 Trap Rd., Vienna, VA 22180 (tel. 703/938-2404).

---

2. Williamsburg

Restoration of historic homes, public buildings, and even villages is not unique in the United States. Up and down the eastern seaboard and westward all the way to California, the history of the country has been preserved in buildings where much of it happened. But Colonial Williamsburg *is* unique—there's nothing quite like it anywhere else. It's almost as if, when you walk down Duke of Gloucester Street, the doors of the Raleigh Tavern may swing open at any moment and Patrick Henry will emerge deep in heated discussion with Thomas Jefferson, so true to its original character has this town been restored. And though the faces under bonnets or above 18th-century shirts bear the stamp of today, the clothes, and even the manners, are those of the past. To visit Williamsburg is not to "do" it in the tourist sense, but to become surrounded by and immersed in a way of life that nurtured men who molded, and still mold by works that have endured over the years, the future of this country.

Men in knee breeches and women in long-skirted, white-collared dresses walk the streets on their way to and from enterprises that engaged Williamsburg citizens back in 1699, when Virginia's capital was moved from Jamestown (the first settlement) up to the inland Middle Plantation, which was given the new name in honor of the reigning British monarch. Just as the town bustled then with the commerce of bootmaker, printer, wigmaker, and blacksmith, it is populated now with costumed artisans carrying on these same crafts. And even the crowds of visitors are fitting, for in the old days, when the courts were in session or the Assembly met, inns, taverns, and rooming houses swelled with outsiders.

After Williamsburg became the political and social center of the colony (it already had the 1693-chartered College of William and Mary, second in age only to Harvard University), the royal governor and Assembly laid out an orderly plan for its development on either side of mile-long Duke of Gloucester Street. A capitol building was erected at the east end of the street, and midway between it and the college, a magnificent Governor's Palace went up in a setting of formal gardens. Thomas Jefferson came in 1760 to study at the college and later met many of the men who would join him to put the growing spirit of independence into words that would pull together a nation from fragmented, widely separated groups of colonists: George Washington, Patrick Henry, Richard Bland, and others. Patrick Henry led the fight against England's infamous Stamp Act Resolves. And in May of 1776 the Virginia Convention sent a resolution from Williamsburg to the Continental Congress that resulted in the Philadelphia declaration that the colonies were "absolved from all allegiance to the British Crown." George Mason's Virginia Declaration of Rights, which became the foundation of our constitutional Bill of Rights, was adopted here in June of the same year.

It was a vigorous, stimulating, sometimes rowdy town during those years, and remained so until the capital was moved again in 1780, this time to Richmond, still farther inland where it would be closer to the center of population and safer from attack by the British. After that, things settled down and Williamsburg's days of glory seemed ended forever, a feeling that intensified when federal troops occupied the area for over two years during the Civil War.

It wasn't until 1926, when the Rev. W. A. R. Goodwin, rector of Bruton Parish Church, infected John D. Rockefeller, Jr., with his own enthusiasm for restoring the colonial capital, that wheels were set in motion to give the American people this authentic, carefully researched and restored link with their past. Rockefeller hovered over the project right up to his death in 1960, pouring vast sums of money into the restoration of some 88 still-standing buildings and the faithful reconstruction of hundreds of other structures on their original foundations. And today the nonprofit Colonial Williamsburg Foundation, free from any affiliation with other organizations or governmental agencies, watches over the 173 acres, 276 costumed historical interpreters and craftspeople, 63 or more gardeners, and 3,460 other employees, meeting the $130-million annual operating costs through tourist income, investment returns from the permanent endowment left by Rockefeller, and donations.

What all this meticulous care and expenditure of money means to you and me is the opportunity to wander through this 18th-century "city" and literally feel the heartbeat of our nation when it was new—in candlelight concerts at the Governor's Palace, fife and drum corps parades on Market Square Green, and in tavern meals that recall those long-ago menus.

GETTING THERE

Williamsburg can be reached by U.S. 60 and I-64 from the west, I-95 from the north and south. Greyhound has bus service, and Amtrak provides train service from Boston, New York, Philadelphia, Baltimore, and Washington, as well as excellent package tours. Newport News's Patrick Henry International Airport is only a 20-minute drive, and the Norfolk International Airport is a 50-minute drive.

WHERE TO STAY

Back in its colonial youth, Williamsburg boasted more than 30 inns, taverns, and "ordinaries" to accommodate the men of affairs who rode in from plantations, some several days away by horseback, to attend sessions of the legislature. From the first, it has been a center of hospitality, and in that respect things haven't changed a bit in the last 200 years. The only difference, of course, is in size—today every road leading into Williamsburg is lined with motels; inside the city limits are scores more, offering a total of about 9,000 rooms; there are some 30 privately owned guesthouses; and those who carry their accommodations with them in the increasingly popular campers will find over a dozen campgrounds within easy driving distance. Whatever your budget, there's a suitable place to stay in Williamsburg.

In spite of this, I would again caution: *don't come without a reservation.* Williamsburg's "season" is a long one—mid-March to early November—and visitors from all over the world throng its streets. An excellent way to be sure you will have a place to lay your head is to write for the directory of accommodations, attractions, camping, and dining facilities published by the Williamsburg –Williamsburg Area Convention and Visitors Bureau, P.O. Box GB, Williamsburg, VA 23187 (tel. 804/253-0192), under the title "Visitor's Guide to Virginia's Historic Triangle—Jamestown, Williamsburg and Yorktown." The Williamsburg Hotel and Motel Association (tel. toll free 800/446-9244) can also furnish current reservation information. And Colonial Williamsburg has a toll-free number for information and reservations for lodgings, dining, and group tours: 800/HISTORY. Or you may write Reservations Manager, Colonial Williamsburg, P.O. Box B, Williamsburg, VA 23187.

The Best

If money is no object and you lean toward quiet elegance, there's just one place to stay, the **Williamsburg Inn,** Francis Street, Williamsburg, VA 23185 (tel. toll free 800/HISTORY). Owned and operated by the Colonial Williamsburg Foundation, the sprawling, whitewashed brick inn, located just one block from the restored area, will surround you with the graciousness of the famous 19th-century spa hotels; and its English Regency decor is a sure antidote to any 20th-century tensions you may have brought along. From the moment you step into the lobby, with a fireplace at each end and French doors across the entire rear wall, you'll begin to experience the relaxation that is the inn's keynote. Walk through those French doors and you're on a brick veranda that overlooks swimming pools, croquet grounds, tennis courts, lawn bowling greens, a putting green, a driving range, and two golf courses. Follow a courteous bellboy to your room and you'll find it spacious, modern in every convenience, furnished in the same Regency style as the public rooms. You might well fancy yourself a pampered guest at a Virginia country estate! Or maybe you'll feel like one of the kings and queens who've stayed here (Queen Elizabeth II and Prince Philip are on the royal heads-of-state guest list). U.S. presidents Harry S Truman and Dwight Eisenhower and foreign presidents also have enjoyed the inn's hospitality. Winston Churchill came to dinner, then reluctantly —audibly so—traveled on to Richmond.

If you stay in the main building, you'll find that rates for double occupancy start at $150, with a bed-sitting room costing $250 and a suite at $325. The most luxurious of the inn's rooms are in the newer (1972) Providence Hall, set in a wooded area just east of the main building. There's a private balcony or patio for each room, and each has a superb view. Double-occupancy tariff starts at $160, with suites ranging from $320 up.

There are several package plans at special rates: inquire about the Williamsburg Tavern Plan, Leisure Season, Colonial Weekends, and Tennis or Golf Plans.

Rates at the **Williamsburg Lodge,** a short distance away on South England Street, and only a little less elegant (the decor is modern, not Regency), are a more modest $87 to $150.

Very Special

For a truly unique vacation experience, reserve at one of the **Colonial Houses** operated by the Williamsburg Inn, Francis Street, Williamsburg, VA

23185 (tel. toll free 800/HISTORY). There are 28 of them, ranging in size from a tiny cottage tucked away in a garden to a 16-room tavern. They're all in the historic area, furnished in period manner, and carry with them full guest privileges at the inn, at rates beginning at $120 for a room and $150 and up for a suite or complete house. For full details and reservations, call the toll-free number.

Motels

The **Best Western Patrick Henry Inn,** York and Page streets, P.O. Drawer S, Williamsburg, VA 23187 (tel. 804/229-9540 or toll free 800/582-8910 in Virginia, 800/446-9228 elsewhere), is ideally situated, just a half block from the restored area. This is a full-service hotel, a moderately priced restaurant, lounge with live entertainment April to December, swimming pool, game room, and playground. The 301 attractive guest rooms are nicely furnished, some with king-size beds, and some suites have whirlpool tubs. Seasonal rates for doubles range from $49 to $85, and there are several good-value package rates available.

Out from the center of town, the **Best Western Williamsburg Outlet Inn,** P.O. Box 3108, Williamsburg, VA 23187 (tel. 804/565-1000 or toll free 800/922-9277), is convenient to the Williamsburg Pottery Factory, and amenities include a moderate-priced restaurant, lounge, swimming pool, and playground. Guest rooms include cable/movie TV, and there are attractive honeymoon suites. Season rates range from $18 to $30 per person.

The **Gov. Spottswood,** 1508 Richmond Rd., Williamsburg, VA 23185 (tel. 804/229-6444, or toll free 800/368-1244, 800/572-4567 in Virginia), has 17 kitchen units and in-room coffee in the remainder of its 58 rooms. Rates are a moderate $45 to $95, and there's a pool and playground on the wooded premises, a coffeeshop and restaurant just across the street. It's one mile from the historic area.

The **Motor House** is operated by Colonial Williamsburg Hotel Properties, Inc. (tel. toll free 800/HISTORY), and is located at the visitor center. This sprawling, casual-contemporary complex is ideal for families. Doubles and singles run $71 to $81; corner studios are $90 and up.

The **Cascades,** P.O. Box B, Williamsburg, VA 23187, is operated by Colonial Williamsburg Hotel Properties, Inc. (tel. toll free 800/HISTORY), and is located behind the Motor House at the visitor center on SR 132, just off U.S. 60 bypass. These rustic two-story buildings are located in a wooded area and offer mini-suites, all in a contemporary design. Doubles cost $50 to $98.

There are picture-window views from every room; and facilities for swimming, horseshoe pitching, table tennis, badminton, a 9-hole putting green, an 18-hole miniature-golf course, a playground, and shuffleboard are available, as well as guest privileges at the Golden Horseshoe Club, which has two golf courses. Two restaurants serve the Cascades and Motor House: The Cascades, specializing in Chesapeake Bay delicacies, and a cafeteria grill for quick service.

A welcome addition to the Williamsburg scene is the spiffy 210-room **Days Inn East,** 90 Old York Rd. (P.O. Drawer GQ), Williamsburg, VA 23185 (tel. 804/253-6444 or toll free 800/635-5366). It nestles in a quiet, woodsy setting on Va. 199 (Exit 57B, off I-64) across from Water Country USA. Youngsters under 12 dine free with adult guests in the casual, candlelit dining room, which showcases old Williamsburg and southern delicacies. And their parents can enjoy live weekend entertainment, late-night Friday to Sunday dancing. Doubles range from $58 to $62 May through September and drop considerably after that. Add $3 for each child under 18; those under 1 stay free.

The **Comfort Inn Historic Area,** 120 Bypass Rd., Williamsburg 23185 (tel. 804/229-2000 or toll free 800/228-5150), is, as its name implies, handy to the restored area of Williamsburg, yet not right in the hubbub of downtown. Rooms are attractively decorated (some in colonial style) and comfortably furnished, and there's a coin laundry, as well as a heated pool. Seasonal rates range from $35 to $69 for doubles.

In the super-budget category, the three-story, 169-room **Motel 6,** 3030 U.S. 60, Williamsburg, VA 23185 (tel. 804/565-3433), is popular with travelers seeking clean, comfortable "no-frills" lodging. This doesn't mean austerity by a long shot: there's a swimming pool, and a color TV (for a nominal nightly charge). A nearby restaurant is open from 7 a.m. to 11 p.m. Rates are $24 for singles, plus $6 for each additional adult. This fast-growing national chain consistently keeps its rates down and offers a great buy for the travel dollar. From I-64, eastbound or westbound, take Va. 646 south (Lightfoot exit) to U.S. 60 east (about two miles).

Bed and Breakfast

For B&B accommodations in some 20 private homes, contact **Benson-house of Williamsburg Bed & Breakfast,** 2036 Monument Ave., Richmond, VA 23220 (tel. 804/648-7560).

Campgrounds

Located 4½ miles west of Williamsburg on U.S. 60, **Williamsburg Campsites,** P.O. Box 357, Norge, VA 23127 (tel. 804/564-3101 or 564-9637), has 300 sites, and there's no charge for water or electric hookups. The swimming pool is also free and there are hot showers, toilets, a laundry, grocery, and disposal station; $11.50 minimum for up to four people. Additional persons, $1 each; $1 extra for sewer. Rates are subject to change. Open year round and just across the road from Williamsburg Pottery (Exit 53 off I-64).

The **Jamestown Beach Campsite,** on Va. 31 South (P.O. Box CB), Williamsburg, VA 23185 (tel. 804/229-7609 or 229-3300), is set on 200 lovely acres along the James River, just 3½ miles from Williamsburg on Va. 31 South. There are 600 sites, plus amusement equipment, swimming in the pool or river, modern rest rooms, showers, miniature golf, groceries, and ice. Rates are $12 and up for up to four people, $2 for each additional; trailer hookups are extra.

Four miles west of Williamsburg on Va. 646 between U.S. 60 and I-64, the **Best Holiday Trav-L-Park Fair Oaks,** 901 Lightfoot Rd., Williamsburg, VA 23185 (tel. 804/565-2101), has 450 camping sites in a very attractive, open, shaded site. Amenities include a grocery store, firewood, laundry, tiled hot showers, a pump station, and metered LP gas. There are two pools, two wading pools, fishing pond, recreation hall, playgrounds, four sheltered pavilions, nature and bike trails, and a mini-golf course. Clubs and caravans are welcome. The site is near the popular Williamsburg Pottery outlet shops (show $50 or $100 in pottery sales receipts for camping-fee discounts at certain seasons).

Rates are $11.50 to $15 nightly for a group of four; extra persons pay $1. Reservations are strongly recommended at this popular, well-maintained campground, which remains open all year.

WHERE TO EAT

"This is the place to come if you really like good food," a Williamsburg native told me—and he's right. Good eating has been a tradition here since the early days, and you can find almost any cuisine your appetite fancies, in settings as varied as a colonial tavern and a New York deli.

True Elegance

The **Williamsburg Inn** (tel. toll free 800/HISTORY) ranks first again, with its handsome **Regency Room** highlighted by bronze and crystal chandeliers, hand-painted Chinese wall paintings, tranquil green walls, and curved windows. There's dancing, and gentlemen are, of course, required to wear a jacket and tie at dinner. Breakfast in this elegant setting can be a simple repast for about $7, or you can go all the way with a champagne breakfast for two for $40. And somehow, a champagne breakfast seems appropriate! Lunch consists of sandwiches, salads, fresh fish, or meat and vegetable plates ($8 and up).

But it's at dinner that the Regency Room outdoes itself—both cuisine and wine list are internationally respected. You might start with bouquet of shrimp suprême or Virginia ham on Boston lettuce with condiments, move on to lobster bisque Chantilly, then select from a dazzling array of seafoods—perhaps the croustade of lobster au whisky—or French lamb chops with minted pears from the grill. The salads are true creations, and rolls and breads are all fresh baked and of the melt-in-your-mouth variety. Desserts (if you're still hanging in there) include an extraordinary list of homemade pies, cakes, pastries, and such exotic ice creams (also homemade and *very* rich) as black walnut and rum (made with the real thing, of course). Entrees will run $22 to $30 on the à la carte menu. All in all, it's a rare epicurean experience. Reservations required.

The **Bay Room** at the **Williamsburg Lodge** (tel. 229-1000) also serves breakfast, lunch, and dinner, and features fresh seafood. On Friday and Saturday evenings its renowned Chesapeake Bay Feast draws hosts of regulars, as well it should. The overflowing buffet has a full array of appetizers—seafood soups and chowders, clams on the half shell, steamed shrimp, etc.—and there are as many seafood main dishes as the imagination can conjure up, plus sugar-cured Virginia ham and prime ribs of beef, with side dishes like spoon bread and European-blend vegetables. Each trip to the buffet will doubtless bring on an agony of indecision, and my advice is to keep your helpings small and try to sample some of each. The cost is $18 for adults, $10 for children, and beverages and desserts are extra (there's a very complete list of both alcoholic and nonalcoholic drinks, and try to save room for one of the yummy desserts). The Feast is served from 6 to 9:15 p.m. Call for reservations.

The Hunt Breakfast Buffet at the **Cascades Restaurant,** Information Center Drive, is as sumptuous as the Chesapeake Bay Feast, only here it's early-morning fare. As one Williamsburg devotee advised, "You really should starve the day before so you can appreciate it fully!" Served Monday through Saturday from 7:30 to 10 a.m., the buffet is a modern-day version of the old plantation breakfast, with eggs, sausage, bacon, ham, fried chicken, grits, scalloped oysters, muffins, etc. Again there's no limit to the times you can visit the table, and the $7 ($5 for children) charge includes beverage. They also have an equally good Sunday brunch from 8:30 a.m. to 2:30 p.m. at $9 for adults, $6 for children.

The Taverns

Part of the fun of a Williamsburg visit is eating in one of the four restored taverns that specialize in 18th-century food served by waiters in knee breeches and gaiters. You can eat in the garden at two, and have dinner by candlelight at all three. Prices are surprisingly moderate. Dinner reservations are required and can be made at all three taverns by calling 229-2141.

Josiah Chowning's Tavern, adjacent to Market Square (tel. 229-2141), serves lunch and dinner in the garden when weather permits. The Brunswick stew that is traditional here is $4.50 at lunch, $10.25 at dinner. Welsh rarebit ($5) is also a specialty, but prime ribs, ham, and barbecued pork ribs are all very, very good. Breads and desserts come from the same bakeshop that serves the inn (true of all three taverns). Count on spending $4 to $7 for lunch, $11 to $17 for dinner. But the best part of your meal at Chowning's might well be after it's over, when the "Gambols" begin at 9 p.m. You can sit back, order up a clay pipe exactly as Patrick Henry or Thomas Jefferson did, and enjoy the "diversions"—balladeers and games (backgammon, if you like). In fact, even if you dine elsewhere, you can amble over for the Gambols, only don't amble late —seating is on a strictly first-come, first-served basis. Lunch is from 11:30 a.m. to 3:30 p.m. The three dinner sittings are at 5, 6:45, and 8:30 p.m.

Christiana Campbell's Tavern, Waller Street (tel. 229-2141), was one of George Washington's favorites. Brunch (from 10 a.m. to 2:30 p.m.) includes such plantation fare as pecan waffles, country sausage, specialty omelets, and chicken dishes, costing from $6 to $8. Ale, beer, lemonade, cider, and iced tea are served, and dinner (with strolling musicians) is 5:30 to 9:30 p.m., with prices in the $14 to $18 range. Spoon bread, muffins, and homemade fig ice cream add just the right exclamation point.

READER'S TAVERN SELECTION: "**Christiana Campbell's Tavern** gives out their recipe for sweet potato muffins—in fact, they're already printed and readily available. We found 9 o'clock Sunday morning the loveliest time to visit areas of restored Williamsburg, before the crowds and while waiting to have that nice brunch at Christiana's" (G. Salassi, Baton Rouge, La.).

At the **King's Arms Tavern,** on Duke of Gloucester Street across from the Raleigh Tavern (tel. 229-2141), your costumed waiter will likely be a college student—it's a tradition that dates from the beginning of the restoration. Lunch (it might be Yorkshire meat pie or Virginia ham) is from 11:30 a.m. to 2:30 p.m. Dinner hours are 5:30 to 9:30 p.m. The evening menu includes Cornish game hen, filet mignon stuffed with oysters, and colonial game pie (venison, duck, and rabbit), with prices ranging from $12 to $18.

Shields' Tavern, on Duke of Gloucester Street next door to the King's Arms (tel. 229-2141), dates back to 1710, but was not reconstructed until the 1940s and underwent further extensive restoration in 1988. Nowadays, diners face a menu filled with Chesapeake Bay specialties: clams, oysters, shrimp, and a marvelous seafood platter that comes with a cornbread cake. For a real treat, try the "Sampler: A Tasting of the 1750s Foods," which changes almost daily, with small portions of several dishes such as buttered crabmeat and crab fritters. For dessert, you can't outdo the lemon cheesecake or a yummy sour-cherry trifle. Hours are 11:30 a.m. to 2:30 p.m., and 5:30 to 9:30 p.m., with prices of $5 to $8 at lunch, $11 to $20 at dinner. It's a large place, but so popular that reservations are a good idea.

Other Choices

The **Old Chickahominy House,** 1211 Jamestown Rd. (tel. 229-4689), used to be in an old house on the river of that name, but the new location has every bit as much charm as the original. Dale and Maxine Henderson serve breakfast and lunch from 8:30 a.m. to 3 p.m. in a country setting of 18th-century antiques, many of which you can buy and take home if you've a mind. Besides the things for sale in the dining room, there's a large adjoining shop full of unusual items. Service is family style at large tables, which seat from 6 to 10 people (I found it a neat way to meet interesting people), and reservations are not necessary. You can breakfast simply on Miss Melinda's pancakes or fill up on the grits, hot biscuits, and coffee or tea. My own lunch favorite is Miss Melinda's special, which starts with a fruit salad, followed by a cup of Brunswick stew, smoked Virginia ham on hot biscuits, homemade pie (try the buttermilk pie for something different), and a beverage. They'll sell you Brunswick stew to take home or smoked Virginia ham, cured bacon and sausage, and water-ground cornmeal. Prices are moderate to cheap. It's hard to say whether the charm of this place or the food comes out on top!

Beethoven's Inn, 467 Merrimac Trail, (tel. 229-7069), is that New York deli I mentioned, and during its short life it has attained a place in the hearts of locals that's just short of beloved. About eight years ago Jim Wesson decided he'd had it with the business world in Washington, D.C., and moved his family here for a pressure-free lifestyle. True to his "quality of life" philosophy, Jim will tell you, "this is the most personality-oriented place you'll run into." He serves the deli food he loves himself, plays only his favorite classical records (most of them works of the great Ludwig, naturally), and even has a modest library of books for sale, but only those by authors of his personal choice. In the pleasant, red-carpeted dining room whose walls are hung with signed photos of performing artists and writers on one side and oil portraits of you-know-who, Mark Twain, Edgar Allan Poe, and the like on the other, you're likely to see students, college faculty, and local residents all munching happily on thick sandwiches of pastrami, liverwurst, and knockwurst with sauerkraut, or smiling over the superb onion soup that's a house specialty. There is even New York cream-cheesecake that rivals my Manhattan favorite. And like its "up nawth" counterparts, it has a take-out service. Reservations aren't necessary—come any time from 11 a.m. to 8 p.m., until 9 p.m. on Friday and Saturday. You will eat well here for under $10.

A longtime favorite with both townspeople and William and Mary faculty members is the **Green Leafe Café,** 765 Scotland St. (tel. 220-3405). The rustic oak interior is an indoor garden (true to its name), accented by stained-glass windows from old Richmond homes that have yielded to the wrecker's ball. The cuisine is continental, ranging from veal parmesan to sausage lasagne to vegetarian dishes, and there are daily specials. Prices are in the $6 to $12 range. Hours are 4 to 9 p.m. daily. There's a late-night menu after 9 p.m.

Executive chef and co-owner Marcel Desaulniers has garnered wide acclaim as one of the up-and-coming new breed of American chefs for the fine contemporary cuisine of the **Trellis Café, Restaurant and Grill,** on Duke of Gloucester Street (tel. 804/229-8610), in Merchants Square just outside the historic district. Personable, award-winning Marcel, who grew up in a French-Canadian family in Woonsocket, Rhode Island, insists that all ingredients be fresh and "impeccable." His seasonal menus change four times a year to take advantage of the freshest ingredients the region has to offer: local catfish, sea scallops, Virginia ham and peanuts, duck. And from what he modestly calls a "simple" cooking style emerge such wonders as grilled sea trout filet with tomatoes and cactus leaves on jalapeño-chile rice; sautéed shad roe with lump backfin crabmeat, cucumbers, leeks, and scallion butter; sautéed venison with white trumpet mushrooms, Barlette onions, and chive butter on chive and roasted-garlic fettuccine; freshly shucked oysters and shiitake mushrooms served in warm brioche. Simple? Simply wonderful! Surprisingly, dinner entrees range from $11 to $20. It's possible to have a salad, entree, and one of the most expensive desserts and stay under $20 per person. The average lunch—which runs to quiche, burgers, grilled chicken, and nutty-tuna sandwiches—costs about $9. "We're talking basic food at lunch," chef Marcel explains. But it's basic with superbly imaginative touches.

The Trellis has five rooms, each with a distinctive personality: the Café Bar, awash with Mexican and Italian tiles; the elegant Garden Room, with a lavish Venetian glass chandelier and mirrors; the Grill Room, with handmade oak tables and an open-hearth Texas mesquite grill; the Vault Room, which gives the impression of dining inside a wine barrel; and the airy Trellis Room, with its ceiling, booths, and floors of century-old pine from a Gimbels department store in Philadelphia. Sit wherever most pleases your fancy, but don't miss this one!

Italian dishes, as well as southern specialties and steak, star on the menu at the **Jefferson Inn,** 1453 Richmond Rd. (tel. 229-2296). Hot breads are home-baked, and à la carte prices run $7 to $22. Hours are 5 to 11 p.m., and reservations are advised.

The **Dynasty,** 1621 Richmond Rd. (tel. 220-8888), is a local favorite for Hunan, Szechuan, Mandarin, and Cantonese dishes in a pagoda-like setting of understated elegance. Prices are under $22, and hours are 5:30 to 10 p.m. There's also a Sunday buffet from 11:30 a.m. to 3 p.m.

Budget Eating

For a good, inexpensive meal or snack, head for the **Marketplace** in the campus center of the College of William and Mary. It's a popular "gourmetisserie" of food bars selling pizza, burgers, hot dogs, submarine sandwiches, ice cream, and the like.

Morrison's Cafeteria, 1851 Richmond Rd. (tel. 253-0292), serves food of dependable quality at reasonable prices (a meal will seldom run as much as $10). Hours are 7 to 10 a.m. and 11:30 a.m. to 9 p.m.

WHAT TO SEE

The **Colonial Williamsburg Visitor Center,** Colonial Parkway and Va. 132 (tel. 229-1000)—just follow the signs posted all over town—is the place to start. A 35-minute color film, titled *Williamsburg—The Story of a Patriot,* is shown continuously until 6 p.m. each day, and do take time to see it. This is the best possible introduction and shouldn't be missed.

Three types of admission tickets are available for Colonial Williamsburg attractions. The popular **Patriot's Pass,** good for one year from date of purchase, provides unlimited admission to all exhibition buildings, the historical film, Carter's Grove Plantation, Governor's Palace, Public Hospital of 1773, DeWitt Wallace Gallery, the one-hour guided Patriot's Tour, Abby Aldrich Rockefeller Folk Art Center, and Bassett Hall (Williamsburg home of the Rockefellers), as well as shuttle bus transportation. It costs $24.50 for adults, $12.25 for ages 6 to 12.

The **Royal Governor's Pass,** good for up to four consecutive days, provides admission to all exhibits in the historic area, including the Governor's Palace, DeWitt Wallace Gallery, and Patriot's Tour. Cost is $19.50 for adults, $9.75 for ages 6 to 12.

The **Basic Admission Ticket** admits you to up to 12 exhibition buildings in the historic area and includes a one-hour guided tour, and rides on the shuttle bus. It costs $14.50 for adults, $7.25 for ages 6 to 12. Major credit cards may be used to purchase all passes and tours.

All exhibition buildings are open from 9 a.m. to 5 p.m. in summer and 9:30 a.m. to 4:30 p.m. in winter. Some shops have evening hours during July and August.

For more complete information on points of interest before you come, contact Colonial Williamsburg Foundation, P.O. Box C, Williamsburg, VA 23187, or phone the visitors center (tel. 804/229-1000).

The foundation operates a special bus, which circles the historic area, and your admission ticket allows you to catch it at any of the designated stops and ride as far as you like.

In fact, going the full circle is a good way to begin, after which you can get off at the first of the nine stops, spend as much time as you like, then reboard to ride to the next one. There are also horse-drawn carriages and wagon rides. Occasionally there are oxcart rides too.

Organized tours (most are available only on specified days of the week, and some are offered only during summer months) include: According to the Ladies, two-hour walking tour with a costumed guide who presents the feminine perspective of colonial Williamsburg; The Other Half, two-hour walking tour that explores 18th-century African and African/American culture in Williamsburg; Colonial Life in Virginia, walking tour of the historic area for family groups; and Lanthorn Tours, evening tour of selected craft shops. For the children, ask about the Once Upon a Town Tours (for ages 4 to 6), Time Trippers (for ages 7 to 10), and the Young Apprentice Tours (for ages 11 to 14).

Here are not-to-be-missed highlights:

The **Raleigh Tavern** was the scene of heated political debates, rollicking nighttime gaiety, and grand balls (in the Apollo Room).

The **Capitol** is one of the reconstructed buildings, but is faithful in detail to the original modified-Renaissance style. This is where so much pre-Revolution political activity took place.

The **Governor's Palace** was home to seven royal governors and both Patrick Henry and Thomas Jefferson when they served as governor of the new state. What you see is a reconstruction of the original, which was destroyed by fire in 1781; Jefferson's detailed floor plan of 1779 was followed to ensure accuracy in the reconstruction.

The craft shops scattered throughout the historic area are functioning work museums, where costumed artisans use hand tools and colonial-vintage methods. There's an apothecary, basketmaker, miller, weaver, musical-instrument maker, harnessmaker, and a long list of others.

Largest Williamsburg reconstruction in 51 years, the **Public Hospital of 1773,** which was opened in 1985, was the first American institution devoted to treating mental illness.

The **DeWitt Wallace Decorative Arts Gallery,** also added in 1985, was made possible in large measure by a gift of the founders of *The Reader's Digest,* as was the Public Hospital. Designed by renowned architect Kevin Roche, it displays over 8,000 priceless antiques and is one of the world's greatest collections of decorative arts.

The **Abby Aldrich Rockefeller Folk Art Center,** just outside the restored area, houses fascinating traditional arts ranging from paintings, drawings, and furniture to pottery, weather vanes, and toys.

And don't leave out the beautiful old walled campus of the **College of William and Mary**—look especially for the **Christopher Wren Building,** oldest academic building in America (1695) still in use.

Colonial Williamsburg is open year round, but if you can get there during the quiet months of January and February you'll not only avoid the crowds, you'll have the benefit of many reduced rates and special programs.

SIGHTS AND SITES NEARBY

Jamestown Settlement (write: Superintendent, Colonial National Historical Park, P.O. Box 210, Yorktown, VA 23690; tel. 804/898-3400), is six miles away by way of the Colonial Parkway. Admission to the island is $5 per car, and the entrance gate is open from 8:30 a.m. to 4:30 p.m. Jamestown was the first permanent English settlement in America (May 1607), capital of the Virginia colony from 1607 to 1699, and the place where Capt. John Smith became acquainted with the young Pocahontas through her father, Powhatan. Stop at the visitor center for a film, tour information, and exhibits, before setting out to see the old Church Tower (1639) and other historic sites in the old village. The settlement is a year-round exhibit that includes replicas of the *Susan Constant* (you can go on board and poke around), the *Godspeed,* and the *Discovery,* the three tiny sailing ships in which Jamestown's colonists crossed the Atlantic. The latter two are 1984 seaworthy replacements of earlier vessels. There's also a replica of the 1607 Jamestown fort, an Indian lodge, and a $2.8-million museum expansion devoted to the native Indians and early settlers. Open from 9 a.m. to 5 p.m. every day. Admission is $5 for adults, $2.50 for ages 6 to 12.

When Cornwallis surrendered at **Yorktown** in 1781, the fight for American independence was finally over. The free National Park Service visitors center (open 8:30 a.m. to 6 p.m. in the summer months; closes at 5 p.m. Labor Day through March) has walking tours of the battlefield daily, as well as a film and a lot of interesting exhibits. The Yorktown Victory Center puts on an absolutely smashing sound and light show to dramatize the military goings-on here, for which there is a small charge.

Just for fun, visit Europe on this side of the Atlantic at **Busch Gardens,**

The Old Country, P.O. Drawer FC, Williamsburg, VA 23187 (tel. 804/253-3350), located just three miles east of Williamsburg. It's a 360-acre family-entertainment amusement park that re-creates 17th-century villages of England, France, Italy, and Germany, and throws in shows, a celebrity concert series, restaurants, and rides like the famous Loch Ness Monster. Billed as the tallest, fastest, fiercest roller coaster in the world, the Loch Ness Monster has double interlocking loops and a 114-foot drop where speed reaches 70 mph. New shows are presented each year. (In 1989, *Stage Struck,* a Broadway-style musical revue, and *The Enchanted Laboratory,* a computer-animated show featuring magnificent special effects and automated animal characters were introduced.) Open weekends from mid-March to mid-May and September 4 to October 29, and daily from mid-May to early September. One-day tickets (age 3 and up) are $19.95, two days cost $25.95, and there's a reduced rate after 5 p.m.

Carter's Grove, a 1755 restored plantation house that has been called "the most beautiful house in America," overlooks the James River just six miles to the southeast on U.S. 60. It's open daily March through November; $6.50 for adults, $3 for children to 12.

The **James River** between Williamsburg and Richmond might well be called "plantation row," since both Va. 5 and 10, on their north and south sides, are dotted with restored homes, many of which you can visit for a small fee. Highway markers are posted all along the way, giving directions for turning off the main road to reach them. Some of the more interesting ones are Shirley Plantation, Berkeley Plantation, Evelynton Plantation, Bacon's Castle and archaelogical center, and Flowerdew Hundred.

3. Richmond

The state capital since 1780, Richmond is 49 miles northwest of Williamsburg on I-64, and is well worth a day—or several more. Even before it became a proper town, Indians and white settlers were fighting over rights to the location, a tradition that lingered down through the centuries. It was here, in 1775, that Patrick Henry made his famous "Give me liberty or give me death" speech defying British rule, and during the Revolution (having been named capital of the state in 1780), it was plundered mercilessly by soldiers of the Crown. During the Civil War, it served as capital of the Confederacy from 1861 to 1865, and was under almost constant attack by Federal troops. Finally, in 1865, the city was abandoned, and fleeing Rebel soldiers actually burned down large portions of the city rather than have them fall into the hands of the enemy.

Today's Richmond has risen from those ashes to represent the New South in its most positive sense. Its turbulent past is far from forgotten, and historical sites are maintained with all due respect. Modern-day Richmond is, however, very much a creature of the present and the future, with tall skyscrapers as well as historical buildings, and an active industrial climate based on tobacco, paper, publishing, and chemicals. There's also a strong emphasis on cultural and educational affairs.

WHERE TO STAY

One of the South's most heralded "new" hotels is the magnificently restored 1895 **Jefferson Sheraton Hotel,** a national historic landmark at Franklin and Adams streets, Richmond, VA 23220 (tel. 804/788-8000). Upon entering the massive, fanciful white-brick structure, you're greeted in the soaring Palm Court Lobby Rotunda by the famed Edward Valentine statue of the hotel's "patron saint," Thomas Jefferson; it stands under a luminous stained-glass skylight. Just off the Rotunda is one of Richmond's favorite rendezvous spots, T.J.'s restaurant and bar. In the Jefferson's specialty restaurant, Le Maire, guests dine in seven intimate formal rooms, one a library with the hotel's original leather-bound book collection. Fare is primarily continental, with a few regional touches. Another historic touch: the restaurant is named for the third president's French maître d'hôtel, who introduced cooking with wine to the fledgling nation. And if you're fond of french fries, you can thank Mr. Jefferson, who reputedly became captivated with them in France and brought the preparation back home with him. The hotel's 274 spacious rooms and suites are pleasingly decorated in mulberry, dusty rose, and mint green, and beautifully appointed with period reproduction furnishings. Doubles range from $104 to $125, and attractively priced weekend packages are available.

The **Hyatt Richmond at Brookfield,** 6624 W. Broad St., Richmond, VA 23230 (tel. 804/285-1234, or toll free 800/238-9000), has a very attractive suburban location in a west-end park just off I-64. There's a resort-like setting, indoor/outdoor pools, lighted tennis courts, sauna, jogging course, and playground. All rooms have free cable TV, and parking is also complimentary. Lightfoot's offers live entertainment and dancing, and Hugo's is the elegant main dining room. Rates, double occupancy, range from $59 to $145, $125 on the Regency Club concierge floor. On weekends, rates can drop to $65 a night, single or double occupancy.

The **Residence Inn by Marriott,** 2121 Dickins Rd., Richmond, VA 23230 (tel. 804/285-8200 or toll free 800/331-3131), is in Richmond's West End, and, in addition to the amenities standard for this chain (see Introduction), there's a microwave in every suite, barbecue facilities, and suites for nonsmokers. Rates range from $55 to $75 for studio suites, depending on length of stay ($75 to $85 for stays of six nights or less), $75 to $100 for penthouse suites.

Located a bit out of town (about six miles from the city center) on U.S. 60, the English Tudor–style **Best Western Governor's Inn,** 9848 Midlothian Turnpike, Richmond, VA 23235 (tel. 804/323-0007 or toll free 800/528-1234), offers rooms and suites of a high standard in both decor and furnishings, with cable TV and movies, and refrigerators in some. An all-day restaurant is moderately priced, and there's a pool as well as a whirlpool.

Courtyard by Marriott, 6400 West Broad St., Richmond, VA 23230 (tel. 804/282-1881 or toll free 800/321-2211), is a small hotel not unlike European inns that create the feeling of being "at home." Rooms are attractively decorated and comfortably furnished, with cable TV and movies. There's a pool, whirlpool, exercise room, and coin laundry. The dining room serves all three meals at moderate prices. Rates range from $64 to $70, with special weekend rates available.

The always-reliable Days Inn chain has four locations in the area, including the **Days Inn West Broad,** W. Broad Street at 2100 Dickens Rd., Richmond, VA 28230 (tel. 804/282-3300, or toll free 800/325-2525). It's a handsome seven-story 185-room brick structure with some extra-large rooms, a gift shop, and a pool. Health center privileges are offered, and there's a restaurant nearby. Nonsmoking rooms are available, and some rooms are equipped for wheelchair travelers. Double rates range from $40 to $48; add $5 for each additional adult, $1 for each child under 18. Also ask about special features for business travelers.

Motel 6, 5704 Williamsburg Rd., Sandston, VA 23150 (tel. 804/222-7600), has a swimming pool, and rooms that are standard for this dependable economy chain (see Introduction). Convenient to Richmond Airport, on U.S. 60. Rates are $26 single, $32 double.

Another good "value for dollar" chain is represented by the **Red Roof Inn,** 4350 Commerce Rd., Richmond, VA 23234 (tel. 804/271-7240 or toll free 800/848-7878). Rooms are average in size, comfortably furnished, with extra-long double beds, and there's free sports and movies TV. A limited number of nonsmoking rooms available. Rates are $31 to $45 for doubles, and those over 60 are given a 10% discount.

Guesthouses

If you're as fond of guesthouses as I am, you'll be delighted to know about the **Carrington Row Inn,** in the historic Church Hill district, 2309 W. Broad St., Richmond, VA 23223 (tel. 804/343-7005). In adjoining 1818 rowhouses, four guest rooms, two with private bath or fireplace, are lovingly furnished in period decor with four-poster twin, full, or queen-size mahogany beds. If privacy is your preference, request the upper level, which has its own sitting room adjacent to two guest rooms. Guests are welcomed with a glass of sherry before a fireplace which lends a welcome glow to nippy evenings. Continental breakfast is served each morning. Doubles with shared bath are in the $60 to $65 range, and with private bath about $75. One night's deposit is required to hold a reservation.

The owners, Dr. and Mrs. Abbott, also operate the equally engaging **Catlin-Abbott House,** another Federal structure, at 2304 E. Broad St. (tel. 804/780-3746).

READER'S ACCOMMODATION SUGGESTION: "For travelers who want to stay over in Richmond, meet someone local, and enjoy a home atmosphere, I can heartily recommend the guesthouse reservation service of **Lyn Benson,** who can book you into a private home, guest cottages, or apartments in Richmond. She has a variety of accommodations and neighborhoods and is very nice about trying to find just what you're looking for, and almost all her listings include a full breakfast. Rates are comparable to or lower than motels. Her address is Lyn M. Benson, Bensonhouse of Richmond, P.O. Box 15131, Richmond, VA 23227 (tel. 804/648-7560)" (S. Caliri, Wayne, N.J.).

WHERE TO EAT

One of the South Atlantic's fastest-growing cities, Richmond offers an almost baffling choice of excellent dining rooms. For a good rundown, pick up the latest "Dining & Shopping Guide" from the Convention and Visitors Bureau, 300 E. Main St.

The **Tobacco Company Restaurant,** 1201 E. Cary St. (tel. 804/782-

9555), one of the city's abidingly popular dining spots, is ensconced in an 1870s tobacco warehouse in historic waterfront Shockhoe Slip. It's an amalgam of period furnishings, stained-glass windows, vintage signs, and an old brass elevator, guarded by a stern-faced carved wooden Indian. The first level, in an "old Richmond" atmosphere, encompasses an action-packed cocktail area with live entertainment; if you're in a quieter mood, head for the more sedate Victorian Lounge. The second- and third-floor dining rooms overlook a large airy atrium filled with suspended plants and a massive chandelier. Service is deft and friendly, and food choices include such specialties as prime rib, seafood, pasta, and veal at prices that average $20 to $30. There's nightly entertainment in the atrium, and dancing in the lower-level Tobacco Company Club. Lunch hours, Monday through Saturday, are 11:30 a.m. to 2:30 p.m.; dinner, Monday through Friday, 5:30 to 10:30 p.m., to midnight on Saturday, to 10 p.m. on Sunday. Sunday brunch is served from 10:30 a.m. to 2 p.m.

If you have a sense of history or if you just like good food in pleasant surroundings, make time for lunch or dinner at **Traveller's,** 707 E. Franklin St. (tel. 804/644-3976). It's located where the famed Confederate general's horse was stabled, and you'll enter through the basement of Lee's Richmond home, now a cocktail lounge. The rather limited menu runs to steaks, beef, and fresh seafoods. It's just a very relaxing place, and costs are moderate to somewhat expensive. Lunch is served from 11:30 a.m. to 2:30 p.m. Monday through Friday, and dinner is from 6 to 10 p.m. Monday through Saturday. Reservations are a good idea.

Since way back in 1903 residents have been flocking to Richmond's oldest continuously operating restaurant, the **Chesterfield Tea Room,** 900 W. Franklin St. (tel. 804/359-0474)—and with good reason! It's one of those wonderfully welcoming spots where you feel as if time has been reversed, or at least stopped in its tracks. Traditional southern fare is offered, along with newer "Williamsburg-style" selections of seafood, veal, chicken, and beef. Saturday night is a favorite with romantics—the room is candlelit and classical music is gently played. Lunch is served from 11 a.m. to 2 p.m., and dinner from 4 to 8 p.m. Monday through Friday; that magical Saturday dinner is on from 5 to 9 p.m.; and a full-course dinner is offered from 11 a.m. to 3 p.m. Prices are in the modest $6 to $15 range. Reservations are suggested.

Richmond also boasts one of the South's most acclaimed rib houses, the cozy neighborhood **Commercial Café,** at 111 N. Robinson St. (tel. 804/643-7427), which dates back to 1902 and specializes in Virginia hickory-smoked meats. Co-owners Ken Scott and Skip Doane (he's also the chef) jealously guard the recipe for their tangy, fruit-based sauce—and estimate that they sell over 40 tons of ribs a year. At dinner, serious eaters can order the pig-out plate for $14, a feast for $11.75, dinner for $9.75, or a "taster" for $7.50. There's a good choice of chicken, barbecue, ribs, and combination platters, along with barbecue and country Virginia ham sandwiches. Prices drop somewhat at lunch when soups and salads make for a lighter meal. So popular is the Commercial's fare that, at this writing, the owners are planning other locations in the West End (near Reynolds Metals Southside) and The Midlothian Village area. Call for specific addresses.

When your mood turns elegant, **La Petite France,** 2912 Maywill St. (tel. 804/353-8729), will greet you in a beautiful faux marbre entrance, usher you into one of Richmond's loveliest dining rooms, and present a menu of exquisite French dishes (seafood and veal are specialties). Lunch is served from 11:30 a.m. to 2 p.m., dinner from 5:30 to 10 p.m., every day except Sunday and Monday; and you'll pay under $10 for lunch, between $15 and $25 for dinner. There's a dress code, and reservations are advised.

If the mood is casual, the **Strawberry Street Cafe,** 421 N. Strawberry St. (tel. 804/353-6860), is just the place. A relaxed neighborhood café, it dishes up very good lunch and dinner meals, with brunch on the weekends, all at moderate prices ($17 and under for dinner).

Two "drop in" chains that can quell hunger pangs almost any time or place they strike (at moderate-to-cheap prices) are: **Aunt Sarah's Pancake House** (tel. 804/264-9189 for the five locations), serving breakfast, lunch, and dinner daily (try their honey-dipped chicken); and **Bill's Barbecue** (tel. 804/353-2757 for eight locations), where Virginia-style, slow-cooked pork and beef barbecue and heavenly homemade cream pies take top billing.

Two **Morrison's cafeterias,** at 2949 Emerywood Parkway (tel. 804/672-6016) and 8220 Midlothian Turnpike (tel. 804/272-9314), offer good-value meals at inexpensive prices. Hours at both are 11 a.m. to 8:30 p.m., Monday through Thursday, to 9 p.m. Friday and Saturday.

THINGS TO SEE AND DO

Begin your exploration of Richmond's rich historical heritage with a stop at the **Metro Richmond Visitors Center,** 1700 Robin Hood Rd., Exit 14 off I-95/64 (tel. 804/358-5511), where they can not only point you in the direction of historic and cultural attractions, shopping areas, restaurants, and hotels, but can also make reservations and furnish information about organized tours of the city and vicinity. They can also furnish discount combination sightseeing tickets for many museums. Other visitors centers are located in the Sixth Street Marketplace downtown, and at the airport.

A good beginning point for sightseeing is **Capitol Square,** with the State Capitol (9th and Grace streets), designed by Thomas Jefferson in 1785 and modeled after an ancient Roman temple. This is the meeting place for this country's oldest continuous legislative body. It has been the setting for numerous historic events that include Aaron Burr's treason trial, Virginia's secession from the Union, meetings of the Confederate Congress, and Robert E. Lee's assumption of command of the state's armed forces at the beginning of the Civil War. The Governor's Mansion, on the northeast corner of the square, dates from 1813; and on the northwest corner, there's a splendid equestrian statue of George Washington.

Patrick Henry left his footprints over much of colonial Richmond. It was at **St. John's Church,** 24th and E. Broad streets (tel. 648-5015), that he proclaimed so defiantly, "Give me liberty or give me death." The church sits in a 19th-century residential neighborhood, and the many restored homes of historic vintage merit a stroll through its streets. Other sites important in Patrick Henry's Richmond life are his home during the Revolution, **Scotchtown Plantation,** 11 miles west of Ashland (tel. 227-3500), which is open daily from April through October for a small fee; and **Hanover Courthouse,** U.S. 301 North in Hanover (tel. 798-6081), where the young lawyer presented his first case. No doubt he also patronized the **Hanover Tavern** (which dates from

1723) and visited a client or two at the **old jail,** now a museum—you'll find both adjacent to the courthouse.

The **Hollywood Cemetery,** Albemarle and Cherry streets, is the final resting place for Presidents James Monroe and John Tyler, along with Jefferson Davis (president of the Confederacy), generals J. E. B. Stuart and George E. Pickett, and some 18,000 Confederate foot soldiers. Other distinguished Virginians buried here include John Randolph and Matthew Fontaine Maury.

On a happier note, at the corner of Leigh and Adams streets, there's a marvelous **statue of Bill "Bojangles" Robinson,** whose agile tap dancing captivated the world during the '30s and '40s and who was born in Richmond's Jackson Ward neighborhood, at 915 N. 3rd St.

Chief Justice Marshall built the imposing house at 818 E. Marshall St. (tel. 648-7998) in 1790, and it was his home until his death in 1835. Many of the original furnishings still remain, and it is impossible to wander through the rooms without gaining a distinct insight into the life and times of this country's first chief justice. Hours are 10 a.m. to 5 p.m. Tuesday through Saturday, 1 to 5 p.m. on Sunday, with a small admission charge.

The first woman in the country to found a bank is honored at the **Maggie L. Walker National Historic Site,** 110-A E. Leigh St. (tel. 780-1380 or 226-1981). This fascinating woman, who was physically handicapped in addition to being black (daughter of an ex-slave) and female, opened the St. Luke Penny Savings Bank and was a very vocal advocate of black women's rights. Her accomplishments are astounding in view of the social climate in which she lived. Open Tuesday through Sunday (call for hours).

Perhaps the best overall look at Richmond's history and daily life over the centuries comes with a visit to the **Valentine Museum,** 1015 E. Clay St. (tel. 649-0711). Extensive collections depict the lives of those who have shaped the city's destiny through more than half a million photographs, furnishings, clothing, silver, china, and crystal. Running through 1991 is a remarkable exhibition exploring the issue of race and the integral role of Richmond's blacks, a part of the Richmond History Project. In the adjoining **Granville Valentine Building,** there are more collections and exhibitions, as well as food service during summer months. There are hourly guided tours Monday through Saturday from 10 a.m. to 5 p.m., Sunday from 1 to 5 p.m. Admission is $3.50 for adults, $3 for senior citizens, $2.75 for students with ID cards, $1.50 for ages 7 through 12, and there's a family rate of $8.

The **Virginia Museum of Fine Arts,** Boulevard and Grove Avenue (tel. 367-0844), is the largest art museum in the Southeast, and is noted for its art nouveau and art deco collections. Five of the fabulous jeweled Fabergé Russian Easter eggs are here, along with other Russian items. Hours are 11 a.m. to 5 p.m. Tuesday through Saturday (till 10 p.m. on Thursday), 1 to 5 p.m. Sunday, closed holidays. No set admission, but there's a suggested donation of $2.

The **Edgar Allan Poe Museum,** 1914 E. Main St. (tel. 648-5523), occupies an old stone house dating from 1737 that's believed to be Richmond's oldest house. The writer was a longtime resident of Richmond (his mother is buried in the graveyard of St. John's Episcopal Church), and you'll find a wealth of artifacts in the Raven Room and throughout the house. The old-fashioned Enchanted Garden is just that: enchanting. A slide show is presented in the carriage house. Open 10 a.m. to 4 p.m. Tuesday through Saturday, 1:30 to 4 p.m.

Sunday and Monday. Admission is $3 for adults, $2 for senior citizens, and $1 for students (under 6, free).

The **Museum of the Confederacy,** 12th and E. Clay streets (tel. 649-1861), is next door to the White House of the Confederacy, where Jefferson Davis dwelt during most of the Civil War. As is only fitting, this museum houses the world's largest collection of memorabilia from that conflict. Hours are 10 a.m. to 5 p.m. Monday through Saturday, 1 to 5 p.m. Sunday, and it's closed on holidays. Adults pay $3; senior citizens (over 62), $2.50; and ages 7 through 12, $1.25.

Any visitor who is intrigued by the Civil War will want to visit the **Richmond National Battlefield Park,** whose headquarters are at 3215 E. Broad St. (tel. 226-1981). The 10 separate units that make up the park are relics of the 7 Federal attacks on Richmond. Following maps furnished at headquarters, a 97-mile drive will take you through Hanover, Henrico, and Chesterfield sites. In the summer, several special "living history" programs bring the era to vivid life.

Tours

The Visitors Center (see above) can furnish guides for walking tours, and various sightseeing tours are offered by: the **Richmond-on-the-James Heritage Center,** 1805 E. Broad St. (tel. 780-0107); **Phillip Morris & Co.,** Commerce and Bell roads, Exit 8 off I-95 (tel. 274-3342 or 274-3329), has guided tours of its cigarette-factory weekdays; **Gray Line Tours,** 1617 Brood Rd. (tel. 644-2901), offers both city and area tours (including Williamsburg, Charlottesville, and Monticello); and as we go to press, the **Heritage Cruise Line** (tel. 804/222-5700) plans to begin cruises down the James River on board the *Annabel Lee,* with visits to three historic plantations.

Especially for Families

If you're traveling with youngsters, they'll probably insist that you veer off the historical-cultural circuit one day and head for **Kings Dominion Theme Park,** Doswell, VA 23047 (tel. 804/876-5000), which is reached via Exit 40 on I-95 to Va. 30. In the 400-acre park, there are no less than 43 rides; 5 theme areas; a Broadway-style revue; white-water rafting; a bobsled run; and Safari Village, which features a monorail ride through a wildlife preserve that holds about 50 wild animal species, including lions, tigers, elephants, and white rhino. The all-inclusive admission is $16.95, with discounts for those over 55, and no charge for under 3. Parking costs $2. Hours are 9:30 a.m. to 10 p.m. daily during July and August, shortened hours the rest of the year.

After Dark

While after-dark spots are subject to the winds of change, local newspapers can tell you if the following are still going strong at the time of your visit: the **Cellar Lounge** of the Holiday Inn Midtown, 3200 W. Broad St. (tel. 359-4061), has a casual atmosphere for drinks, food, and entertainment; the Holiday Inn Downtown, 301 W. Franklin St. (tel. 644-9871), is home of **Shu's Lounge,** a great favorite with locals, with live entertainment; and there's dancing at the **Tobacco Company,** 1201 E. Cary St., at historic Shockoe Slip, every night except Monday.

AN EXCURSION TO PETERSBURG

Due south on I-95 at Exit 3 is Petersburg, yet another Virginia town involved in the early history of this country. It's worth a visit to see the beautiful Victorian **Centre Hill Mansion,** 400 E. Washington St. (parking at Tabb and Adams streets), and **Old Blandford Church,** 321 S. Crater Rd., with its 15 Tiffany glass windows. You can wander through the **Siege Museum,** 15 W. Bank St., which depicts the 10-month siege of the city during the Civil War; the **National Battlefield Park,** off Va. 36; the **U.S. Army Quartermaster Museum,** at nearby Fort Lee on Va. 36; the old **Farmers Bank,** 19 Bollingbrook St.; and the rather eccentric early 1800s **Trapezium House,** 244 N. Market St., with its interior completely devoid of right angles. Admission costs to Centre Hill, Old Blandford Church, and the Siege Museum are $2 for adults, $1 for children ages 6 to 12, for each visit. Trapezium House and Farmers Bank admission is $1 for adults, 50¢ for children ages 6 to 12. Hours at all these attractions are 9 a.m. to 5 p.m. Monday through Saturday, 12:30 to 5 p.m. on Sunday, and they're closed only on Christmas and New Year's days although opening hours vary during months.

You can write ahead for maps and brochures to the **Petersburg Information Services,** P.O. Box 2107 (FP), Petersburg, VA 23804 (tel. 804/733-2400), or drop by the **Visitors Center** at 425 Cockade Alley, Old Market Square (tel. 804/733-2400).

---

4. Tidewater Virginia and the Eastern Shore

To Virginians, the term "Tidewater" means that whole area around the mouth of the great Chesapeake Bay, which stretches all the way up to Delaware. It encompasses Norfolk, an important port and U.S. naval base; Portsmouth, with its huge shipyard; Hampton and historic old Fort Monroe; Newport News, home of the world's largest shipbuilding company; and Virginia Beach, one of the most popular beach resorts in the Southeast. The 14-mile-long stretch where the Elizabeth, York, James, and Nansemond rivers come together into the bay is known as Hampton Roads and is one of the best natural harbors in the world.

The Eastern Shore, across the bay from Tidewater (accessible only by ferry until the 17.6-mile-long Chesapeake Bay Bridge-Tunnel opened in 1964 to connect Cape Charles with Norfolk), has superb surf fishing, with charter boats going out in fleets for the albacore, channel bass, white marlin, bluefish, and other fish that populate waters offshore around uninhabited barrier islands. Pre-Revolution towns, wild ponies near Chincoteague, fishing villages, large strawberry farms, and some of the best oysters and clams to be found on the coast combine to make it a fascinating area to visit.

Virginia Beach makes an ideal base from which to explore both these interesting areas and has the added benefit of an ocean dip at the beginning or end of any sightseeing foray, even in the fall (you can swim comfortably until late September or early October). Driving is also easier from the beach, away from Norfolk's traffic congestion, and all points of interest can be reached on easy day trips. In case you prefer **Norfolk,** however, I've also included several lodging and dining suggestions in this fine old city.

GETTING THERE

Two excellent highways (U.S. 58 and U.S.60) plus the Virginia Beach Expressway (Va. 44) lead to the beach from Norfolk. USAir (Piedmont) and United fly into Norfolk from New York, and Amtrak reaches Newport News from Boston, New York, Philadelphia, and Washington. Greyhound serves most of the Tidewater area

WHERE TO STAY IN VIRGINIA BEACH

New luxury hotels, older ones that wear their age with dignity and comfort, full-size apartments, efficiencies, hospitable guesthouses—directly on the beach or a little bit away from it at lower prices—you'll find them all at Virginia Beach. For a complete list, including rates, write the **Virginia Beach Visitors Bureau,** P.O. Box 200, Virginia Beach, VA 23458 (tel. toll free 800/446-8038), for their free accommodations directory.

The Best

"The hotel that made Virginia Beach famous." That's how **The Cavalier** bills itself. But these days, it's the new Cavalier, Oceanfront at 42nd Street (P.O. Box 885), Virginia Beach, VA 23451 (tel. toll free 800/446-8199, 800/582-8324 in Virginia). In the days of my Virginia youth, it was the "old" Cavalier, a majestic structure situated across the highway from the ocean on a rise that put it literally head and shoulders above everything else at the beach. The dashing, swashbuckling Cavalier dominated the landscape and the social scene, drawing patrons in the upper brackets from the entire eastern seaboard. Over the years, however, its "swash" "buckled" somewhat and, while not exactly shabby, the grand old building relinquished its prestige to the new building across the road, an 11-story high-rise with 270 superbly appointed rooms, each with an ocean view and private balcony.

But now the more-than-60-year-old hotel on the hill has been restored to its former elegance. For those who value graciousness above an oceanfront location, this is a "must." When booking, be *sure* to specify that it's the older hotel you want. The spaciousness of guest rooms was accomplished by knocking out the walls to double their size, leaving all bath and closet facilities intact—that means *two* full baths and closets in each. Closets are cedar lined, baths have retained their huge porcelain fixtures from the old days, and many beds are of the king-size variety. Smaller rooms for single occupancy are cozy, not tiny, and just as beautifully decorated with period furniture as the larger ones. Some are interesting, irregular shapes, following the contours of the building. Banquet service is available in the basement Hunt Room with its mammoth fireplace. The 20-acre wooded property has tennis courts and shuffleboard, and the oceanfront isn't all *that* far away. Golf privileges are available at nearby courses. Rates for doubles begin at $97.

Of course, if you come to the beach to *be* at the beach, the new Cavalier is for you. This is elegance in the modern style, and I found the staff as friendly and gracious as you might expect in the older establishment. Most rooms have 2 double beds (some king-size), and children under 12 stay free in the same room with their parents. There's platform tennis, deck shuffleboard, volleyball, archery, a game room, and a children's playground. The list of "extras" is impressive: baby cribs at no charge, irons and ironing boards, a copying service for businesspeople, valet and laundry service, airport limousine, and special arrangements for fishing, golf, and water sports. They'll even plan a birthday or anniversary celebration. The Cavalier Lounge is just off the main lobby. The Sand Dollar Restaurant, also off the lobby, serves all three meals and cocktails, with outdoor dining in season at The Breeze overlooking the pool and beach. Orion's (Top of the Cavalier) is one of Virginia Beach's "special" places for dining and dancing (see "Where to Eat"). Rates are seasonal: for double occupancy May 15 through September 15 the charge is $97, oceanview, $134 oceanfront; lower other months.

Also Good

The **Four Sails Hotel,** 3301 Atlantic Ave., 33rd and Atlantic Avenue, Virginia Beach, VA 23451 (tel. 804/491-1800), has oceanfront suites, all nicely appointed, with whirlpool baths, queen-size beds, cable TV, and refrigerators in every room. In addition to the oceanfront restaurant and lounge, there's an indoor pool, sauna, and a health club. They'll also furnish transportation to and from the airport. Rates begin at $150 double during summer months, but off-season rates drop to as low as $55; there's a discount for seniors, and weekly rates are available.

At the **Beach Quarters Hotel,** 501 Atlantic Ave., Atlantic Avenue at 5th Street, Virginia Beach, VA 23451 (tel. 804/422-3186; toll free in Virginia 800/468-1108, in other states, 800/345-3186), all rooms and two-room apartments are oceanfront. All apartments have fully equipped kitchens, and all units have balconies, cable TVs, and refrigerators. There's a restaurant, heated pool, sauna, whirlpool, health club, and coin laundry. Rates run $99 to $120 for doubles during high season, but drop to $40 to $49 from October to March. Ask about golf-package rates.

The **Courtyard by Marriott,** 5700 Greenwich Rd., Virginia Beach, VA 23462, (tel. 804/490-2002), has both high-quality, attractive guest rooms and suites, all with either a balcony or patio. Cable TV and in-room movies, a heated pool, whirlpool, exercise room, and a moderately priced restaurant are features here. Double-room rates start at $70 from Sunday through Thursday, at $60 Friday and Saturday.

Comfort Inn Oceanfront, 2015 Atlantic Ave., Virginia Beach, VA 23451 (tel. 804/425-8200 or toll free 800/228-5150), is a member of Quality Inns' upmarket chain, and has nicely appointed rooms, as well as suites with kitchen facilities. There's a heated indoor pool, whirlpool, exercise room, and coin laundry. No restaurant, but there's one just across the road. Doubles run $100 to $150 from June to September, drop to as low as $40 to $80 off-season, and there's a discount for seniors. No-smoking rooms available.

The **Hilton Inn,** 8th Street and Oceanfront, Virginia Beach, VA 23458 (tel. 804/428-8935), is a sleek six-story semicircular structure wrapped around a sun-struck oceanfront terrace. There are heated outdoor and indoor pools, as well as a kiddie pool, sauna, whirlpool, and weight room. All 124 rooms have

pleasing ocean views. There's a poolside cocktail/snack bar and seasonal entertainment in the lively Laverne's Lounge. The hotel dining room offers breakfast, lunch, and dinner; evening meals range from $10 to $25. All rooms of this
impeccably maintained mini-resort are attractively decorated, and spacious
family rooms are available. In season (May 23 to August 31), double rates range
from $99 to $130; they drop considerably off-season. There's no charge for children 12 and under in their parents' room.

The **Avamere,** 26th Street and Oceanfront, Virginia Beach, VA 23451 (tel.
804/428-2112), has been operated by Clarence Smith's family for nearly half a
century, and he maintains the same atmosphere of easy informality that has
made it a favorite on the beach. There are connecting rooms for families, an exceptionally fine dining room, and oceanfront verandas. Rates from mid-June
through Labor Day begin at $110 for modified American plan (includes break-
fast and dinner), lower May 15 to mid-June and the rest of September.

The **Dunes Motor Inn,** Oceanfront at 10th Street (P.O. Box 467), Virginia
Beach, VA 23451 (tel. 804/428-7731), is a six-story motel that also offers
kitchen units. There's a pool and a wading pool for the small fry. For a small fee,
they'll provide a crib for children in the same room with their parents. The on-
premises restaurant is open for all three meals and for room service. Rates for
doubles start at $84 from June to August, lower other months. Closed mid-
October through late March.

Days Inn Oceanfront, Oceanfront at 32nd Street, Virginia Beach, VA
13451 (tel. 804/428-7233 or toll free 800/325-2525), has exceptionally attractive and comfortable rooms, as well as a few (9) efficiencies. Cable TV and
in-room movies are features of guest rooms, and other amenities include a
heated indoor pool, whirlpool, bike rentals, and a restaurant that's open from 7
a.m. to midnight. Rates $45 to $60 for doubles, $50 to $60 for efficiencies,
during high season (slightly lower other months), and there's a senior citizens'
discount.

Econo Lodge has two budget-priced locations: **Econo Lodge Expressway,** 3637 Bonney Rd., Virginia Beach, VA 23452 (tel. 804/486-5711 or toll
free 800/446-6900); and **Econo Lodge Amphibian Base,** 5173 Shore Dr.,
Virginia Beach, VA 23455 (tel. 804/460-1151 or toll free 800/446-6900).
Seasonal rates for doubles run $36.95 to $38.95, with a $5 charge for each
additional person, the same for rollaway beds.

A Guesthouse

Conveniently located in the heart of Virginia Beach, just one block from
the ocean, **Angie's Guest Cottage,** 302 24th St., Virginia Beach, VA 23451
(tel. 804/428-4690), is run by Barbara Yates. It has six nice bedrooms (one
with private bath—the others convenient to two central baths) and two apartments. All have air conditioning, and some rooms have small refrigerators.
There's a sundeck, barbecue pit, and picnic tables. All in all, this is a friendly
family-type place to stay, just across the street from the Greyhound bus station,
and you won't believe the low rates—$38 to $52 per night (including continental breakfast) from Memorial Day to Labor Day, $25 to $40 (without breakfast) at other times. Backpackers and bikers will find dormitory bunks for only
$10 in season, $7 off-season, for AYH members ($13 and $10 respectively for
nonmembers). Open April 1 to October 1.

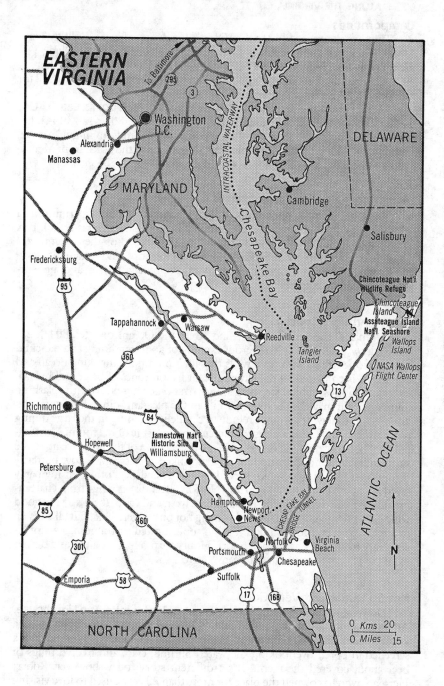

EASTERN VIRGINIA

To Baltimore

295

3

Washington D.C.

DELAWARE

Alexandria

Manassas

MARYLAND

INTRACOASTAL WATERWAY

Cambridge

Salisbury

Chesapeake Bay

Fredericksburg

95

Chincoteague Nat'l
Wildlife Refuge

Chincoteague
Island

Assateague Island
Nat'l Seashore

Tappahannock

360

Warsaw

Reedville

Tangier
Island

Wallops
Island

NASA Wallops
Flight Center

13

Richmond

64

Jamestown Nat'l
Historic Site

Williamsburg

Hopewell

Petersburg

85

460

Hampton

Newport
News

CHESAPEAKE BAY BRIDGE TUNNEL

301

Norfolk

Virginia
Beach

ATLANTIC OCEAN

Portsmouth

Chesapeake

Emporia

58

Suffolk

17

168

N

NORTH CAROLINA

0   Kms   20
0   Miles   15

Campgrounds

The closest campground to the Virginia Beach oceanfront is **Holiday Trav-L-Park,** 1½ miles south of Rudee Inlet Bridge at 1075 Gen. Booth Blvd., Virginia Beach, VA 23452 (tel. 804/425-0249). It has 1,000 sites, full hookups, a recreation building, store, pools, laundry, and LP gas. Prices are $15 to $22 for two people, $3 for each additional. There's free beach parking.

Also very near the beach (less than five minutes), the **Virginia Beach KOA,** 1240 Gen. Booth Blvd., Virginia Beach, VA 23451 (tel. 804/428-1444), has 750 sites, full hookups, three swimming pools, playgrounds, mini-golf, a store, and dump stations. They also furnish free bus service to the beach from Memorial Day through Labor Day. Prices run $14 to $29.

WHERE TO EAT IN VIRGINIA BEACH

Virginia Beach has restaurants of all persuasions. Space will permit only a very subjective listing, but write the Virginia Beach Visitors Bureau, P.O. Box 200, Virginia Beach, VA 23458 (tel. 804/428-8000), for their *Restaurant Guide* (free), a full roster of pancake houses, coffeeshops, and restaurants serving Chinese, American, French, Greek, Mexican, Italian, Jewish, and, not surprisingly, seafood cuisines.

Fancy and Very Special

Orion's, at the new Cavalier, 42nd Street and Oceanfront (tel. 804/425-8555), is *the* place for a splendiferous evening of gourmet dining and dancing. The rooftop setting, with glass walls that look out on breathtaking ocean and city views, is enhanced by the elegant decor in soft tones of beige and brown. Entering via mosaic-tiled stepping stones over reflecting pools with splashing fountains, you may choose to sit a while in the pleasant, dimly lit lounge and just enjoy the view. It's a nice prelude to candlelight dining in the large dining room, where an orchestra plays for dancing on one side of the room. Most important, both the menu selections and the preparation of the food live up to the surroundings. Seafood dishes are a treat. I liked the scampi Savoy, butterfly shrimp in a special wine sauce served over seasoned rice; others in my party raved about the crabmeat and shrimp Norfolk. Beef dishes range from chateaubriand for two to beef brochette. Salads are fresh and crisp, there's a very good wine list, and rolls come to the table piping hot on a covered plate. It all adds up to a marvelous evening of good food in sophisticated surroundings—not always easy to come by at a beach resort. Hours are 6 p.m. to 1 a.m., and dinner from the à la carte menu can run from $16 to $45.

Not So Fancy, But Very Good

Down at the very end of Virginia Beach, at Rudee Inlet, **The Lighthouse,** Atlantic Avenue at 1st Street, (tel. 804/428-9851), began many years ago in a small wooden building with one dining room that held about 20 people, plus a screened-in porch overlooking the water. Shrimp, crab, and frosted mugs of beer about covered the menu. It's a different story today, however. Robert Herman, who has owned the place for more than 20 years, used to love visiting it with his wife, saw its potential, and never seems to be quite finished with improvements, additions, and innovations such as an outside patio, upstairs rooms overlooking the water, and a very nice lounge. Decor is, of course, nautical, but that doesn't begin to describe the interior. Divided into eight separate rooms to prevent a "barny" feeling in the large building, it has grown from that tiny wooden shack to such proportions that they can, and often do, feed 600 at once! There's an almost whimsical touch in the way standing brass ship compasses, mounted blue marlin and other fish (most are caught by Robert or members of the staff), a free-standing aquarium, ship lanterns, etc., are scattered around the place. One of the newer rooms, The Deck, has a heavenly view through bowed skylights. Every table has a sea view. It's simply impossible to summarize the long menu, much less to pick a personal favorite. But to list a few: deluxe lump crabmeat or shrimp sautéed in parsley butter (with soup, salad, baked potato, and coffee or tea); whole fresh flounder broiled or fried, or stuffed with crabmeat (both with all the accompaniments listed above); and a whopping fried seafood platter (fresh flounder, scallops, oysters, shrimp, crab cake, and fried clams). Lunch can run from $5 to $10; dinner, from $10 to $23. There's also a full range of sandwiches, beef, salads, and even hot pastrami. Locals have loved this place from its screened-porch days. Open from 10 a.m. to 11 p.m. Saturday and Sunday, from 5 p.m. weekdays, or "whenever the last customer is through eating."

The **Three Ships Inn,** 3800 Shore Dr. (tel. 804/460-0055), resembles a weathered old inn, with an early-English decor and candlelit tables. There's gourmet eating here, with such delicacies as chicken Kiev, quail, roast duckling, frogs' legs, Maine lobster, and fresh rainbow trout stuffed with backfin crabmeat, all at prices of $12 to $30. Flounder and sea trout are caught fresh daily in their own nets. Open for dinner from 6 to 11 p.m. daily.

Henry's Seafood Restaurant, 3319 Shore Dr. (tel. 481-7300), is at the eastern end of the Lessner Bridge at U.S. 60 overlooking Chesapeake Bay and the Lynnhaven River. The decor is as nautical as the menu, with a huge, two-story, 8,000-gallon saltwater aquarium right smack in the middle of the dining room. Exotic fish and other sea creatures furnish the entertainment as you tuck into local seafood, lobsters, or—if you dare in such an environment—steak. Hours are 11 a.m. to 11 p.m., and you can expect to pay anywhere from $3 to $15 at lunch or dinner from the à la carte menu.

When the "I've had it with seafood" syndrome hits, a beefy alternative is **Aberdeen Barn,** 5805 Northampton Blvd. (tel. 464-1580). The rustic decor is a perfect setting for excellent steak, prime ribs, and (just in case the finny critters begin to beckon) lobster tails. There's also a good salad bar, and entertainment most nights except Sunday. Open from 11:30 a.m. to 11 p.m. except Christmas Day.

For more elegant dining, **La Broche,** 608 Birdneck Rd. (tel. 428-0655), offers intimacy enhanced by candlelight and lovely old Flemish tapestries. The menu is continental, with veal escalope a standout, and bread is home-baked. Very European in ambience, and open from 11:30 a.m. to 2 p.m. for lunch, 6 to 11 p.m. for dinner (when it's a good idea to make advance reservations). Prices run about $5 to $7 at lunch, $15 to $19 at dinner.

For truly inexpensive eating when you're tired of the fast-food spots, there's a **Morrison's Cafeteria** at the Hilltop East Shopping Center, 1532 Laskin Rd. (tel. 422-4755), with hours of 11 a.m. to 9 p.m., and the **Piccadilly**

Cafeteria, 701 Lynhaven Pkwy. (tel. 340-8788), with hours of 11 a.m. to 8:30 p.m.

READER'S RECOMMENDATION: "We found an excellent restaurant, **Tandom's Pine Tree Inn,** at 2932 Virginia Beach Blvd. (tel. 340-3661). The food and service were good, the prices reasonable, the decor pleasant, and there was a piano player" (J. Wiener and S. Hunt, New York, NY).

WHERE TO STAY IN NORFOLK

The **Omni International Hotel,** 777 Waterside Dr., Norfolk, VA 23510 (tel. 804/622-6664, or toll free 800/228-2121), was the first hotel in this fast-growing luxury system. It's so impeccably maintained that it might just have opened its doors. There are two fine dining rooms, the Riverwalk Café and the Esplanade (see "Where to Eat in Norfolk" for description of the latter). The lobby bar with its wide sweep of window wall overlooks the always-bustling harbor, and there's evening piano or trio entertainment here. Rooms are furnished in a warm, contemporary motif, with soft muted tones of rose, gray, beige, and blue predominating. There's valet parking (for a fee), a pool, and a jogging track. The Omni has some accommodations for wheelchair travelers, along with the special check-in and checkout, concierge services, and other touches this system provides. It's located adjacent to the Waterside Festival Marketplace and within walking distance of the Scope Convention Center. Double rates range from $81 to $141 for rooms facing the city, $119 to $129 for those with views of the harbor.

The **Hotel Madison,** Granby and Freemason streets, Norfolk, VA 23510 (tel. 804/622-6682, or toll free 800/522-0976, 800/552-6353 in Virginia), is a beautifully restored old hotel that reflects an era of bygone elegance. With its rich dark woods, crystal chandelier, hand-woven carpet, and baby grand piano, the lobby resembles that of an intimate small European hostelry. The Embassy Lounge features a raw bar and daily happy hour, and there's dining in the light and airy atmosphere of Dolley's or the sophisticated surroundings of the Embassy Restaurant. All 135 spacious guest rooms and suites are handsomely furnished and decorated in tones of gold, beige, cream, and burnt orange. Mornings, complimentary fresh-brewed coffee, orange juice, pastries, and the daily paper are delivered to your room. There's concierge service, valet parking, and express check-in/out, and a free trolley takes guests to the waterside and harbor. Doubles range from $85 up, and suites are $95 to $125.

The excellent Econo Lodge budget system has six motels in Norfolk. An especially pleasant location is the **Norfolk Ocean View,** 1111 E. Ocean View Ave., Norfolk, VA 23503 (tel. 804/480-1111, or toll free 800/446-6900); take I-64 through the Hampton Roads Tunnel to Ocean View and Exit 60. The lodge is across from the beach, and a fishing pier and charter fishing are nearby, as is a popular seafood restaurant. All rooms have refrigerators and free cable color TVs with HBO, and there's free morning coffee. Doubles range from $46.50 to $48.50, and there's a $4 charge for each extra person, (also a $4 charge for a rollaway). Pets are welcome, with a deposit fee.

There's an attractive 160-room **Days Inn** at 5701 Chambers St. (U.S. 13 and I-264), Norfolk, VA 23502 (tel. 804/461-0100, or toll free 800/325-2525). It's just a 10-minute drive to downtown and the Waterside. Some rooms are equipped for wheelchair travelers, and there's a pool, free cable color TV, and the 24-hour Day Break Restaurant. Summer rates are $58 double, and they drop considerably in winter.

Bed and Breakfast

For information on home stays in this area, contact: **Bed and Breakfast of Tidewater Virginia,** P.O. Box 3343, Norfolk, VA 23514 (tel. 804/627-1983).

WHERE TO EAT IN NORFOLK

This burgeoning city offers a variety of dining experiences, from basic good down-home cookery to fine fresh seafood, continental, and nationality restaurants. Write the **Norfolk Convention Visitors Bureau,** 236 E. Plume St., Norfolk, VA 23510 (tel. 804/441-5266, or toll free 800/368-3097 outside Virginia), for its "Norfolk-by-the-Sea Dining Guide."

The Esplanade, in the Omni International Hotel, 777 Waterside Dr. (tel. 804/623-0333), is a perfect choice if you're celebrating something special or just want to treat yourself to a memorable evening. In this exquisite small dining room overlooking the hotel's larger dining room, comfortable wing chairs surround intimate tables for two or four. Service is impeccable in this quiet enclave where you have a sense of absolute privacy. A recent memorable dinner included such choices as papillote of sea trout baked in parchment with shrimp and crab, veal Lafayette with sautéed sea scallops, and fresh breast of chicken stuffed and roasted with backfin crab and tarragon. The presentation was artful, with carrots honey-glazed with tomatoes, red cabbage, and sautéed green beans beautifully arranged as accompaniments on a separate plate. There's a memorable lobster bisque en croûte, and appetizers are such imaginative delights as galatoire of salmon and sole or oysters with Smithfield ham. Mr. Lynnwood B. Craig, the personable maître d'hôtel, welcomes diners as if they were guests in a private home. The Esplanade is open from 6 to 11 p.m. Monday through Saturday, with prices ranging from $15 to $28. Reservations, and coat and tie for men, are requested.

A Norfolk institution, the **Ship's Cabin,** 4110 E. Ocean View Ave. (tel. 804/480-2526), is a large airy series of rooms decorated with Tiffany-style lamps and hanging baskets. It always seems crowded, but you'll never be rushed and service is especially pleasant. This is a wonderful spot to sample crab Norfolk ($14.50); or other such luscious entrees as shrimp Stella Oceanis topped with tomato, spices, and feta and parmesan cheeses; and angel-hair pasta and backfin crabmeat with sun-dried tomatoes. Mesquite grilling adds a delicious flavor to halibut, salmon, and swordfish, as well as steaks. It's open from 6 to 10 p.m. daily; closed major holidays (call for seasonal hours). There's an excellent choice of Virginia and California wines. Prices are in the $10 to $25 range.

Il Porto of Norfolk, 333 Waterside Dr. (tel. 804/627-4400), is an ideal place in which to relax and view the passing waterside scene as you enjoy your favorite pizza or pasta dish. It has a colorful, lively European taverna ambience, and just smells so great as you enter that you realize I'm talking honest-to-goodness hearty Italian cooking here. Lunch prices range from $5 to $8; dinners, from $7 to $15. It's open continuously from 11:15 a.m. to midnight, and there's live ragtime piano entertainment from 8:30 p.m. to 1:30 a.m. daily.

Café 21, at 21st Street and Colley Avenue (tel. 804/625-4218), near the Ghent restoration area, is one of those great local spots that makes you feel as if you've made a real discovery. It's small, and everybody seems to know everybody else. Fare ranges from salads, sandwiches, and pizza to chicken, pasta, and other Italian dishes. It's moderately priced and serves both lunch and dinner. Hours are 11 a.m. to 11 p.m., Monday through Thursday, to midnight Friday and Saturday, and to 10 p.m. Sunday.

The **Banque,** 1849 East Little Creek Rd. (tel. 804/480-3600), is another aspect of "southern" culture, with a country/western ambience rather than the historical or coastal emphasis found in so many other Virginia establishments. It is a large place, with a huge dance floor, live entertainment, and even free dancing lessons (of the western genre, of course). If it weren't for the great homespun food offerings, the Banque would qualify primarily as a nightclub—as it is, you can go for a soul-satisfying meal and stay the night for toe-tapping entertainment. Hours are 6 p.m. to 2 a.m., and prices are moderate.

Suddenly Last Summer, 9225 Granby St. (tel. 804/587-0077), is a pleasant, oak-paneled café that dishes up homemade pasta, seafood, and continental specialties such as poivre Dijon at prices of $7 to $12 at lunch, $14 to $39 at dinner. Hours are 11:30 a.m. to 3 p.m. weekdays and 5 to 11 p.m. every day except Sunday and Monday, when it's closed, as it is for major holidays.

Budget meals are available at **Morrison's Cafeteria,** 530 N. Military Hwy. (tel. 461-2477).

NIGHTLIFE

Both at Virginia Beach and nearby Norfolk, nightlife is found mostly in restaurants and motel or hotel lounges. Prime examples are **Orion's** at the top of the New Cavalier, 42nd and Oceanfront (tel. 804/425-8555), **Shipmates,** in the Ramada Inn, Atlantic Avenue at 7th Street (tel. 804/425-5151), and **Alexander's,** in the Omni International Hotel, 777 Waterfront Dr. at St. Paul's Boulevard (tel. 804/622-6664). The **Tidewater Dinner Theater,** 6270 Northhampton Blvd. (tel. 804/461-2933), is in the Quality Inn; reservations are necessary and shows change frequently. If you're in a country/western mood, go straight to The Banque (see above).

THINGS TO SEE AND DO

When I was growing up in Norfolk, all of Tidewater and the Eastern Shore seemed like one big playground to me. The beaches came first, of course; my father liked to fish, both surf casting and deep sea; there were the amusement parks at Virginia Beach and Ocean View; I played tennis on the courts at City Park; and there was always the excitement of living in a navy town, where new friends passed in and out of our lives regularly. It wasn't until my teen years that I began to appreciate the deeper, more meaningful attractions that lay around my hometown. History is all around, of course, but now there's space technology and industrial developments to add a new dimension to the area, and artistic and cultural events are housed in sparkling new edifices. The only way to get a handle on the widespread panorama of things to see and do is to break them up into localities:

At Virginia Beach

The beach itself, complete with boardwalk, fishing piers, bowling, tennis, miniature golf, waterskiing, and surf-riding, makes this the complete resort, especially when you add the seafood that's out of this world (in my case, I can't get enough of those Lynnhaven oysters, whether they're on the half shell, fried, or in a creamy stew). And I've always fantasized about the *Norwegian Lady* statue that stands at the very center of town on the oceanfront, a memorial to a sea captain's wife who was rescued by townspeople when her husband's ship broke up during a storm. The **Information Center** is located at 19th Street and Pacific Avenue (tel. 804/425-7511, or toll free 800/446-8038) and will furnish specifics about restaurants, amusements, etc.

For sightseeing, there's the **Old Cape Henry Lighthouse** in the Fort Story Military Reservation, a little north of Virginia Beach on the shore drive. It was the first government-built lighthouse in the U.S. (1791). And close by is the plain **First Landing Cross** that marks the spot where the colonists who were to settle at Jamestown landed on April 26, 1607.

The **Adam Thoroughgood House,** thought to be over 300 years old, is at 1636 Parrish Rd., eight miles northeast via Va. 166 and U.S. 13 on Lynnhaven Bay. Restored to its original design, it's a lovely old brick cottage-type house with a high-pitched roof, surrounded by ancient trees and boxwood. It's open Tuesday through Saturday from 10 a.m. to 5 p.m. and on Sunday from noon to 5 p.m. April 1 through December; Tuesday through Saturday from noon to 5 p.m. January 1 to March 31. Admission is $2 for adults, $1 for children 6 to 12; under 6, free.

Lynnhaven House, another 18th-century house, eight miles north off U.S. 225 on Wishart Road, is one of the nation's best-preserved 18th-century middle-class dwellings. Open Tuesday through Sunday from noon to 4 p.m. April through October; admission is $2 for adults, $1 for senior citizens, students, and children under 12; under 6, free.

The **Virginia Beach Maritime Historical Museum,** 24th Street and Oceanfront (tel. 804/422-1587), in the recently restored 1903 Seatack Lifesaving Station, has an excellent collection of nautical artifacts, scrimshaw, and ship models. Its well-stocked gift shop includes nautical brass and works by local artists. It's open from 10 a.m. to 9 p.m. Monday to Saturday, and noon to 5 p.m. on Sunday, Memorial Day to October; closed Monday the rest of the year. Admission is $2 for adults, $1 for seniors and military, 50¢ for children ages 6 to 18.

At the splendid "hands-on" **Virginia Marine Science Museum,** 717 General Booth Blvd. (tel. 804/425-FISH), you can explore the depths of the Atlantic Ocean, walk under waves of the Chesapeake Bay, see the life of a salt marsh firsthand, and visit a coastal plains "river," which is a 10,000-gallon aquarium brimming with local aquatic species. One of the South's finest marine exhibits, it's not to be missed! Open from 9 a.m. to 5 p.m. Monday through Sunday, September through May; call for extended summer hours. Admission is $4 for adults, $3.50 for seniors, and $2.50 for children.

Wildwater Rapids Water Park, 1049 General Booth Blvd. (tel. 804/425-1080), offers splashy great times for all the family on 10 acres of flumes, slides, rapids, pools, and wave ponds. It's open from 10 a.m. to 10 p.m. Sunday through Saturday, late May through early September, and weekends in May, weather permitting. Admission is $12 for adults, $9.50 for 62 and over, $6 for ages 4 to 6.

Virginia Beach is a marvelous place to get in some deep-sea fishing, and there are daily charter boat full- and half-day trips that venture as much as 40 miles into the Atlantic during the summer from Virginia Beach Fishing Center, 200 Winston-Salem Ave., Rudee Inlet (tel. 425-9253). Call at least one day in advance to reserve space.

Norfolk

Norfolk is first, last, and always a seaport; from its earliest days (which is pretty early—the site was purchased for 10,000 pounds of tobacco in 1682), ships have come and gone in one of the best natural harbors in the world. Commercial ships still make up a great deal of water traffic, but in addition, the town, together with Portsmouth, is the site of one of the oldest U.S. Navy facilities in the country. The Norfolk Naval Base and Naval Air Station, combined with Portsmouth's Naval Shipyard, make up one of the largest naval facilities of any nation in the world, and the city's streets are filled at any given time with naval uniforms, both U.S. and foreign. It has been, in its time, a rough, rather rowdy liberty town for sailors (I remember seeing signs on lawns warning "Sailors and Dogs Keep Off the Grass"), but when World War II brought respectability to servicemen, all that changed and there's little left of the seamier sections that used to be the only place enlisted men found a welcome.

Without doubt, **Granby Street** is the main thoroughfare in downtown Norfolk. Old-fashioned brick walkways are lined with boutiques and shops, and nearby you'll find the fascinating **d'Art Center,** 125 College Place, Norfolk, VA 23510 (tel. 804/625-4211): a complex of artists' studios located in several renovated turn-of-the-century buildings. It's open seven days a week, year round, with hours of 10 a.m. to 5 p.m. Monday through Friday, until 6 p.m. on Saturday, and noon to 6 p.m. Sunday.

The **Scope Convention and Cultural Center,** at Brambleton Avenue and St. Paul's Boulevard, covers some 14 acres in the downtown area, and houses a 12,000-seat convention hall and Chrysler, a 2,400-seat theater that presents concerts, Broadway plays, and the Virginia Symphony Orchestra. The Waterside complex, a giant marketplace that has risen from the ruins of dilapidated buildings on the waterfront, holds more than 100 shops, restaurants, and a bevy of street entertainers during summer months. Incidentally, if you arrive in mid-June, you'll find the waterfront alive with **Harborfest** festivities, including sailboat races, water-skiing shows, fireworks, and a host of other entertainments —it's Norfolk's annual bow to its seafaring heritage, and loads of fun.

All in all, it's quite a different town from the one I knew, but it has a lot to see and do, and it's well worth a day or two of exploration. Look for blue and gold signs pointing the way to historic sites.

Before setting out, however, by all means stop by the downtown **Norfolk Convention and Visitors Bureau,** at 236 E. Plume St., Norfolk, VA 23510 (tel. 804/441-5266 or toll free 800/368-3097 outside Virginia). Or, even better, write before you come. They do a terrific job of supplying details on the entire Tidewater area and can furnish combination discount tickets for several sightseeing attractions.

One of my favorite spots is the lovely **Norfolk Botanical Gardens,** which I knew in my youth as the Azalea Gardens. These botanical gardens are eight miles east of the city, adjacent to the airport, on Azalea Garden Road near the junction of I-64 and Military Hwy. Don't miss the 4,000-plant, award-winning rose garden or the 300-flowering-tree arboretum. A special feature is the fragrance garden for the blind, and there are narrated boat rides and train tours ($2 each, or $3 for a combination ticket) from mid-March to October.

There's a 1½-hour narrated cruise of the Norfolk-Portsmouth harbor aboard the *Carrie B*, replica of a 19th-century Mississippi riverboat. It leaves from Waterside behind Phillip's Seafood Restaurant, and fare is $9 for adults, children, $4.50). From Portsmouth, you can tour Hampton Roads by boat, leaving from the foot of North Street at Portside in Historic Olde Towne for the same fares. Write **Harbor Tours,** End of Bay Street, Portsmouth, VA 23704 (tel. 804/393-4735).

You can tour by bus the gigantic **U.S. Naval Station** and the **U.S. Naval Air Station,** Hampton and Admiral Taussig boulevards (I-564), and even go aboard one or more naval vessels on Saturday and Sunday from 1 to 4:30 p.m. Tours leave from Waterside and the Naval Base Tour and Information Center at 9809 Hampton Blvd. in Norfolk, and you should call (tel. 804/444-7955) for exact times, since they change according to the time of year. There's a $4 charge for adults ($2 for ages 6 to 12; under 6, free) for the naval base tour. Ship visits are free.

You can hop aboard the **Norfolk Trolley Tour** May through September for an hour-long narrated orientation jaunt through the historic downtown district. At various stops, you can get off, explore, and catch a later trolley. Cost is $1.50 for adults, 75¢ for children under 12, seniors, and handicapped. Phone 623-3222 for a schedule, which varies with the season.

The **Moses Myers Home** (1792) is at 323 E. Freemason St. (at Bank Street) and is a beautiful old Georgian home filled with over 60% of the original furnishings. From April through December, hours are 10 a.m. to 5 p.m. (noon to 5 p.m. on Sunday) every day except Monday. The rest of the year, it opens at noon. Cost is $2 for adults, $1 for ages 6 through 18; under 6 and military with ID, free.

The **Willoughby-Baylor Home** at 601 E. Freemason St. is a splendid 18th-century Georgian-Federal town house on a 1636 land grant. It showcases fine period furnishings, and its formal gardens are outstanding. Hours and costs are identical with the Moses Myers Home (see above).

The **Hermitage Foundation Museum,** 7637 N. Shore Rd. (tel. 423-2052), near the intersection of Hampton Boulevard (Va. 337) and Little Creek Road (Va. 165) is an elegant and unusually furnished riverside mansion housing an outstanding collection of Oriental and Western art. Built in 1908 by textilist William Sloane, this Tudor-style structure is highlighted by ivories, jade, and Chinese tomb figures from the T'ang Dynasty. It's open from 10 a.m. to 5 p.m. Monday through Saturday and 1 to 5 p.m. on Sunday. Admission is $3 for adults, $1 for ages 6 to 18; under 6 and military with ID, free.

In a restored old courthouse, the **General Douglas MacArthur Memorial,** City Hall Avenue and Bank Street, known as MacArthur Square (tel. 804/441-2965), holds the general's tomb and memorabilia of his life and military career. There's an interesting film biography. It's free and open from 10 a.m. to 5 p.m. Monday through Saturday, from 11 a.m. on Sunday.

The **Chrysler Museum,** Olney Road at Mowbray Arch (tel. 804/622-1211), has been acclaimed as "one of the 20 top museums in the country" by the *Wall Street Journal*. Art from nearly every important culture, civilization, and historical period of the last 5,000 years is included in the collection. The museum also houses a 10,000-piece glass collection, considered one of the foremost worldwide; the only museum photography gallery in the state; and a fine collection of Worcester porcelain. Family programs, films, lectures, and concerts are offered in the museum theater on a regular basis. Admission: free but donations are encouraged. Hours: 10 a.m. to 4 p.m. Tuesday through Saturday, 1 to 5 p.m. on Sunday.

St. Paul's Church, 201 St. Paul's Blvd. (tel. 804/627-4353), dates back to 1739, and its southeastern wall still holds a British cannonball from the 1776 bombardment led by Lord Dunmore. The beautiful Tiffany stained-glass windows are a turn-of-the-century addition. The church is open from 10 a.m. to 4 p.m., Tuesday through Saturday, with admission by donation. During summer months, you can attend Sunday services at 8 a.m. and 10 a.m.; 8 a.m. and 11 a.m. other months.

You can reach Portsmouth, across the harbor from Norfolk, by tunnel or the ferry that leaves from The Waterside (the ferry is faster; and fares are 50¢ for adults; 25¢ for children, seniors, and the handicapped). The city dates from a king's grant in 1620, and throughout its history has been the center of shipbuilding. The **Portsmouth Naval Shipyard Museum,** at the foot of High Street on the waterfront (tel. 804/393-8591), is the repository of paintings, models, and exhibits tracing Portsmouth's role in U.S. naval history. It's open 10 a.m. to 5 p.m., Tuesday through Saturday, from 1 p.m. on Sunday (closed major holidays), and admission is free. For a glimpse of Portsmouth homes from the past, take the **Olde Towne Tour,** 6 Crawford Pkwy. (tel. 804/393-5111), for a trolley tour of interesting old residences. On the waterfront, **Portside** (6 Crawford Pkwy., tel. 804/393-5111) is a marketplace complex with a visitors center, open-air restaurants, and entertainment.

Newport News

During the world wars, Newport News's docks were the jumping-off point for men and supplies headed into battle; they also served as a huge repair shop for naval vessels that had been damaged. Then, as now, it was dominated by the **Newport News Shipbuilding Company,** the world's largest, which has constructed some of our most famous ships—the *United States,* the *Enterprise,* and the *Kennedy* among them. The proud **Victory Arch,** at 25th Street and West Avenue, stands as a memorial to American men and women who have served in all the wars of our history. Incidentally, the "News" in this city's name was of the arrival back in the early 1600s of one Capt. Christopher Newport with supplies and settlers from England to join the tiny Jamestown colony. For all kinds of sightseeing assistance, contact: Virginia Peninsula Tourist Information Center, 13560 Jefferson Ave., Newport News, VA 23603 (tel. 804/886-2737).

If you've any interest at all in seafaring affairs, you won't want to miss the **Mariners' Museum,** Newport News, VA 23606 (tel. 804/595-0368). It's located three miles off I-64, Exit 62-A to the intersection of J. Clyde Morris and Warwick boulevards (well signposted), and it's one of the largest maritime museums in the world. Located in a 550-acre park with picnic areas, it holds a marvelous collection of ship models, figureheads, small boats, and much more, all dedicated to preserving the heritage of the sea that has been so important to this part of Virginia. The grounds are actually a wildlife sanctuary, with a lake for fishing, and scattered about are old anchors, cannons, and sculpture. Hours are 9 a.m. to 5 p.m., Monday through Saturday, from noon on Sunday; $4 admission for adults, $1.50 for ages 6 through 16, under 6 free, and discounts for seniors and the military. An ideal morning's sightseeing topped off by a picnic lunch under the trees.

At the **Virginia Living Museum,** 524 J. Clyde Morris Blvd., Newport News, VA 23601 (tel. 804/595-1900), you can stroll a lakeside boardwalk to view carefully maintained wildlife exhibits in an eight-acre outdoor "living habitat." Indoor living displays include marine life, nocturnal animals, and microscopic life. There's also an aviary with songbirds and water fowl, a planetarium and observatory. Open from 9 a.m. to 5 p.m. Monday through Saturday (and 7 to 9 p.m. on Thursday), and 1 to 5 p.m. on Sunday. Adult admission is $4 for the museum, $2 for the planetarium, $5 for a combination ticket; for children under 12, admission is $2 for the museum, $1.50 for the planetarium, $2.50 for a combination ticket (under 4, admission is free).

Fort Eustis is located on **Mulberry Island** at the northwest end of the city and is headquarters of the U.S. Transportation Center. Both the fort and the **Army Transportation Museum** (which traces the development of transportation from the wheel to the flying saucer) are free, and the museum or the Public Affairs Office can give you directions for a self-guided auto tour of the grounds.

Hampton

Your first order of business in Hampton (or even before you come) should be to go by (or write) the **Hampton Tourist Information Center,** 710 Settlers Landing Rd. (via I-64, on the downtown waterfront), Hampton, VA 23669 (tel. 804/727-6108).

You can tour **Fort Monroe,** three miles southeast of Hampton (it's clearly marked from almost any point in town), free, and it makes for a fascinating day for the whole family. The battle between the *Monitor* and the *Merrimac* was fought just off the fort in Hampton Roads on March 9, 1862, ending in a draw between the first two ironclads. The fort was held by Union troops throughout the Civil War—Abraham Lincoln plotted strategy against Norfolk here in May of 1862—and Jefferson Davis was imprisoned here following the downfall of the Confederacy. Ironically, Robert E. Lee, as a young engineer in the U.S. Army, helped with the construction of Fort Monroe, but was never able to effect its capture when he commanded Confederate forces. The **Casement Museum** (free) depicts these and many other stories in a panoramic painting, and there are all sorts of intriguing documents, pictures, and models on display. Kids will love the fact that the old fort was encircled by a moat.

The famous **Hampton University** (formerly known as the Hampton Institute), at the east end of Queen Street (exit off I-64), was established in 1868 by the Freedman's Bureau to teach former slaves how to read and write. Today it specializes in science, the liberal arts, business, teaching, nursing, architecture, and graduate studies. Don't miss the **museum** (free) in the Academy Building —it has an outstanding collection of Native American and African artifacts.

Also free are the film and special exhibits at the **NASA Langley Research Center,** three miles north on Va. 134 (tel. 804/865-2855), where you can see moon rockets, space suits, an Apollo command module, and many more space-age items. Open Monday through Saturday from 8:30 a.m. to 4:30 p.m., from noon on Sunday. Closed on major holidays. If you're space-minded, go by the **Air Power Museum,** 413 W. Mercury Blvd., and see their impressive display of jet aircraft, rockets, missiles, and satellites.

THE EASTERN SHORE

The old Cape Charles ferry used to take almost three hours to cross Chesapeake Bay. Today you can "Follow the Gulls" (a neat blue-and-white sign with a white silhouetted seagull that points you to the 17.6-mile-long Chesapeake Bay Bridge-Tunnel from almost anywhere in the Tidewater area) and make the crossing in 23 minutes! And the trip is unforgettable—miles and miles of causeway, one rather high bridge, and two mile-long tunnels. This remarkable engineering feat was completed in 1964 and takes you from Norfolk to **Cape Charles.** Cross another causeway and bridge, and you'll reach **Assateague Island National Seashore,** one of the newest of our national parklands. U.S. 13 runs through the long peninsula that has come to be known as **Delmarva** because it holds tiny portions of Delaware, Maryland, and Virginia. The toll is $9 per car each way, including passengers.

As an aside, let me point out that when you spend your day—and it will take a whole one—on the Eastern Shore, there's a very good restaurant at **American House** at the Cape Charles end of the bridge-tunnel which serves all three meals at reasonable prices. However, you're likely to find interesting places to eat also at **Chincoteague** (the town, not the island) or perhaps in other villages along the shore. I personally couldn't eat anything but the oysters, clams, and crabs that are such a specialty out here, and there are several small seafood restaurants scattered around. But America House is a sure thing, so keep it in mind. If you're an island person or just plain intrigued by this coastal country, you may want to plan more than just one day, in which case see "Where to Stay," below.

If you want to fish on the Eastern Shore, the pier at Cape Charles can furnish bait and tackle. You don't need a license, and there's no limit on the catch. For charter-boat fishing, go on to **Wachapreague** or Chincoteague and look for the charter signs.

For a comprehensive listing of all the delights of this region, obtain a copy of the "Eastern Shore Travel Guide" from the Tourism Commission, 1 Courthouse Ave. P.O. Box 147, Accomac, VA 23301 (tel. 804/787-2460). It includes accommodations, shopping, restaurants, charter fishing, game laws, and even a four-day tour if you decide to tarry here.

Now, back to that national seashore—it's Va. 175 (from U.S. 13) that will lead you the 10 miles to **Chincoteague Island** and on to Assateague. There are two very special times of year to arrive on the islands: the first Wednesday in May is set aside for the Eastern Shore Annual Seafood Festival, which has gained such popularity since it began in 1969 that reservations start coming in as soon as tickets go on sale in October for the next year's festival. If you're early enough, you can (ticket in hand) wander from booth to booth sampling a seaside feast. But you *must* have that ticket, and be warned: they sometimes sell out the very first day they're offered! For ticket information, contact the Chamber of Commerce, P.O. Box 258, Chincoteague, VA 23336 (tel. 804/336-6161). Then, on the last Wednesday and Thursday in July, comes the "penning" of wild Chincoteague ponies, and it's really something! The shaggy little ponies, larger than a Shetland but smaller than a horse, are descendants of horses that swam ashore from a Spanish galleon that perished in these waters, so the legend goes. Through the centuries their growth became stunted from a steady diet of marsh grass. All year they roam wild on Assateague Island, but at the end of July Chincoteague citizens turn into cowboys, herd them into the water for the swim across the channel, and sell the foals for prices that range from $75 to $300 (all proceeds go to the volunteer fire department), then drive the mares and stallions back to Assateague for another year of breeding. It's a fun time to be here, with carnival amusements and general hilarity prevailing.

Other lively annual happenings include the well-known Columbus Day weekend Oyster Festival, and a juried Easter Decoy and Art Festival, which draws about 100 top exhibitors from throughout the East.

Those are highlights of the year on the Eastern Shore. But no matter when you come, there's much to fill your days. Across the bridge from Chincoteague, the island of **Assateague** was cut off from the longer extension of barrier islands (which runs from Massachusetts to Florida and includes many in South Carolina and Georgia —which we'll get to later in this book) by a storm in 1933. It's about 37 miles long, and its width varies from one-third of a mile to a little over a mile. Its gently shelving sand beach is just spectacular, and swimming is not perilous because the undertow here is very light. Virginia and Maryland share ownership of Assateague, and you can enter via bridges at either end. The State Park Information Center and Campground Registration Office is located at the north end, and there's a visitors center just over the bridge from Chincoteague. If you begin your trip from the north, plan to go over to Assateague from near Ocean City, Md. And you should know that because some 22 miles of roadless beach and marsh lie between the two entrances, you won't be able to drive from one end to the other, but must return to the mainland to reach the other end (about a 1½-hour drive). Assateague State Park and Assateague Island National Seashore (for further information, contact Superintendent, Assateague Island National Seashore, Rte. 2, Box 294, Berlin, MD 21811; tel. 301/641-1441) are at the northern end, Chincoteague National Wildlife Refuge at the southern. (Contact Refuge Manager, P.O. Box 62, Chincoteague, VA 23336, tel. 804/336-6122.)

Up at **North Assateague,** you'll find camping sites (see "Where to Stay," below), bathhouses (in summer), bait and tackle shops, limited food service, and picnic tables. Also in summer, there are lifeguards stationed on those marvelous beaches. One of the two herds of wild ponies roams freely over this part of the island, and they are a thrilling sight running in groups or feeding quietly. Remember, these are *wild* animals—keep a respectable distance (they just may bite or kick if crowded), and *don't try to feed them*.

From Chincoteague, a paved road leads three miles through the **Chincoteague National Wildlife Refuge** (a small entrance fee) before it reaches the beach. What you're likely to see along the way depends on the time of year: snow geese, Canada geese, and tundra swans regularly winter here, and there are always the shorebirds, some of which are seldom found anywhere else but along this stretch of coast. And, of course, there's that other herd of wild ponies (the ones that make the swim to Chincoteague each year).

At both ends of Assateague there is excellent fishing, clamming, and crabbing in addition to swimming. Canoe launch areas and camping are permitted on the Maryland portion (the northern end) of Assateague. The Chincoteague National Wildlife Refuge located on the southern end (the Virginia portion) prohibits the landing of a boat anywhere other than at Fishing Point at the very southern tip of the island. Each year, over 305 species of birds visit the refuge, and nature trails that wind through loblolly pines and freshwater marshes provide excellent opportunities to observe bird life, as well as many different mammals, reptiles, and amphibians.

Wildlife-oriented auditorium programs and walks are presented daily during the summer and on weekends during the spring and fall. Island Cruises, a concession operation of the Fish and Wildlife Service, conducts cruises and land safaris at various times during the year. For specific information on tours or programs, write Refuge Manager, Chincoteague National Wildlife Refuge, P.O. Box 62, Chincoteague, VA 23336 (tel. 804/336-6122).

This is old, old country, and if its history interests you, stop at **Accomac** to see the debtor's prison (there's another one at **Eastville).** Incidentally, the Eastville Courthouse, built in 1730, houses court records which date, unbroken, back to 1632!

Where to Stay

There are motel facilities on the Delmarva Peninsula and in Chincoteague, campsites on both ends of Assateague. But my first recommendation may, at first blush, not belong in a guide to the Southern Atlantic. I'm putting it in for two reasons: first of all, many readers will be coming to the Eastern Shore from points north; and second, I've found the inn so completely charming that I think you should know about it.

The **Mainstay Inn,** 635 Columbia Ave., Cape May, NJ 08204 (tel. 609/884-8690), is convenient to the Cape May–Lewes, Delaware ferry, one of the most enjoyable ways to reach the Eastern Shore (fare is $10 per car and driver, $5 for each passenger over age 6), and a delightful place to begin or end a visit there. A lovely old Victorian mansion built in 1872, the Mainstay was once a "gaming parlor" known as Jackson's Clubhouse, where a sweet little old lady was stationed in a rocking chair on the veranda as a lookout for the law. Since then, it has been a rooming house and a local museum. But Tom and Sue Carroll have given it a new, and one hopes a lasting, identity by refurbishing 12 rooms with Victoriana and the warmth of patchwork quilts, braided rugs, and potted plants everywhere. The furnishings are impressive, with the 10-foot gilt mirror in the parlor a decided focal point. All rooms have private bath. In the guesthouse tradition, Tom and Sue serve a marvelous breakfast (included in the rates) and afternoon tea. Sue is usually the chef and sets a breakfast table that rates raves—strawberry crêpes, cheese soufflé, and fried apples are just some of the items that may appear. Rates run from $70 to $112, and that includes both breakfast and afternoon tea. This is a no-smoking inn, and they ask that you not bring pets. They'll provide beach tags for the city beaches if you bring your own beach towels.

In Chincoteague, the **Channel Bass Inn,** 100 Church St., Chincoteague, VA 23336 (tel. 804/336-6148), is another hostelry loaded with charm and spiced by the enthusiasm of its owners. Jim and Kathleen Hanretta bought the rambling old house back in 1972, leaving careers as a classical and flamenco guitarist (Jim) and schoolteacher (Kathy) to devote themselves to converting the former boarding house into a first-class inn. The eight rooms and two suites have all been done over and furnished with antiques, reproductions, and original artwork. The Hanrettas have developed an internationally known restaurant that utilizes the best of all that fresh seafood on the island to turn out gourmet dinners with specialties such as backfin crab soufflé and prices that average $200 for two with tax and tip. Breakfasts are also available, by appointment. Doubles range from $125 to $250. Weekly rates are available, and all are lower January through March. Just one thing: Don't bring the children under 10, and leave Fido home.

Also in Chincoteague, **The Refuge,** one block west of Assateague Bridge, (P.O. Box 378), Chincoteague, VA 23336 (tel. 804/336-5511), is a family owned and operated, two-story, 68-room building that overlooks the wildlife refuge and has rental bicycles as well as a guest laundry, picnic tables with hibachis, a pool, whirlpool, sauna, and exercise room. Doubles here start at $65 in season, lower the rest of the year.

For budget accommodations in Chincoteague, you can't do better than the **Lighthouse Motel,** 224 N. Main St., Chincoteague, VA 23336 (tel. 804/336-5091). They have both rooms and efficiency apartments, and there's free coffee and a fridge in rooms, a pool, cookout area, heated spas, and outdoor games. No pets. Doubles run $35 to $50, and efficiencies run $34 to $50 in season, as low as $25 and $30 in winter.

America House Motor Inn, P.O. Box 472, Rt. 13, Cape Charles, VA 23310 (tel. 804/331-1776), is located on U.S. 13 not far from the Eastern Shore side of the Chesapeake Bay Bridge-Tunnel. Situated on 40 acres, with 10 of them a private sandy beach, America House has spacious rooms that are modern in furnishings, but colonial in atmosphere due to prints, wall hangings, and other decorative touches that recall the Revolution. There's a high observation tower from which to get the lay of the land, and recreational facilities include sailboats, swimming pool, indoor shuffleboard, putting green, golf driving range, picnic areas, children's playground, and a game room with Ping-Pong and a pool table. Their restaurant, also in colonial decor, serves outstanding meals at very reasonable prices. Doubles here run $52 to $60, and studios are $54 to $60 in season (summer); all rates drop a bit off-season.

Camping

On the northern end of **Assateague** there's a modern campground with hot showers, flush toilets, and 311 spaces for campers (no electric or water hookups), which are open most of the year. Space is usually allocated on a first-come, first-served basis, although some sites in summer may be reserved for a full week by contacting the Superintendent, Assateague State Park, Rte. 2, Box 293, Berlin, MD 21811 (tel. 301/641-2120).

Immediately south of the state park, the National Park Service operates smaller, primitive campgrounds (portable toilets and cold water only) year round. These family campgrounds and three backcountry, hike-in sites are always available on a first-come, first-served basis, and reservations eight weeks in advance are available through local Ticketron outlets. Four bayside canoe-in sites are also available. Contact: Superintendent, Assateague Island National Seashore, Rte. 2, Box 294, Berlin, MD 21811 (tel. 301/641-3030).

IV

THE BLUE RIDGE MOUNTAINS

1. THE SKYLINE DRIVE (VIRGINIA)
2. THE BLUE RIDGE PARKWAY
(VIRGINIA AND NORTH CAROLINA)

There's something about mountains! "Majestic" is overworked, but it applies. A sense of timelessness—of patience and endurance. And there's just no better antidote to today's impatient rush toward tomorrow than the nearly 600-mile drive along the ridgecrest of the Blue Ridge Mountains that stretches down the western extremities of Virginia and North Carolina.

Beginning at Front Royal, Virginia, the Skyline Drive leads southward through 105 miles of the Shenandoah National Park at the eastern boundary of the Shenandoah Valley region of the state, to meet the Blue Ridge Parkway at Rockfish Gap, between Charlottesville and Waynesboro. The parkway then goes on for some 470 miles south, still along the crests of ancient mountains, until it reaches the Great Smoky Mountains National Park near the North Carolina–Tennessee border.

It's a drive of incredible beauty, with stunning mountain views and that increasingly rare commodity, a look at nature's face where "civilization" has been smart enough to protect it. All sorts of wild animals live here—bobcat, fox, white-tailed deer, and black bear, to name a few. Streams are clear and forests of birch, poplar, beech, hickory, and oak (some more than 300 years old) are undisturbed. To come in late spring is to see green creeping up the peaks as trees leaf out. In summer, wildflowers blossom to make a carpet of colorful blooms. Fall brings vivid reds and yellows and oranges to give a flame-like hue to every mountainside. And the miracle is that although men and women have made their homes here since that first push westward, it is *nature* that endures. In fact, even the broad, well-paved highway, the carefully planned overlooks, the lodges and cabins and restaurants seem only to enhance what was here to begin with. The rigors of wilderness travel have been eliminated to leave only a natural, unspoiled area that can be traveled in comfort. For most of the year, that is. Fog is a problem at times, and some of the higher sections are closed during icy or snowy weather. It's best to plan this drive between mid-May and mid-November, when conditions are almost consistently good.

You *could,* of course, drive straight down the entire length of this gorgeous roadway. But if you did, you'd miss a wealth of sightseeing. All along the way there are not-to-be-missed historic sites and caverns and bridges that have been sculpted by the centuries just a few miles off the drive and parkway on either side. If time is a problem—it's a *long* drive and there are a lot of side trips—it's best to take one section at a time and come back later for the others. Personally, I prefer seeing it in small chunks (if those enormous vistas could be called "small"). So let's look at it that way.

1. The Skyline Drive (Virginia)

I find **Charlottesville,** at the southern end of the drive, a perfect base. It's a full day's trip up to Front Royal and back, but accommodations are more plentiful, and it's so central to sightseeing that I can leave the suitcase unpacked for a few days. An appealing alternative is to begin your journey about 15 miles north of Front Royal on I-81 in the little town of Middletown for no other reason than to stay at a very special inn dating back to Revolutionary days. Also, if you plan far enough in advance, the lodges at Big Meadow and Skyland are lovely—read on.

WHERE TO STAY

Both these lodges are almost at the center of the drive and both are closed during the winter months. For full details on these and all other accommodations along the drive, write: ARA Virginia Sky-Line Co., Inc., P.O. Box 727, Luray, VA 22835 (tel. 703/999-2266).

Skyland Lodge, P.O. Box 727, Luray, VA 22835 (tel. 703/999-2211), is open from early April until mid-November. It's 10 miles south of the Thornton Gap entrance from Va. 211. This is the highest point on the drive, and the glass-enclosed lobby takes full advantage of the spectacular view, with a fireplace to add just the right note of coziness on cool nights. There are rooms in the main lodge, as well as in separate cottages, and all are comfortable and attractive. Some suites have their own fireplaces. This is a great place for children: a playground, recreation room, lawn games, horses available (with trail maps) for hour-long, half- or full-day rides, and a planned children's program. The café serves all three meals and there's entertainment in the bar every night except Sunday. Doubles run $55 and up, with suites for two to six people beginning at $72. Children under 7 stay free in the same room with their parents. Pets are welcome, but must be kept on a leash.

Big Meadows Lodge, P.O. Box 727, Luray, VA 22835 (tel. 703/743-5108), 19 miles south of the Thornton Gap entrance, is smaller than Skyland and is open from March through December. Besides the main lodge, there's an annex and cottages. Rooms are quite nice and many have fireplaces. For children there's a playground and planned activities, a recreation room, and both horses and bicycles are available. All meals are served in the café (no room service) and the bar has entertainment every night except Wednesday. The leash rule applies to pets here, too. Rates are $33 to $55 for double lodge rooms, $49 to $55 for motel rooms, $47 to $88 for cabins, $72 to $121 for suites that will sleep up to six (children under 16, free).

Campsites

Campers will find tent and trailer sites at **Matthews Arm, Big Meadow, Lewis Mountain,** and **Loft Mountain,** but none have hookups. The rate is $8 per day and there's a 14-day limit. Write Superintendent, Shenandoah National Park, Rte. 4, Box 348, Luray, VA 22835 (tel. 703/999-2229), for full details.

In Middletown, Va.

The **Wayside Inn Since 1797,** 7783 Main St., Middletown, VA 22645 (tel. 703/869-1797), began life in 1797 as Wilkinson's Tavern, offering bed and board to weary travelers in the Virginia wilderness. With the advent of the Shenandoah Valley Turnpike some 20 years later, it became a relay station for stagecoach drivers, as well as a welcome stop for their passengers. During the Civil War, Yankees and Rebels both frequented the place, and one of the war's fiercest battles was fought at nearby Cedar Creek. Today's motorcar travelers find the same warm hospitality, comfortable rooms, and outstanding food as did those earlier move-abouts. Rooms are decorated in a mixture of styles: heirlooms from England, lovingly brought over by early settlers; locally made "Early American" furniture; relics of the Victorian era; and touches of Oriental bric-a-brac brought home by wandering sea captains. There are canopied beds in some rooms, and even fireplaces in a few. Each room has its own personality, and when booking, you might specify if you'd prefer colonial, Chinese, Empire, or Victorian decor (no promise you'll get it, but the friendly owners do all they can to please, so it's worth a try). There are no elevators, so be prepared for stairs. There are seven dining rooms (I can't resist the Slave Quarters, with its crackling fire, high-back chairs, and bare wooden tables) and the Coachyard cocktail lounge, a throwback to the English pub tradition. As for the food, it's famed all through the valley—country-cured ham, peanut soup, pan-fried chicken, hot breads, and even chicken gumbo. And if sitting on the veranda in one of the white rocking chairs is a little too tame for your tastes, you can walk just a few yards to the Wayside Theater, where professional actors perform from June to December. The Wayside has become one of the most famous hostelries in Virginia, and in my book that's a reputation well earned. Singles and doubles range from $70 to $132; suites are $90 to $132. A crib is $10. No pets.

In Charlottesville, Va.

Call 804/293-6789 for a free local reservation service.

The **Boar's Head Inn,** P.O. Box 5185, Charlottesville, VA 22903 (tel. 804/296-2181), is one mile west of Va. 250-W Bypass and is one of the finest resort inns in the commonwealth. An inn has stood here since 1763 when Terrell's Ordinary greeted travelers, and the present building dates its west wing from 1834. Decor is, as you'd expect, colonial, with a liberal supply of antiques in the attractive public areas. Rooms are beautifully decorated, some with lovely views of the mountains or the lake with its ducks and swans. There are facilities for tennis, squash, paddle tennis, and swimming (in season), plus exceptional health facilities. The tavern features live entertainment, and the dining room is considered one of the best places to eat in these parts (see "Where to Eat").

Doubles start at $100 and suites (some with fireplaces) at $160, and if you want to stay in this exceptionally beautiful place, you'd best reserve at least a month ahead. Children under 18 stay free with their parents, but there's an added charge for pets.

If you're interested in going the full luxury route, the sumptuous **Omni Charlottesville Hotel,** at 235 W. Main St., Charlottesville, VA 22901 (tel. 804/971-5500, or toll free 800/228-2121), is heartily recommended. In a historic redevelopment area in the heart of downtown, the seven-story brick-and-glass contemporary structure is something of a surprising contrast to its surroundings. But it's tastefully done, and the 65-foot-atrium lobby lounge is a real attention-getter. There's an elegantly appointed multilevel dining room with colonial touches, where dinners range from $10 to $22. A cocktail lounge, also bilevel, offers nightly entertainment, and there's an indoor/outdoor pool and complete health-fitness center. All in all, this 208-room charmer offers the amenities you can expect from this top-scale system, including special check-in and checkout and concierge services. Double rates for all this opulence will cost $125 a night, but seasonal package rates are available.

The **English Inn of Charlottesville,** 2000 Morton Dr., Charlottesville, VA 22901 (tel. 804/971-9900), is modeled on the small inns of England in a sort of modern-Tudor style. Suites have oversize beds and refrigerators, and other amenities include cable TV and in-room movies in all guest rooms, an indoor pool, restaurant, cocktail lounge, health club, and free transportation to and from airport, bus, and train terminals. Double-room rates begin at $86, suites run $80 to $88, and all rates include a full cooked breakfast.

The **Charlottesville Days Hotel,** 1901 Emmet St., Rt. 29, Charlottesville, VA 22901 (tel. 804/977-7700 or toll free 800/325-2525), is located out toward the airport. Guest rooms are nicely decorated and comfortably furnished, as is typical of this chain, and there's a pool and moderate-priced restaurant. Rates range from $39 to $62, with superior rooms on the Executive Floor running $49 to $65.

The **Comfort Inn,** 1807 Emmet St., Charlottesville, VA 22901 (tel. 804/293-6188 or toll free 800/228-5150), has guest rooms of a high standard, a pool, and a free continental breakfast. Rates are $43 to $52 for doubles.

The **Quality Inn,** Rt. 9, Box 428, Charlottesville, VA 22901 (tel. 804/977-3300 or toll free 800/228-5151), is located at the junction of I-64 and U.S. 250, Exit 25. Located some three miles from Monticello and Ash Lawn, it offers such amenities as cable TV and movies in guest room, a swimming pool, miniature golf, and a moderately priced restaurant and lounge. Doubles run $40 to $65.

Most of the large, convenient rooms at **Howard Johnson's,** 1309 W. Main St., Charlottesville, VA 22903 (tel. 804/296-8121), have balconies and attractive, modern decor. Directly across from the University of Virginia, the motel has indoor parking, an indoor pool, and a restaurant. Doubles run $52 to $65, and the only time advance reservations are necessary is at graduation time at the university (June).

The **Best Western Cavalier Inn,** 105 Emmet St., Charlottesville, VA 22905 (tel. 804/296-8111 or toll free 800/528-1234), is also across from the university and has a pool, a nearby 24-hour pancake house, and a family restaurant specializing in seafood and pasta. A continental breakfast is served in the lobby. They can also furnish a list of babysitters. Doubles here start at $59, but go up during special university events. Special vacation package rates are available.

Rooms at the budget-priced **Econo Lodge,** 2014 Holiday Dr., Charlottesville, VA 22901 (tel. 804/295-3185 or toll free 800/446-6900), are clean and comfortable and the inn offers free morning coffee and doughnuts. It's close to the university and a large shopping center. Advance reservations are advisable during June, July, and August. A double room here costs $39 to $45. Children under 12 stay free.

There's another **Econo Lodge** on the south side of town at 400 Emmet St., Charlottesville, VA 22903 (tel. 804/296-2104 or toll free 800/446-6900), with similar facilities and rates.

Bed and Breakfast

Bed and Breakfast, Inc., P.O. Box 5737, Charlottesville, VA 22905 (tel. 804/979-7264 Monday through Friday, noon to 5 p.m.), can book you into rooms, suites, and even estate cottages in Charlottesville, Luray, and points in between.

The **200 South Street Inn,** 200 South St., Charlottesville, VA 22901 (tel. 804/979-0200), is a lovely old restored inn in the historic district. English and Belgian antiques are used throughout, and guest rooms feature some fireplaces, whirlpools, and canopy beds. Rates range from $80 to $150, and include breakfast, wine, and afternoon tea.

An Alternative Sightseeing Base

Sometimes known as the "Capital of the Shenandoah Valley," Staunton (pronounced "Stanton") is the oldest city west of the Blue Ridge and presents quite a nice base for your stay along this part of the Skyline Drive. If you should opt for this alternative, take U.S. 250 west to Staunton, then continue westward for 12 miles (pass through Churchville) to reach a charming and historic guesthouse that will give you a firsthand taste of genuine Virginia hospitality. The **Buckhorn Inn,** Star Rte., Box 139, Churchville, VA 24421 (tel. 703/337-6900), has welcomed travelers for more than 200 years, having been first a popular carriage stop, later a rather famous gambling spot as well as an inn, and a center for the sick and wounded during the Civil War. Today, the two-story inn, with wide verandas across the front upstairs as well as downstairs, is most famous for its antique-filled guest rooms and old-fashioned, Shenandoah Valley country cooking. A terrific full country breakfast is included in room rates and served to overnight guests only. Lunches and dinners are open to the general public and served both buffet and family style, at prices well under $10. As for guest rooms, each one is different and furnished with antiques, and the star of the inn is the two-room suite with private Jacuzzi. Rates for doubles, which include that great breakfast, run from $45 to $55, with the suite going for $65.

In Staunton itself, there's a **Comfort Inn,** 1302 Richmond Rd., Staunton, VA 24401 (tel. 703/886-5000 or toll free 800/228-5150), with nice guest rooms, a free continental breakfast, and a discount for seniors on rates of $39.95 double; and the **Econo Lodge Staunton,** 1031 Richmond Rd., Staunton, VA 24401 (tel. 703/885-5158 or toll free 800/446-6900), that accepts pets and has a restaurant on the premises, with rates of $32 to $37. For a comprehensive listing of historic lodgings and restaurants in and near Staunton, contact the **Staunton Augusta Chamber of Commerce,** 30 N. New St., Staunton, VA 24401 (tel. 703/886-2351).

WHERE TO EAT

On the Skyline Drive itself, you'll find good food at moderate prices at both the lodges listed in the previous section. In addition, you'll be able to eat reasonably well at **Panorama,** or if a picnic seems like a good idea (it is!), you can pick up light lunches and groceries at **Elkwallow, Big Meadow,** and **Loft Mountain Waysides.**

In Charlottesville, Va.

The Old Mill Room at the **Boar's Head Inn,** one mile west of Va. 250-W Bypass (tel. 804/296-2181), is in an 1834 gristmill now incorporated into the inn's west wing, and this is colonial-style dining at its best. Waitresses in colonial dress add to the early-days atmosphere in the candlelit room with its yellow-pine beams, fireplace, and antique furnishings. Escalope of veal Oscar is a favorite with patrons (appetizers, salads, and desserts extra). Dinner prices range from $12 to $25, and reservations are absolutely necessary. Lunch runs $5.50 to $10 and breakfast costs $3.50 to $6. Sunday brunch is $12.50. Hours are 7:30 to 10:30 a.m., noon to 2 p.m., and 6 to 9:30 p.m.—and best reserve. On the premises you'll also find a wine shop and country store.

The **Ivy Inn,** 2244 Old Ivy Rd., one mile from the University of Virginia, just off Va. 250 Bus. (tel. 804/977-1222), is in a 19th-century brick house. It, too, has fireplaces, and there's pleasant background music for candlelight dining. Featured dishes are veal, lamb, seafood, and steaks, and prices are in the $12 to $18 range. Dinner begins at 5 p.m., and reservations are a good idea. Closed Sunday.

Janice Amiss is now the owner-operator of the longtime favorite **Martha's Café,** just across from the university at 11 Elliewood Ave. (tel. 804/971-7530). This pleasant, homey restaurant attracts an appealing local clientele, many of them students, with its homemade dishes and friendly service. Quiches, muffins, and salads are excellent, and vegetables are always fresh. Lunch and dinner prices are surprisingly moderate (about $4 to $6 for lunch, $6 to $9 for dinner). It's a small, inviting restaurant with only 45 seats and reservations are not accepted, so you may have a bit of a wait (the outdoor patio adds 24 seats in summer); but for a light lunch or dinner, this is the place to go. Hours are 11:30 a.m. to 2 p.m. and 5:30 to 8:30 p.m. weekdays, to 2:30 and 9 p.m. on weekends.

The **Garrett,** 102 14th St. NW (tel. 804/295-6060), is "on the corner," and is a favorite spot for the university and professional community. It's rustic, yet not without elegance, with a six-foot TV screen for major sports events. Specialties, all at moderate prices, vary daily. There's an above-average bar offering seasonal concoctions of their own, which add to the general sparkle of the place. Sunday brunch is a local tradition (served from 10:30 a.m. to 2:30 p.m.). The Garrett is open from 11 a.m. to 4 p.m. for lunch Monday through Friday, and daily from 4 to 10:30 p.m. for dinner, with a late-night menu until closing. They also accept Visa and MasterCard.

Le Snail, 320 W. Main St. (tel. 804/295-4456), in a restored turn-of-the-century house in downtown Charlottesville is a refreshing change of scene from the area's prevailing colonial ambience. There's a main candlelit dining room and several smaller ones; the comfortable, rather eclectic decor might best be described as homey French provincial. Cuisine is highlighted by such impeccably continental specialties as la truite du chef, a luscious boned trout with assorted herbs and spices, wrapped in pastry and baked, and a classic beef Wellington. My favorite appetizer is special snails of the house in a delicate puff pastry. There's a dress code, only fitting in such a top-scale establishment. A la carte entrees, which include vegetables of the day, run from about $15 to $21. There's a $16.95 table d'hôte dinner Monday through Thursday. Le Snail is open Monday through Saturday from 6 to 10 p.m.; it closes December 25 to mid-January and the first three weeks of August. Reservations are urged!

For a moderate-priced lunch, there's historic old **Michie Tavern** (see "Things to See"), with a café that serves from 11:15 a.m. to 3 p.m.

THINGS TO SEE

If you're based at **Charlottesville**, plan at least one day to explore the historic sites and homes in this beautiful mountain town.

Make your first stop the **Thomas Jefferson Visitors Bureau** on Va. 20 South, P.O. Box 161, Charlottesville, VA 22902 (tel. 804/293-6789 or 977-1783) for free brochures, maps, and self-directed automobile and walking tours of the Charlottesville area. It's open from 9 a.m. to 5 p.m. Monday through Friday; closed major holidays. There's also a free local reservations service.

You can't miss the **University of Virginia** at the west end of Main Street, and certainly you *shouldn't* miss the experience of rambling around its campus for an hour or two. There are also free historical tours of the grounds and main points of interest that leave from the Rotunda Monday through Friday during the school term (call 804/924-1019 for times). Thomas Jefferson founded the school and drew plans for its grounds as well as many of its early buildings. Set in broad lawns with huge old trees and sweeping vistas, the handsome red-brick buildings with their white trim have an impressive, simple dignity. A classic example of Jefferson's architectural genius is the Rotunda, focal point of the oldest part of the campus, and the one-brick-thick serpentine wall and the columned porticoes that front student living quarters. Hostesses at the Rotunda will arrange student-guided tours on weekdays during the school year. The university opened its doors in 1825 with a student body of 68 and eight faculty members. Three of the first five U.S. presidents (Jefferson, Madison, and Monroe) served on its first board of trustees! Smaller today than many American universities, it has an annual enrollment of about 16,000 — out of which it awards more graduate degrees than any other institution of higher learning in Virginia.

Monticello and Vicinity

Jefferson's beloved home, **Monticello** (pronounced "Mont-i-*chell*-o"), is on a mountaintop three miles southeast of Charlottesville on Va. 53 (tel. 804/295-8181). He designed and built the house, using materials made right on the spot, from bricks right down to nails, on land that had come to his father in a land grant. Begun in 1769, it wasn't completed until 1809, although he lived in it from 1772. Jefferson died here on July 4, 1826, exactly 50 years after the signing of the Declaration of Independence, and his tomb is in the family cemetery. Restoration continues throughout the house, which contains many original furnishings. The gardens are extensive and include the newly replanted orchard. Open from 8 a.m. to 5 p.m. March to October, from 9 a.m. to 4:30 p.m. the remainder of the year. Admission is $7 for adults, $2 for children 6 to 11, and $6 for senior citizens.

A recently added exhibit, "Thomas Jefferson & Monticello," in the **visitors center** on Va. 20 South offers fascinating glimpses into Mr. Jefferson's life and times via multimedia displays, artifacts, and family memorabilia. It's open from 9 a.m. to 5:30 p.m., March through October, to 5 p.m. the rest of the year. Closed Christmas Day. Admission is free.

Just 2½ miles southeast of Monticello (off Va. 53 on County Road 795) is where the fifth U.S. president, James Monroe, lived at **Ash Lawn** ("Highland"), a modest country house on a 535-acre estate. Thomas Jefferson selected the house site and planted orchards for his neighbor. Now restored by the College of William and Mary, Ash Lawn offers tours of the house with its late-18th- and early-19th-century furnishings, including Monroe's furniture, periodic home-craft demonstrations, kitchen gardens, and truly magnificent boxwood hedges. There are peacocks among the boxwood, a Piccirilli statue of Monroe, quiet picnic spots, and great views of the Blue Ridge foothills. Special events include summer festivals of music and drama, and Christmas celebrations. Open daily from 9 a.m. to 6 p.m. March through October, from 10 a.m. to 5 p.m. November through February (closed Thanksgiving, Christmas, and New Year's days). Admission is $6 for adults, $5.50 for seniors, $2 for ages 6 to 11, with special rates for groups of 15 or more.

Another American president, James Madison, also made his home in the Charlottesville area. **Montpelier,** now an imposing Georgian mansion some 35 miles northeast of Charlottesville on Va. 20, was built by the president's father as a modest, two-story house in the mid-1700s. It was James Madison's childhood home, to which he returned after completing his second term of office in 1817. His widow, the colorful Dolley Madison, was forced to sell the estate to pay off gambling debts of her son by a first marriage, and Montpelier passed through many hands until it was bought by one of the Du Ponts in 1901. That illustrious family enlarged, improved, and renovated the original home almost beyond recognition, and it remained one of the family's residences until the mid-1980s, when it was deeded to the National Trust for Historic Preservation by a Du Pont daughter. The mansion, by that time, had grown to 55 rooms, and the 2,700-acre estate held stables, a sawmill, steeplechase course, bowling alley, and steam laundry. In 1987 Montpelier was opened to the public, and although it is far from the home James and Dolley Madison called home for some 19 years, historical mementoes abound, and the home is well worth a visit. For full details, contact the National Trust for Historic Preservation, P.O. Box 67, Montpelier Station, VA 22957 (tel. 703/672-2728). Hours are 10 a.m. to 4 p.m. daily, and admission is $6 for adults, $5 for seniors, and $1 for children over 6; under 6 free.

Located high on a mountainside near Monticello, one mile south of town on Va. 20, historic **Michie Tavern** (tel. 804/977-1234) is one of the oldest homesteads remaining in the state. A Scotsman, John Michie, purchased the land from Patrick Henry's father in 1746 and built his home on what was a popular stagecoach route. In 1784 the commodious dwelling became a tavern and inn. Until 1910 Michie's descendants owned the property, but in 1927 the inn was dismantled and moved by horse and wagon and truck to its present site near Jefferson's Monticello. After a painstaking reconstruction, it opened in 1928 as a museum. Inside you'll find such handcrafted wooden household gadgets as a cheese press, apple peeler, potato cutter, etc., and a folding "Murphy bed" in an upstairs closet. The ballroom, keeping hall, ladies' and gentlemen's parlors, bedroom, and tap bar hold colonial and Revolutionary furniture and artifacts. Outbuildings include a log kitchen, "necessary," dairy, well house, and smoke house, as well as the Meadow Run grist mill that dates from about 1797. A colonial-style buffet is served daily in the "Ordinary," a 200-year-old slave house, from 11:30 a.m. to 3 p.m. The museum is open daily from 9 a.m. to 5 p.m., and admission is $4.50 for adults, $4 for seniors, $2 for children 6 to 12 (under 6, free).

In Staunton

Stop by the **Staunton-Augusta Chamber of Commerce,** 30 N. New St., Staunton, VA 24401 (tel. 703/886-2351), for walking-tour maps of downtown, the 19th-century warehouse district, and historical residential areas of the city.

President Woodrow Wilson was born in Staunton, and his birthplace, a Greek Revival–style home that was built in 1846 as the **First Presbyterian Church** manse, is at Coalter and Frederick streets (tel. 703/885-0897). There's a good documentary film for visitors, as well as loads of Wilson family memorabilia, and the president's Pierce Arrow limousine. After seeing the house, stroll through the lovely Victorian garden. Hours are 9 a.m. to 6 p.m. during summer months, to 5 p.m. other times of the year, and admissions are $3.50 for adults, $3 for seniors, and $1 for ages 6 to 12.

Trinity Episcopal Church, 214 W. Beverley St. (tel. 886-9132), was built in 1855 on the site of a 1746 church that served for several days as the Revolutionary capitol of Virginia in 1781.

Those keen on shopping will want to stop in nearby Waynesboro at the **Shenandoah Village Outlet Mall,** a cluster of 17 buildings modeled after Shenandoah 18th-century homes, barns, and inns. Very much 20th century, however, are the 50 retail outlets with savings of 50% to 70%, small restaurants, and tourist center. Hours are 10 a.m. to 9 p.m. weekdays, 10 a.m. to 6 p.m. Sunday.

On and Near the Skyline Drive

There's a $5 charge per car to enter the drive (for detailed information and pamphlets, contact: Superintendent, Shenandoah National Park, Rte. 4, Box 292, Luray, VA 22835; tel. 703/999-2266), and an *enforced* 35-mph speed limit (you won't want to speed through, anyway). The southernmost entrance at Rockfish Gap is 20 miles west of Charlottesville on U.S. 250. Other entries are at Swift Run Gap, between Stanardsville and Elkton on U.S. 33; Thornton Gap, on U.S. 211 between Luray and Sperryville; and at Front Royal (U.S. 340), its northernmost end.

At Big Meadows (Mile 51), the **Harry F. Byrd, Sr., Visitor Center** features a movie exploring man's relationship to the mountains and a historical and cultural museum. It's open every day, but only part-time during January and

February. From April to November the **Dickey Ridge Visitor Center** near Front Royal is also open daily. **Shenandoah National Park headquarters** is five miles east of Luray on U.S. 211, and they'll send informative pamphlets if you write: Superintendent, Shenandoah National Park, Rte. 4, Box 292, Luray, VA 22835 (tel. 703/999-2266).

There are free **picnic grounds** with fireplaces, water, tables, and rest rooms at Dickey Ridge, Elkwallow, Pinnacles, Big Meadows, Lewis Mountain, South River, and Loft Mountain.

You can **trout fish** in some of the park streams from April to October 15, but you'll need a five-day state license (get them at park concession units).

If you bring Fido along, be *sure* to keep him on a leash—this is one regulation that's rigidly enforced.

You'll need at least one day—another if you plan to take in all the attractions just off the drive—to drive to Front Royal and back. The views are breathtaking all along the way—across the Shenandoah Valley on your left lie the Massanutten Mountains, and beyond, the Alleghenies. There are parking overlooks at the most spectacular ones, and I defy you to drive right on by without making at least one stop! When you reach the north entrance to **Skyland,** you'll be at the highest point on the drive: 3,680 feet above sea level. And not far from Thornton Gap, you'll pass through a 700-foot tunnel at **Mary's Rock.**

At Thornton Gap, you can turn west on U.S. 211 for a 10-minute drive to the **Luray Caverns** (tel. 703/743-6551). Its gigantic underground rooms—there's one that measures 300 feet wide, 500 feet long, and 140 feet high—are connected by natural corridors, and one features stereophonic music produced on an organ that uses reverberating stalactites instead of pipes! Be sure to bring that camera, for the lighting system makes color photos possible, and the staggering array of stalactites and stalagmites will arouse the photographer in you. About every 20 minutes or so, hour-long guided tours leave from the entrance of this majestic U.S. natural landmark, beginning at 9 a.m. The last tour leaves at 7 p.m. June 15 through Labor Day, at 6 p.m. March 15 to June 14 and after Labor Day to November 14, and at 4 p.m. Monday through Friday and at 5 p.m. on Saturday and Sunday the rest of the year. Adults pay $9 to explore this underworld magical kingdom, senior citizens pay $8, children 7 through 13 pay $4, and those under 7 are admitted free with their parents. Cost also includes admission to the **Car and Carriage Caravan,** a fascinating collection of antique cars, coaches, and costumes dating from 1625. There's no charge for the 45-minute (June through August) **carillon concerts** played every Tuesday, Thursday, Saturday, and Sunday by a world-famous carillonneur at the Luray Singing Tower, whose largest bell weighs 7,640 pounds and the smallest, 12½. Concerts are given weekends only, March through May and September through October.

Back on the drive, ride on up to **Front Royal** (which got its name, incidentally, from the order of an out-of-patience drill sergeant to ill-trained local militia to "front to the royal oak," meaning the "royal" tree of England, when they had trouble following his regulation military command). The excellent **Thunderbird Museum and Archeological Park** (tel. 703/635-7337) is six miles south on U.S. 340, then half a mile west (you'll see the entrance signs), and here, for a fee of $3.50 (children 8 to 12, $2), you can watch archaeologists at work during summer months. The museum displays some of their finds and explains exhibits, which show that early man was living here thousands of years before the Roman Empire. It also features an outdoor replica of an early Native American house.

The **Skyline Caverns**, P.O. Box 193, Front Royal, VA 22630 (tel. 703/ 635-4545), just one mile south of Front Royal on U.S. 340, have beautiful calcite formations known as "anthodites," which look like flowers, and whose estimated growth is only one inch every 7,000 years. The caverns are well lighted, there's a 37-foot waterfall, and you'll enjoy their sound and light show. Topside, a miniature train chugs around the wooded grounds ($2), and there are picnic grounds. Admission to the caverns is $8 (ages 7 to 13, $4), and they're open from 9 a.m. to 5 p.m. or 8 a.m. to 7 p.m., depending on the time of year. These are the nearest major caverns to the Skyline Drive.

One of nature's greatest curiosities is at picturesque **Mount Solon,** 11 miles north of Staunton on U.S. 11, then west on Va. 646 to Va. 747. "Natural Chimneys" are seven huge limestone columns, rising to a height of 120 feet, which have been carved out of solid rock by the Shenandoah River over millions of years. From some vantage points they do indeed look like chimneys, but my fancy turns to the turrets and towers of a medieval castle. And I'm certainly not alone in that fancy, for back in 1821 people hereabouts started an annual jousting tournament in which "knights" with long lances attempt to spear a small, suspended ring while on horseback. Each knight gets three "tilts" and the winner is king of the tournament. If you're in these parts on the third Saturday in August, it's a fun day.

2. The Blue Ridge Parkway (Virginia and North Carolina)

From Waynesboro south, the Blue Ridge Parkway (write for maps and detailed information to: Superintendent, Blue Ridge Parkway, 700 BB&T Building, One Pack Square, Asheville, NC 28801; tel. 704/259-0779) takes up where the Skyline Drive leaves off, winding and twisting along the mountain crests right on through most of western North Carolina. You'll drive at elevations ranging from 649 to 6,053 feet above sea level. There's no toll on the parkway, and there are rather frequent exits to nearby towns.

There are 11 visitor contact stations, nine campgrounds (open May through October only, except for limited winter camping at Otter Creek, Roanoke Mountain, Price Park, and Linville Falls) with drinking water and comfort stations, but no shower or utility hookups (on a first-come, first-served basis— no reservations); restaurants and gas stations; and three lodges plus one location featuring rustic cabins for overnight accommodations (reservations are recommended). Opening and closing dates for campgrounds and cabins are flexible, so be sure to check with the parkway in advance. At many overlooks you'll see a squirrel-rifle-and-powder-horn symbol and the word "trail," which means that there are marked walking trails through the woods. Some take only 10 or 20 minutes and provide a delightful, leg-stretching break from the confines of the car. Others are longer and steeper and may take an hour or more if you go the entire way.

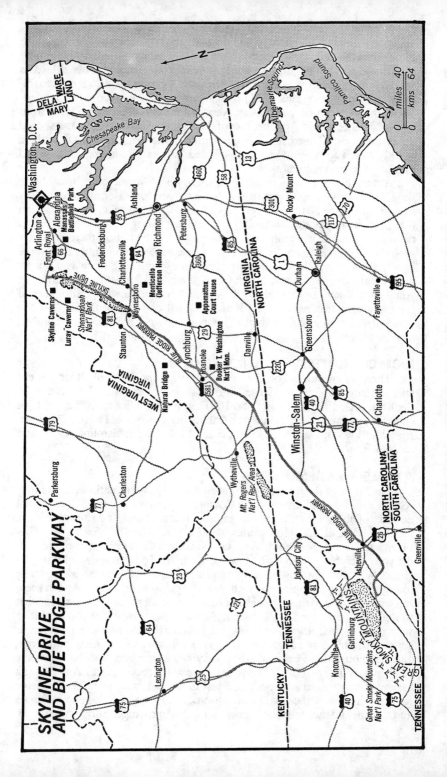

SKYLINE DRIVE AND BLUE RIDGE PARKWAY

Washington, D.C.

DELA WARE
MARY LAND

Chesapeake Bay

Albemarle Sound

Pamlico Sound

0 miles 40
0 kms 64

Arlington
Front Royal
Alexandria
Manassas Battlefield Park

Fredericksburg
Ashland
Richmond
Petersburg

Charlottesville
Monticello (Jefferson Home)

Rocky Mount

VIRGINIA
NORTH CAROLINA

Skyline Caverns
Luray Caverns
Shenandoah Nat'l Park
SKYLINE DRIVE

Waynesboro

Staunton

Appomattox Court House

Durham
Raleigh

Fayetteville

Lynchburg
Roanoke
Booker T. Washington Nat'l Mon.

Danville

Greensboro

WEST VIRGINIA
VIRGINIA

Natural Bridge

BLUE RIDGE PARKWAY

Winston-Salem

Charlotte

Parkersburg

Charleston

Wytheville
Mt. Rogers Nat'l Rec. Area

BLUE RIDGE PARKWAY

NORTH CAROLINA
SOUTH CAROLINA

Greenville

Johnson City
Asheville

KENTUCKY
TENNESSEE

Lexington

Knoxville
Gatlinburg
GREAT SMOKY MOUNTAINS
Great Smoky Mountains Nat'l Park

TENNESSEE

There are a few simple rules laid down by the National Park Service, which administers the parkway: no commercial vehicles are permitted; no swimming in lakes and ponds; no hunting; pets must be kept on leash; and above all else, *no fire except in campground or picnic area fireplaces.* A good rule of your own to follow is to keep your gas tank half filled at all times—it's no place to be stranded! The higher sections of the parkway, west of Asheville, are usually closed from mid-November to mid-April because of the danger of ice and snow, and should dangerous conditions exist at any other time of the year, sections affected are quickly closed to traffic. Oh, yes, the speed limit is 45 miles an hour—and they're quite serious about that.

Although Roanoke is just 120 miles south of Waynesboro, it probably should be your first overnight stop in order to spend at least one day at nearby Lexington and the Natural Bridge. From Roanoke to Asheville, North Carolina (the next city of any size), is too long to attempt in one day unless you're in a rush. And if you're in a rush, stay off the parkway—first of all, there's that 45-mph speed limit; and second, if you don't have time to amble and drink in the beauty through which you're passing, wait and come back when you do. By breaking the drive at Boone, North Carolina (about 10 miles off the parkway), you'll have time to sightsee along the way and perhaps catch a performance of the outdoor drama *Horn in the West.* The final two legs of the trip—from Boone to Asheville and from there to Fontana Village—are easily accomplished in a day's drive.

FROM CHARLOTTESVILLE TO ROANOKE, VA

There are two lodges on the parkway in Virginia. **Peaks of Otter** (for details and rates, which vary, write Virginia Peaks of Otter Co., P.O. Box 489, Bedford, VA 24523; tel. 703/586-1081), some 86 miles from the northern end of the parkway; and **Rocky Knob Cabins** (write National Park Concessions, Inc., Meadows of Dan, VA 24120), closer to the North Carolina border and south of Roanoke.

A Very Special Detour

For a taste of that celebrated antebellum life, leave the parkway at its intersection with I-64 and drive west to Covington, then north on U.S. 220, a total distance of about 60 miles, to the grand old resort hotel, **the Homestead,** at Hot Springs (U.S. 220, Hot Springs, VA 24445; tel. 703/839-5500). This classic, magnificent château holds over 600 rooms, and the tone is set from the minute you enter the 70-yard-long Great Hall, with its 16 Corinthian columns, 18 chandeliers, and two log-burning fireplaces. There are lobbies galore, many lounges, and two shopping areas, all on a very grand scale, indeed. And in keeping with its grand manner, the Homestead enforces a moderate dress code that though fairly casual, rules out blue jeans and T-shirts (not that you'd *want* to wear them in such elegant surroundings). As for the rooms, there are spacious suites with parlors and big screened porches with magnificent mountain views, and penthouse duplexes in the South Wing, whose bedroom balconies are reached by spiral staircases (I *told* you this was a very special place). And there's a variety of recreational activities that is just simply outstanding: mineral baths or saunas, which were the original attractions; 16,000 acres of mountain forests and streams and meadows; horseback riding, hiking, fringed-surrey rides; an indoor and two outdoor pools; tennis courts (20); and three superb golf courses. Dining here is an experience. Both the cuisine and the service are legendary, and both more than live up to the elegance of the place. And that service doesn't flag even if you opt for room service in a room so beautifully furnished you just can't leave it. All in all, if a splurge is on your agenda or if posh is your natural style of travel, the Homestead is sure to fill the bill: it's been doing that since 1892. What you pay for such pampering is $270 to $350 (add $80 to $115 for those parlor suites) for doubles. There are some golf and tennis package plans—but don't expect huge reductions; it isn't that kind of place.

Where to Stay in Roanoke

Roanoke was just a tiny village (population about 500) until it became a railroad center in the 1880s. One of the remnants of the prosperous times that followed is the **Hotel Roanoke,** 19 N. Jefferson ST. (P.O. Box 12508), Roanoke, VA 24026 (tel. 703/343-6992), two blocks north off U.S. 220, U.S. 11, and I-581 (look for the "Downtown" exit). The large old "railroad hotel" is in the style of an English inn, albeit an elegant one. And both accommodations and service live up to that elegance. You'll really get the feeling of an era now passed when you settle into the groove of being a much-catered-to guest. There are three dining rooms (you can eat from 7 a.m. to 11 p.m.), bars, a heated indoor pool with poolside food service, babysitting service, and golf privileges at nearby courses. Doubles run $75 to $100; suites, $120 to $185.

The **Marriott Motor Hotel,** 2801 Hershberger Rd. NW, Roanoke, VA 24017 (tel. 703/563-9300 or toll free 800/228-9290), is located near the airport and has superior rooms, some with private patios or balconies, refrigerators, and oversize beds. All rooms have cable TV and in-room movies. Amenities include two heated pools, a restaurant, and a bar with entertainment and dancing. Free transportation is available to airport, railway station, and bus depot. The double-room rates range from $58 to $130, and there's a discount for seniors.

There's a **Holiday Inn,** Orange Avenue at Williamson Road NE, Roanoke, VA 24012 (tel. 703/342-8961), in downtown Roanoke, with renovated large rooms and modern furnishings. Prices in the dining room (open for breakfast, lunch, and dinner) are moderate. Amenities include a pool and wading pool, and pets are accepted. Double-occupancy rooms are $60 to $68.

The **Days Inn Roanoke–Civic Center,** 535 Orange Ave. (P.O. Box 12325), Roanoke, VA 24024 (tel. 703/342-4551, or toll free 800/325-2525), at I-581 and U.S. 460, is conveniently located in the heart of downtown. Its 260 rooms offer the clean, comfortable, and spacious accommodations for which this system is noted. There's a pool and two lighted tennis courts, free cable TV, and local phone calls are also free. Dining room costs are moderate, and doubles go for $37 to $42; add $4 for each additional adult, $2 for each child 2 to 18. If Fido comes along, he is charged $4.

The **Comfort Inn,** 3695 Thirlane Rd. NW, Roanoke, VA 24019 (tel. 703/563-0229 or toll free 800/228-5150), is near the airport. The high-quality rooms feature cable TV and in-room movies, there's a pool, cribs are furnished without charge, a complimentary continental breakfast is included in the rate, and there's a restaurant close by. Doubles run $47 to $54.

In a convenient downtown location, the **Econo Lodge,** 308 Orange Ave.,

Roanoke, VA 24016 (tel. 703/343-2413 or toll free 800/446-6900) features free coffee and sweet rolls in the lobby, cable TV with in-room movies in all guest rooms, and free cribs. Doubles go for $35.95, with a $5 charge for each additional person and each rollaway bed.

To the West

Off to the west of the Blue Ridge Parkway and Roanoke, there's the unspoiled scenery and mountain lodge at **Mountain Lake.** This pristine 2,600-acre nature conservancy holds Virginia's largest lake, and it's an idyllic spot for a romantic honeymoon, a back-to-nature family holiday, or simply a few days respite from the toing and froing of the modern world. The hand of man lies lightly on this natural paradise, and the conservancy means to keep it that way. The facilities that let you and me commune comfortably with nature are all designed to blend in, rather than disrupt, Mother Nature's work. There's a stone lodge with 50 tastefully decorated and comfortably furnished guest rooms, some with fireplaces; the 16-room Chestnut Lodge, where every room has a separate sitting area, fireplace, whirlpool, and balcony; 15 cottages (no cooking facilities), most with fireplaces; and a first-rate restaurant. As for what to do in this breathtakingly beautiful setting, there's fishing in the lake, miles and miles of hiking trails, a games room in the large barn, and in the evening, convivial gatherings around the large stone fireplaces in the lodge lobby or the lounge.

You can choose European Plan rates (no meals) or the modified American Plan (breakfast and dinner), and doubles range from $90 to $135 in both the lodge and cottages, depending on the plan you select; in the Chestnut Lodge, the range is $125 to $160. If you opt for the European Plan, dinner in the excellent restaurant will run $19 and up.

To reach Mountain Lake from Roanoke, drive south on I-81 to Exit 37, turn west on U.S. 460 to Blacksburg, then follow U.S. 240 bypass to Rte. 700, and the lake is seven miles to the north. For full details and booking, contact: Mountain Lake, Mountain Lake, VA 24136 (tel. 703/626-7121 or toll free 800/346-3334).

Where to Eat Along the Parkway

Restaurants, cafés, and picnic grounds are all in abundant supply at fairly convenient locations. If you decide on a picnic, however, stock up either before you go or at the first supply store you see — they aren't that plentiful once you're on the parkway.

Where to Eat in Roanoke

The **Hotel Roanoke's Regency Room** (tel. 703/343-6992) is far and away the best place to eat in this area. It's an elegant atmosphere (jacket and tie required at dinner), with entertainment and dancing. And there's a delightful terrace dining when weather permits. Specialties include spoon bread (they do their own baking, so all breads are delicious), tournedos béarnaise, and steak Diane, and the tab will come to somewhere between $12 and $23 on the semi–à la carte menu. Less formal meals are served in their Ad Lib lounge/restaurant.

For less expensive meals, try the dining rooms at the motels listed in the "Where to Stay" section.

La Maison du Gourmet, 5732 Airport Rd. (tel. 703/366-2444), is located in a historic Georgian mansion. Its elegant dining room, where a pianist holds forth in the evening, specializes in continental dishes such as veal Oscar and seafood creations. There's patio dining in good weather, and an intimate lounge for cocktails. Lunch averages $3 to $9, dinner $9 to $20; hours are 11 a.m. to 2:30 p.m. and 4:30 to 11 p.m. every day except Sunday, Christmas, and New Year's Day; and reservations are recommended, especially at dinner.

The **Charcoal Steak House,** 5225 Williamson Rd. (tel. 703/366-3710), features American specialties along with Italian and Greek dishes. There's evening entertainment and dancing, and hours are 11 a.m. to 11 p.m. except Sunday and major holidays, with prices under $10 at lunch, $10 to $30 at dinner.

THINGS TO SEE AND DO

Before setting off down the parkway, there's a side trip you may want to take for half a day or so, especially if you were a fan of TV's Walton family. Some 30 miles south of Charlottesville, just off Va. 6 on a secondary road (800), the little town of Schuyler is where Earl Hamner grew up and the setting for "The Waltons" series. Aside from the absolutely gorgeous Blue Ridge Mountains scenery, you'll see the "Walton Home" and "Mr. Godsey's store" (Jim Bob's son may be behind the counter to sell you postcards or a snack). Or you can walk around the mill, now a soapstone factory. Don't expect guided tours or admission fees—just an easy, informal atmosphere and conversation with very friendly natives.

Now, back to the parkway. About five miles from its northern end you'll come to **Humpback Rocks** and a reconstructed mountain farm. There's also a hiking trail a little farther along that leads three-quarters of a mile to the rocks. At **Yankee Horse,** look for an oldtime logging railroad spur, or take a short walk through the woods to see **Wigwam Falls.**

Lexington

Take the U.S. 60 exit west from I-81 to Lexington, home and burial place of two famous Confederate generals, Robert E. Lee and "Stonewall" Jackson. The **Lexington Visitor's Center,** 102 E. Washington St. (tel. 703/463-3777), will provide self-guided walking tours of historic sites, a short slide show, exhibits, and travel directions in Virginia. It's open from 9 a.m. to 5 p.m. daily except Thanksgiving, Christmas, and New Year's days; open to 6 p.m. June through August.

Robert E. Lee came to Lexington following the Civil War to assume the presidency of the college that is today Washington and Lee University. The Lee family crypt, the famed Edward Valentine statue of General Lee, the Washington-Custis-Lee portrait collection, and General Lee's office, preserved as he left it, are located within the Lee Chapel on the university campus. The chapel is open mid-April to mid-October, Monday through Saturday from 9 a.m. to 5 p.m. (to 4 p.m. the rest of the year), and on Sunday from 2 to 5 p.m. except for major holidays.

Jackson's residence, the **Stonewall Jackson House,** 8 E. Washington St. (tel. 703/463-2552), was the only home he ever owned, and has been faithfully restored to tell the story of the man who was a professor at VMI prior to the Civil War The house has been restored to its appearance when he and his second wife lived there from 1859 to 1861. It's open year round, Monday through Saturday from 9 a.m. to 4:30 p.m. and on Sunday from 1 to 4:30 p.m. There's an admission charge of $4 for adults, $2 for children. Closed Easter, Thanksgiving, Christmas, New Year's Day, and Sunday during January and February. The general, along with other Confederate soldiers, is buried in the cemetery on the east side of Main Street.

The **Virginia Military Institute,** on U.S. 11, has been sending graduates to war since the Mexican War of 1846. During the school year (September to May) you can see the colorful Guard Mount every day at 12:30 p.m. in nice weather and the dress parade on Friday at 4:15 p.m. The VMI Museum (tel. 703/463-6232) one of the finest college museums in the nation, with displays on the history of this unique institution, is free and open daily. During school sessions, guided tours by cadets are available. Gen. George C. Marshall began his military career at VMI (class of 1901), and his personal, military, diplomatic papers and Nobel Peace Prize are housed in the **George C. Marshall Museum,** at the west end of the Parade Grounds, and there's an electric map that traces World War II developments. It's free and open Monday through Friday from 9 a.m. to 4:30 p.m., on Saturday from 9 a.m. to noon and 2 to 5 p.m.; and on Sunday from 2 to 5 p.m.

Lexington Carriage Company tours (tel. 703/463-9500) offer a delightful way to explore this charming city. Horse-drawn carriages ply the main streets, passing the colleges, historic structures, and restored 1860s Lexington. Stops are made at each historic site. Tours last about 40 minutes and leave from the Lexington Visitor's Center from 9 a.m. to 5 p.m. Monday through Saturday April 1 through October 31. Cost is $6 per person.

Twenty miles north of Lexington, **Walnut Grove Farm,** Va. 606, Steeles Tavern, VA 24476 (tel. 703/377-2255), was the childhood home of Cyrus McCormick, inventor of the mechanized reaper in 1831. His invention was perhaps *the* most important agricultural development of his century. The workshop in which he toiled, the family's gristmill, blacksmith shop, and the family home have been restored and opened to the public, while the 634-acre farm is an agricultural research center under the ownership of Virginia Polytechnic Institute. There's a picnic site, and the farm is open year round from 8:30 a.m. to 5 p.m. daily, with free admission. To reach Walnut Grove, take U.S. 11 North to Va. 606, or I-81 to Exit 54.

For a breathtakingly beautiful scenic interlude, head for the **Goshen Pass,** a great mountain gorge that passes through three miles of magnificent forests of pine and other evergreens, maples, mountain ash, and maples. Rhododendron and dogwood add splashes of color in the spring. The area is a game forest preserve, and at the wayside park, you'll find a pavilion with picnic shelter, fresh water, and bathroom facilities. To reach the pass, take U.S. 11 North to Va. 39, about 12 miles from Lexington.

Natural Bridge

South of Lexington on U.S. 11 you'll find one of the Seven Natural Wonders of the World, **Natural Bridge.** The 215-foot-high arch was an object of worship by Native Americans, and when Thomas Jefferson bought it for "20 shillings of good and lawful money" from King George III of England, he built a small cabin for visitors and hired a caretaker. His guests included such colonial greats as George Washington (who carved his initials in the limestone), Patrick Henry, James Monroe, and John Marshall. You reach the bridge by natural steps that wind down to Cedar Creek, past arborvitae trees estimated to be 10 centuries old, or via the free shuttlebus. It's open daily year round from 7 a.m. until dusk. The *Drama of Creation,* a depiction of the world's beginning in special music, narration, and lighting, is presented after dark each night. There's a $5 charge for adults for either the day or night drama visit ($4 for seniors, $2.50 for ages 6 to 15); special combination tickets for both visits are $6, $5, and $3. Also on premises are a **Wax Museum and Caverns,** with special combination rates for all attractions.

At the **Natural Bridge Hotel, Motor Lodge, and Inn** (tel. 703/291-2121, or toll free 800/336-5727, 800/533-1410 in Virginia), a full-service dining room, cafeteria, and snackbar adjoin. Rates begin at $38 for doubles.

You can rejoin the parkway from Natural Bridge and follow it on to Roanoke.

In and Around Roanoke

First thing on your agenda should be a visit to the **Roanoke Valley Convention and Visitors Bureau,** 14 W. Kirk Ave., Roanoke, VA 24011 (tel. 703/342-6025), for all sorts of helpful literature and information on current events. One block away, check out the bustling city market.

Across the Walnut Avenue Bridge, off Va. 220, the **Mill Mountain city park** has a marvelous panoramic view of the city and its surroundings. There's also a children's zoo and a miniature train. Even if you don't visit the park, you'll be aware of it, for every night a 100-foot-high electric star is visible for miles around.

Drop by the 100-year-old downtown **Market Square,** longtime showcase for the fresh vegetables, fruits, and flowers of Shenandoah Valley farmers. Rescued after a period of rather sleazy decline, it has taken on new life as centerpiece of an exciting urban resurgence. Facing the square, the historic **City Market Building** has been transformed into a delightful festival marketplace, with oldtime gas lights and brick sidewalks lined with a bevy of smart shops, taverns, and restaurants. And, yes, farmers still come in from the country to hawk their fresh produce. Also facing the square is the impressive **Center in the Square,** which houses five cultural organizations under one roof and boasts both a theater and state-of-the-art planetarium.

At the **Virginia Museum of Transportation,** 303 Norfolk Ave. (tel. 703/342-5670), you can see steam, diesel, and electric locomotives amid one of the Southern Atlantic's most comprehensive collections of transportation artifacts. Other exhibits in this renovated 1917 Norfolk and Western Railway freight depot range from horse-drawn carriages to space rockets. The museum is open from 10 a.m. to 5 p.m. Monday through Saturday and from noon to 5 p.m. on Sunday. Admission is $2 for adults, $1.60 for seniors, and $1 for children 3 to 12. Group rates are available.

The **Mill Mountain Theatre,** at Center in the Square, performs nightly, with Saturday and Sunday matinees, from December through August. Call 703/342-5740 for information about performance and reservations.

Check on current concerts and performances at the **Roanoke Civic Center,** 710 Williamson Rd. NE, Roanoke, VA 24016 (tel. 703/981-1201).

Booker T. Washington's birthplace is 20 miles southeast of Roanoke. Drive south on Va. 116 to Burnt Chimney, then take Va. 122 north (follow the signs). A visitor center has a 14-minute audiovisual biography of the black leader's life and accomplishments, as well as other exhibits, and there's a short, self-guiding trail walk past replicas of farm buildings that were on this tobacco farm where he was born as a slave in 1856. The farm is now worked much as it was when he lived here, and you'll see crops and animals similar to those he knew as a boy. The visitor center is open from 8:30 a.m. to 5 p.m. daily except for major holidays. Admission is $1 for ages 17 to 61, $3 for family groups. For advance information, write: Booker T. Washington National Monument, Rte. 3, Box 310, Hardy, VA 24101 (tel. 703/721-2094).

If you're in Roanoke around July 4th, do take in part of the **Roanoke Valley Horse Show** at the nearby Salem Civic Center. It's one of the best in the country, and a fun way to celebrate the holiday.

For a worthwhile brush with history, take U.S. 460 East from Roanoke, past Lynchburg to the little town of **Appomattox.** Three miles northeast of town, on Va. 24, is **Appomattox Court House National Historical Park,** where the sun set on the Confederacy and the Civil War ground to a halt. It was here that General Robert E. Lee surrendered what was left of the Army of Northern Virginia to Gen. Ulysses S. Grant, commander of the Army of the Potomac, on April 9, 1865. Stop by the visitor center, browse through the museum, and take a look at the short audiovisual program on the second floor before setting out on a self-guided tour, aided by the helpful free brochure. The entire village has been restored to its 1865 appearance, and among significant restored and preserved attractions to look for are the **Clover Hill Tavern, Lee and Grant headquarters, the county jail, Woodson Law Office, Meek's Store and Storehouse, the Kelly House,** and the **Confederate cemetery.** The **McLean House,** where the two generals actually met, has been reconstructed. During summer months, there are living history programs, with costumed soldiers and village residents acting as guides. The park is open from 9 a.m. to 5 p.m. from March through December, closed for major holiday. Admission is $1, free for ages 61 and over or under 17. For further information, contact: Superintendent, Appomattox Court House National Historical Park, P.O. Box 218, Appomattox, VA 24522 (tel. 804/352-8782).

FROM ROANOKE TO BOONE

Although it's only a 175-mile drive from Roanoke to Boone, you won't want to rush along this scenic route, and a stop at Boone is just about right to give you a full, unhurried day getting there.

On the Parkway

The only licensed American Youth Hostel along the Blue Ridge Parkway is about 10 miles southeast of Galax, Virginia, just 2 miles north of the North Carolina border and 100 feet off the parkway (milepost 214.5). The hostel building is a faithful copy of an ancient Yorktown house, and there's a 19th-century log cabin adjacent. Accommodations consist of dormitory-style quarters, a kitchen where hostelers do their own cooking, and a common room for relaxing and socializing. There's a mountain stream flowing through the 25 acres on which the hostel sits, and panoramic views are stunning. The overnight fee is $7 per person in summer, $10 in winter. American Youth Hostels membership is a requirement (for applications, contact American Youth Hostels, Dept. 854, P.O. Box 37613, Washington, DC 20013-7613, tel. 202/783-6161). Book by contacting: Blue Ridge Country–AYH Hostel, R.R. 2, Box 449, Galax, VA 24333 (tel. 703/236-4962 after 5 p.m.).

Where to Stay in Boone

One of the most exclusive resort lodges in this part of the country is near Boone, and if "deluxe" is your travel style, it will be a mountain visit par excellence if you reserve at **Hound Ears Lodge,** P.O. Box 188, Blowing Rock, NC 28605 (tel. 704/963-4321), which gets its unusual name from a nearby rock formation. It's five miles southwest of Boone on N.C. 105, then three-quarters of a mile south on County Road 1568 (follow the signs). The setting is gorgeous, the rooms and suites are the ultimate in luxury, and this complete resort, surrounded by beautifully landscaped grounds, has a pool and facilities for golf, tennis, fishing, and skiing (in winter months, of course). Prices are steep—a whopping $226 per day for doubles, modified American plan—but very good value for the dollar.

Holiday Inn, 710 Blowing Rock Rd., Boone, NC 28607 (tel. 704/264-2451, or toll free 800/465-4329), has a heated pool, health-exercise club, and running track, as well as a restaurant which serves moderately priced meals. Double-occupancy rooms are typical of this chain and range from $53 to $79.

Where to Eat in Boone

Head straight for the **Dan'l Boone Inn,** 105 Hardin St. (tel. 704/264-8657), for family-style breakfasts, lunches, or dinners that are really something special—and at prices that won't hurt. Everything is home-cooked, and the fare is definitely southern: country ham and biscuits, fried chicken, and the like. Prices run from $5.50 for a family-style breakfast to $8 for dinner. Children's plates average $2.50.

The **Holiday Inn,** 710 Blowing Rock Rd. (tel. 704/264-2451), has an exceptionally nice dining room that specializes in steaks and other beef dishes at moderate prices ($7 to $12 for complete dinners). Like most of this chain's dining rooms, it serves all three meals, with hours from 6:30 a.m. to 10 p.m.

Things to See and Do

Between Roanoke and the North Carolina border, be sure to stop at **Mabry Mill.** There's a lovely cluster of log cabins, farm buildings, a blacksmith shop, a church, and a water-powered gristmill straight out of pioneer days. The restaurant makes a good lunch stopover too.

If you're theater-minded, there's a detour off the parkway onto I-81 that you really should take. In the town of **Abingdon,** something happened back in 1933 that has profoundly influenced the American theater ever since. A young enthusiastic actor, Robert Porterfield, figured out that hungry professional actors all over the country would be happy during those depression years to exchange their talents for a place to work and food to eat. At the same time, he believed the theater-hungry mountain people (who had food aplenty) would welcome a chance to swap it for live productions when they didn't have the 40¢ admission. He was right, and the Barter Theatre he established on a "ham for

Hamlet" basis has been a rousing success since those first days when playwrights like Austin Strong, Noel Coward, Thornton Wilder, Robert Sherwood, and Maxwell Anderson accepted hams and other country produce in payment for scripts, and one day's door receipts showed up on the little company's table the next day.

Since 1946 the Barter has been the **State Theatre of Virginia,** supported in part by legislative funds, and admissions nowadays are in the form of coin of the realm (I don't really know what would happen if you showed up with a ham, but they *do* invite you to call for barter procedure!). Many of our theatrical leading lights have had their early training here, among them: Hume Cronyn, Patricia Neal, Fritz Weaver, Ernest Borgnine, and Gregory Peck. Across the street, the Barter Playhouse has now become a full-fledged member of Actor's Equity and presents established works. The regular season runs from April to October, and people come from several hundred miles around (tourists often make this a primary stop). To find out about schedules and tickets, write the Barter Theater, Abingdon, VA 24210 (tel. 703/628-3991, or toll free 800/368-3240, 800/572-2081 in Virginia).

For an Overnight Stay in Abingdon

It is not inconceivable that the Barter Playhouse will entice you to stay overnight for a performance. If that happens, run—don't walk—over to the **Martha Washington Inn,** 150 W. Main St., Abingdon, VA 24210 (tel. 703/628-3161). Housed in what was built in 1830 as a private residence and then served nearly 100 years as a college, the inn was completely renovated in 1985, yet still retains the feeling of graciousness and hospitality native to those long-gone days. Lobbies and sitting rooms are furnished with antique grandfather clocks and glistening chandeliers. An elegant colonial staircase sweeps down into the wide central hall. Upstairs, many rooms have four-poster beds (some with canopies) and fireplaces, and all are beautifully and comfortably furnished. Whether you stay here or not, plan on at least one meal in the dining room, which features country ham and other southern specialties. Doubles are $85, and children under 12 stay free. Deluxe rooms range from $100 to $120, and suites are $135 to $365.

Sights In and Around Boone

There's so much to see and do here that it might be a good idea to make this a two- or three-day stop, especially during the summer months. Be sure to check with the **Boone Area Chamber of Commerce,** 350 Blowing Rock Rd., Boone, NC 28607 (tel. 704/264-2225).

The **Boone–Banner Elk–Blowing Rock** area, sometimes called "The High Country," has been a summer resort retreat for Southerners since the 1800s. But in recent years, skiers have been attracted to the high slopes during winter months as well. There are now excellent skiing facilities and a wealth of winter accommodations, restaurants, and entertainment spots at **Ski Beech Ski Resort,** P.O. Box 1118, Banner Elk, NC 28604 (tel. 704/387-2011). While I've never been attracted to the sport myself and cannot judge the quality of the snow (there are snowmakers to help out Mother Nature), runs, etc., friends who head for the hills every winter weekend tell me this is the best skiing in the South. Day-long lift rates, subject to change, are in the $22 range, and increase to $27 on weekends and holidays. Rentals are $11 to $15 per day. The top-flight professional ski-school staff offers class lessons as well as private lessons. There's also a children's ski program, and nonskiing tykes can stay and play in the Land of Oz Nursery.

Boone itself (named for Daniel, of course—he had a cabin here in the 1760s) draws hunters and fishermen to the abundantly stocked streams and forests. For the sportsman and nonsports-minded summer visitors alike, there's a beautifully produced outdoor drama, Kermit Hunter's *Horn in the West,* staged in the **Daniel Boone Theatre,** P.O. Box 295, Boone, NC 28607 (tel. 704/264-2120), every night except Monday from late June through mid-August. It tells a vivid story of pioneer efforts to win the friendship of native Cherokee Indians. Performances begin at 8:30 p.m. and admission is $8 to $9 (age 13 and under, half price).

Located adjacent to *Horn in the West* is the **Hickory Ridge Homestead Museum** (tel. 704/264-2120), an 18th-century living-history museum in a re-created log cabin. It's open from 6 to 8:30 p.m. Tuesday through Sunday during late June through mid-August performance season. Traditional craftspeople demonstrate their skills, and there's a homestead store. An apple festival is held on the grounds in late October, and Christmas events lighten mid-December.

In the immediate vicinity, don't miss **Blowing Rock,** two miles southeast of the town of the same name on U.S. 321 (tel. 704/295-7111), where you can stand on The Rock, as it's affectionately called, throw a handkerchief or some other light object off the edge, and have it sent right back up to you by strong updraft winds. And when you're not playing that rather fascinating game, the observation tower, gazebos, and gardens offer really splendid views of the **John's River Gorge** and nearby Blue Ridge peaks. The observation tower is open every day from 8:30 a.m. to 6 p.m. in April and May, from 8 a.m. to 8 p.m. June through August, and from 8 a.m. to 6 p.m. in September, October, and November (as long as weather permits). Adults pay $3.50; ages 6 to 11, $1. Another natural phenomenon at Blowing Rock is **Mystery Hill,** where balls roll and water runs uphill. The **pioneer museum** is interesting and you'll get a kick out of the mock grave marked simply "He Wuz a Revenoor"—a pile of dirt with boots sticking out one end!

Don't think the **Tweetsie Railroad** (tel. 704/264-9061), halfway between Boone and Blowing Rock, is for the kiddies only; the whole family will enjoy this old narrow-gauge train (I love every toot of the sweet-toned whistle) as it winds through the mountains, suffering mock attacks by "Indians" and "outlaws." Mountain music and other entertainment waits at **Tweetside Palace,** and the Junction and Mining Company are straight out of a history book. The train makes daily runs from 9 a.m. to 6 p.m. from late May to mid-October. Fare is $10 for adults, $9 for seniors, and $7 for ages 4 to 12.

Grandfather Mountain (one mile off the parkway on U.S. 221 near Linville) is the highest peak in the Blue Ridge. You can see as far as 100 miles from the **Mile High Swinging Bridge,** and the **Environmental Habitat** is home to Mildred the Bear and her black bear friends. In spacious separate sections you can also view native deer, cougars, and bald and golden eagles (which have been injured and cannot live in the wild on their own). This is the place where kilt-clad Scots gather (from Scotland as well as all parts of North America) early in July for the **Annual Highland Games and Gathering of the Clans.** Exciting bagpipe music, dancing, wrestling, and tossing the cabar (a telephone-pole-like shaft) contests—as well as the colorful mix of people bent on two days of fun—make it a spectacle not to be missed.

FROM BOONE TO ASHEVILLE, N.C.

A worthwhile detour from the parkway at this point is **Burnsville,** where a delightful town square is surrounded by vintage buildings. From Burnsville you can return to the parkway and stop at Little Switzerland overnight at **Big Lynn Lodge,** Rte. 226A, P.O. Box 459, Little Switzerland, NC 28749 (tel. 704/765-4257 or 800/654-5232), with doubles from $75 to $90 (including breakfast and dinner) in summer, or at **The Chalet,** off the Blue Ridge Pkwy., milepost 334, P.O. Box 399, Little Switzerland, NC 28749 (tel. 704/765-2153), where high-season doubles range from $36 to $75.

Where to Stay in Asheville

Mountain vacationing can be rustic and at the same time luxurious. If you don't believe that, reserve at Asheville's **Grove Park Inn and Country Club,** 290 Macon Ave., Asheville, NC 28804 (tel. 704/252-2711, or toll free 800/438-5800), a favorite of southern gentry since 1913; host over the years to such notables as F. Scott Fitzgerald, F.D.R., Woodrow Wilson, Thomas Edison, and Henry Ford; and listed in the National Register of Historic Places.

Built on the side of Sunset Mountain at an elevation of 3,100 feet, the rambling main building is constructed of huge native boulders and its "great hall" lobby is flanked on each end by 14-foot fireplaces. The comfortably padded chairs and sofas create a feeling of coziness despite the 120-foot-long dimensions of the room. On crisp evenings (even in summer, nighttime temperatures are often in the 50s and 60s), when fires are lit, a sort of magic takes over as special events are held here, transforming travelers from strangers into warm friends.

With an extensive renovation and expansion project completed in 1984, the resort is open on a year-round basis. It now includes 389 guest rooms, 5 restaurants, 4 lounges, a shopping arcade, 7 tennis courts, both indoor and outdoor swimming pools, a sports center, and an 18-hole championship golf course.

Notable among the fine restaurants are the famed Sunset Terrace, an outdoor veranda overlooking the Blue Ridge Mountains and serving lunch and dinner with dancing in season; the Dynasty Restaurant and Lounge, featuring international cuisine and dancing; the Fox & Hounds, for continental dining in an English country setting; and the Carolina Café for light meals and continuous service. After dark, Elaine's Nightclub swings into action with variety shows and dancing.

Various package plans are offered for sports enthusiasts, special holidays (Thanksgiving, Christmas, etc.), or for couples with something special to celebrate (perhaps a honeymoon, as was the case with my own parents). Room rates begin at $95 double until mid-April, $115 to $130 thereafter. If you prefer, there's a higher rate that covers all meals.

Deluxe accommodations are also on tap at the **Great Smokies Hilton,** 1 Hilton Dr., Asheville, NC 28806 (tel. 704/254-3211). In addition to the high-quality guest rooms (some with wet bars) that are typical of Hilton hotels, there are also a heated pool and sauna, tennis courts, and an 18-hole golf course. Rates from April through October are in the $65 to $80 range for singles, $75 to $95 for doubles, with family package rates available. Other months, rates are somewhat lower.

At the **Haywood Park Hotel,** 1 Battery Park Ave., Asheville, NC 28801 (tel. 704/252-2522 or toll free 800/845-7638, 800/922-7638 in North Carolina), it's suites only in a sophisticated setting in the heart of downtown Asheville. Suites are a nice blend of luxury (such as marble baths, oversize tubs, Jacuzzis, mini-bars, and fridges in some) and practicality (computer hookups in all). Brenna's Restaurant and Lounge provides both casual and more formal dining. Rates begin at $80 single for a studio and run $100 to $225 double for one-bedroom superior suites.

If the budget calls for moderate rather than deluxe, head for Lloyd and Leone Kirk's **Forest Manor Motor Lodge,** U.S. 25 South, Asheville, NC 28803 (tel. 704/274-3531), 3½ miles from the city center. In a scenic, wooded setting, the bungalow-style rooms are pine paneled and attractively furnished, and each has an inviting front porch entrance bordered by well-tended flower beds. And the Kirks so pride themselves on cleanliness that if you find any evidence of dirt, there's no charge! The sounds of song birds and gentle breezes sighing through pine trees predominate over highway noises, which are reduced to a faint hum by the set-back location. It's a relaxed, very friendly place to stay, open year round. Rates are $58 to $88 double, April through October; $40 to $58 the rest of the year. There are kitchenettes available for a minimum of one week, and rollaway beds or cribs are furnished at a small additional charge.

Asheville has a **Days Inn,** I-40 and U.S. 70 East, P.O. Box 9708, Asheville, NC 28805 (tel. 704/298-5140), situated on a hillside with mountain views that are especially spectacular, especially when autumn foliage begins to turn. There's a pool, kiddie playground, restaurant, gift shop, and laundry service. Only five miles from Biltmore House. Seasonal rates range from $28 to $42 for singles, $33 to $47 for doubles.

The **Red Roof Inn,** 16 Crowell Rd., Asheville, NC 28806 (tel. 704/667-9803 or toll free 800/843-7663), has cable TV, oversize beds in some rooms, and a restaurant nearby. Double rooms run $41 to $43 from May to October, lower other months.

Bed and Breakfast in Asheville

A stay at **Cedar Crest,** 674 Biltmore Ave., Asheville, NC 28803 (tel. 704/252-1389), is a lovely trip back to the Victorian era. Built in 1894, this grand mansion is a fantasy of leaded glass, ornately carved fireplaces, antique furnishings, and a massive oak staircase. Owners Barbara and Jack McEwan have indulged their romantic and whimsical imaginations in furnishing the 11 guest rooms—all have period antiques and the decor in each is unique, with a canopied ceiling in one, marvelous carved walnut bed in another, and brass bedsteads in another. All have private or semiprivate baths. Evening coffee and chocolate are served in the parlor, and a continental breakfast is included in the rates, which begin at $65 for singles and $70 for doubles with shared bath, and rise to $80 to $90 single, $90 to $100 double and for private bath. Adjacent to the main house, there's a cottage with a two-bedroom suite at $125 and a one-bedroom suite at $80. Cedar Crest does not accept children under 12 or pets, and smoking is permitted only in designated areas.

Reed House, 119 Dodge St., Asheville, NC 28803 (tel. 704/274-1604), is another delightful old mansion that welcomes guests. Mrs. Marge Turcot presides over the 1892 house on a hill overlooking Biltmore Village. The five guest rooms come complete with working fireplaces and rocking chairs, and the complimentary continental breakfast features homemade, low-sodium muffins and rolls with homemade jam—a real southern treat! Rates at this friendly place begin at $35 single, $40 double for rooms with shared baths, $50 for those with private baths. Open from May 1 to November 1.

Two Nearby Mountain Retreats

About 45 miles south of Asheville, the **Greystone Inn,** P.O. Box 6, Lake Toxaway, NC 28747 (tel. 704/966-4700, or toll free 800/824-5766), is just the sort of getaway spot for which your heart and soul begin to yearn as the richness of Mother Nature's gifts to the scenic wonderland of the Blue Ridge Mountains unfolds around you. Set on a wooded peninsula on Lake Toxaway, this 1915 mansion has been restored to welcome guests with 15 rooms that feature an engaging mix of antique furnishings and modern comforts (there are even Jacuzzi baths in all but one!). Each has its own unique character, and many have working fireplaces. The stone fireplace is also a focal point in the gracious oak-paneled living room; the library is a beautifully appointed oasis that promises hours of reading pleasure; and the terrace is the perfect setting for before-dinner drinks. For dedicated do-nothings, there are wicker rocking chairs on the glassed-in sun porch overlooking the lake. For those of a more active nature, there are tennis courts, fishing, waterskiing, swimming, sailboating, and golf at the adjacent Lake Toxaway Country Club (membership is included in the inn rates). Meals in the Hearthsides dining room feature gourmet entrees such as veal française Scandi and rainbow mountain trout amandine. In addition to main-house guest rooms, there are six lovely cottages (two or three bedrooms) that come with full kitchens. Rates (which include a sumptuous country breakfast, midafternoon tea or coffee and cakes, and dinner) are in the $125 to $350 range, plus a 15% service charge and state and local taxes. The Greystone Inn is just off N.C. 64 between Brevard and Cashiers.

To the west of Asheville, on a ridge overlooking the village of Maggie Valley, the **Cataloochee Ranch** is a working mountain ranch, with horses and cattle, timberlands, and vegetable gardens. Accommodations here are, to coin a phrase, high-class rustic, with pine-walled guest rooms in a two-story lodge and guest cottages, and stone fireplaces that bring welcome warmth to mountain evenings. The ranch offers units with full kitchens; and an excellent dining room in the lodge dishes up sumptuous family-style meals, outdoor buffets, and picnic lunches to be taken along on hiking or horseback treks. Activities also include tennis, trout fishing, table tennis, badminton, and croquet. Only a mile away is the Cataloochee Ski Area. From time to time, there's mountain music entertainment and square dancing. Doubles range from $90 to $140, cottages the same, and suites are $120 to $150. A 15% service charge is added to all rates in lieu of tipping, which is just not done.

Needless to say, the mountain scenery and serenity come at no extra charge at all, making Cataloochee Ranch truly good value for your dollar. To reach this idyllic vacation spot, take I-40 to Exit 27, then follow U.S. 19S through Maggie Valley westward to Fie Top Road, and the ranch is three miles farther on.

Camping from Boone to Asheville

There are three campgrounds operated by the National Park Service on the Blue Ridge Parkway between Boone and Asheville. None has showers, and other facilities are limited, varying from one location to another. Rates are $7 per site and availability is on a first-come, first-served basis. For full details, you can contact each at these addresses:

Open year round: Linville Falls Campground, Rte. 1, Box 798, Spruce Pine, NC 28777 (tel. 704/259-0701); Julian Price Memorial Campground, Blowing Rock, NC 28605 (tel. 704/259-0701).

Open May through October: Blue Ridge Parkway, National Park Service, Doughton Park Campground, Rte. 1, Box 263, Laurel Springs, NC 28644 (tel. 919/259-0701).

Where to Eat in Asheville

Some of the best eating in Asheville is to be found at the **Grove Park Inn,** 290 Macon Ave. (tel. 704/252-2711). Even if you stay elsewhere, you really should plan at least one meal at this great old hostelry. Sunday brunch in the **Blue Ridge Dining Room and Terrace** is an Asheville tradition, with a sumptuous southern breakfast buffet table laden with so many plantation "extras" (fried chicken, grilled trout, etc.) that any thought of sticking to a diet will evaporate at the mere sight. Priced at $15, it is extremely popular with locals, so reserve as early as possible. Equally popular is the Friday night seafood buffet for $18. If an elegant, gourmet meal is what you're after, reserve at the Inn's **Dynasty Restaurant,** where polished, professional service complements such specialties as veal Cordon Bleu and Peking duck. It's open for dinner only (7 to 10 p.m.), prices are $30 and under, and there's dancing. For more casual meals, there's the lovely **Sunset Terrace** looking out to the mountains, with light lunches (salads, sandwiches, quiches, burgers, etc.) for under $10 and a very good dinner menu featuring sautéed scampi, fresh mountain trout, and the like for $25 and under, and in summer months, there's dancing. In the **Carolina Café,** either lunch or dinner will run no more than $10 for a simpler menu of salads, burgers, etc.

Brenna's Restaurant and Lounge, 1 Battery Park Ave. (tel. 704/252-2612), is an attractive, pleasant restaurant that serves excellent meals in a casual front room, as well as in the slightly more formal cozy back dining room. A specialty here is grilled salmon in red-pepper butter, but no matter what you order, you can be sure it's prepared from fresh ingredients, obtained locally whenever possible. Lunch will run from a moderate $3 to $5; dinner is in the $10 to $18 range. Hours are 7 to 10 a.m. for breakfast and 11 a.m. to 2 p.m. for lunch, Monday through Friday; 6 to 9 p.m. for dinner Tuesday through Saturday. Reservations are advisable (but not always necessary) at this popular restaurant.

In Biltmore Village, the charming **Depot Restaurant,** 30 Lodge St. (tel. 704/274-4826), is housed in the 1896 railway station. It's a relaxed place, with a large menu that includes chicken, seafood, pork, veal, and beef dishes. Most folks hereabout, however, come for the prime rib (which are offered at the remarkable price of $7 in a six-course special on weekends!). Prices average around $4 at lunch, $12 to $15 at dinner. Hours are 11:30 a.m. to 10 p.m. Monday through Thursday, until 11 p.m. on Friday and Saturday, and to 7:30 p.m. on Sunday.

Also in Biltmore Village, the **Corner House Café,** 6 Boston Way (tel. 704/274-3086), is a delightful restaurant/bakery/deli. Casual diners love the glassed-in front porch, and there's more formal dining in bright inside rooms. In addition to moderately priced, delicious meals featuring seafood, poultry, beef, pork, and a vegetarian menu, there's a wide selection of salads and sandwiches, as well as fresh-baked croissants, assorted breads, muffins, etc., from their bakery. They'll also provide boxed picnic lunches and cheese-and-wine baskets to go. Hours are 8 a.m. to 6 p.m. Monday through Saturday.

If it's *real* southern mountain food you're after, you'll find yourself going back again and again to **Bill Stanley's Barbeque and Blue Grass,** 20 S. Spruce St. (tel. 704/253-4871). The large dining room has the look of an authentic "mountain rustic" decor, and the friendly staff brings a real "down-home" ambience right along with some of the most mouthwatering barbecue (beef, pork, and chicken) you're likely to encounter in the entire state. Piled-high dinner plates come with that scrumptious barbecue or smoked chicken, catfish, sliced ham, or sliced turkey, all at prices under $10! Side orders include such southern favorites as corn on the cob and potato salad, and it goes without saying that hush puppies are highlights of any meal. At lunch there's a large selection of sandwiches priced under $3.50, with side orders of coleslaw, corn on the cob, potato salad, french fries, etc., and a good choice of bottled beers. There's also a nice salad bar for under $3, and a marvelous "all you can eat" buffet for $8.50 at lunch. Hours are 11 a.m. to midnight Monday through Thursday, to 1 a.m. on Friday, and 6 p.m. to 1 a.m. on Saturday. One word of caution: If you come along after 8 p.m., be prepared to shake a leg or two to some of the best footstomping mountain music in the South (see "Things to See and Do," below) that has been known to entice even the most timid of diners out onto the floor.

Things to See and Do in the Asheville Area

For detailed information on Asheville's many attractions (including the Blue Ridge Parkway), write or visit: **Asheville Area Chamber of Commerce,** 151 Haywood St. (P.O. Box 1011), Asheville, NC 28802 (tel. 704/258-5200).

Since 1797, Asheville has grown from a tiny mountain trading village at the confluence of the French Broad and Swannanoa rivers into a year-round resort, gaining along the way architectural gems from several eras and cultural features that make it such an interesting place to visit. In recent years there's been a vigorous movement afoot to preserve and restore those remnants of the city's colorful past, and a concise "Asheville Heritage Tour" brochure, available from the Asheville Chamber of Commerce, will guide you through such points as the historic downtown district, **Biltmore Village** (a cluster of some 24 English-village cottages built in conjunction with Biltmore Estate and now housing interesting boutiques, craft shops, and restaurants), the **Chestnut Hill** historic district, with its more than 200 turn-of-the-century residences, and a number of outlying points of interest. In the downtown area, keep an eye out for marvelous art deco buildings now being restored, the **Lexington Park** area that is attracting artists and artisans whose studios and workshops are tucked away down a little alleyway, and **Pack Place,** which is being developed as a center for all sorts of cultural activities.

Incidentally, you shouldn't make the mistake of dismissing Biltmore Village as just one more shopping complex—the buildings are of interest in themselves, and browsing is a sightseeing adventure as you stop by such shops as the **Early Music Shop,** 3 Biltmore Plaza, that trades in oldtime instruments such as dulcimers and Celtic harps. At **Fireside Antiques,** 32 All Souls Crescent, owners Robert Griffin and Ronald Clemmer present a fine collection of European, Oriental, and American antiques and unique gift items, and stand ready at a drop of a question to wax enthusiastic about the preservation of Asheville's unique heritage. Book-lovers will want to drop in at the **Book Mart,** 7 Biltmore Plaza, for a look at their old and rare books. Other shops are equally interesting, and there's good eating handy when stomach and feet call for a halt.

I've fantasized as long as I can remember about the life of the really rich and what it would be like to have unlimited money. Well, while my chances of ever knowing that lifestyle firsthand are nil (not *practically* nil, all-the-way nil), the fantasies get a shot in the arm every time I go to see the overwhelmingly magnificent **Biltmore Estate,** One North Pack Square, Asheville, NC 28801 (tel. 704/255-1700), on U.S. 25, two blocks north off I-40. The French Renaissance château built by George W. Vanderbilt has 250 rooms! And talk about the "grand manner"—it fills every nook and cranny of this house and its gardens. There just isn't an ordinary spot in the place, not even the kitchen. Vanderbilt, a man who lived out *my* fantasies, gathered furnishings and art treasures from all over the world for this palace (for instance, Napoleon's chess set and table from St. Helena are here) and then went further to plant one of the most lavish formal gardens you'll ever see. There are more than 200 varieties of azaleas alone, plus thousands of other plants and shrubs. Admission to the house and gardens is $17.95 for adults, $14 for children 12 to 17 (under 12 free with their parents). You should allow a minimum of two hours for the self-guided tour. If you plan to make a day of it, there's a charming restaurant in a renovated barn, as well as an interesting winery. Biltmore is closed Thanksgiving, Christmas Day, and New Year's Day. Special events during the year include a spring Festival of Flowers, September Take-off, and Christmas at Biltmore—inquire ahead for specific dates.

There's no charge to visit a pet project of Mrs. Vanderbilt's, the **Biltmore Homespun Shops,** two miles north of town on Macon Street via Charlotte Street, on the grounds of the Grove Park Inn (tel. 704/253-7651). Mrs. Vanderbilt wanted to preserve the ancient wool-manufacturing skills of the mountains and help the weavers turn those skills into a paying industry, so she set up the cluster of old-world-style buildings, found local orders for the beautiful hand-woven fabrics, and eventually a mail-order business evolved which still thrives. You can visit the buildings, now covered with ivy to add to their charm, and see the whole wool-making process, from dyeing and carding to spinning to weaving on homemade oak looms to the final washing and sun-drying. There's an **Antique Automobile Museum,** also free, which holds cars dating back to 1905.

Thomas Wolfe grew up in Asheville and immortalized the town and its citizens (much to their dismay) in his *Look Homeward, Angel.* The boarding house, "Dixieland," that figures so prominently in the book, is at 48 Spruce St. and is maintained as a literary shrine, with hours that vary seasonally (call 704/253-8304 for details). Adults pay $1; children through high school, 50¢. Both Wolfe and William Sydney Porter (O. Henry) are buried in **Riverside Cemetery** (entrance on Birch Street off Pearson Drive).

A few miles from Asheville on N.C. 70, you'll find **Black Mountain,** a small mountain community that seems suspended in time. Stop by the Old Depot, which has been turned into a center for the work of local craftspeople and where you'll often hear the sweet music of oldtime dulcimers played by local musicians who also sing traditional ballads of these hills. If you should be in the area the first weekend in December, don't miss the heart-lifting lighting of a Christmas tree that floats on the small lake just back of the Old Depot—it's a lovely gathering of mountain people who begin the holiday season with this touching event. In mid-October, there's the three-day Black Mountain Festival, when traditional music and dance make for an ideal family event.

Some five miles east of downtown Asheville, at milepost 382 on the Blue Ridge Parkway, the **Folk Art Center,** P.O. Box 9545, Asheville, NC 28815 (tel. 704/298-7928), is operated by the Southern Highland Handicraft Guild, a nonprofit organization of craftspeople of the nine-state Southern Appalachian region. The contemporary native-wood and stone structure houses the finest in both traditional and contemporary handcrafts of the region, the **Allanstand Craft Shop** (one of the oldest craft shops in the country, established in 1895), and exhibition and museum areas. Throughout the year, special events include **Celebrate Folk Art and Fiber Day** in May, the **World Gee Haw Whimmy Diddle Competition** in August, and **Christmas with the Guild,** in December. In July and August, try not to miss *Mountain Sweet Talk,* a two-part, two-act play presented by Barbara Freeman and Connie Regan-Blake, two talented ladies who are among this country's best mountain storytellers. Call ahead for dates and times of special events.

Chimney Rock Park is 25 miles southeast of Asheville on U.S. 74 at N.C. 64 and N.C. 9. The huge granite monolith rises to a height of 315 feet, and you can reach its top by a stairway, a trail, or (as in my own case) by an elevator. There's an observation lounge open every day from mid-March through November (weather permitting), and the charge is $7 for adults, $4 for children 6 to 15. Trails lead to Needle's Eye, Moonshiner's Cave, and Devil's Head (on the way to Hickory Nut Falls, twice the height of Niagara). Food service is available, as are picnic facilities. For full details and a free vacation brochure and map, contact: Chimney Rock Co., P.O. Box 39, Chimney Rock, NC 28720 (tel. 704/625-9611).

Stately **Mount Mitchell** (highest point in the East) is in the **state park** that bears its name, some 33 miles northeast on the parkway, then five miles north on N.C. 128. There are a museum, a tower, and an observation lodge at Mount Mitchell; camping and picnicking facilities are available in the park.

About 30 miles southeast of Asheville on U.S. 25 is the little town of **Flat Rock,** home to the **North Carolina State Theater's Flat Rock Playhouse,** which stages performances from late June through August. It is better known, however, as the last home of two-time Pulitzer Prize–winning writer/poet/historian Carl Sandburg, who lived at **Connemara Farm** (on Little River Road, just west of U.S. 25) for some 22 years, longer than he'd ever lived in one place before. His home and the farm are preserved just as they were in his lifetime—the typewriter still sitting on an orange crate in his top-floor hideaway and his guitar propped against a chair in the living room—and there's no charge to visit and stroll around the grounds.

There are things to do in Asheville other than sightsee, however. For instance, if you land here the first week of August, don't miss the **Annual Mountain Dance and Folk Festival** held at the **Asheville Civic Center** on Haywood Street. It begins at sundown and goes on until the last fiddler, banjo picker, ballad singer, dulcimer player, and clog dancer has called it quits and there's nobody interested in one more square-dancing set. This is the oldest such festival in the country, everybody is invited, and you're encouraged to join in even if you don't know a "do-si-do" from a "swing-your-partner."

If you miss the festival, every Saturday night from early July through August (except for the first weekend in August), there's something called a **Shindig-on-the-Green** at the **City County Plaza,** where you'll find many of those same mountain musicians and dancers having an old-fashioned wingding. It's free, lots of fun, and again, you're invited to join in the fun. If sitting on the ground isn't your thing, take along a blanket or chair.

On a more personal level, lovers of mountain "hoedown" sessions should head for **Bill Stanley's,** 20 S. Spruce St. (tel. 704/253-4871), any night but Sunday, where local clog dancers often go through their spirited paces to the music of honest-to-goodness mountain musicians, and patrons are lured to join the ranks of square dancers even when they've never before even *seen* a set danced. Residents from miles around congregate here for the kind of traditional free-spirited fun that is a hallmark of the Blue Ridge Mountains. It's a good idea to phone ahead to find out just when the music begins. This is definitely a "don't miss"! (It's also a mecca for barbecue lovers—see "Where to Eat," above.)

And in **Brevard,** 27 miles southwest of Asheville, there's a **music festival** held throughout the summer months (late June through mid-August) at the **Brevard Music Center,** during which you can hear nationally and internationally famous artists perform in symphony, chamber music, band, recitals, choral works, musical comedy, and opera every night. Write P.O. Box 592, Brevard, NC 28712, or call 704/884-2019, for schedules and reservations.

FROM ASHEVILLE TO FONTANA DAM

The Blue Ridge Parkway comes to an end at **Cherokee,** the largest organized Native American reservation in the East (see below). Just west of the reservation, on N.C. 28, is **Fontana Village,** Fontana Dam, NC 28733 (tel. 704/498-2211 or toll free 800/438-8080), a mountain resort that makes a perfect ending for your parkway trip. Built near a 30-mile-long lake formed by the construction of Fontana Dam, the resort has a 94-room inn, a 30-room lodge, and 257 cottages with one to three bedrooms. Sports-minded people will be in their element here, with stocked trout ponds, tennis courts, riding horses, and miniature golf (plus a par-three course) right at hand. In addition, there are all sorts of crafts workshops with a charge for materials only and square dances from June through August. It really has something for almost anyone who loves the outdoors and an oldtime atmosphere. During the summer (June 1 through October 31), rates begin at $60 in the inn, $45 for a one-bedroom cottage (which will accommodate up to three if you use the living-room studio couch as a bed). The rest of the year, rates drop considerably, making it one of the best fall vacation spots I know of.

As for dining facilities, if you don't cook your own meals in the fully equipped cottage kitchens, there is a cafeteria and the Pioneer Dining Room, where the whole family can eat reasonably.

Things to See and Do

A little south of Asheville on the parkway, a turn east at Wagon Road Gap will take you down a steep, winding road to the first **forestry school** in the U.S. There's an interesting museum for visitors. Along the way, you go past **Sliding Rock,** where children often delight in sliding down the glass-slick surface, and **Looking Glass Falls.**

Nearer the end of the parkway, at Maggie Valley on U.S. 19, the **Ghost Town in the Sky,** P.O. Box 790, Maggie Valley, NC 28715 (tel. 704/926-1140), entertainment center is great fun. Separate western, mining, and mountaineer towns have been re-created on different levels of the mountaintop, and there's something going on in each one all the time. Shows are staged in the saloons, there are street gunfights, and all sorts of western and mountaineer types wander about. You reach the park (3,364 feet up) by means of twin inclined railways or a chair lift. Kids will enjoy the rides. It's open from 9 a.m. to 6 p.m. daily from early May to early November (weather permitting). Admission is $11.95 for adults, $9.95 for ages 3 to 9.

From the middle of December until snow disappears in the spring, there's very good skiing at the **Cataloochee Ski Area** at Maggie Valley. For full information, write Rte. 1, Box 502, Maggie Valley, NC 28751 (tel. 800/843-1686). A base lodge serves three hearty meals daily in ski season.

As mentioned, the Blue Ridge Parkway comes to an end at Cherokee, right at the entrance to the **Cherokee Indian Reservation,** where Indian life has moved into the 20th century with all kinds of modern inventions and conveniences, but has held on to age-old traditions. You can see competitions in archery and blowguns, for example, or watch a game of Cherokee stickball, one of the roughest games anywhere. If you're there at the right time, you'll also see dances that have been handed down from generation to generation. The some 8,000 Cherokee who live on the reservation are descendants of a proud tribe, many of whom hid out in the Great Smokies in 1838 to escape that blot on American history, the removal of all eastern tribes to the West. A government Indian agent, one William H. Thomas (part Indian himself), bought part of the land that is now reservation and gave it to the Cherokee who'd managed to stay, and later a total of 50,000 acres was handed over to the tribe by the U.S. government.

A powerful drama, *Unto These Hills,* now tells the moving story of those tragic days when so many Indians traveled the "Trail of Tears." It is presented at the outdoor **Mountainside Theater,** off U.S. 441 (P.O. Box 398, Cherokee, NC 28719; tel. 704/497-2111), from mid-June through late August at 8:45 p.m., Monday through Saturday—and many of the actors are portraying their own ancestors. Tickets are $7 to $9.

The **Museum of the Cherokee Indian,** on U.S. 441 at Drama Road (tel. 704/497-3481), tells the story of the Cherokee through exhibits of such items as spear points several centuries old and multimedia theater shows. It's open daily except major holidays year round for $3 (children 6 to 12, $1.50). Rates are lower from January through May.

But to really see Indian life among the Cherokee 250 years ago, you have to visit **Oconaluftee Indian Village,** off U.S. 441 (Cherokee, NC 28719; tel. 704/497-2111 or 497-2315). It's an authentic Cherokee community whose residents wear the tribal dress (most wear conventional clothes in the town of Cherokee and throughout the reservation) and practice the same crafts as their ancestors. You'll see dart guns being made or a log canoe being shaped by fire, and beautiful beadwork taking shape under skilled fingers. And the seven-sided Council House conjures up images of the leaders of seven tribes gathered to thrash out problems or to worship their gods together. It's a kind of living museum of a way of life and a period of our country's history that is all too often distorted by fiction writers and Hollywood scenarios. You can visit the village any day from mid-May through late October for $6, $3 for children 6 to 12.

Youngsters will find Christmas alive and well even in the summer at **Santa's Land Park and Zoo,** (tel. 704/497-9191) 2½ miles east of Cherokee on U.S. 19. Santa and his helpers are busy getting ready for December 25 in a charming Christmas village, and there's a zoo with (what else?) reindeer and other domestic and exotic animals. And just for fun, there are some amusement rides. It's open for visitors from early May through October; and adults pay $8.95 (children 2 through 12, $7.95).

A Side Trip for Rubies

Gem-quality blood-red rubies are found in only two places in the world—the Magok Valley in Burma and the **Cowee Valley** north of Franklin, N.C. While these ruby and sapphire mines are played out for commercial purposes, rock-hounds are still finding many thousands of dollars in gem-quality stones every year. For an admission charge of about $5 a day (8 a.m. to 5 p.m. seven days a week, April through October) and about 25¢ a gallon, you can sort through the gem-bearing gravel—and keep anything you find. Two of the most reliable are the **Holbrook Ruby Mine** (tel. 704/524-3540), one of the original mines in the area, and the **Shuler Ruby Mine** (tel. 704/524-3551), both of which have only native stones and provide assistance to novice gem-seekers. Then stop in at **Ruth and Bud's Cowee Gem Shop** (tel. 704/369-8233), where Bud Schmidt, a former hobbyist rockhound himself, will examine your finds and offer expert faceting and mounting services. If you want to stay for more than a day, bunk in at **Miner's Rest** (within walking distance of the mines), where Ruth and Bud Schmidt provide three completely furnished efficiency apartments, each fully heated and air-conditioned, at $40 a day for three and $50 for four people (weekly and monthly rates available). For reservations, call 704/369-8233 (days) or 704/524-3902 (evenings), or write to Miner's Rest, 206 Ruby Mine Rd., Franklin, NC 28734.

To get to the mining area, take U.S. 23 from Asheville or U.S. 441 from Cherokee to Franklin, then N.C. 28 north for about six miles. After passing the Cower Creek Road, keep right at the next two intersections, and you will be on Ruby Mine Road. The mines are about three miles beyond Cowee Baptist Church.

INTRODUCTION TO NORTH CAROLINA

1. BY WAY OF BACKGROUND
2. TRAVELING TO NORTH CAROLINA
3. TRAVELING WITHIN NORTH CAROLINA

We felt so sorry for her," the lady from California told me, "that we came all the way across the country to cheer her up." She was speaking of her daughter, a brand-new lieutenant in the air force who had joined up primarily for the travel benefits. "North Carolina was not exactly what she had in mind," my newfound friend related. The whole family had been disappointed when news came of her assignment to Pope Field, close by Fort Bragg in the center of the state. "But since we've been here, it's a different story," the mother went on with a beaming face, "this state has *everything!* It's been a whole new experience for us, and well worth the trip just to get to know it."

This reaction by first-time visitors to the state that bills itself as the "Variety Vacationland" is not unusual. Although Southerners have long known and enjoyed North Carolina's resorts, "Yankees," Midwesterners, and those from the Far West have for the most part tended to think of it merely as a place to pass through on the way to points farther south. Yet within its borders lie tourist and vacation attractions numerous enough and varied enough to offer an appeal to almost any traveler, regardless of his or her special interests.

1. By Way of Background

FROM SIR WALTER RALEIGH TO THE WRIGHT BROTHERS
There's history aplenty, for it was here, on tiny Roanoke Island, that Sir Walter Raleigh's colony of 150 English settlers was "lost" in 1587, a full 20 years before Englishmen arrived farther north in Virginia's Jamestown. What

happened to them (including Virginia Dare, the first child born of English parents in the New World) remains a mystery, since the only clue—if that's what it is—to their fate was the word "Croatan" (the name of a tribe of friendly Indians) carved on a tree.

Along the coast are stately old plantation homes, some with formal gardens still lovingly tended and open to visitors, which housed the planters who came and stayed to plow prosperity from the rich soil. And farther inland, at Winston-Salem, an entire village—Old Salem—has been restored to depict the lifestyle of Moravians who arrived in 1753 and created a community that has lived through the centuries.

To the west in the mountains (the Blue Ridge, Great Smokies, Nantahalas, and others that form the southern Appalachians), history lives in the form of the Cherokee reservation—teeming with residents whose ancestors were here eons before a white face appeared—and towns like Boone (named for you-know-who) and Banner Elk (see Chapter IV for details on all these) that speak of the persevering frontiersmen whose restless western wanderings cleared the way for those who followed to settle down, bringing "civilization" with them.

In more recent times, man literally took off into the Age of Flight right here in North Carolina when Wilbur and Orville Wright made the first powered flight in 1903 at Kitty Hawk.

WITH A VIEW TO THE PRESENT

But if history isn't your thing, the Old North State has an ample supply of other attractions in its grab bag.

Its beaches, from Nags Head to Ocean Isle, are a delight, with broad stretches of white sand, waving sea oats, waves big enough to challenge the most skillful surfer, and seaside resorts located on outer banks, peninsulas, or offshore islands that face sounds and rivers as well as the Atlantic. Fishing, boating, waterskiing, sand-skiing, and even hang-gliding from gigantic dunes are all part of the fun up and down the coastline. (And if you're a "sea nut," enamored of its mystery and many moods, you'll *love* the tales of Blackbeard, that fierce pirate who sailed these waters and met his end here, and looking for relics of the more than 2,000 shipwrecks claimed by the "Graveyard of the Atlantic.")

Tennis and golf lovers will find a home in the state too. Indeed, who doesn't equate the very word "golf" with Pinehurst? And no one would deny that the sport is at its best there, but neither should the fact be overlooked that the whole state has excellent courses and courts from one end to the other.

Equestrians will find some of the country's finest horses in North Carolina, along with miles and miles of riding trails. You'll see horses on the beaches, on sandy paths shaded by softly sighing long-leaf pines, and following ancient Indian routes through mountain passes.

And the mountains beckon hikers, climbers, skiers (the snow kind), and campers, then throw in Fontana, where square dancing and other oldtime recreations still hold sway (again, see Chapter IV).

Naturalists and others who'd rather bed down in a tent than in the fanciest resort hotel will find an embarrassment of riches in the Great Smoky Mountains National Park, as well as 2 national seashores, 4 national forests, 36 state parks and recreation areas, 60 public and more than 300 privately owned campgrounds in the state.

THREE STATES IN ONE

As you may have gathered from the foregoing, North Carolina's geographical makeup divides into three distinct regions: the Coastal Plain, the Piedmont Plateau, and the Mountains. You can take your pick or sample all three: either way you're almost certain to be surprised by the sheer number of things to see and do.

AND THEN THERE ARE THE PEOPLE

One of your biggest surprises may well be the people who live here—"Tar Heels" they like to call themselves. (It is said that Gen. Robert E. Lee originated the name when North Carolina troops stuck so tenaciously in the front lines of battle during the Civil War.)

While all three regions have produced certain "personality" characteristics in the natives, there are some traits that all North Carolinians share, and they are a definite bonus to anyone visiting the state. Along with the courtesy and friendliness found among most southern people, those in North Carolina possess an engaging lack of pretense—you'll find few "phonies" here—and a delightful sense of humor. Basic good manners make them helpful at the drop of a question, and a sort of native sophistication may surprise you with the quality of the help. A resourcefulness and determination of high degree has, down through the years, been responsible for North Carolina's position as one of the most progressive southern states in industry, education, and agriculture; and even in remote areas you'll find the latest methods being employed by knowledgeable, well-informed citizens. Whether it's a fisherman at Ocracoke, a businessman in Raleigh, or a craftsman in the mountains at Brevard who winds up being a special friend during your visit (and you're bound to find one), the friendship is sure to be a lively, enjoyable, and lasting one.

TO SUM UP

North Carolina, then, does have a little bit of everything—something for everyone—and, as my friend from California said, it's well worth the trip.

NORTH CAROLINA TELEPHONE AREA CODES

Raleigh, 919; Winston-Salem, 919; Nags Head, 919; Wilmington (Wrightsville Beach), 919; Asheville, 704; Charlotte, 704.

VISITOR INFORMATION

For a packet of specific information brochures and bulletins before coming to North Carolina, contact: **North Carolina Travel and Tourism Division,** 430 N. Salisbury St., Raleigh, NC 27611 (tel. 919/733-4171, or toll free 800/VISIT-NC). Whether it's sightseeing, golf, fishing, or almost any other facet of travel you're interested in, you're likely to receive very complete, thorough answers to your questions.

NORTH CAROLINA HOTELS

You can find just about any-priced hotel accommodation in North Carolina, from the expensive Hyatt House in Winston-Salem to the budget Days Inn chain detailed in the introduction to this book. Aside from price, there is also a

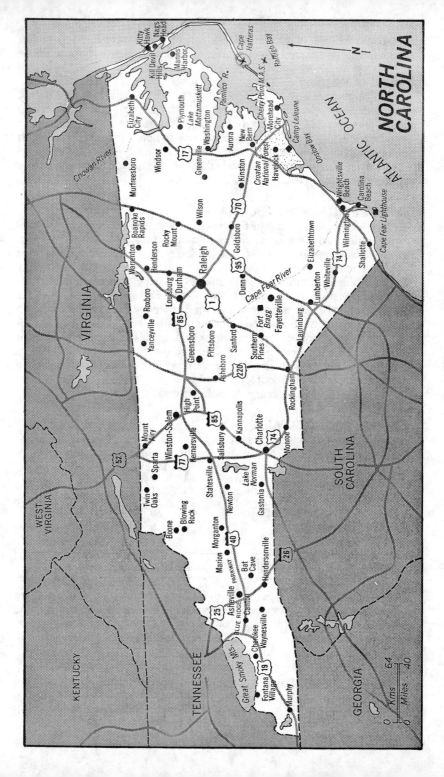

wide choice of *type* of accommodation: there are country inns, mountain lodges, tourist homes, and motels and hotels with a distinctive regional flavor.

A Word of Warning

Just because *you* may not have thought of North Carolina as a prime tourist area, don't be deceived into believing that you can come without reserving ahead. 'Taint so, and I can attest to that fact on the basis of my own experience when I arrived "out of season" at the coast, only to find that the nearest room to be had was 40 miles inland, because of the Annual Mullet Fishing Tournament! So, no matter when you plan to travel in the state, do yourself a favor and be sure your accommodations will be waiting.

DINING OUT IN NORTH CAROLINA

North Carolina's food is just as varied as its vacation attractions. And restaurants range all the way from fancy establishments that would rival the best in New York in decor to plain, road-house–looking cafés such as the one I found at Carteret. At either end of the spectrum, you're likely to find well-prepared, tasty North Carolina specialties: barbecued pork (the spicy, minced-up kind that's unique to this state—in particular, look for the Parker's chain, which serves some of the best barbecue on earth at very moderate prices), country ham, fresh seafood served with hush puppies (cornmeal batter-fried in deep fat), and always, grits served with breakfast (don't knock them until you've tried them served with globs of melting butter). I've tried to point out my own personal finds, but in this state especially, you stand a very good chance of running into a "special" place if you ask about local favorites.

You must be 21 to order any alcoholic beverage.

NORTH CAROLINA CLIMATE

North Carolina's climate is generally moderate, as can be seen from the following yearly mean highs and lows for various locations in the state:

	High	Low
Cape Hatteras	84	40
Raleigh	88	31
Winston-Salem	88	32
Asheville	85	30

---

2. Traveling to North Carolina

The best way for *you* to get to North Carolina depends, of course, on where you start, how much you can spend on transportation, and just how much time you have. These are the options that will let you find the mode of travel that best fits your circumstances.

BY AIR

Eastern, United, Delta, American, and USAir (Piedmont) have direct flights into major North Carolina cities, and USAir (Piedmont) has the largest number of North Carolina destinations from out of state, though not all are direct: Raleigh, Wilmington, Jacksonville, New Bern, Kinston, Fayetteville, Greensboro, Winston-Salem, Hickory, Charlotte, and Asheville.

BY TRAIN

North Carolina is on Amtrak's New York/Miami and Tampa runs, with stops in Raleigh, Hamlet, Southern Pines, Rocky Mount, Wilson, Selma, and Fayetteville. The New York/Washington/New Orleans *Southern Crescent* stops in Greensboro, High Point, Salisbury, Charlotte, and Gastonia. Be sure to check for excursion fares or seasonal specials.

BY BUS

Greyhound has good direct service to major cities in North Carolina from out of state, with connections to almost any destination within the state.

BY CAR

From Virginia and South Carolina, you can enter North Carolina on either I-95 or I-85, and I-27 and I-77 also lead in from South Carolina. The main Tennessee entry is I-40. All major border points have attractive, helpful welcome centers, some with cookout facilities and playground equipment in a park-like setting.

---

3. Traveling Within North Carolina

BY AIR

USAir (Piedmont), as noted above, has a number of in-state destinations, with connecting flights possible between most.

BY BUS

There are few places you can't reach by Greyhound.

BY CAR

Driving is a pleasure on North Carolina's 76,000 miles of toll-free, well-maintained highways. Most interstate and U.S. highways and some state roads have periodic rest areas with picnic tables and outdoor cooking facilities. For a map that is one of the easiest to use I've come across, as well as a fount of tourist information on the state, write to Travel and Tourism NC, Dept. of Commerce, 430 N. Salisbury St., Raleigh, NC 27611, for the **Official Highway Map and Guide to Points of Interest.**

Special Note: North Carolina law is quite specific that *all* traffic must come to a standstill when a school bus is stopped on a highway, and this is stringently enforced. So if you see a bright-yellow school bus stopped—whether or not you see children getting on or off—save yourself a stiff fine and stop, and that applies whether you're meeting it or following behind.

You will find Thrifty Rental Car locations in Charlotte, Greensboro, and Raleigh.

BY FERRY

I'd go out of my way just to travel on one of this state's most enjoyable transportation facilities, the system of toll-free auto ferries that ply the sounds and rivers of the coastal area. You can cross Currituck Sound from Currituck to Knotts Island, Hatteras Inlet, Pamlico River at Bayview, and Neuse River at Minnesott Beach. All schedules are printed on that wonderfully complete Official North Carolina Highway Map. For an up-to-date printed ferry schedule before you leave home, write: Director, Ferry Division, Room 120, Maritime Bldg., 113 Arendell St., Morehead City, NC 28557 (tel. 919/726-6446 or 726-6413).

VI

NORTH CAROLINA'S COASTAL PLAIN

1. NAGS HEAD AND THE OUTER BANKS
2. MOREHEAD CITY AND ATLANTIC BEACH
3. IN AND AROUND WILMINGTON

The beaches along North Carolina's Atlantic coastline are, to say the least, unusual. Many of them, in fact, lie technically offshore on the long string of narrow islands that make up the Outer Banks. And what beaches they are! The strand is wide, dunes are breathtakingly high, and interspersed with resort centers that have slowly developed over nearly 200 years are long stretches of natural beach where you can walk and swim and surfcast far from the madding crowd. But to begin at the beginning:

1. Nags Head and the Outer Banks

In 1899, when Nathaniel Gould emigrated from Cape Cod to Roanoke Island, he advised arriving guests at his newly opened Hotel Roanoke to take "any one of the Merchant and Miners Transportation Company's or the Old Dominion Steamship Company's boats, both lines stopping at Norfolk, Virginia, which connects with trains of the Norfolk & Southern Railroad to Elizabeth City, which connects with Steamer to Roanoke Island. In coming from the south, take Steamer from New Bern, N.C. Carriages will be in waiting at the steamboat wharf on the arrival of every boat, taking guests direct to the Hotel."

It's a much simpler matter today to reach the Outer Banks, thanks to a superb network of highways, bridges, and toll-free ferries. U.S. 158 eliminates the need for steamships from the north, and U.S. 64 provides easy access to visitors from the south.

NAGS HEAD
This largest resort in the Outer Banks area is ideal as a place to headquarter during your visit. Its odd name, according to local legend, comes from the prac-

tice of canny land pirates who in the old days would hang lanterns from the necks of ponies, parade them along the dunes at night, and lure unsuspecting ships onto shoals where they were grounded and their cargoes promptly stripped by the waiting robbers. Another theory holds that it was named for the highest point of Scilly Island, the last sight English colonists had of their homeland.

However it got its name, Nags Head has been one of the most popular beach resorts in North Carolina for over a century. The town itself is a semitacky collection of the usual beach houses, motels, and modern luxury hotels, but it has one of the finest beaches to be found in the state. **Jockey's Ridge,** highest sand dune on the East Coast, is located here also. Its 138-foot-high smooth, sandy slopes are popular with the sand-skiing and hang-gliding crowd, and since it is now a state park, it's open to all. And at **Kill Devil Hills** (named for a particularly potent rum once shipped from here), the Wright Brothers made that historic first flight back in 1903.

Roanoke Island is where Sir Walter Raleigh's colony of more than 100 men, women, and children settled when they landed here in 1587 in what was to be England's first permanent foothold in the New World. Virginia Dare, granddaughter of the little band's governor, John White, was born that year, the first child of English parents to be born in America. When White sailed back to England on the ships that had brought the settlers, it was his intention to secure additional provisions and perhaps more colonists, then return within the year. Instead, he found England so threatened by the Spanish Armada that Queen Elizabeth I refused to allow any large ships to leave. It wasn't until 1590 that White was able to get back to Roanoke, and what he found there was a mystery —one that remains to this day. The rude houses he had helped build were all dismantled and the entire area enclosed by a high palisade he later described as "very fort-like." At the entrance of the enclosure, crude letters spelled out the word "CROATAN" on a post from which the bark had been peeled.

Since their prearranged distress signal, a cross, was not there and no evidence suggested violence, his conclusion was that those he'd left on Roanoke Island must have joined the friendly Croatan Indian tribe. An unhappy chain of circumstances, however, forced him to set sail for England before a search could be made. Despite all sorts of theories about their fate, no link was ever established between the "lost" colonists and the Indians, nor was there ever any clue unearthed to reveal exactly what did happen. It would be 1607, at Jamestown, Virginia, before England could claim that permanently established settlement.

The **Fort Raleigh National Historic Site** was named in 1941, and its visitor center tells the story in exhibits and film. Paul Green's symphonic drama *The Lost Colony* brings it to life in the amphitheater that has been constructed at the edge of Roanoke Sound.

From **Whalebone Junction** at South Nags Head, the **Cape Hatteras National Seashore** stretches 70 miles down the Outer Banks barrier islands. The drive along N.C. 12 takes you through a wildlife refuge, pleasant little villages, long stretches of dunes with designated parking areas and ramps leading over to sand beaches that can only be called gorgeous, and on to **Buxton** and the **Cape Hatteras Lighthouse,** tallest on the American coast. It has stood since 1870 as a beacon for ships passing through these treacherous waters that have earned the title "Graveyard of the Atlantic," claiming more than 1,500 victims of foul

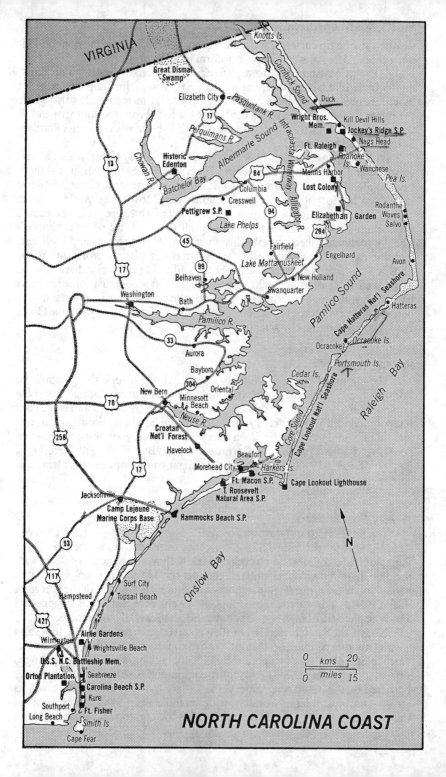

NORTH CAROLINA COAST

weather, strong rip currents, and shifting shoals. This is where the ironclad Union gunboat *Monitor* went down in a storm in December of 1862.

At the little village of **Hatteras,** a free auto ferry makes the 40-minute crossing to **Ocracoke Island,** where more than 5,000 acres, including 16 miles of beach, are preserved by the National Park Service for recreation. It's also where the pirate Edward Teach (Blackbeard) met his end. From the southern end of the island, a toll auto ferry takes you on a 2 ¼-hour voyage across **Pamlico Sound** to **Cedar Island.**

With no stops, it's about a 4 ½-hour drive—but by rights, it's an all-day trip or several half-day trips from a Nags Head base. Otherwise, you'll miss those beaches for swimming, fishing, or just walking along the sand, the breathtaking view from the top of Cape Hatteras Lighthouse. Most of all, you'd miss the chance to stop for lunch or a respite or to shop, all of which are perfect excuses to get to know the marvelous people who call this necklace of sand "home." They're hardy "Bankers" who've lived with winds and storms and high seas, and who can—and will, to friendly souls—recount tales of heroism at sea, the ghostly light that bobs over Teach's Hole, and wild ponies that have roamed Ocracoke Island for at least 400 years, all in the soft accent that some say harks back to Devon, home of shipwrecked sailors who came ashore here and stayed to become ancestors of those you'll meet today. If you miss the *people* of the Outer Banks, you'll miss the character of these islands. Take the day!

WHERE TO STAY

The choice of beach accommodations is wide, but one thing should be borne in mind: while the beaches are lined with cottage rentals, many of them are spoken for on a year-to-year basis, and it is absolutely essential to make your reservations well in advance. I'll list a few in the hotel-motel category in this area, but if you'd like to settle down for a week or more, your best bet is to write the **Outer Banks Chamber of Commerce,** P.O. Box 1757, Kill Devil Hills, NC 27948 (tel. 919/441-8144), which can put you in touch with cottage and apartment owners.

A Very Special Place

The **Sanderling Inn Resort,** Box 319Y, Duck, NC 27949 (tel. 919/261-4111) is wishful thinking fulfilled for those of us who remember the Outer Banks as a haven of rambling wooden hotels with wide verandas complete with rocking chairs, spacious rooms, and the sort of old-fashioned hospitality that invites you to sink into seaside rhythms and shuck the tensions of the everyday, inland world. These days, those long-ago havens have just about disappeared amid the plethora of high-rise structures and plasticky, all-alike motels.

Not so, the Sanderling. First of all, it is surrounded only by sand dunes and a wide, mind-expanding beachfront, with glimpses of private homes in the distance. Not a neon sign in sight, nor will there ever be, since the Sanderling is situated on 12 acres of a 300-acre private community of single-family residences bordered by the 3,400-acre Audubon sanctuary to the north. Then there's its architecture—wonder of wonders, wide verandas wrap around both floors of the two-story wooden building that even has the comfortable sprawl of those fondly remembered hostelries and rocking chairs aplenty invite leisurely hours of "rockin' and thinkin'." Guest rooms are unbelievably spacious, all beautifully decorated and furnished, with Audubon bird prints in every room, and all have tea- and coffee-making facilities. Public rooms are graciously appointed, and focal point of the Green Gallery is a magnificent portfolio of Audubon prints. Fireplaces are sprinkled about public spaces and put to good use on cool evenings, and there's a guest library, as well as VCR films for guests' use. Adjacent to the inn itself, there's a handsome 1899 building that was once a Coast Guard station (now a registered historic landmark), and which has been beautifully restored to house the Sanderling restaurant and bar. Across the road is a small, but complete, health center.

Space limitations, of necessity, cut short my personal rave for the Sanderling—suffice it to say that extras such as wheelchair access to all facilities (including a special ramp to the beach), periodic barbecues on a sundeck, picnic lunches packed by the restaurant, and organized sightseeing tours to Roanoke Island, Cape Hatteras, Edenton, and a scenic cruise along the Outer Banks, are just a few examples of the care and attention guests receive from one of the friendliest staffs on the North Carolina coast.

Rates at this highly recommended inn all include a complimentary continental breakfast and wine and hors d'oeuvre service. Doubles range from $135 to $250 during summer months, $80 to $160 in the spring and fall, and $70 to $160 in winter.

Also Good

The Best Western Armada is at the south end of Nags Head where U.S. 158 and U.S. 64 meet, Milepost 17 (P.O. Box 307), Nags Head, NC 27959 (tel. 919/441-6315, or toll free 800/334-3302, 800/233-5922 in North Carolina). Children 12 and under stay here *free,* and rates for double occupancy, oceanside, start at $97 Memorial Day through Labor Day, with much lower rates other seasons. Bayside rooms are a better buy at considerably lower rates. All rooms in the seven-story hotel are attractively decorated in a modern manner and oceanfronts have private balconies. The oceanside restaurant is especially pleasant, with above-average food. Henry's Pub, also on the ocean, features top entertainment and dancing during the summer months. They'll pack you a box lunch for day trips, or you can stay put on their private beach or the two oceanside pools. There's a playground for children, tennis courts for their parents, and access to two PGA-approved golf courses.

At the other end of the beach—in price as well as distance—is the **Quality Inn John Yancey,** P.O. Box 422, Kill Devil Hills, NC 27948 (tel. 919/441-7141 or toll free 800/228-5151). Considerably fewer frills, but the moderate price range is a joy, as are the efficiencies, which come completely equipped, right down to the coffee pot. There's no charge for children under 12 if they share a room with their parents, and the double-occupancy rates for a room (oceanfront) are from $80 in season all the way down to $30 off-season. Efficiencies cost $75 and up, depending on the time of year. A swimming pool provides swimming for those too fainthearted to brave the surf. Management here is especially friendly and helpful, and the rooms are cheerful.

The **Quality Inn Sea Ranch,** P.O. Box 325, Kill Devil Hills, NC 27959 (tel. 919/441-7126), at Milepost 7, has a posh oceanfront tower, with glass-enclosed balconies and rooms decorated with real flair. Each has two double beds or one king-size bed, and there are efficiencies (with mini-kitchens—not really meant for cooking full dinners). Oceanfront luxury apartments have two bedrooms, two baths (one with full Jacuzzi), full kitchens, and glass-enclosed balconies. In the main building, you can choose rooms that come with one double and one single bed, or with sitting room area, and two double beds; all rooms have a mini-refrigerator and a microwave oven. There's a quality boutique, a Nautilus health spa, an enclosed pool with a sliding-glass roof, and an indoor tennis club. Golf is just minutes away on two 18-hole championship courses. The window-walled Top of the Dune dining room serves all three meals (dinner is by candlelight), and there's dancing and entertainment in the cocktail lounge. Doubles start at $90 from mid-June to early September and drop by stages to around $50 from late November through mid-March.

At Milepost 11, the **Beacon Motor Lodge,** 2617 S. Virginia Dare Trail (P.O. Box 729), Nags Head, NC 27959 (tel. 919/441-5501), is a low, rambling complex offering rooms, efficiencies, cottages, and apartments. There are two swimming pools, and tennis and golf privileges at nearby facilities. Rooms are comfortably furnished and decorated in welcoming beiges and browns. All rooms have phones and refrigerators. There's a children's playground and coin-operated laundry. There's no restaurant on the premises of this oceanfront family motel, but there is one opposite and several more nearby. Doubles start at $60 from late May to early September, and drop during other months. Cottages (with kitchens) run $450 to $550 per week in season. Apartments are in the $500- to $600-per-week range in season, with daily maid service and linens furnished. Open late March through late October.

The **Nags Head Inn,** 4701 S. Virginia Dare Trail, P.O. Box 501, Nags Head, NC 27959 (tel. 919/441-0454), is on the oceanfront at milepost 14. Guest rooms are nicely done up, with contemporary decor and furnishings, refrigerators, and cable TV and in-room movies. Oceanfront rooms have balconies. There's a small heated pool, whirlpool, and golf privileges at nearby courses. Doubles range seasonally from $35 to $110 (starting at $75 in high season), and weekly rates are available.

The **Days Inn,** 3919 Croatan Hwy., P.O. Box 1096, Kitty Hawk, NC 27949 (tel. 919/261-4888) is one block from the ocean between mileposts 4 and 5. The nicely appointed guest rooms have cable TV and in-room movies, and there's a small pool. Doubles run $35 to $80, depending on the season.

The **Carolinian,** Beach Road, P.O. Box 370, Nags Head, NC 27959 (tel. 919/441-7171) is a charming older hotel at milepost 10.5. Rooms are comfortably furnished, and rates range seasonally from $30 to $85 for doubles.

WHERE TO EAT

Dining out is no problem anywhere along North Carolina's coast, and Nags Head has plenty of small, good seafood restaurants. I'm listing only four, recognizing that the day's activities influence beach eating more strongly perhaps than in other locations.

The Seafare, at Milepost 5.2, U.S. 158 Bypass, in Seagate North Shopping Center (tel. 919/441-5554), is the worthy successor to the original restaurant in Old Nags Head, which, alas, burned some years ago. The same owner-management assures that you'll still find the fine cuisine, atmosphere, and service that has led local residents to patronize it since 1960, when descendants of Nathaniel Gould (the one who gave such explicit steamship instructions to his hotel guests) opened the Seafare after years of operating hotels whose dining rooms had become noted all up and down the coast. Although it's not quite as large as the original, it's a very attractive, spacious, tastefully decorated place with nautical touches, and the famous Seafare smörgåsbord is still being served—a truly groaning board heaped with fresh seafoods, roast beef, fresh salads and vegetables. The menu for table service is surprisingly extensive, featuring everything from several combination platters to a surf-and-turf plate of beef tenderloin (eight ounces) and a six-ounce rock lobster tail to a chateaubriand for two. Dinner, on the semi–à la carte menu, can run from $9 to $25. There are also nightly dinner specials for a low, low $9! But it's the food, not the price, that's the attraction here—it's *all* good!

The Seafare doesn't take reservations, and dress is casual. Incidentally, don't bother asking for the recipe of their famous she-crab soup—that's the one recipe they won't give out. The selection of fine wines and international beers is outstanding. It's open seven days a week from 6:30 a.m. for breakfast, and 11:30 a.m. to 10 p.m., with continuous service. Call for seasonal hours in fall and winter.

Owens' Restaurant, Milepost 17, on the Beach Road in Nags Head (tel. 919/441-7309), is one of those great local favorites that just keeps getting better with the years. Just across from Owens' Motel, it has been owned by the same family for over 40 years. There's a welcoming family atmosphere you sense the moment you step inside this homey spot decorated with nautical relics and artifacts from the Outer Banks' "olden days." Fresh seafood is the specialty, and dinners range from $11 to $23. There's a child's menu as well, and if the kids prefer burgers and fries to broiled flounder, they can have them. You can enjoy nightly entertainment and your favorite libation in the Station Keepers Lounge. The restaurant is open from 5 to 10 p.m. mid-March to December 1; closed Thanksgiving Day.

A little farther south, next door to the Sea Oatel near the junction of U.S. 158 and U.S. 64, is another longtime Nags Head favorite, the **Dareolina Cove Restaurant** (tel. 919/441-7477). There are three dining rooms, but the one I especially like has wide windows opening to the Atlantic. It's a pleasant place during the day and downright romantic at night. Open from 7 a.m. to 2 p.m. and 5 to 10 p.m. in the summer, to 9 p.m. the rest of the year, the Dareolina serves all three meals and will fix box lunches for picnics or fishing trips. The menu is a long one, and prices are moderate. As you might expect, fresh seafood is featured, along with prime steaks and home-baked pies and breads. My personal choice is the Nags Head crab (served on avocado halves). Breakfast will run under $6, lunch under $10, and dinner prices are in the $8 to $25 range. Like the Seafare, no reservations are required (at either place, you'll wait no more than 15 to 20 minutes). There's live entertainment on Friday and Saturday nights.

Dinner at **A Restaurant by George,** Milepost 11, Nags Head (tel. 919/441-3535), is a real treat. In an elegant East Indian setting, gourmet dishes are brought to the table by attentive, well-trained waiters. Prices are surprisingly moderate in light of both food and service, ranging from $12 to $30 (there's a children's menu with lower prices). Open all year, from 5:30 to 9:30 p.m. mid-September through May, 5:30 to 10 p.m. June to mid-September. Exotic drinks are a specialty, and the lounge is open from 5:30 p.m. to 1 a.m.

There's a very good restaurant over at Wanchese (that's the south end of Roanoke Island), serving the freshest seafood, steaks, and chicken at moderate prices, and overlooking the harbor. **Fisherman's Wharf** (tel. 919/473-5205) also has a connected retail seafood market. Hours here are 11 a.m. to 3 p.m. for lunch, 5 to 9 p.m. for dinner, and it's closed Sunday.

At Hatteras

The **Channel Bass,** on N.C. 12 at Hatteras (tel. 919/986-2250), has a clam chowder that will have you calling for seconds. In fact, all their seafood is fresh and cooked to perfection. The menu is semi–à la carte, and dinner can run as low as $8 or as high as $25. It's closed from December 1 through March 28, and open 5:30 to 9:30 p.m. the rest of the year (to 9 p.m. on Sunday).

At Ocracoke

The **Island Inn,** on Ocracoke Island, N.C. 12 (tel. 919/928-4351), has been a part of the island since 1901 when it was built as an Odd Fellow's Lodge and housed the first public school on its ground floor. Over the years it has been moved across the street, served as a private home, been converted to a small inn, played host to naval officers during World War II as their officers' club, had wings added to accommodate more travelers, and wound up under the capable management of one native and another confirmed island lover. Larry Williams (he's the native) and his partner, Foy Shaw, have refurbished the rooms with plain but comfortable furnishings, added a heated swimming pool, and opened a restaurant that's earned an enviable reputation all along the Outer Banks. During the summer, it serves all three meals at moderate prices, breakfast 7 to 11 a.m., lunch 11 a.m. to 2 p.m., and dinner 5 to 9 p.m. Breakfast runs from $2 to $3.50 (and it's an islander's breakfast—hearty); lunch (including salads, sandwiches, and a couple of hot seafood platters), from $3 to $9, and dinner—where almost anything that comes from the sea is served up, with sautéed crabmeat, clam chowder, and an enormous seafood platter sharing honors—from $7.50 to $16. This is fishhouse eating as it should be, and if you find a soul response to the little fishing village, you can stay over here for $35 to $85, double occupancy, depending on the season.

THINGS TO SEE AND DO

The Nags Head area has more than its share of things to keep you occupied when not on the beach, and the Outer Banks hold their own special appeal. For sightseeing particulars, contact the **Outer Banks Chamber of Commerce,** P.O. Box 1757, Kill Devil Hills, NC 27948 (tel. 919/441-8144).

In and Near Nags Head

A little to the north, on U.S. 158 Bypass, at **Kill Devil Hills,** the **Wright Brothers National Memorial** is open to the public at no charge. Both the hangar and Orville and Wilbur's living quarters have been restored, and the visitor center holds a replica of that first airplane, as well as exhibits that tell the story of the two brothers who came here on vacations from their Dayton, Ohio, bicycle business to turn their dream into reality. It's an inspiration to see where they worked while you listen to the drone of modern airliners as they fly over this place where it all began.

From Whalebone Junction, U.S. 64-264 leads to **Roanoke Island** and the village of **Manteo.** Four miles west, you'll reach **Fort Raleigh National Historic Site,** where the old fort has been excavated and reconstructed just as it stood in 1585. The **visitor center** (tel. 919/473-5772) is a fascinating first stop, and they'll arrange guided tours by appointment. It's open 8 a.m. to 8 p.m. from mid-June to September 1, closing at 4:30 p.m. the rest of the year.

It is here, where it all happened, that Paul Green's moving drama, *The Lost Colony,* is presented in the **Waterside Theater,** Monday through Saturday at 8:30 p.m. from mid-June to late August. It's been running since 1937 (this country's first outdoor drama), and leaves you with a very real sense of what life was like for that courageous little band. The **Elizabethan Gardens** nearby, as well as the Tudor style of auxiliary buildings, remind all of us that this was the first connection between Elizabethan England and what was to become the United States of America. All seats for the outdoor drama are reserved (P.O. Box 40, Manteo, NC 27954; tel. 919/473-2127) and cost $10 for adults, $9 for seniors, the military, and handicapped, $4 for those under 12. There's a $2.50 charge to enter the gardens (tel. 919/473-3234), and children under 12 go in for free.

Also when you're in Manteo, don't miss one of North Carolina's newest state historic sites, *Elizabeth II* (tel. 919/473-1144), moored across from the nicely renovated waterfront. This 69-foot-long three-masted bark was built with private funds for the 400th anniversary commemoration of the settlement of the Lost Colony. The proud beauty, a composite design of 16th-century ships, was presented to the state on July 13, 1984. Before boarding her, you'll first enter the visitor center, where exhibits describe exploration and shipboard life during those tenuous years. "A Roanoke Voyage" realistically depicts life aboard such a ship from the perspective of its voyagers. During the summer, living-history interpreters portray roles of colonists and mariners. The site is open daily from 10 a.m. to 6 p.m. April through October, and Tuesday through Sunday from 10 a.m. to 4 p.m. November through March; closed major holidays. Admission is $3 for adults, $2.50 for seniors, and $1.50 for students.

About an hour and a half away from Nags Head (take U.S. 64, turn right at N.C. 37, then left when you reach N.C. 32), a later phase of this country's hisrory is preserved at **Edenton,** a lovely old town whose streets are lined with homes built by the planters and merchants who settled along the Albemarle Sound. The women of Edenton held their own "tea party" in 1774, one of the first recorded instances of American women taking a purely political action. Stop by the **Barker House Visitor Center** (tel. 919/482-3663) on South Broad Street (signs are posted throughout the town) to view a free 14-minute slide show. Here you can also purchase a historic district map for a nominal fee. The visitor center is open from 10 a.m. to 4:30 p.m. Monday through Saturday and from 2 to 5 p.m. on Sunday; closed major holidays. Guided tours of four historic buildings—the 1767 Chowan County Courthouse, 1725 Cupola House, 1773 James Iredell House State Historic Site, and restored St. Paul's Episcopal

Church—are conducted from 10 a.m. to 2:30 p.m. Monday through Saturday, and at 2:30 p.m. Sunday. The package tour is $5 for adults, $2.50 for ages 6 to 18; admission to individual buildings is $3.50 for adults, $1.50 for ages 6 to 18.

Along the Outer Banks

The **Outer Banks Chamber of Commerce,** P.O. Box 1757, Kill Devil Hills, NC 27948 (tel. 919/441-8144), will send information about outdoor activities and the "Cape Hatteras Visible Shipwrecks" booklet that tells you where to look for the remains of wrecked ships along the beaches (they appear and disappear with shifting tides and sands).

Turn left off N.C. 12 about eight miles south of U.S. 158 to reach **Coquina Beach,** where there are bath shelters, lifeguards (from mid-June to Labor Day), picnic shelters, and beach walks guided by National Park Service naturalists.

Farther south, across **Oregon Inlet** (there's a bridge), the **Pea Island Wildlife Refuge** attracts birdwatchers from all over the country to see the snow geese, which winter here, and wading shore and upland birds in the summer months. There's a parking area and overlook.

All along N.C. 12, you'll see places to pull off and park to reach the beaches, which are hidden from view by huge protective sand dunes. A word of warning: *Don't* try to park anywhere else—the sands are very soft and it's easy to get stuck!

There are also **campgrounds** at various spots, but you should know in advance that they're flat, sandy areas with no shade and that you'll need tent stakes longer than you'd normally use. And no hookups are provided. Sites are on a first-come, first-served basis, and the maximum stay is 14 days from May 25 through September 10. Fees are $8 nightly for up to six people at all sites.

For private campgrounds in the area, which do have hookups, call the Outer Banks Chamber of Commerce at 919/441-8144 and they'll supply full information.

Whether you're camping or just stopping at the beaches where there are no lifeguards, you should always keep in mind that tides and currents along the Outer Banks are *very* strong, and ocean swimming can be dangerous at times.

When you get to **Buxton,** turn left off N.C. 12 to see the **Cape Hatteras Lighthouse.** Its rotating duplex beacon has a 1,000-watt lamp in each side, and the 250,000 candlepower is visible 20 miles.

The little village of **Hatteras** exists now, as it has from the 1700s, as a fishing center, and there are large commercial and sport fleets that operate from its docks and marinas. In the spring and fall the boats bring in catches of sea trout, king and Spanish mackerel, bluefish, red drum, and striped bass, and in summer most of the action is offshore, where blue marlin and other billfish are in plentiful supply. Even if you're not fishing yourself, it's fun to watch the boats come in between 4 and 6 p.m. And if you'd rather be one of those coming in than be a bystander, the **Outer Banks Chamber of Commerce,** P.O. Box 1757, Kill Devil Hills, NC 27948 (tel. 919/441-8144), can supply a list of charter boats available, as well as fishing information.

From Hatteras, a free auto ferry crosses the inlet to **Ocracoke** in 40 minutes. Especially during the peak summer tourist season, however, be prepared to wait in line to board the ferry.

Ocracoke has shown up on maps as far back as the late 1500s, when Sir Walter Raleigh's Roanoke Island party made a landfall here. It is rumored to have been Blackbeard's sailing headquarters, and it was definitely his downfall. That wily pirate—who would braid pieces of hemp dipped in tallow into his long black beard and set them afire as he sailed into battle against merchant ships— made his peace with the Crown in 1712, receiving a full pardon from the king. Then, pretending to settle down to a peaceful life in the little town of Bath, he worked hand in glove with Gov. Charles Eden and Tobias Knight, the secretary of the colony, to go right on preying on ships from the Caribbean to the Virginia Capes. That fearsome head ended up, however, in 1718 adorning the prow of a sloop commanded by Lt. Richard Maynard, of the British Royal Navy, after he had engaged the pirate in a bloody duel in Ocracoke Inlet and captured his ship and crew. Maynard then sailed back to Virginia displaying his trophy to let ships along the coast know that the sea lanes were safe once more. Tales persist to this day of treasure stashed away or buried along the coast of North Carolina, but none has ever been found, and it's far more likely that Blackbeard sold his spoils quickly and squandered the proceeds.

When Ocracoke Island was isolated from the mainland and few visitors came by boat, as many as a thousand wild ponies roamed its dunes. Where they came from is uncertain, whether from shipwrecks, early Spanish explorers, or from original English settlers. At any rate, as more and more people traveled to and from the island, more and more ponies were rounded up, shipped to the mainland, and sold. The remnants of the herd—about a dozen—now live on a range seven miles north of Ocracoke village, where the National Park Service looks after them.

In a quiet little corner of Ocracoke Island, there's a bit of England, the **British Graveyard** that holds four British navy seamen whose bodies washed ashore when H.M.S. *Bedfordshire* was torpedoed offshore by a German submarine in 1942. It's leased by the British government, but lovingly tended by towns-people.

Ocracoke village has seen some changes since World War II, when the U.S. Navy dredged out Silver Lake harbor (still called "Cockle Creek" by many natives) and built a base here. They also brought the first public telephones and paved roads. In spite of the invasion of 20th-century mainland improvements, Ocracoke is essentially what it has always been—a fishing village whose manners and speech reflect 17th-century ancestors. It is by far the most picturesque spot on the Outer Banks.

To reach North Carolina's more southerly beaches, there's a ferry from Ocracoke to **Cedar Island**. Not only is there a toll; you have to make a reservation for the 2¼-hour trip! If you're leaving from Ocracoke, you must call within 30 days of departure (tel. 919/928-3841) and reserve space on one of the scheduled sailings; coming from Cedar Island, call 919/225-3551. The fare is $10 per car and occupants, $2 for bicycle and rider, and $1 for pedestrians. It's a wonderful, semi-ocean voyage on boats with names like *Pamlico, Silver Lake,* and *Sea Level,* manned by natives of the region whose creed is friendliness. For a complete list of ferries, schedules, and fares, write: Ferry Division, Dept. of Transportation, 113 Anendell St., Morehead City, NC 28557 (tel. 919/726-6446).

2. Morehead City and Atlantic Beach

From the Cedar Island ferry landing—where, incidentally, the **Pirate's Chest Restaurant** at the Driftwood Motel serves very good food at moderate prices, if you hit at eating time—it's almost a two-hour drive south to Morehead City and Atlantic Beach. Not that the distance is that long, it's just that the two-lane highway winds and curves through historic old fishing towns like Atlantic and Sealevel, under huge old water oaks hung with Spanish moss, emerging at intervals for long, straight patches of marshy savannahs of sea grass: it altogether discourages hurrying along.

Atlantic Beach is the oldest of the resorts on a 24-mile stretch of **Bogue Banks,** and most North Carolinians use the name Atlantic Beach to include the newer vacation centers of Pine Knoll Shores, Indian Beach, Emerald Isle, and Salter Path. The long, thin island began to develop back in 1927 when the first bridge was built across Bogue Sound to Morehead City, and it is now one of the state's most popular coastal areas, with fishing festivals and tournaments in the early spring and late fall making it virtually a year-round resort.

Morehead City, which has been an important port for oceangoing vessels since 1857, is the world's largest tobacco export terminal. Just across the sound, **Beaufort** (pronounced "*Bo*-fort") is a quaint old seaport that seems frozen in time, with narrow streets lined by white-frame houses built when the town was young (it goes all the way back to 1709) in a distinctive, almost West Indian, style. It was once, believe it or not, a whaling center.

Less than 50 miles inland, **New Bern** was the provincial capital for several years. Swiss colonists gave it its name, perhaps in a fit of homesickness. When William Tyron was royal governor, he built a splendid "palace" here, considered at the time the "most beautiful building in the New World." Both the palace and the gardens around it have been restored to their former splendor.

But overshadowing everything else, the ocean is the focal point in the area. There is an almost complete preoccupation with fishing and water sports, with historic sites sort of thrown in as a bonus for the tourist, who will have come, the natives have no doubt, to enjoy the sea.

WHERE TO STAY

Take your choice: headquarter in historic old Beaufort, Morehead City, or along the string of beaches known collectively as Atlantic Beach.

In Beaufort

From the looks of the **Inlet Inn,** 601 Front St., Beaufort, NC 28516 (tel. 919/728-3600), you'd think it has been a part of this historic old town from the very beginning. The truth is, however, that it was built within the last decade, but with due respect for the ambience and architecture of Beaufort's Historic District. The 36-room, L-shaped wooden structure faces the water, with wide front porches across its first and second floors. All rooms overlook the harbor, and all have unique features, such as French doors that open onto those private porches (they come with rocking chairs, a nice touch), or fireplaces, or window seats. Furnishings are in the colonial style, with some antiques; and rooms feature a seating area, bar with refrigerator/ice maker, cable TV, and ceiling fans. There's a courtyard garden at the rear, and a rooftop Widow's Walk Lounge. A continental breakfast is included in the rates, and complimentary wine and cheese are served every afternoon. Boat skippers have the use of transient boat slips. Special activity weekends (literary, native music, etc.) in spring, fall, and winter are offered at package rates. Seasonal rates for doubles range from $79 May through September; to $59 March and April and October and November; and $49 December, January, and February. Add $10 for rooms with fireplaces. Recommended.

Katie and Bruce Etheridge run the **Beaufort Inn,** 101 Ann St., Beaufort, NC 28516 (tel. 919/728-2600) as a labor of love, and they've managed to give the inn the look of history, though it is of recent vintage. The 41-room inn is located at the eastern end of the Grayden Paul drawbridge on U.S. 70, and its rooms are tastefully decorated, with lots of homey touches. Some 15 boat slips are provided for guests who arrive by water, and the inn has bicycles for rent. A full cooked breakfast is included in the rates, and there are several good restaurants within walking distance. Seasonal rates for doubles range from $49 to $69.

In Morehead City

The **Buccaneer Motor Lodge,** 2806 Arendell St., Morehead City, NC 28557 (tel. 919/726-3115 or toll free in NC 800/682-4982), has some in-room whirlpools, free coffee, free local telephone calls, a pool, and a moderately priced restaurant on the premises. Double-room rates are in the $35 to $69 range, depending on season.

The **Comfort Inn,** 3012 Arendell St., Morehead City, NC 28557 (tel. 919/247-3434 or toll free 800/422-5404 in NC, 800/228-5150 in other states), is on U.S. 70 East at Morehead Plaza, just across the causeway from Atlantic Beach. There are some in-room whirlpools, and a complimentary continental breakfast is included in rates, which range from $40 to $69 for doubles, depending on the season.

Atlantic Beach

There are excellent motels spread up and down Bogue Banks, and, like the natives, I'll use "Atlantic Beach" as a catch-all name.

The **Islander Motor Inn** at Emerald Isle (P.O. Box 1035), Swansboro, NC 28584 (tel. 919/354-3464, or toll free 800/354-3464 in North Carolina), has 80 rooms directly on the ocean and has become one of the most popular motels on the island. Its swimming pool sits right at the edge of a broad sand beach, and there's a sundeck with comfortable lounging chairs. The rooms, some with kitchenettes, are easily accessible to pool, beach, and restaurant. The manager will help arrange charter fishing or golf at the Star Hill Golf and Country Club. There's a lounge with entertainment and dancing on weekends. From April 1 through Labor Day, doubles start at $70, dropping after Labor Day.

At Atlantic Beach proper, and also directly on the ocean, the **Oceanana Resort Motel,** P.O. Box 250, Atlantic Beach, NC 28512 (tel. 919/726-4111), completely won me over as the perfect family vacation "home." There are so many extras here that it's hard to know where to start listing them. For starters, there's a free fishing pier for guests. Then, to make it easy for fishermen to turn the day's catch into the evening meal, there's a huge bin out by the pool that holds charcoal, grills, firestarter, and even ketchup and mustard (not for fish—they're for the hot dog/hamburger crowd). And there's never a charge for any of them. Picnic tables are right there also to make outdoor eating a pleasure. For the small fry, there's a playground with an attractive assortment of play equipment (like the pirate's lookout tower, swinging bridge, and pioneer wagon). For all ages, the semiweekly watermelon party out by the pool is a festive occasion, and you just have to see the free tropical breakfast spread under an open poolside pavilion to believe it—more than 15 fresh fruits! It's served every morning from 8 to 10 a.m. The coffeeshop is open from 5 a.m. to midnight, and there's a grill for fast-order foods out by the fishing pier. Every room has a refrigerator, some have stoves. And those portable grills may be brought to the lawn area in front of your room (but not on upper-floor decks) to cook dinner right at your front door. Doubles range from $52 to $60, and kitchen units from $73 to $154 from May 20 to Labor Day, then drop.

A. B. Cooper, the owner-manager, tells me that reservations are necessary at least a month in advance—people keep coming back each year, and the place stays pretty well booked. And that's been going on so long, over 45 years, that he keeps a "growing scale" posted to measure the height of children who come each year. It really is a super vacation spot, even if the only "family" you bring along is yourself.

Facing 1,000 feet of broad ocean beach on Salter Path Road, the **John Yancey Motor Hotel,** P.O. Box 790, Atlantic Beach, NC 28512 (tel. 919/726-5188, or toll free 800/533-3700, 800/682-3700 in North Carolina), has more than 95 rooms, a games room, free coffee and doughnuts, a pool, and nearby golf and tennis privileges. I find this chain's rooms much more spacious than most, and the rates modest. Doubles during the peak season are $57 to $90. From Labor Day to April 15, they drop considerably, and there's always a 10% discount for senior citizens. Youngsters 18 and under stay free in their parents' room.

For a very comprehensive listing of motels, restaurants, and attractions, write the **Carteret County Chamber of Commerce,** P.O. Box 1198, Morehead City, NC 28557 (tel. 919/726-6831), and ask for their free vacation guide.

Campgrounds

The **Salter Path Campground** on Salter Path Road (P.O. Box 721), Morehead City, NC 28557 (tel. 919/247-3525), overlooks the ocean on one side, Bogue Sound on the other. There are full hookups, a boat ramp, bathhouses, and a playground. Rates are $13 and up. For reservations, send a deposit.

Also on Salter Path Road, the **Arrowhead,** Rte. 1, Box 792, Morehead City, NC 28557 (tel. 919/247-3838), has showers, a store, pier fishing, a playground, drive-through waterfront sites, and golf nearby. Rates begin at $13.

WHERE TO EAT

Beaufort House, 502 Front St., Beaufort (tel. 919/728-7541), is on the boardwalk, overlooking the harbor. It's a pleasant, relaxed sort of place, specializing, of course, in fresh seafood from local waters, but with a large menu that includes beef tips, a wide variety of prime steaks, and southern fried chicken. There's also an excellent salad bar, and breads are home-baked (do try southern-style biscuits or cornbread). Service is friendly and efficient, and most entrees come with a choice of two fresh vegetables. Wine and beer are served, as are setups for mixed drinks. During the summer, there's live music on weekends. Hours are 11 a.m. to 2:30 p.m. and 5 to 9 p.m., to 10 p.m. on weekends; closed from December 22 to March 1. Lunch prices will average well under $10, dinner $6 to $19, and Sunday brunch is $9. Recommended.

The **Spouter Inn,** 218 Front St., Beaufort (tel. 919/728-5190), is a waterfront eatery popular with locals and visitors alike. Dine by candlelight in the evening from a menu that specializes in fresh seafood, as well as a selection of continental dishes that are rather rare in this region. Prices are moderate to expensive, and reservations are recommended for dinner. Lunch hours are 11:30 a.m. to 2 p.m., dinner from 5:30 to 9:30 p.m., and there's a champagne brunch on Sunday.

In Morehead City, **Captain Bill's Waterfront Restaurant,** 701 Evans St. (tel. 919/726-2166), overlooks fishing boats on Bogue Sound. It's a family-style restaurant that retains its popularity year after year. Locals look forward to the conch stew on Wednesday and Saturday, as well as all-you-can-eat nightly specials for $5.50 to $8, which are likely to feature fried fish on Monday, popcorn shrimp on Tuesday and Thursday, and fish and shrimp on Friday. As you can see, prices are moderate to cheap, and nonseafood-lovers will find a good selection of nonfinny dishes. Desserts, sauces and salad dressings are all home-made.

Tony's Sanitary Fish Market and Restaurant, 501 Evans St., Morehead City (tel. 919/247-3111), has been family owned and operated since 1938. Located right on the waterfront, this large eatery (seats some 650 diners) offers no less than 50 items on its menu, most—as you would expect—related to the waters just outside. Broiled and fried seafoods, homemade clam chowder and she-crab soup are beloved favorites of locals, who patronize this moderately priced restaurant that serves continuously from 11 a.m. to 8:30 p.m. Closed December and January.

Mrs. Russell Willis's family has been serving the public since 1952 at **Mrs. Willis Restaurant** on 3002 Bridges St., Morehead City (tel. 919/726-3741). There's seafood, as you'd expect in this fishing center, but in addition, you'll find pit barbecue and choice charcoal steaks on the semi-à la carte menu, at prices that start at $4 and go up to $17. It's a cozy place, rather rustic, with a fireplace, background music, and very friendly service. You'll need to bring your own liquor; mixers are available. Open from 11:30 a.m. to 9:30 p.m.

Less than 20 miles south of Morehead are two eating places worth looking up. The **T & W Oyster Bar and Restaurant,** N.C. 58 North, Cape Carteret, (tel. 919/393-8838), is five miles north of the Emerald Isle bridge, and looks like a country roadhouse from the outside. Inside, however, the sloping, beamed ceiling and two large dining rooms, each with a fireplace, have a simplicity bordering on sophistication. Seafood is featured, reservations aren't necessary, and dress is casual. Prices for a regular dinner are $6 to $10, and seafood combination plates run $8 to $10 depending on the assortment you wish to order. The oyster bar is very popular here, with a half dozen on the half shell costing only $3.50 (a fact that made me cringe when I remembered New York prices). And they sell steamed oysters and clams by the half *peck*. It isn't too hard to find. Just take N.C. 24 south from Morehead City, turn right on N.C. 58, and T & W is about five miles down the road. It opens at 5 p.m. and closes around 10 p.m. Monday through Saturday; on Sunday it's open after church to 10 p.m.

When the time comes that you simply cannot face another meal of things that used to swim, look for the **New York Deli,** Causeway Shopping Center, Atlantic Beach (tel. 919/726-0111). It's a deli/restaurant that features sliced deli meats and cheeses, a whole slew of sandwiches, homemade salads, desserts, specialty food items, and a nice selection of imported beers and wines. They'll make up box lunches and specialty trays, as well as providing take-out service for virtually everything.

THINGS TO SEE AND DO

Beach activities, naturally, are the top attraction along the coast. And fishing is especially good here—the Gulf Stream brings in blue marlin, tarpon, and other prizes in addition to inshore fish. There are some 80 miles of surf in this area and 400 miles of protected waterways. If you're a boat owner, there's an excellent marina on **Harkers Island,** Calico Jack's Marina (tel. 919/728-3575). And if you don't have your own boat, there's a ferry that leaves from Harkers Island Fishing Center (tel. 919/728-3907) for Cape Lookout (a 35-minute trip) between April and December for a day of surf fishing or beachcombing (for details, write: Superintendent, Cape Lookout National Seashore, P.O. Box 690, Beaufort, NC 28516). The fee is modest, and once at the cape, you can use the jitney service that roams up and down the sands between Cape Point and the lighthouse to move fishermen from one spot to another. Bring a picnic, insect repellent, and your own water supply. I love the "get-away-from-it-all" island atmosphere, and it's perfect for anyone who likes sailboats, lots of sun, and miles and miles of sand beach. Incidentally, the unique diamond-patterned lighthouse has stood here since 1859.

A near-perfect day or evening on the water can be arranged by contacting the *Carolina Princess,* 8th Street Waterfront, P.O. Box 1663, Morehead City, NC 28557 (tel. 919/726-5479 or toll free 800/682-3456). The *Princess* is a trim vessel that can accommodate up to 100 passengers. It has a snackbar, a sundeck, and coolers to hold the day's catch on ice. Full-day deep-sea fishing trips run around $45, and from May to October, they offer dinner cruises down Bogue Sound and the Inland Waterway for a seafood or steak dinner at the Galley Stack Restaurant, at prices of $20 for adults, $15 for children. For the ultimate in coastal cruising, inquire about their Ocracoke Excursion, which sets sail at 7 a.m. from Morehead City for the island of Ocracoke. A continental breakfast and afternoon champagne reception are on-board affairs, while lunch is ashore, with time allowed for sightseeing.

When you begin to feel a bit waterlogged, plenty of sightseeing is within easy reach. For instance, down at the very tip of **Bogue Island** (you're on it if you stay at Atlantic Beach) sits old **Fort Macon,** a Civil War landmark now restored and open to the public at no charge. The jetties (designed by Robert E. Lee), moats, gun emplacements, and dungeons make up terrific exploring territory. The museum is quite good, though small, and the public beach has bathhouses, a snackbar, and lifeguards.

A trip to **Beaufort** is really—that overworked phrase—"a trip back in time." North Carolina's third-oldest town, it dates back to 1713 and still reflects its early history. There are two 200-year-old houses and more than a hundred that are over 100 years old along the narrow streets. The old graveyard (still called the "Burying Ground") positions its occupants facing east so they will be facing the rising sun on "Judgment Morn"; and it holds the remains of a British officer who wanted to be buried with his boots on, so was lowered into the grave in a standing-up position. The earliest markers that are still legible are dated 1756, and the headquarters of the **Beaufort Historical Association** in the 1825 Josiah Bell House, 138 Turner St. (tel. 919/728-5225), will furnish a map of the cemetery. The last weekend in June, Beaufort holds an **Old Homes Tour** and a reenactment of the Pirate Invasion of 1747. Any time, you can stop by the historical association headquarters for self-guiding tour maps of the **Beaufort Restoration Area,** which includes the 1767 Joseph Bell House, 1796 Carteret County Courthouse, 1829 county jail, 1859 apothecary shop, and 1778 Samuel Leffers House, home of the region's first schoolmaster. The 1830 Rustell House functions as an art gallery from June through Labor Day. Charming costumed hostesses guide visitors through the restored area of the state's third-oldest town, which is open from 9:30 a.m. to 4:30 p.m. Monday through Saturday. Admission is $3 for adults, $1.25 for ages 8 to 12.

And don't miss the fine, new, state-owned **North Carolina Maritime Museum** at 315 Front St. (tel. 919/728-7317). It has splendid natural and maritime history exhibits, ship models, and shell collections, and offers intriguing field trips, lectures, and programs for all ages. The Wooden Boat Show is held here annually the first weekend in May, and on the third Thursday in August it's the site of one of the South's zaniest events, the Strange Seafood Festival. It's your golden opportunity to chow down on marinated octopus, squid, stingray casserole, and other deep-sea delicacies. Admission is $5, and it's so popular you must reserve in advance! Museum admission is free, and it's open from 9 a.m. to 5 p.m. Monday through Friday, from 10 a.m. to 5 p.m. on Saturday and from 2 to 5 p.m. on Sunday; closed major holidays.

New Bern, a little inland on U.S. Bus. 70 and U.S. 17, was once the capital of North Carolina when it was a royal colony. The **visitors center,** 101 Middle Street, (tel. 637-3111) can rent you a taped walking-tour guide and furnish detailed information on historic sites. The 48-room **Tryon Palace,** 613 Pollock St. (tel. 638-1560), built as both the capitol and residence for the royal governor, has been authentically restored and beautifully furnished. It's easy to see, walking through the elegant rooms, why this mansion was once called the most beautiful in America. It was built in 1767–1770; then the main building burned in 1798. After that it lay in ruins until the restoration in 1952–1959. The handsome grounds and gardens surrounding Tryon Palace are designed in 18th-century style. Two other exhibition landmarks in the 13-acre Tryon Palace Restoration and Gardens Complex are the **John Wright Stanly House** (1780), a sophisticated late-Georgian-style mansion, with town-house gardens, and the **Stevenson House** (1805), built by a merchant and noted for its rare Federal antiques. Costumed hostesses guide tours Monday through Saturday from 9:30 a.m. to 4 p.m., from 1:30 to 4 p.m. on Sunday. Closed Thanksgiving Day, December 24 to 26, and New Year's Day. The combination savings ticket (good for all tours, the landmarks, and the gardens) is $9 for adults, $4 for children through high school; for the palace and gardens only, it's $6 for adults, $2 for children. On the grounds, craftsfolk demonstrate 18th-century home arts. Historical dramas supplement the regular hostess interpretation during the summer months. Special events, including candlelight tours of the complex, are held at Christmas and other seasons.

The **New Bern Firemen's Museum,** 420 Broad St. (tel. 919/637-3105), is 2½ blocks from the Tryon Palace Restoration and Gardens Complex. Firefighting equipment dating back to the early 19th century, memorabilia from the mother city of Bern, Switzerland, and Civil War artifacts make this a memorable, small museum. Admission is 75¢ for adults, 25¢ for children. Open Tuesday through Saturday from 9:30 a.m. to noon and 1 to 5 p.m., on Sunday from 1 to 5 p.m.

Historic **Christ Episcopal Church, First Presbyterian Church,** and **National Cemetery** are among the many sites that may be visited in old New Bern. There are over 180 18th- and 19th-century structures in New Bern listed on the National Register of Historic Places.

South of New Bern, the little town of Swansboro borders the White Oak River, and is a real charmer, with interesting little shops and renovated waterfront buildings and docks. The **Mullet Festival,** held here every October, draws huge crowds from around the Southeast. A free passenger ferry runs from Swansboro to Bear Island, where Hammocks Beach is a state park dominated by high sand dunes, a maritime forest, and more than four miles of unspoiled beach.

Almost due east of Swansboro, Jacksonville sits inland, but only a 20-minute drive from choice beaches. Focal point of the city is the adjacent New River Marine Base, universally known as Camp LeJeune. The 110,000-acre reservation is one of the world's most complete amphibious military training centers, and you can obtain a pass to drive through unrestricted parts of the grounds if you present your driver's license and car registration to personnel at the information center next to the main gate on N.C. 24. Organized tours can be arranged for groups, and in June, the Marine Corps Air Station stages a spectacular demonstration of parachuting and free-fall acrobatic skills; call 919/451-2197 for exact dates and other details about the base.

For a true North Carolina coastal seafood experience, drive south of Jacksonville to the little fishing village of Sneads Ferry, which is loaded with eateries featuring right-off-the-boat entrees, steamed, broiled, or fried to perfection.

For further information about the Swansboro/Jacksonville area, contact the Greater Jacksonville/Onslow Chamber of Commerce, 1 Marine Blvd. North, P.O. Box 765, Jacksonville, NC 28541-0165. They can also help you with accommodations, places to eat, etc.

3. In and Around Wilmington

Down near the southern end of North Carolina's coast is Wilmington, a city that has figured prominently in the state's history since 1732. Known first as New Carthage, then New Liverpool, New Town, and Newton, in 1739 it was given its present name in honor of the Earl of Wilmington. Technically it isn't even on the coast—it's inland a bit at the junction of the Cape Fear River's northeast and northwest branches. And given the treacherous shoals that guarded the mouth of the Cape Fear when explorers first arrived in 1524, it's a wonder upriver Wilmington ever developed into an important port. But its protected riverfront site gave access to a valuable waterway for the movement of goods to and from Europe during colonial days, and since then the town has grown steadily as a commercial shipping center.

The first English settlers, from the Massachusetts Bay Colony, actually landed on the west bank of the river in 1662, and they were followed shortly by another group from Barbados. But they suffered mightily from Indian conflicts and from virtual abandonment by England. Pirates roamed the river freely and there wasn't much of a settlement until Brunswick Town was founded about 16 miles south of Wilmington in 1725 and a fort built to guard the passageway up Cape Fear. Soon surrounded by large, thriving plantations (some of them still intact today), Brunswick prospered until the British tried to destroy it by fire in 1776. It never really recovered, and it ceased to exist as a town about 1830, becoming a part of the landholdings of Orton Plantation until it was named a state historic site in this century.

Wilmington, too, played a part in the Revolution. In 1765, eight years before the Boston Tea Party, patriots here refused to allow the unloading of stamps to implement the infamous Stamp Act and forced the resignation of the stamp master. But in 1780 the city fell to Lord Cornwallis, and he headquartered in a house (still standing) all that winter before leaving for Yorktown and ultimate defeat.

This was one of the principal ports of the Confederacy during the Civil War, and many blockade runners, who eluded both northern ships that patrolled the coastline and the Cape Fear shoals to bring in supplies to the South, found a home berth here. So important was Wilmington that Fort Fisher, on the eastern shore of the river, sustained one of the heaviest bombardments of the war, falling just 90 days before the Confederacy met defeat.

During both world wars, Wilmington was a major port for the export of naval stores. Today the river is busier than ever with industrial shipping, and the town has become an important rail center as well.

The city holds on to its history in the visible remnants that are lovingly restored and maintained. All those exciting events from the past seem very close to the present when you walk through the old residential section of town (now an official "historic area"), around the grounds of Orton Plantation, among the excavated foundations of Brunswick Town houses, or examine blockade-runner relics at Fort Fisher. And just a hop, skip, and a jump away over on the coast, Wrightsville Beach (a family-oriented resort for generations) is the perfect place from which to explore the whole region—in between swimming, beachcombing, fishing, sailing, or just plain loafing, that is.

WHERE TO STAY

The **New Hanover County Convention and Visitors Bureau,** P.O. Box 266, Wilmington, NC 28402 (tel. 919/762-2900, or toll free 800/222-4757 in the eastern U.S., 800/922-7117 in North Carolina), will do more than just send you their "Accommodations Guide." If you're in the market for an apartment or cottage for a week or more (a dollar-saving method of vacationing that's hard to beat), and will write them far enough in advance describing just what you have in mind, they'll circulate your requirements in a bulletin that goes to owners and managers in the area who will then contact you directly.

If you want to stay in Wilmington rather than at Wrightsville Beach, the **Hilton Inn,** 301 N. Water St., Wilmington, NC 28401 (tel. 919/763-9881), has superior rooms with doubles ranging from $70 to $92.

Next door to the Coast Line Convention Center, the **Coast Line Inn,** 503 Nutt St., Wilmington, NC 28401 (tel. 919/763-2800), has been designed to complement the restored historic rail depot for which it is named. Indeed, its adjacent full-service restaurant actually occupies one of the original railroad buildings, and, in addition to daily lunch and dinner service, has a nice bar and periodic live entertainment. The inn's 51 rooms all have good views of the Cape Fear River, and suites afford two river views. In decor, the Coast Line Inn features lots of mahogany, brass, and rich leather, and guest-room furnishings go beyond mere comfort. Rooms adapted for the handicapped are available, and double-room rates are in the $60 to $75 range, with suites starting at $90.

Two good, less expensive motels are the **Days Inn,** U.S. 17 and U.S. 74, 5040 Market St., Wilmington, NC 28405 (tel. 919/799-6300, or toll free 800/325-2525), where doubles range from $33 to $49; and the **Heart of Wilmington Motel,** 311 N. 3rd St. (P.O. Box 195), Wilmington, NC 28401 (tel. 919/763-0121), with doubles from $38 to $55.

At the **Sheraton Wrightsville Beach Hotel,** 1706 N. Lumina Ave., Wrightsville Beach, NC 28480 (tel. 919/256-2231, or toll free 800/325-3535), all rooms have an ocean view, all have balconies or patios, and all are attractively furnished. Those that actually face the ocean are especially nice, with glass sliding doors opening directly to the beach on the first floor and individual balconies on upper levels. A large, oceanside pool has shade areas and a refreshment bar, and there's a wading pool for young children. The lounge offers dancing and seasonal entertainment. Dinners in the charming dining room are good and moderately priced in the $10 to $20 range. Guests enjoy golf privileges at a nearby private course, and would-be sailors will find sailboat rentals available. The hotel will also arrange golf-package weekends and charter-boat fishing trips. In fact, I found the staff here exceptionally friendly and helpful in all respects during my stay. Seasonal rates for doubles are $95 to $140 June through August, considerably lower other months.

About a mile down the beach, the seven-story **Blockade Runner Resort Hotel & Conference Center,** 275 Waynick Blvd., P.O. Box 555, Wrightsville Beach, NC 28480 (tel. 919/256-2251), has luxury rooms, heated oceanside pool, nightly entertainment, a playground for children, and sailboats for rent. The bright, cheerful dining room serves continental cuisine at moderate prices. Double rooms are $90 and up mid-May to mid-September, lower the rest of the year.

A Nearby Beach Village

South of Wrightsville and Carolina beaches, the little settlement of Kure Beach still retains much of its fishing village past, and the **Dockside Inn,** 210 N. 2nd St., P.O. Box 373, Kure Beach, NC 28449 (tel. 919/458-4192), offers the sort of low-keyed beach accommodations that fit right into the easygoing ambience of the area. The owner, personable Kip Darling, says he "psychologically retired" at the age of 38, fled the rigors of Chicago winters, traded in his

Cadillac and BMW for a four-wheel-drive truck, and watched his blood pressure drop dramatically "the moment I drove into Kure Beach." He lives on the property and takes a personal interest in the welfare of his guests, making this a warm, friendly place to stay. The long, U-shaped motel has a dozen oceanfront rooms (all with private porches) that accommodate up to 4, 11 efficiencies, and 13 standard guest rooms. All are attractively decorated in beach colors of blue, gray, and mauve; and most have a coffee pot, popcorn popper, toaster, and all the tableware, cookware, and various other utensils you'll need for light snacking. The smashing Captain's Cabin that goes for $10 above other rates is without question the star of the Docksider, with its queen-size bed romantically ensconsed on a raised platform looking out to sea. The pool, surrounded by a wooden deck, which sports a gazebo for shade, is the setting for Sunday-morning coffee, juice, and doughnuts, and The Sunketch, a topside sundeck, is another popular focal point for convivial gatherings. Golfers have three superb local courses within a 15-minute drive.

Summer rates range from $77 to $92 per room (up to four people per room, $5 per additional person per night); in winter, they run $50 and under. There are weekly rates at a 10% discount, and singles pay $5 less per night for any accommodation. Recommended.

An Island Retreat

A 45-minute drive southeast from Wilmington on U.S. 17 South, with a left turn onto N.C.87, will bring you to the little town of Southport, jumping-off point for the passenger ferry to Bald Head Island (the terminal is on Moore Street. You must call ahead to book on the ferry (tel. 919/457-5006), and day trippers pay a $20 fare; resident visitors and golfers, $12.

For nature-lovers, it's a trip not to be missed, and Bald Head Island invites a much-longer-than-one-day visit. Some 3,000 pristine acres, with 14 miles of sandy beachfront, miles and miles of salt marshes, tidal creeks, and maritime forests also hold an 18-hole championship golf course, the Village of Bald Head Island with shops and restaurants, private homes, and condominiums.

Still, man's intrusion has been kindly. For example, no cars are permitted on the island—transportation is strictly provided by golf carts and similar jitneys used to transport arriving and departing guests. Sea oats, yucca, beach grasses, live oaks, red cedar trees, palmetto, sabal palms, loblolly pines, and a lovely yellow wildflower called galardia still thrive, seemingly undisturbed by the human touch. Birds like the white ibis, great blue heron, snowy egret, black ducks, mallards, and pintails frequent the island, and naturalist Bill Brooks works with the Bald Head Conservancy to protect the loggerhead sea turtles who nest here. All in all, Bald Head Island (which takes its name from a high, bare dune that was a much-used lookout point during both the Revolution and the Civil War) is a happy coming together of mankind and the natural world in a remarkable family resort setting.

Private homes, as well as condominiums in communities with names like Swan's Quarter, Timber Creek, and Royal James Landing, are available as rentals, as are two rather rustic houses that were home to lighthouse keepers and their families from 1903 to 1958. All units are beautifully furnished, with full kitchens, TV, and other modern conveniences, and most rates include the use of one of the electric-cart passenger vehicles. Activities on the island include swimming (there's a pool as well as all those miles of beaches), biking, tennis, golf, canoeing, fishing, and just plain beachcombing or bird-watching.

Daily rates are in the $120 to $200 range during summer months, $105 to $180 other months; weekly rates run $700 to $910 in summer, $400 to $720 off-season. For full details and bookings, contact: Bald Head Island, P.O. Box 10999, Bald Head Island, NC 28461 (tel. 919/457-5000 or toll free 800/722-6450 in North Carolina, 800/443-6305 elsewhere.

Campgrounds

The **Camelot Campground** (formerly the Wilmington Safari Campground), 7415 Market St., Wilmington, NC 28405 (tel. 919/686-7705), sits on 43 wooded acres on U.S. 17. There's a pool, recreation room, playground, laundry, grocery store, and propane gas. Rates start at $12.

WHERE TO EAT

As is true of so many coastal towns, Wilmington's best dining spots are at the beaches or on its fringes, and you'll find more seafood spots (most of them excellent) than you'll have time to sample.

In-town exceptions are topped by **Stemmerman's,** 138 S. Front St. (tel. 919/763-7776), a charmingly converted 1855 grocery store. There are such unexpected features as stained-glass windows, chandeliers, and a river view. Under one roof, this amazing complex holds a grocery, bakery, café, deli, seven-suite inn, cocktail lounge and raw bar, Rathskellar pub, and a very good restaurant. In addition to the fresh seafood (try the broiled flounder with shrimp and oyster sauce), there's a steak menu and weekly chef specials such as rock Cornish game hen stuffed with wild rice and a raspberry sauce, curried chicken, and shrimp scampi. Lunch will run under $10, dinner under $20.

The popular **Pilot House Restaurant,** 2 Ann St. in Chandler's Wharf (tel. 919/343-0200), is lively at lunchtime when shoppers, downtown workers, and tourists surge in for crab quiche or Carolina seafood chowder. Dinner specialties range from fresh local seafoods to veal, beef, and fowl entrees, all prepared with deft special touches. Save room for the Caribbean fudge pie! Lunch ranges from $2.75 to $6.50, and dinner is in the $9 to $18 bracket. It's open from 11 a.m. to 3:30 p.m. and 5:30 to 10 p.m. Monday through Saturday.

For distinctively "down east" North Carolina barbecue, make a bee-line for **Skinner & Daniels,** 5214 Market St. (tel. 919/799-1790). Its heaping plates of barbecued pork, chicken, beef, short ribs, or Brunswick stew will satisfy the strongest "Q" craving at amazingly modest cost. It's open from 10 a.m. to 9 p.m. Monday through Saturday, and you can place take-out orders until 9 p.m.

The **King Neptune** is right in the center of Wrightsville Beach at 11 N. Lumina St. (tel. 919/256-2525), and is a very informal, very nautical place with two large dining rooms and a lounge to one side. Pictures of Wrightsville Beach in the '20s and '30s, along with colorful fish motifs adorn the walls. The menu announces that "It's fun to eat at the King Neptune," and indeed it is, for sometimes it seems that about half the permanent residents and almost all the tourists in town congregate here. The atmosphere is lively, and the food is superb. You can probably guess what gets star billing, but there is also a good selection of beef and even a pizza. Lunch prices can run anywhere from $3.50 to $8.50. Most dinner entrees on the à la carte menu are in the $8 to $16 range. Service is continuous from 11:30 a.m. to 11:30 p.m., and they don't accept reservations (except for large parties in the private room).

Right at the Wilmington edge of the Wrightsville Beach–Wilmington drawbridge (on your left if you're coming from the beach), is the **Bridge Tender,** Airlie Road on the Sound (tel. 919/256-4519). I found it the best possible way: someone told me about it! "It's reasonable," she told me, "yet has an elegant feeling, and it's relaxing to watch the boats go past and the bridge when it's raised." I found the Bridge Tender all of that, and in addition the food was just superb. The policy here is to keep the menu limited in order to serve top-quality meats and seafoods cooked by expert chefs. And it *is* limited in the number of items, but certainly not in imaginative preparation. There's an excellent Polynesian chicken, tender filets of chicken breast marinated in a special teriyaki sauce and broiled just right, and tender Alaskan king crab legs served on long-grain and wild rice with drawn butter. Prices run $11 to $22 at dinner, $4.75 to $10 at lunch. And there's a very good salad bar (you serve yourself there with every dinner or lunch entree). The walnut layer cake brought back fond memories of those my grandmother used to make; it's a very southern dessert and I've rarely run into it in northern climes. They're open seven days a week for lunch (11:30 a.m. to 2 p.m.) and dinner (5:30 to 10 p.m., 'til 11 p.m. on Friday and Saturday). It's a good idea to reserve for dinner or the locally popular Sunday buffet.

Everybody in the area knows and loves **The Raw Bar,** at 13 E. Salisbury St. at the beach, right where U.S. 74 meets the ocean. This highly informal and very-often crowded restaurant serves oysters and clams, both on the half shell and steamed, as well as delicious seafood platters, either broiled or fired. Prices range from downright inexpensive to moderate. This "drop-in" place is open from 5 to 10 p.m.

Windows Oceanfront Restaurant, 2700 Lumina Ave. (tel. 919/256-5050) adds mesquite-grilled steaks, chicken, and pork entrees to a menu that features the freshest of seafood. Dinner hours are 5:30 to 10:30 p.m. daily, and prices are in the $12 to $20 range.

It's candlelight dining in a sanctified setting at the **Steeple Restaurant,** 205 Charlotte Ave., Carolina Beach (tel. 919/458-4939), which began life as a church. Seafood comes broiled, char-grilled, sautéed, or steamed, and the menu is rounded out with steak, chicken, and veal. Hours are 5:30 to 10:30 p.m., with prices of $12 to $25. On weekends, there's live music in the lounge.

For inexpensive Mexican food, stop by **Tijuana Fats' Great Mexican Food and Bar,** 232 Causeway Dr., Wrightsville Beach (tel. 919/256-8048). Eat on the premises, or take out. Hours are 11 a.m. to 2 a.m. daily.

Sooner or later you're bound to hear the name **Calabash** in connection with food. Well, that's a town about 35 miles south of Wilmington (almost to the South Carolina border, in fact) on U.S. 17 that's so small it wasn't even shown on state maps for years. What literally put it on the map is the cluster of about 20 seafood restaurants that vie with one another to serve the biggest and best platter of seafood at the lowest price. The 150 residents of this small village use family recipes handed down from generation to generation, and last year they served 1½ *million* people some 668,000 pounds of flounder and 378,000 pounds of shrimp, to say nothing of tons and tons of oysters, scallops, and other fish. That's an impressive record, and although I found the Wrightsville Beach area more than adequate when it comes to food, a Calabash trip is an experience.

Recommendations for specific restaurants? I wouldn't even try! And you won't need them—according to locals, you can't miss, no matter which one you choose.

THINGS TO SEE AND DO

To get a delightful overview of the historic Wilmington waterfront, hop aboard the **Capt. J. N. Maffitt riverboat** (tel. 919/343-1776), which departs from the foot of Ann Street at Chandler's Wharf for a five-mile loop of the Cape Fear River. It skirts the busy harbor, passes the Cotton Exchange renovation, the new Waterfront Park, the U.S. Coast Guard icebreaker *Northwind,* and stops at the dock for passengers who wish to disembark to tour the battleship U.S.S. *North Carolina.* The half-hour trips leave daily at 11 a.m. and 3 p.m. June through August, and at 3 p.m. in May and September. Cost is $3 for adults, $1.50 for ages 1 to 12.

Before you begin any sort of sightseeing tour, I strongly suggest that you stop by the **New Hanover County Convention and Visitors Bureau** (tel. 919/762-2900, or toll free 800/222-4757 in the eastern U.S., 800/922-7117 in North Carolina), to pick up their free brochures on the many attractions of Cape Fear County. This super-efficient staff is located at 24 N. 3rd St., or you may want to write for information in advance to P.O. Box 266, Wilmington, NC 28402. There's a self-guided walking tour of historic Wilmington in great detail, giving background information on everything you'll want to see, including the **Cotton Exchange.** That's an in-town shopping center of malls, arcades, and courtyards in the old cotton exchange with its two-foot-thick brick walls and hurricane rods. The small shops and restaurants are a delight, and the wrought-iron lanterns and benches add to the charm of their setting. It's right on the riverfront, just across from the Hilton Inn, and there's an ample parking deck adjacent.

Another "must" is **Chandler's Wharf,** also on the riverfront, at the southern end. It encompasses a fine nautical museum with a two-masted schooner, the 147-foot-long *Harry W. Adams,* and four other vessels, along with spiffy specialty shops in renovated and restored buildings. Across the street, two warehouses are home to more shops, galleries, and restaurants. Wooden sidewalks, white picket fences, and cobblestone alleyways lend the shopping-museum complex a distinctive 19th-century ambience.

If you'd rather have a guide for that walking tour, they're available at **Thalian Hall** from Historic Wilmington Tours, 3rd and Princess streets (tel. 919/763-9328). Tickets are $6 for adults, $1 for students; children under 6 are free. Those prices cover an audiovisual orientation and admission to all buildings, as well as your guide.

In the **Historic Wilmington** old residential area, bounded roughly by Nun, Princess, Front, and 4th streets, the **Burgwin-Wright House,** 224 Market St. (tel. 919/762-0570), was built in 1771 and used by Lord Cornwallis as his headquarters in 1781. It's a perfect, beautifully restored example of a colonial gentleman's town house. You can tour the interior Tuesday through Saturday from 10 a.m. to 5 p.m. Adults pay $3; children, $2.

Also at 3rd and Market is **St. James Episcopal Church,** a beautiful building erected in 1839 to replace the 1751 church, which had been used by the British as a stable during the Revolution. The Spanish painting *Ecce Homo* that hangs inside was taken from a captured pirate ship in 1748 and has been estimated to be between 400 and 600 years old.

The **New Hanover County Museum,** 814 Market St. (tel. 919/763-0852), showcases the lower Cape Fear region's social and natural history. Especially fascinating are the Civil War artifacts and dioramas from the former Blockade Runner Museum. Followers of fashion will appreciate the fine collection of 19th- and 20th-century costumes. It's free and open from 9 a.m. to 5 p.m. Tuesday through Saturday, and from 2 to 5 p.m. Sunday. Extensive renovations are planned in 1990, which will close the museum temporarily, but dates were not set as we went to press.

These are only highlights—just walking the old tree-shaded streets is an exercise in imagination.

Outside Wilmington, take U.S. 76 toward the beach and watch for **Airlie Gardens.** Once the plantation home of a wealthy rice planter, Airlie is surrounded by huge lawns, serene lakes, and natural, wooded gardens that hold just about every kind of azalea in existence. Admission is $5 per adult, $2 for children, and the gardens are open during the daylight hours from early March until late fall. The blooms are at their height in the early spring, but even when they've faded, this is a lovely spot that will set you dreaming of Old South life.

Poplar Grove Plantation, a restored Greek Revival manor house and estate dating from 1850, is nine miles northeast of town on U.S. 17 (tel. 919/686-9518). Outbuildings include a smokehouse and slave quarters, and there's a country store and tea room. "Living History" tours are conducted (adults pay $3.50, under 12, $2) daily: from 9 a.m. to 5 p.m. Monday through Saturday, and from noon to 6 p.m. on Sunday, except for the month of January, when it's closed. Outbuildings, gardens, farmyard, farm animals, picnic tables, craft artists-in-residence, and a country store are all covered by the admission charge. Moderately priced meals are served from 11 a.m. to 3 p.m. weekdays and noon to 5 p.m. on Sunday in the Plantation Tea Room.

Greenfield Gardens, just off U.S. 421 South, is Wilmington's largest municipal park justly famous for its scenic millpond, a sunken garden of native North Carolina flowers, and the Venus fly trap, which is found naturally in the Carolinas and no other place in the world. In the spring and summer, camellias, azaleas, and roses bloom in profusion, and the five-mile drive around Greenfield Lake is beautiful any time of the year.

Follow U.S. 421 South from the park and you'll reach the **Fort Fisher State Historic Site,** P.O. Box 68, Kure Beach, NC 28449 (tel. 919/458-5538). One of the Confederacy's largest, most technically advanced forts, Fort Fisher protected Blockade Runners bringing in vital goods to the port of Wilmington. After withstanding two of the heaviest naval bombardments of the Civil War, the fort finally fell to Union forces in the conflict's largest land-sea battle. The visitor center displays artifact exhibits of that era, and an audiovisual program is given. Costumed tour guides welcome visitors, and seasonal living-history events are depicted. The fort and visitor center are open from 9 a.m. to 5 p.m. Monday through Saturday and from 1 to 5 p.m. on Sunday; closed Monday in winter. Admission is free.

Not far from Fort Fisher, a toll ($5 for car and passengers) ferry makes the half-hour crossing of the Cape Fear River and deposits you at the quaint little village of Southport. Turning north on N.C. 87, then left at N.C. 133, you'll reach **Brunswick Town State Historic Site.** The excavated home foundations have been left as archeological exhibits, but there are displays that re-create colonial life here, and the walls of St. Phillip's Anglican Church are still partially standing. The visitor center is open from 9 a.m. to 5 p.m. Monday through Saturday and from 1 to 5 p.m. on Sunday, April through October; the rest of the year it's open from 10 a.m. to 4 p.m. Tuesday through Saturday and from 1 to 4 p.m. on Sunday. Admission is free. For information, write Rte. 1, Box 55, Winnabow, NC 28479 (tel. 919/371-6613).

Orton Plantation, between Southport and Wilmington on N.C. 133 (tel. 919/371-6851), is a private residence, and the mansion is not open to the public. But the magnificent gardens, bordered by long avenues of live oaks and planted with camellias, azaleas, and thousands of other ornamental plants, can be seen March through November (8 a.m. to 5 p.m.) for an admission of $5 ($2.50 for children 6 to 12). The formal and informal gardens are in a lovely setting overlooking old rice fields and the Cape Fear River.

Back at Wilmington, you'll see signs on U.S. 74 (it's also U.S. 17 and U.S. 76 at this point) leading to the **U.S.S.** *North Carolina* **Battleship Memorial** (tel. 919/762-1829). The ship, which was commissioned in 1941, is permanently berthed here as a memorial to the state's World War II dead. You can tour most of the ship, and the museum presents a pictorial history of the *North Carolina's* Pacific campaigns. It's open daily from 8 a.m. to sunset, and costs $5 for adults, $2.50 for children 6 to 11. From early June through Labor Day, there's a 70-minute sound and light show, *The Immortal Showboat,* at 9 p.m. every night, at a cost of $3 for adults, $1.50 for children. A visitor center has a large gift shop and snackbar, as well as an auditorium where a 10-minute orientation film is shown.

North Carolina's first battle of the Revolution took place 20 miles northwest of Wilmington (via U.S. 421 and N.C. 210) at **Moores Creek.** The site is now a national battlefield, as well it might be, since the victory of local patriots squelched a Tory scheme to invade and seize all the southern colonies. The earthworks and bridge have been reconstructed, and there's a visitor center and museum.

VII

PIEDMONT NORTH CAROLINA

1. RALEIGH, DURHAM, CHAPEL HILL
2. WINSTON-SALEM
3. CHARLOTTE

Perhaps nowhere in the South do the old and the new come together quite so dramatically as in that section of North Carolina that lies between the coastal plains and the mountains. The Piedmont, as this region is called, holds mementos of American history that predate the Revolution (it was in 1771 that some 2,000 farmers of Alamance County organized to protest British taxation and were savagely subdued by a royal governor at the Battle of Alamance near Burlington), as well as the first nuclear-reactor building in the country devoted exclusively to the peaceful use of the atom (on the North Carolina State University campus in Raleigh).

The contrast is especially marked in cities such as Winston-Salem, where the mammoth tobacco industry is represented by R. J. Reynolds Tobacco Company, manufacturers of several major cigarette brands and pipe blends, and where the Joseph Schlitz Brewing Company produces over four million barrels of beer each year in one of the largest such plants under a single roof; while in another part of town the streets and buildings of Old Salem are perfectly restored to reflect the life of Moravians who planned the community in 1766.

The land itself is as varied in this region as the industry, agriculture, and recreation that utilize it. From the red clay hills around Raleigh and Greensboro, to the flat fields of tobacco, peanuts, and vegetables in the midlands, to the rolling sand dunes alive with long-leaf pines and peach orchards in the Sandhills farther south, there is a pleasant, ever-changing character to the landscape. Some of my most cherished childhood memories were formed against the background of wind softly sighing through those pines, and the white blossoms of dogwood growing wild in wooded stretches along the highways always reminded me of snowdrifts sprinkled among other just-greening trees in early spring. Azaleas, camellias, and a host of summer-blooming flowers add to the visual beauty of this part of the state.

Higher forms of education are also an important part of the Piedmont character, where the "Research Triangle" you'll run across so often in conversation and directions refers to Duke University in Durham, the University of North Carolina in Chapel Hill, and North Carolina State in Raleigh. Wake Forest University, founded in 1834 in the town of that name near Raleigh and relocated to the western edge of Winston-Salem in the 1950s, is another leading educational institution. And literally scores of small private colleges and junior colleges are located throughout the region.

For the visitor, the Piedmont has sophisticated entertainment in its cities, the simplicity of rustic, outdoor life in fishing camps along the Catawba, Cape Fear, and Neuse rivers, the excitement of intramural collegiate sports competitions, and the challenge of some of the world's greatest championship golf courses. Throw in sightseeing trips that will delight any history buff, and you have in this one 21,000-square-mile region much of the "variety" of that "Variety Vacationland" slogan.

1. Raleigh, Durham, Chapel Hill

RALEIGH

State government has been the principal business conducted in Raleigh since 1792, when it became the state's capital. A five-acre square that holds the state capitol is the focal point for a cluster of state office buildings in the heart of the city. From it radiate wide boulevards and lovely residential streets shaded by trees that frame some of the older homes. Downtown Raleigh has been transformed by a $2-million mall, where trees and fountains and statuary create a park-like shopping oasis from the capitol to the civic center. No fewer than six college campuses dot the city streets with wide lawns and impressive brick buildings. The oldest, St. Mary's College, was founded in 1842; and the "youngest," North Carolina State University, in 1887. New suburbs and gigantic shopping centers dominate the outskirts, but they somehow escape the "little boxes" image of so much suburban construction, with nicely designed homes blending into a landscape that retains much of its original wooded character.

Raleigh has, of course, witnessed much of the state's history: It was the setting for fiery legislative debate just prior to the Civil War that led at last to North Carolina's secession from the Union in 1861 (the last southern state to pull out); it endured Union occupation by General Sherman in 1865; and it saw the west wing of its imposing Grecian Doric capitol building turned into a rowdy barroom by "carpetbagger" and "scalawag" legislators during Reconstruction days, its steps permanently nicked from whisky barrels rolling in and out of the building. It was the stage on which Gov. Charles Aycock launched his campaign for education revival in the early 1900s, and from its state buildings has come strong support for industrial development that makes North Carolina one of the most progressive of the southern states.

All of this, plus the abundance of good accommodations, makes Raleigh the ideal base from which to explore the Triangle area—which is what we'll do here. Both Chapel Hill and Durham are within easy reach for day trips, and after a day of sightseeing, the capital city becomes an entertainment center for anything from smart, supper-club shows and dancing to Broadway theater to cultural events.

Where to Stay

If you're going first class or feel the need to splurge for a night or two and want a truly "southern" ambience, your best bet is **Plantation Inn,** 6401 North Blvd. (P.O. Box 11333), Raleigh, NC 27604 (tel. 919/876-1411, or toll free 800/992-9662, 800/521-1932 in North Carolina), located in a restful, pine-wooded setting on U.S. 1 North, some five miles out of town. The main building, a colonial, white-columned structure, evokes visions of the Old South. And that legendary southern hospitality is embodied in a coffee bar which dispenses free cups 24 hours a day in the gracious lobby (sporting portraits of Robert E. Lee and Stonewall Jackson), which opens onto a terrazzo terrace overlooking the lake and wooded lawn. Rates for the large, handsomely furnished rooms begin at $65 for a double; and the tastefully appointed restaurant serves everything from a hamburger to a superb buffet at lunch or dinner featuring roast prime rib of beef au jus at $18. Other dinner entrees range from $9 to $20. There's live organ music during dinner hours, and the Carriage Club Lounge on the lake level of the main building is a pleasant before- or after-dinner retreat. This is a favorite of international business travelers, and you may well encounter an Arab executive in native dress or a Japanese technician and his family quartered here while looking for a permanent home. Because it is so popular, it's advisable to reserve rooms at least three weeks in advance.

More centrally located, and a great local favorite, is the **Velvet Cloak Inn,** 1505 Hillsborough St., Raleigh, NC 27605 (tel. 919/828-0333), within a few blocks of both downtown and the North Carolina State University campus. A pseudo–New Orleans motif is carried out with wrought-iron balconies and in the room decor. There is an indoor swimming pool, and the Charter Room Restaurant and Baron's Supper Club are both on the premises. Rates here range from $78 to $103 for doubles.

The **Pickett Suite Hotel,** 2515 Meridian Parkway, P.O. Box 14067, Research Triangle Park, NC 27709-4067 (tel. 919/361-4660 or toll free 800/PICKETT), is located in the Research Triangle Park, at the intersection of I-40 and N.C. 55, within a few minutes' drive of Raleigh, Durham, and Chapel Hill. Set in rambling landscaped grounds whose focal point is the lake just behind the hotel, the Pickett has luxury two-room suites with coffee- and tea makers, a fridge stocked with complimentary juices and soft drinks, *three* color TVs (one in the bathroom!), hairdryer, oversize beds, ample-size desk, and spacious living/dining room area. Other amenities include the excellent restaurant serving American cuisine, indoor/outdoor pool, rental paddle boats for the lake, whirlpool, exercise facilities, and a guest library. This is one of the most beautiful accommodations in the area, and the setting provides a welcome relief from city streets at the end of a day's sightseeing. Rates, which include a complimentary buffet breakfast, run $115 to $135 for doubles, with weekend specials as low as $64.95. Ask about honeymoon package rates, corporate rates, and other specials.

The **Residence Inn by Marriott,** 1000 Navaho Dr., Raleigh, NC 27609 (tel. 919/878-6100 or toll free 800/331-3131), has high-standard one- and two-bedroom units with fully equipped kitchens, some with fireplaces. Amenities on the premises include heated pool, whirlpools, a sports court and fitness center, and barbecue and picnic facilities. There's a complimentary wine-and-cheese reception every evening, and a weekly cocktail party. Nonsmoking units are available, and double-occupancy rates range from $82 to $102 for studios, $99 to $119 for penthouse suites; all rates decrease for stays longer than six nights.

The **Holiday Inn North,** on U.S. 1 North, 2815 North Blvd., Raleigh, NC 27604 (tel. 919/872-7666, or toll free 800/465-4329), is an exceptionally nice member of this chain, having added a tower, renovated all older guest rooms, built a Holidome that encloses an indoor pool, Jacuzzi, mini-golf, exercise room, and assorted games, all surrounded by an abundance of plants and trees and fountains. The Brandy's Holidome Restaurant serves all three meals, and there's dancing in Brandy's Lounge every night except Sunday. Doubles here start at $75 for standard rooms, $77 in the Holidome; king-size doubles start at $78.

At the Raleigh-Durham Airport (2½ miles west of U.S. 70), the **Best Western Triangle Inn/Airport,** P.O. Box 10951, Raleigh, NC 27605 (tel. 919/840-9000), has well-decorated rooms in a moderate price range. Beds here are extra-long, and a special feature is a wheelchair ramp for the disabled. There's a pool, and a 24-hour café is just a block away. Doubles start at $55.

The **Courtyard by Marriott,** 1041 Wake Town Rd., Raleigh, NC 27609 (tel. 919/821-3400 or toll free 800/321-2211), is an attractive complex built around a courtyard area with pool. Rooms are tastefully decorated and comfortably furnished, and some have poolside balcony or patio; and some even have refrigerators. There's a whirlpool and exercise room, as well as a heated pool, and the dining room serves all three meals at moderate prices. Rates for doubles start at $64 weekdays and Sunday, $44 Friday and Saturday; lower weekly rates are available.

The **Comfort Inn Crabtree,** 3921 Arrow Dr., Raleigh, NC 27612 (tel. 919/782-7071 or toll free 800/228-5150), offers a complimentary continental breakfast and a few rooms with refrigerators. There's good shopping at the nearby Crabtree Valley Mall, as well as several good eateries. Doubles go for $44.95 to $58.95, and there are discounts for seniors.

The **Fairfield Inn by Marriott,** 2641 Appliance Court, Raleigh, NC 27604 (tel. 919/856-9800 or toll free 800/228-2800), sits high on a hill, just a short drive from downtown Raleigh. The 132 rooms, all with attractive decor, pleasing furnishings and seating area, and work area with desk, include nonsmoking rooms and those with facilities for the handicapped. All are good sized, but those on the third floor are more spacious. There's complimentary coffee in the lobby, and several good restaurants are in the immediate vicinity. Double-room rates begin at $38.95.

The **Red Roof Inn,** 3520 Maitland Dr., Raleigh, NC 27610 (tel. 919/834-8968 or toll free 800/848-7878), is east of downtown, opposite the Tower Shopping Plaza. Rooms are standard for this chain, and there's a cafeteria next door. Doubles go for $33.95 to $38.95; seniors get a discount; and there are rooms for the handicapped.

The **Econo Lodge/West,** 5110 Holly Ridge Dr., Raleigh, NC 27611 (tel. 919/782-3201), is right next door to the Oak Park Shopping Center. Rooms are especially nice for the budget price, and while there's no restaurant on the premises, there are an even dozen within a half mile. Doubles run from $33.

Where to Eat

The cuisine of provincial France (chef Jean-Claude hails from the Burgundy region) flavors the menu at **Jean-Claude's French Café,** 6112 Falls of Neuse Ave., in the North Ridge Shopping Center (tel. 919/872-6224). The freshest ingredients are used for every dish, and among nightly specials you might encounter is fresh salmon in a puff pastry or seafood crêpe Wilmington (provincial NC?), or an exquisite roast duck with orange sauce. There's a very good wine list. Lunch is served from 11 a.m. to 2 p.m., dinner from 5:30 to 9 p.m. (till 9:30 p.m. on Friday), closed Sunday and holidays. Dinner prices will run $11 to $23.

For southern Italian cuisine, it's **Casa Carbone Ristorante,** in the Oak Park Shopping Center, Glenwood Avenue (tel. 919/781-8750). Traditional Italian pasta, veal, and chicken dishes are featured, and the homemade breads, sauces, and desserts furnish the finishing touches. Hours are 5 to 10 p.m. Monday through Saturday, 4 to 10 p.m. Sunday. Prices are in the moderate, $12 to $24, range.

The **42nd Street Oyster Bar and Seafood Grill,** 508 W. Jones St., (tel. 919/831-2811) is a large, lively place set in a restored warehouse that dates from the 1930s. Oysters on the half shell share menu honors with platters of fried or steamed fish and lobster, prime rib, and fried chicken. Servings are plentiful, and there's a children's menu for the small fry. Prices range from $12 to $25, and hours are 11 a.m. to 11 p.m. Monday through Friday, 5 to 11 p.m. Saturday, and 5 to 10 p.m. Sunday. Closed major holidays.

Mountain Jacks, 2711 North Blvd. (tel. 919/872-2300), is a large, rustic eatery that features prime rib and choice steaks. The extensive menu, however, lists a large selection of seafood, and adds chicken and a lovely rack of lamb that comes with a rosemary-mint glaze. Among steaks to look for are the top-grade filet mignon, whisky peppercorn steak, and a tender roasted château filet, which is coated with herbed breadcrumbs, oven roasted, and served with a port-wine sauce. Prices in this popular place are good value for money: hefty portions, with entrees all $18 or under. Combination orders (prime ribs and seafood, perhaps—you choose two menu items) are specials at $17.95. Hours are 11:30 a.m. to 2:30 p.m. Monday through Friday, 5 to 10 p.m. Monday through Thursday, till 11 p.m. on Friday, and 4:30 to 11 p.m. on Saturday, 11 a.m. to 2 p.m. and 3 to 10 p.m. on Sunday. There's also a cocktail lounge with periodic entertainment.

For dinner in an elegant setting (French provincial furnishings, gold-framed mirrors, candlelight, and fresh flowers on each table), do reserve at the three-star **Scotch Bonnets Restaurant** in the Marriott Hotel, 4500 Marriott Dr. (tel. 919/781-7000). The menu is continental, with emphasis on fresh seafood dishes such as stir-fried shrimp, scallops, or salmon poached or sautéed to perfection and served with a béarnaise sauce. For meat-eaters, there are steak, veal, and chicken offerings as well, and each night there's a chef's special of the day. Prices range from $14 to $22. To top off your dinner with an elegance that matches its setting, however, you really should order one of their luscious flambéed desserts (bananas Foster or pineapples in a peppered fruit sauce) and finish with one of the exotic coffees, prepared at your table from a tray of condiments such as chocolate bits, brown sugar, lemon rind, cinnamon sticks, etc. Hours are 6 to 11 p.m.

For the younger crowd (of any age), it's **Darryl's 1849 Restaurant,** N.C. 70 West (tel. 919/782-1849), **Darryl's 1906 Restaurant and Tavern** at 1906 Hillsborough St. (tel. 919/833-1906), or **Darryl's 1840 Restaurant** at 4309 Old Wake Forest Rd. (tel. 919/872-1840). All are rustic in atmosphere and feature first-rate Italian dinners, a wide variety of sandwiches, beef and pork ribs, steak, seafood, and pizza. Beer comes by the mug or pitcher, cocktails are served, and prices are moderate. This is a popular chain, with branches in Durham, Greensboro, Greenville, Charlotte, and Winston-Salem.

About 12½ miles northwest on U.S. 70 West, you'll find the **Angus Barn** (tel. 919/787-3505), one of the best places for charcoal-broiled steak or choice ribs of beef in these parts. There's also an excellent selection of fresh seafoods. The setting is rustic (it's a restored 19th-century barn), but you'll not feel like one of the "overalls" set here. Fireplaces add a grace note and the food is superior. Semi–à la carte prices range from $12 to $25, with beer, wine, and cocktails available. It's open from 5 to 11 p.m. every day (closes at 10 p.m. on Sunday) and is well worth the drive. Better reserve.

Special Note: I've eaten barbecued pork in a lot of places, but nowhere on earth does it taste quite like that of Piedmont North Carolina. Slow-cooked in an open pit over hickory chips and basted all the while with a highly seasoned sauce, then finely chopped (no slabs of pork slathered with sauce, such as you get in New York, for instance), it is truly a food fit for kings. But you really have to know your cook, even in North Carolina, and almost every locality has a favorite. In Rocky Mount, it's **Bob Melton's;** in Wilson, it's **Parkers,** etc. Well, the word in Raleigh is that **Cooper's Barbecue,** 109 E. Davie St., is *the* place. My best advice is GO! Even if you're a fan of that Texas stuff, you'll leave Cooper's a convert. Prices are reasonable and portions are generous. One final word: Don't expect anything elegant by way of decor—part of the mystique of North Carolina barbecue is that it's always served in plain surroundings, with lots of hush puppies and coleslaw. And that's what you'll find here, plus the bonus of a handy parking lot just across the street.

For good food at truly budget prices, look for the **K & W Cafeteria** in the North Hills Shopping Center on Six Forks Road, about five miles out the U.S. 1/64 Bypass (tel. 919/782-0353), where lunch will run about $4 to $5, and dinner no more than $7. Hours are 11 a.m. to 8 p.m. daily.

Nightlife

There's nighttime entertainment and dancing at the **Brownstone Hotel** (formerly the Hilton Inn), 1707 Hillsborough St. (tel. 919/828-0811), every night except Sunday. Dancing every night except Sunday, also, at the **Holiday Inn North,** 2815 North Blvd. (tel. 919/872-7666). And the **Velvet Cloak Inn,** 1505 Hillsborough St. (tel. 919/828-0333), has both entertainment and dancing except Sunday. Check local newspapers for the current disco scene, which tends to change too frequently to report in this book.

The **Raleigh Little Theatre,** one of the best community playhouses in the country, presents Broadway productions (check local newspapers for current shows and prices), and during fall and winter months the **North Carolina Symphony** is heard at **Memorial Auditorium.** Nationally and internationally known concert artists also appear at the auditorium during the season, and while most seats are sold on a subscription basis, it's sometimes possible to obtain single tickets.

Things to See and Do

For sightseeing brochures, maps, etc., on Raleigh, write or go by the **Raleigh Convention and Visitors Bureau,** 225 Hillsborough St., Suite 400, (P.O. Box 1879), Raleigh, NC 27602 (tel. 919/834-5900).

Besides sightseeing, which I'll get to in a minute, there are several recreational possibilities in the Triangle area. **William B. Umstead State Park,** halfway between Raleigh and Durham on U.S. 70 (Rte. 8, Box 130, Raleigh, NC 27612), has camping (on a first-come, first-served basis) and picnicking facilities (for details call 919/787-3033). You can fish or just enjoy boating at the municipally owned and operated **Lake Wheeler,** five miles southwest of Raleigh on Rhamkatte Road, from 10 a.m. until sundown every day except Monday for a modest fee (phone 919/772-1173 for details).

Now, for the best possible tour of the capital city, your first stop should be the **Capital Area Visitor Center.** It's in a 1918 mansion called the **Andrews-London House** at 301 N. Blount St. (tel. 919/733-3456). It's open from 8 a.m. to 5 p.m. Monday through Friday, 9 a.m. to 5 p.m. on Saturday, and 1 to 5 p.m. on Sunday. They'll start you off with an orientation film, arm you with brochures and loads of background information, and coordinate walking or driving tours of the area. For further information, write the **Visitors Bureau,** 800 S. Salisbury St., P.O. Box 1879, Raleigh, NC 27602 (tel. 919/833-3005).

The **state capitol** (tel. 919/733-4994), a stately Greek Revival structure (constructed 1833–1840), has been named a national historic landmark and is currently being refurbished to its 1840–1865 appearance. All state business was conducted here until 1888. The building now contains the offices of the governor and secretary of state as well as restored legislative chambers. Beneath the awe-inspiring 97½-foot copper dome there's a duplicate of Antonio Canova's marble statue of George Washington, dressed as a Roman general. The capitol, on Union (Capitol) Square, is open from 8 a.m. to 5 p.m. Monday through Saturday (from 9 a.m. Friday), and 1 to 5 p.m. on Sunday, is free, and takes about 30 to 45 minutes to tour.

Across from the capitol, on Bicentennial Plaza, the **North Carolina State Museum of Natural Sciences** is so full of fascinating displays of the state's gems, Native American artifacts, animals, and plants that you'll need at least an hour to explore its contents. There's even a bird hall and live snake collection. One of my favorites here is the whale fossil found near the center of North Carolina, evidence of a long-ago coastline quite different from that of today. There's no charge here, and it's open from 9 a.m. to 5 p.m. Monday through Saturday and 1 to 5 p.m. on Sunday. Closed holidays.

The **legislative building,** on Jones Street between Wilmington and Salisbury streets, is a striking contemporary building designed by Edward Durrell Stone, the same architect who drew plans for the Kennedy Center for the Performing Arts in Washington, D.C. Allow about 45 minutes to go through it, longer if you happen to hit there when the legislature is in session (that's every other year, unless it's called into special session), since you'll be able to watch the proceedings. It's free and open from 9 a.m. to 5 p.m. Monday through Friday, 9 a.m. to 5 p.m. on Saturday, and 1 to 5 p.m. on Sunday.

Be sure and save a half hour or so to see the **governor's mansion** at 200 N. Blount St. You'll have to make an appointment through the visitor center, but the grand old Victorian home shouldn't be missed. It's built of North Carolina brick and wood, and although it was begun in 1883, the first occupant didn't move in until 1891. There's no charge for a look around. Tours are offered only at certain times: Tuesday and Friday morning and afternoon, March through May; Tuesday and Friday mornings only, September through November.

At 109 E. Jones St., the state's history is pictured in relics of colonial, Revolutionary, and Civil War eras at the **North Carolina Museum of History,** which is also free to visitors. It closes on Monday, and is open 9 a.m. to 5 p.m. Tuesday through Saturday and 1 to 6 p.m. on Sunday, and you'll want to plan about an hour and a half here.

The **North Carolina Museum of Art,** 2110 Blue Ridge Blvd., houses an important collection of European paintings. There are American, 20th-century, ancient, African, Oceanic, Judaica, and New World collections. A variety of special exhibitions and programs is offered. Hours are 10 a.m. to 5 p.m. Tuesday through Saturday (to 9 p.m. on Friday) and noon to 5 p.m. on Sunday, and there's no admission charge.

One of North Carolina's three native sons who became president, Andrew Johnson, was born in a small cabin about a block from the capitol building. The 17th president's birthplace has been moved to **Mordecai Place** and is open to visitors.

And speaking of Mordecai Place, be sure to see the restored 1785 **Mordecai House,** at 1 Mimosa St. off Wake Forest Road (tel. 919/834-4844). Five generations of one of North Carolina's oldest families lived here (until 1964, in fact), and the original furnishings give it a "lived in" look. There's no admission charge, although donations are accepted. A guide will show you around from 10 a.m. to 2 p.m. Tuesday through Friday and 1 to 4 p.m. on Saturday and Sunday. Closed January and February, and Tuesday in September.

Christ Episcopal Church, at 120 E. Edenton St., is a lovely Gothic Revival building which dates back to the 1840s. When Sherman's troops left town after occupying Raleigh and the state capitol building during the 1860s, they had so stripped the town that it was said the weathercock on this church's steeple was the only chicken left in town.

By contrast to all that history, the "age of the atom" is very much a part of the Raleigh scene, and you can visit the first college-owned reactor in the country on the North Carolina State University campus. Emphasis here is on *peaceful* utilization of atom-splitting. The university is on Hillsborough Street, and you can't miss it. Once on campus, ask for directions to the nuclear-reactor building.

One final note about Raleigh: If you can get there in mid-October, you're in luck, for the **North Carolina State Fair** is a real oldtime event that draws crowds from all over and is fun from one end of the fairgrounds to the other (they're located one mile west of town on Blue Ridge Boulevard and I-40). For exact dates the year you plan to come, contact: North Carolina State Fair, 1025 Blue Ridge Blvd., Raleigh, NC 27607 (tel. 919/733-2145).

RESEARCH TRIANGLE PARK

By the time you leave Raleigh for Durham or Chapel Hill, you'll have seen highway signs pointing to the Research Triangle Park, which is located on 5,200 acres in the center of a rough triangle formed by the three cities. While it doesn't qualify as a true "sightseeing" destination, it's worthwhile to turn off the highway and drive around, for this is one of the largest research centers in the country. Some of our brightest scientific minds work here in an atmosphere that carries the "think tank" concept a step further to application of research principles to industry, environment, and government.

Over 50 institutions (including the Environmental Protection Agency, General Electric, DuPont, the National Institute for Environmental Health Sciences, the Burroughs-Wellcome Foundation, and I.B.M. Corporation) represent a constantly increasing multimillion-dollar investment in projects under way, completed, or projected. The payroll (to more than 25,000 staffers) exceeds $700 million annually.

To reach the park, turn off the East-West Expressway from Raleigh to Durham onto N.C. 54—actually, you don't have to bother with highway numbers, the markers are that numerous and prominent. Accommodations in all price ranges make this an ideal central base for exploring the region (see "Where to Stay").

DURHAM

A real-life "American dream" success story was played out in Durham back in the late 1880s, when Washington Duke walked 137 miles back to his farm after being mustered out of the Confederate forces at the end of the Civil War and took up life again as a tobacco farmer. That first year, he started grinding and packaging the crop to sell in small packets. Then, in 1880, Duke decided there was a future in the novelty "cigarettes" and set to work with his three sons to manufacture them on a small scale. By 1890 business had grown so that they formed the American Tobacco Company, and a legendary American manufacturing empire was under way. Durham, which was a small village when Duke came home from war, blossomed into an industrial city, taking its commercial life from the "golden weed." And it still does. From September until the end of December, tobacco warehouses ring with the chants of auctioneers moving from one batch of the cured tobacco to the next, followed by buyers who indicate their bids with nods or hand signals (remember that "Sold American" commercial back in the heyday of radio?). And there's a constant traffic all year of bright-leaf tobacco coming into the city and cigarettes and pipe tobacco leaving it.

Even Duke University, the cultural heart of Durham, owes its life's breath to tobacco, for it was little noticed as Trinity College until national and international prominence came with a Duke family endowment of $40 million in 1924. Along with a change in name, the university gained a new West Campus, complete with massive Gothic structures of native stone, flagstone walks, and box hedges that would do justice to Oxford or Cambridge. Its medical center has become one of the most highly respected in the world.

Where to Eat in Durham

You'll find **Claire's,** 2701 Chapel Hill Rd. (tel. 919/493-5721), in a lovely 1909 house that has been renovated to accommodate five dining rooms, with outdoor dining during warm months. There's a nice selection of appetizers (try the escargots or crêpes Florentine). The cuisine, which is primarily continental, features fresh seafood, beef tenderloin, prime rib, veal, lamb, and duckling preparations. For such quality, prices are moderate: $11.95 to $16.95. Claire's is open for dinner only, nightly from 5 to 10:30 p.m. There's a large and varied wine list, and the comfortable Claire's Lounge serves beer and cocktails.

The atmosphere is casual at **Another Thyme,** 109 N. Gregson St. (tel. 682-5225), and the menu is creative, crossing ethnic culinary borders in innovative dishes with an emphasis on vegetarian entrees and seafood. Charcoal-grilled swordfish steaks and seafood kabobs are among the more popular items with locals. This fashionable place is one of the few in the region with a late-night menu (somewhat limited in scope) from 10 p.m. to 1 a.m. Monday through Friday, lunch hours are 11:30 a.m. to 2:30 p.m.; dinner hours are 6 to 10 p.m. Monday through Thursday, and, till 10:30 p.m. Friday and Saturday; and there's a Sunday brunch from 10:30 a.m. to 2:30 p.m. Prices are in the high moderate range, and reservations are advised.

Oliver's, 2800 Middleton Ave. (tel. 383-8575, ext. 525), is an elegant eatery located in Durham's Sheraton University Center. Specialties are keyed to what's fresh for the season, and there are always original creations like the fettuccine Outer Banks. Prices run from $20 to $30, and hours are 6 to 10 p.m., Monday through Saturday, closed Sunday.

Rosebud's Italian Restaurant, 2514 University Dr. (tel. 493-4150), dishes up northern Italian dishes such as chicken saltimbocca and veal piccata, along with luscious homemade desserts, plus a nice variety of other international dishes. Prices are in the moderate range ($11 to $20), and hours are 11:30 a.m. to 2 p.m. Monday through Saturday and 5:30 to 10 p.m. Monday through Thursday, till 11 p.m. Friday and Saturday.

Things to See and Do in Durham

Stop by the **Greater Durham Chamber of Commerce,** 201 N. Roxboro St., P.O. Box 3829, Durham, NC 27702 (tel. 919/682-2133), for detailed sightseeing information.

Duke Homestead, where it all began, has been named a state historic site and national historical landmark, and you can visit the home, the original factory building, and farm. There's a visitor center and it's open at no charge from 9 a.m. to 5 p.m. Monday through Saturday and 1 to 5 p.m. on Sunday April through October; from November through March it's open from 9 a.m. to 5 p.m. Tuesday through Friday, 10 a.m. to 1 p.m. on Saturday, and 2 to 5 p.m. on Sunday. It's located on (what else!) Duke Homestead Road, half a mile north of I-85 and the Guess Road exit. While there, take time to go through the **Tobacco Museum,** which traces the history of tobacco from Indian days to the present. A color film, *Carolina Bright,* is shown on a daily basis as an orientation to the site.

The East and West campuses of **Duke University** cover more than 1,000 acres on the west side of the city, and it's a good idea to keep the car handy to drive from one "walking tour" to another. The **East Campus,** which was the old Trinity College, features Georgian architecture, and its red-brick and lime-stone buildings border a half-mile-long grassy mall. There's an excellent **Museum of Art** on this campus, just off West Main Street, that's free (open 9 a.m. to 5 p.m. Tuesday through Friday, 10 a.m. to 1 p.m. on Saturday, and 2 to 5 p.m. on Sunday) and holds marvelous collections of classical art, and pre-Columbian, African, medieval, European, American, and Oriental art, and coins.

It's the **West Campus** (a short drive away on winding, wooded Campus Drive), however, that really steals the university show. Its Gothic-style buildings and beautifully landscaped grounds are nothing short of breathtaking. And the showplace of this showplace is **Duke Chapel,** which brings back memories of England's Canterbury Cathedral. James B. Duke felt strongly that religion should play a prominent part in university life, and the splendor of this chapel assures a religious emphasis at Duke. The bell tower of the majestic cruciform chapel rises 210 feet and houses a 50-bell carillon that rings out at the end of each work day and on Sunday. There's a half-million-dollar Flentrop organ with more than 5,000 pipes (said to be one of the finest in the western hemisphere) in a special oak gallery, its case 40 feet high. Renowned organists perform at the console in public recitals on the first Sunday of each month.

It's impossible to describe the sheer beauty of the chapel's interior: 77 stained-glass windows light the long nave with soft shades of reds, blues, greens, and yellows, and highlight an ornate screen and carved-oak choir stalls. Visiting hours are 8:30 a.m. to 5 p.m. daily, and there are interdenominational services every Sunday at 11 a.m.

The university's **Botany Department Greenhouses** (some 13 rooms of plants, both native and rare) are open to the public from 10 a.m. to 4:30 p.m. every day of the week and hold the most diverse collection of plants in the Carolinas.

The West Campus is also the setting of **Duke Medical Center,** which has gained worldwide fame for its extensive treatment facilities and varied research programs.

To find out more about Duke, call the Special Events Office (tel. 919/684-3698). They'll be glad to arrange special guided tours, and one I especially recommend is of the **Sarah P. Duke Gardens,** 55 acres of gardens on the West Campus that draw more than 200,000 visitors each year. This beauty spot lies in a valley bordered by a pine forest and features a lily pond, stone terraces, a rose garden, native-plant garden, Asiatic arboretum, wisteria-draped pergola, and seasonal plantings that provide an ever-changing color scheme. It's open every day from 8 a.m. until dark and is a good place to end a day of campus sightseeing.

Durham's **Museum of Life and Science,** 433 Murray Ave., is especially planned for children, but no matter what your age, I'll wager you'll be intrigued by the life-size models of dinosaurs on a "pathway through the past," and the NASA spacecraft that highlights a large diorama of the Apollo 15 lunar landing site complete with a sample of moon rock. And surely no youngster of any age could resist the exciting "hands-on" exhibits in the Science Arcade and Children's Discovery Room. The 78 acres also hold a wildlife sanctuary, barnyard, and mile-long narrow-gauge railroad. Monday through Saturday hours are 10 a.m. to 5 p.m. and 1 to 5 p.m. on Sunday. From Memorial Day through Labor Day the museum is open one hour later each day. Adults pay $3.25, for ages 4 to 12 and senior citizens it's $2.25, and for children 3 and under it's free.

CHAPEL HILL

The third point of the Triangle area is Chapel Hill, a small city that has managed to hold on to its "village" atmosphere in spite of a university that annually enrolls over 22,000 students. Chapel Hill *is* the University of North Carolina, and it has been universally loved by graduates since 1795, when it was the first state university in the country. The 2,000-acre campus holds 125 buildings, ranging from Old East, the oldest state university building in the country (its cornerstone was laid in 1793), to Morehead Planetarium, which was an astronaut-training center in the early days of manned space flights. And its history is as varied as its buildings. When the Civil War erupted, the student body was second only to Yale's in size—until the fighting started and most of the undergraduates and faculty left for battlefields. Reconstruction finished its destruction and it closed down from 1871 to 1875. Since its reopening, however, it has consistently been a leader in American education and a center of liberal intellectualism (rather surprising, since North Carolina is a generally conservative state). So strong is the attachment and affection of those connected with the university that more than once it and Chapel Hill have been described as "the southern part of heaven."

Chapel Hill's appearance may be village-like but its spirit is lively. Those ivy-covered brick buildings have nurtured such mavericks of the literary world as Thomas Wolfe and Paul Green (who wrote the first outdoor drama produced in the country). And the quiet, tree-lined streets lined with homes set in flower-bordered lawns have been "home" to some of the most innovative intellectuals America has produced.

Where to Eat in Chapel Hill

Restaurant La Residence, 220 W. Rosemary St. (tel. 919/967-2506), is in a half-century-old residence surrounded by gardens. Each of the small dining rooms has its own decor, and the menu changes daily in order to utilize the freshest available ingredients (they get fresh mountain trout weekly, and if that's your weakness, call to see which day they expect it). The menu, while limited, is composed of exquisite—and delicious—creations which the chef boasts are "the most innovative food in the Triangle area." You might, for instance, order the chicken stuffed (under the skin) with spinach; or from July through September, North Carolina duck with blackberry sauce. As for desserts, don't pass up their homemade ice creams and sorbets, unless, that is, you yield to the temptation of white-chocolate charlotte with raspberry sauce, or the cappuccino cheesecake. Dinner hours are 6 to 9:30 p.m. Tuesday through Sunday, and it's best to reserve. As you might expect, there's an exceptionally fine (but limited) wine list. Prices for the table d'hôte dinner will run anywhere from $12 to $25.

Elegance in the modern vein best describes dining at **Rubens,** in the Hotel Europa, Europa Drive (tel. 919/968-4900). In a setting of off-white, grays, pinks, beiges, and tan, the atmosphere is one of lighthearted luxury, with a distinctly French accent. An unusual feature of the hotel is its stained-glass elevator! Tea is served in the lounge/lobby every day from 3 to 6 p.m. and features the delicious homemade pastries for which they are locally famous. At lunch, there are light luncheon selections at moderate prices, as well as more substantial fare such as veal, beef, or seafood, most prepared in the French style. The dinner menu is quite extensive, with many specialties. Prices are in the $12 to $26 range at dinner, lower for lunch, and if you just want a touch of elegance, drop in for breakfast, which will run $4 to $8. Hours are 7 to 10:30 a.m., 11 a.m. to 2:30 p.m., and 6 to 10:30 p.m. There's a Sunday brunch from 11 a.m. to 2:30 p.m.

The decor is "elegant eclectic" at the **Pyewacket Restaurant,** in The Courtyard, 431 W. Franklin St. (tel. 919/929-0297). The cozy lounge has comfortable couches and is dimly lit; there are two high-ceilinged rooms done in soft reddish browns; and the greenhouse dining room is windowed all around, and filled with plants (no smokers allowed in this area). There's a nice selection of pasta, soups, sandwiches, omelets, salads, and desserts at lunch with prices that run from $3 to $6, and at dinner seafood, vegetarian, and continental entrees are featured at prices of $6.50 to $15. A wide variety of coffees features espresso made in their own espresso machine. Hours are 11:30 a.m. to 2:30 p.m. and 6 to 10 p.m. Monday through Thursday, to 10:30 p.m. on Friday and Saturday, and 6 to 9:30 p.m. on Sunday.

Behind the rather quirky façade of **Crook's Corner,** 610 W. Franklin St. (tel. 919/929-7643), lurks one of the South's superb restaurants. Young co-owner/chef Bill Neal, formerly chef-manager of Restaurant La Residence, has zoomed to prominence as one of the nation's top up-and-coming chefs. No less a luminary than Craig Claiborne has proclaimed him a "genius of the stove." The restaurant showcases many of the recipes Neal features in his widely acclaimed *Bill Neal's Southern Cooking* (University of North Carolina Press). The menu varies with the season and may include such delights as shrimp and grits or sea scallops sautéed with mushrooms, scallions, sweet red peppers, and new potatoes in a lemon juice–garlic sauce. Side dishes are such down-home delicacies with subtle touches as fresh collard greens or Hoppin' John, which is black-eyed peas and rice with scallions, tomato, and cheddar (both about $2). Entrees range from $8 to $16.

The quirky façade? The roof is adorned with pigs, alligators, rabbits, squirrels, and other critters produced from scrap lumber by an area primitive artist. Inside, the walls are decorated with whimsical art deco–style sculptures of deep-sea denizens. Seating capacity is limited to 70, and there's seating for about 50 more outside in nice weather. Crook's doesn't take reservations, so you may have to wait—but it's worth it. It's open from 5 p.m. to midnight Sunday through Thursday, to 1 a.m. on Friday and Saturday.

Things to See and Do in Chapel Hill

To best arm yourself for sightseeing, contact the **Chapel Hill–Carrboro Chamber of Commerce,** 104 S. Estes Dr. (P.O. Box 2897), Chapel Hill, NC 27514 (tel. 919/967-7075).

Your best introduction to the university community is a free, one-hour campus tour that leaves from Morehead Planetarium (the west entrance) on East Franklin Street (for details, contact the University News Bureau, 210 Pittsboro St., tel. 919/962-2091).

With the tour or on your own, look for the **Old Well,** once the only source of drinking water for Chapel Hill. It stands in the center of the campus on Cameron Avenue, in a small, temple-like enclosure with a dome supported by classic columns. Just east of it is **Old East,** begun in 1793 and the country's oldest state university building. Across the way stands the "newcomer," **Old West,** built in 1824. **South Main Building** is nearby, a structure that was begun in 1798 and not finished until 1814—students lived inside the empty shell in rude huts during that time. And look for the **Coker Arboretum** at Cameron Avenue and Raleigh Street, where five acres are planted in a wide variety of temperate-zone plants. As you walk the campus you'll hear popular tunes coming from the 167-foot **Morehead-Patterson Bell Tower,** whose Italian Renaissance campanile rings throughout the day. And just back of the bell tower is **Kenan Stadium,** in a wooded natural bowl setting, with a 44,000-seat capacity.

And of course you won't want to miss **Morehead Planetarium,** East Franklin St. (tel. 919/962-1248). It was a 1947 gift of John Motley Morehead and houses the first Carl Zeiss instrument located on a U.S. college campus (there are only 12 in the whole country) in a 68-foot domed theater. The "star" of its permanent scientific exhibits is a large orrery showing the simultaneous action of planets revolving around the suns, moons revolving around planets, and planets rotating on their axes. Show times vary considerably, so call for the current schedule. Admission is $3 for adults, $2.50 for seniors and students, $2 for age 12 and under.

Try to catch a PlayMakers Repertory Company production at the **Paul Green Theatre.** You could see classical or contemporary drama, as well as new works—they're professional in both areas.

Off campus, the **North Carolina Botanical Garden,** on Laurel Hill Road and U.S. 15-501 Bypass (tel. 919/967-2246), is open from 8 a.m. to 5 p.m. weekdays 10 a.m. to 5 p.m. Saturday, and 2 to 5 p.m. Sunday and its three miles of easily followed nature trails are lined with native plants of this region. It's free, and a botanical education with herb gardens, and carnivorous plants and native plants in habitat settings.

2. Winston-Salem

Before 1913 the twin communities of Winston and Salem coexisted in perfect harmony, and their incorporation that year into a single city has proved a happy, productive union. Winston, founded in 1849, contributed an industry-based economy, while Salem added the crafts, educational emphasis, and sense of order that its Moravian settlers brought from Pennsylvania in 1766.

Actually, Salem (the name comes from the Hebrew word *shalom,* meaning peace) was the last of three settlements by Moravian clergy and laymen who came to the Piedmont looking for townsites in the early 1750s—the little towns of Bethabara and Bethania came first. But Salem proved to be the main establishment, and the hardworking newcomers laid out a pleasant community with their traditional Single Brothers and Single Sisters houses as focal points for unmarried members of the congregation. Once married, the couples often set up shop right in their own homes. They were hardy, devout, Germanic people who had fled persecution in Europe and brought to the New World their artisans' skills, a deep love of music and education, and absolute rejection of violence in any form.

As "progress" began to encroach on the boundaries of the beautiful, orderly old congregational town, an organized effort was begun in 1949 to restore those homes and shops that were in a state of deterioration and to reconstruct others that had disappeared. Today there are more than 30 buildings restored with meticulous attention to authenticity and still others in the process of renovation. Devout the Moravians were, glum they were not; and the bright, cheerful reds and blues and soft greens and yellows in the restored interiors (exteriors as well) are duplicates of the colors with which they surrounded themselves in those early days. They also loved good food, and that too has been lovingly preserved in Old Salem: today's tourist can sit down to lunch or dinner in the Old Salem Tavern (see below) in an authentic colonial Moravian setting. Most entrees are contemporary American/continental, but you can select such specialties as Moravian chicken pie or ragoût of beef, and one dessert is a wonderful Moravian gingerbread topped with homemade lemon ice cream.

Flowing around the center island of Old Salem, the vigorous new city goes about its business of commerce and industry in a manner that somehow escapes the environmental blight that marks other manufacturing centers. Maybe that's due in part to the fact that it is not too large (latest population figures are 132,000), or maybe it's because its citizens have retained a sense of aesthetic values handed down from those early arrivals. At any rate, although this is the home base for such giants as one of the South's largest banks (Wachovia National), and USAir (Piedmont Airlines), there is a genteel air about the place that almost convinces you progress doesn't *have* to be abrasive.

For the traveler, there are points of interest outside Winston-Salem itself, making Winston-Salem a perfect base for day trips to Greensboro, High Point, and the pottery center at Seagrove, which dates back 200 years.

WHERE TO STAY

It's not in town, but the **Tanglewood Manor House Bed and Breakfast Inn and Lodge,** Clemmons, NC 27012 (tel. 919/766-0591), is an experience not to be missed. It's about 12 miles west of Winston-Salem, just off I-40 (the exit is marked). Once upon a time, Native Americans roamed this lush, wooded section of the Yadkin River Valley. When the Moravians arrived in 1753 and settled the Wachovia tract, one square mile of land was deeded by Lord Linville to the Ellis family, who leased it briefly for "five shillings lawful money of Great Britain in hand and a yearly rent of one peppercorn payment at the Feast of Saint Michael, the archangel." In 1757 the Johnson family acquired it and held on to it until 1921, when William N. Reynolds, the tobacco tycoon, decided it was just the place to build his country home. Never a man to do things on a small scale, "Mr. Will" kept adding acres of contiguous land until the total stood at 1,100. The lovely old Johnson homeplace, built in 1859, sprouted wings on either side and became a true manor house. The Reynoldses named the estate Tanglewood.

Well, five shillings and a peppercorn won't get you far at Tanglewood these days, but the Manor House *can* be your country home, if only for a day—since 1951, Tanglewood (officially, it's the William and Kate B. Reynolds Memorial

Park) has been open to the public, operated as a department of county government. For remarkably reasonable rates, you can sleep in a spacious master bedroom complete with fireplace and canopied double beds, dine in an elegant colonial-style dining room (there are five, one with a mammoth stone fireplace) on gourmet fare, roam the well-kept terraces and lawns, and play the country squire to your heart's content.

There are only 11 bedrooms in the manor house, at rates of $56 to $66, so there's no mob scene to detract you from your fantasy of "lord of the manor," and the nearby motor lodge has just 18 units and an apartment, with rates from $56 to $66. If your idea of country living runs along more rustic lines, there are five vacation cottages in a secluded woodland area overlooking Mallard Lake. The two- and three-bedroom cottages, completely furnished and with fully equipped kitchens, rent for $300 to $340 per week for five or fewer people. More rugged types can reserve one of the 100 family campground sites in one corner of the vast estate. Most have electric and water hookups, all have picnic tables and campfire space, and there are two large bathhouses and a dumping station: $11 a day for those with hookups ($70 per week) and $9 without. All rates include breakfast.

If you think "country" equates with "boredom," 'taint so, at least not here. At Tanglewood, you can play tennis on one of nine courts, swim in a large pool, go paddleboating or canoeing or trail riding. And, of course, there's golf, on an excellent course right on the grounds. There's even steeplechase racing the third Saturday of every April, the last meet of the year on the Carolina circuit; but don't expect to stay at Tanglewood then—all rooms and cottages are held for racing participants. As for other times of the year, better reserve three or four weeks ahead, because the place is a year-round favorite with regulars.

In Winston-Salem

Right in the heart of town at 300 W. 5th St., Winston-Salem, NC 27102, is the **Hyatt Winston-Salem** (tel. 919/725-1234, or toll free 800/228-9000), a winner for travelers going the deluxe route. The nine-story open lobby has the look of an indoor park, and its glass-bubble elevators overlook reflecting pools, fountains, hanging gardens, and a 30-foot waterfall that splashes into the second-story-level swimming pool. For all its modern luxury, the place can lay claim to a southern heritage, since for more than half a century this was the site of the Robert E. Lee Hotel, and a portrait of the general hangs in the lobby, on loan from the local chapter of the United Daughters of the Confederacy (who even imported Robert E. Lee IV for their presentation ceremonies). The Salem Tavern, which hosted George Washington in 1791, is preserved in spirit in the elegant, redecorated Smithfield's on Fifth, with a warm, comfortable atmosphere. The sophisticated and varied menu features some imaginative entrees for the fitness-conscious diner. Luncheons are in the $4 to $10 range, and dinners are about $12 to $20. A testament to the restaurant's excellence is its popularity with the local gentry. The adjoining lounge is a great place to relax and unwind, with live entertainment and dancing. The Greenhouse Restaurant, overlooking the lobby, offers everything from a hearty country breakfast to sandwiches to steaks, and is open from 7 a.m. until 11 p.m.

As for the rooms, each of the 305 has either a balcony view of the lobby or an outside view of the city, but if you're ready for some very special pampering, ask for a room on the ninth-floor Regency Club level. You begin the day there in a graciously appointed drawing room with a continental breakfast buffet and end it with sherry and cheese. Rates on this level are $120 and include the services of a concierge, who will do everything from making travel, rental car, or dinner reservations to finding a babysitter. The *Wall Street Journal* and other out-of-town newspapers can appear at your door every morning—just state your preference. Less elegant rooms (although all are first class) run $90 to $125. Except during special events, some rates drop considerably on Friday and Saturday nights.

In a more moderate price category, the **Holiday Inn North,** 3050 N. Cherry-Marshall Expressway, Winston-Salem, NC 27105 (tel. 919/723-2911, or toll free 800/465-4329), is a good bet. Just across from the center of all major sports events in this area (you guessed it—the coliseum), it also affords easy access to most sightseeing spots. For example, Old Salem is a straight shot through the city center on the expressway (clearly marked) and R. J. Reynolds World and Reynolda House and Gardens are close by. Rooms are large and decor is modern (doubles are $60 and up) and local telephone calls are free, as is transportation to and from the airport. There's piano music in the Open Forum Dining Room on Sunday, where southern fried chicken has brought travelers and local residents back for more over the years. Pets are welcome here if they stay in the kennel.

Special Note: A recent joyful discovery is the **Brookstown Inn,** 200 Brookstown Ave., Winston-Salem, NC 27101 (tel. 919/725-1120). In part of an old 1837 cotton mill that wove and dyed material for Confederate uniforms, this absolute jewel of a 40-room (plus 12 suites) inn offers spacious accommodations with two double beds, a chest of drawers, armoire (hiding a remote-control TV), love seat, desk, chairs, tables, and a live palm tree. The suites have a separate sitting room and hot tub. Silk flowers, quilts, baskets, and wooden decoys adorn the parlor areas, decorated in lovely Wedgwood blue, burgundy, gold, and olive, and accented by old brick and exposed wooden beams. Double rates begin at $75, and you're welcomed with complimentary afternoon wine and cheese, and a continental breakfast highlighted by luscious Moravian lovefeast buns. The inn, on the National Register of Historic Places, is conveniently near the Old Salem restoration. Another area of the mill, its former boiler, is the site of one of the popular Darryl's Restaurants.

The **Residence Inn by Marriott,** 7835 North Point Blvd., Winston-Salem, NC 27106 (tel. 919/727-1777 or toll free 800/331-3131) has upscale suites. In addition, there are fitness-center privileges, golf-club membership, barbecue and picnic facilities, and a weekly cocktail hour. Rates range from $82 to $102 for studio suites, $99 to $119 for penthouse suites, with special weekend and extended-stay rates.

The **Comfort Inn,** 110 Miller St., Winston-Salem, NC 27103 (tel. 919/721-0220 or toll free 800/228-5150), is an attractive motel with a skylighted lobby and nicely decorated rooms. Other on-premises amenities include a pool, sauna, whirlpool, and exercise room. Doubles range from $44 to $52.

In Nearby Greensboro

There's an elegant **Guest Quarters** at 5929 W. Friendly Ave., Greensboro, NC 27410 (tel. 919/292-9821 or toll free 800/424-2900), with one- and two-bedroom suites and all the exceptional service features of this fine chain (see Chapter I). This location has tennis courts and jogging trails, as well as a lovely swimming pool with deck area. Convenient to the airport and the city's corporate centers, Guest Quarters rates here are $94 double for the one-bedroom suites and $102 double for two bedrooms.

The 11-story **Sheraton Greensboro,** 3 Southern Life Center, 301 N. Elm St., Greensboro, NC 27401 (tel. 919/379-8000, or toll free 800/325-3535), right in the heart of downtown, was built around the historic 1926 Greensboro Central Fire Station (which has been renovated to house the elegant Central Station Restaurant). Guest rooms are all beautifully decorated, with mirrored closet doors, built-in headboards, and brass reading lamps. The most striking feature in many are their lovely bay windows. Doubles range from $93 to $108. Continental dishes in the Central Station Restaurant run from $13 to $22, with hours of 4 to 11 p.m. The more moderately priced Café is open from 6:30 a.m. to 10:30 p.m.

Once upon a time, the building that houses the **Greenwich Inn,** 111 W. Washington St., Greensboro, NC 27401 (tel. 919/272-3474), was the rather mundane executive office building for Cone Mills. In a highly successful trans-formation, however, it is today a small, charming, European-style inn, with some 27 rooms and suites. Some rooms are furnished with antique reproductions, and the tasteful decor in all rooms has a distinctive European flavor. Guests are greeted with complimentary champagne, treated with complimentary wine and cheese, and served a continental breakfast that's included in the rate. Doubles run $65 to $90, and there's a discount for seniors.

The **Residence Inn by Marriott,** 2000 Veasley St., Greensboro, NC 27407 (tel. 919/294-8600 or toll free 800/331-3131), has the high-standard suites typical of this chain (see Introduction), and other amenities include health-club privileges, barbecue facilities, complimentary hospitality hour Monday through Thursday, and free airport transportation. The Four Seasons Mall is less than a half mile away, with good shopping and restaurants. Rates for studio suites range from $72 to $94; for penthouse suites, $92 to $110; and there are lower rates for stays beyond six nights.

The **Quality Inn,** 3005 High Point Rd., Greensboro, NC (tel. 919/294-4565 or toll free 800/228-5151), has some rooms with refrigerators, some with whirlpool baths. There's a heated pool, sauna, exercise room, coin laundry, and nonsmoking rooms. A restaurant serves moderately priced meals, and there's a cocktail lounge. Rates for doubles run $76 to $88, rising to $110 for special events at the nearby coliseum, and there's a seniors' discount.

Rates also go up during special events at the **Red Roof Inn–Coliseum,** 2101 W. Meadowview Rd., Greensboro, NC 27403 (tel. 919/852-6560). Rooms are nice sized, with comfortable furnishings and extra-long beds. No restaurant, but a shopping mall across the street has good eateries. Rates for doubles range from $35 to $40; there are nonsmoking rooms, rooms for the handicapped, and discounts for seniors.

WHERE TO EAT

Far and away the most atmospheric place to eat is the **Old Salem Tavern,** 736 S. Main St. in Old Salem (tel. 919/748-8585). Here, as everywhere else in the restored village, authenticity is the keynote. The dining rooms were built in 1816 as an annex to the 1784 Tavern next door, and the simply furnished rooms and colonial-costumed waiters and waitresses provide an appropriate, early-18th-century ambience for your lunch (11:30 a.m. to 2 p.m.) or après-sightseeing dinner (5:30 to 9 p.m. every day but Sunday when hours are 11:30 a.m. to 2 p.m.). During summer months you can eat in the outdoor arbor, which, like the indoor rooms, is candlelit at night. Always available are such favorites as Tavern chicken pie (at lunch), and rack of lamb and roast duckling (dinner only). The pumpkin and raisin muffins are a specialty. Reservations are preferred at dinner and for luncheon parties of five or more. Lunch runs $5 to $10; dinner, $12 to $18.

In a lovely French country setting, **La Chaudiere,** 120 Reynolda Village (tel. 919/748-0269), specializes in both the moderne and classical cuisine of France, and in season also presents regional wild-game dishes. As you'd expect, there's an excellent wine list, and in good weather, patio dining. Prices are in the upper bracket, $30 and up at dinner, and hours are 11:30 a.m. to 2:30 p.m. Tuesday through Friday, from 6 p.m. Saturday and Sunday. Best to reserve ahead at this very popular restaurant.

Ryan's, 719 Coliseum Dr. (tel. 919/724-6132), in a wooded setting overlooking a stream, is rustic in decor as well, but its continental menu leans more toward sophistication. Beef dishes are specialties, as are some excellent seafood creations. Lunch is served 11:30 a.m. to 2:30 p.m. weekdays, dinner from 5:30 to 10 p.m. Monday through Thursday, to 10:30 p.m. Friday and Saturday, 5:30 to 10 p.m. Sunday. Expect to pay between $22 and $30 at dinner, less at lunch. Reservations are a good idea.

Locals flock to **Leon's Café,** 825 South Marshall (tel. 919/725-9593), a low-keyed neighborhood eatery with a surprisingly sophisticated menu. Hours are 6 to 9 p.m., but you can drop by for appetizers and desserts between 9:30 and 11 p.m. Open Tuesday through Saturday; closed Sunday, Monday, and holidays.

Special Note: At 801 Waughton St. is one of those treasures travelers dream about—an inexpensive place to eat with food that's *really* good! At the **Biscuit House** (tel. 919/788-8861), Charles Munday serves a menu that's limited but southern to the core, at prices you won't believe. For less than $2 you can buy two pieces of fried chicken and a large, light, yummy buttered biscuit (as one who grew up with the world's best biscuit-cooking mother, I know my biscuits and can speak with authority!). You can have a full dinner with two pieces, and if you're really a chicken-lover, the four-piece dinner. Mr. Munday also serves biscuits with ham, sausage, and steak for under $3. The chicken is as good as the biscuits, and that says it all—and there's a new addition to the menu, a chicken filet. For just pennies, a bowl of delicious, home-cooked pinto beans accents any of the above. Don't miss this one, even if money is no object.

In Greensboro

Excellent Italian and seafood selections are dished up in two Greensboro eateries: **Giovanni's,** 3938 Market St. (tel. 919/855-8000), with periodic entertainment and hours of 5 to 11 p.m. weekdays, to 11:30 Saturday, and prices $25 and under; and **Cellar Anton's,** 1628 Battleground Ave. (tel. 919/273-

1386), with prices in the $11 to $22 range, a children's menu, and 11 a.m. to 10 p.m. hours, later on weekends, to 9 p.m. Sunday.

The budget-priced **K & W Cafeteria** is in the Friendly Shopping Center on Friendly Avenue (tel. 919/292-2864), with hours of 10:45 a.m. to 8:30 p.m. Southern fried chicken is a specialty here.

THINGS TO SEE AND DO

For detailed sightseeing information, contact the **Convention and Visitors Bureau, Chamber of Commerce,** P.O. Box 1408, Winston-Salem, NC 27102 (tel. 919/725-2361).

Near the very center of the city (just off U.S. 52 on Old Salem Road), **Old Salem** has *got* to be the place you head for first in Winston-Salem. The visitor center, on Old Salem Road, will start you off with exhibits that trace the Moravians' journey from Europe to America and finally to North Carolina. And they'll sell you combination tickets to the restored buildings that are open Monday through Saturday from 9:30 a.m. to 4:30 p.m. and 1:30 to 4:30 p.m. on Sunday at $12 for adults, $6 for students. Of course, if you want to include the **Museum of Early Southern Decoration,** the price goes up—to $15 and $7.50. Individual admission to each building is $2. Costumed hosts and hostesses will show you around, and you'll also see craftsmen in Moravian dress practicing the trades of the original settlement.

And speaking of crafts, when Moravian boys reached the age of 14, they moved into the **Single Brothers House**—the first, half-timbered section of which was built in 1769 and the newer, brick wing in 1786—where they began an apprenticeship to a master artisan for seven years. Academic studies went on as they learned to be gunsmiths, tailors, potters, shoemakers, or whatever. Adolescent girls, too, left home to live in the **Single Sisters House,** diagonally across the town square, and learn the domestic arts they would need when marrying time arrived. Single girls *still* live in this building—it's a dormitory for Salem College—although their present-day education differs considerably.

Be sure to go into the **Tavern.** The one you see was built in 1784 to replace an earlier one which burned, and once inside you'll understand why travelers often went out of their way to stop here and enjoy its hospitality. George Washington spent two nights here in 1791 and commented in his diary on the industriousness of the Moravians. The dining room, sleeping rooms, barns, and grounds are not much different now from when he stopped by, and those cooking utensils you see in the stone-floored kitchen with its twin fireplaces are the real thing.

The **Wachovia Museum** (this whole area was named Wachovia by the original settlers after a district in Saxony that had offered refuge to the sect) was once the boys' school. There are tape recordings of music being played on the old musical instruments you see displayed here, and a host of other historical items. You can also visit the **Market-Firehouse** and the **Winkler Bakery.** Bread and cookies are still baked in the big wood-burning ovens at the bakery. Many of the homes have distinctive signs hanging outside to identify the shops inside, and one of my favorites is the tobacco shop of Matthew Miksch, a sunny-yellow weather-boarded log cottage with a miniature man hanging at the door clutching tobacco leaves and a snuff box.

Like the historic district of Williamsburg, Virginia, Old Salem still functions as a living community, and many of the homes you see restored on the outside are private residences, as modern inside as a contemporary ranch-style. And the young people you see walking the old streets with such familiarity are no doubt students at Salem College, living a 20th-century campus life in an 18th-century setting.

On the square, the **Home Moravian Church,** which dates from 1800, is the center of the denomination in the South. Visitors are always welcome at the services, and hundreds show up for the Easter Sunrise Service (held in Old Salem for over 200 years), the Christmas Lovefeasts (on December 24), and the New Year's Eve Watch Night Service. One block north of the square, the graveyard named "God's Acre" is a visual reminder that death is the great equalizer, since the more than 4,000 graves are marked with almost identical stones—prince and pauper are shown the same respect.

Three miles northwest of Winston-Salem, near Cherry Marshall and University hwys. (just follow the signs), is **Historic Bethabara Park,** 2147 Bethabara Rd., Winston-Salem, NC 27106 (tel. 919/924-8191), the 1753 site of the first Moravian settlement in North Carolina. There are two 18th-century homes, a 200-year-old Moravian church, the excavated foundations of the town of Bethabara, a rebuilt French and Indian War fort, nature trails, and picnic tables. There's also a visitors center, with a slide presentation about Bethabara and the beginnings of Winston-Salem. Guided tours of the buildings are free, and the park is open from April to mid-December from 9:30 a.m. to 4:30 p.m. Monday through Friday, 1:30 to 4:30 p.m. Saturday, Sunday, and holidays.

A prominent citizen of Winston lived at **Reynolda House** (just off Reynolda Road near Wake Forest University): R. J. Reynolds, the tobacco tycoon, built the mansion, which now holds an excellent collection of furnishings and American art, as well as a 1905–1950 ladies' costume display. The gardens are especially lovely in late March or early April, when they're abloom with Japanese cherry trees. The house is open Tuesday through Saturday from 9:30 a.m. to 4:30 p.m. and on Sunday from 1:30 p.m. and costs $4 for adults, $3 for senior citizens, and $2 for students and children. The gardens are free and open every day from 7:30 a.m. to 5 p.m.

No matter where you choose to stay in Winston-Salem, include **Tanglewood** in your sightseeing (see "Where to Stay," above). The beautiful recreation area is 10 miles southwest of town on U.S. 158, and the exit is marked.

Both the **Stroh Brewery,** 5½ miles south on U.S. 52 (tel. 919/788-6710, ext. 375), and the **R.J. Reynolds Tobacco Company,** Whitaker Cigarette Plant, Reynolds Boulevard (tel. 919/773-5718), will show you through their plants.

O. Henry's hometown, Greensboro, is less than 30 miles away. Of course, the short-story writer was known as William Sidney Porter in these parts, and you can see an exhibit illustrating his life and work at the **Greensboro Historical Museum,** 130 Summit Ave. (tel. 919/373-2043). Greensboro was also the birthplace of Dolley Madison. This museum houses a fine collection from her life as the only native-born North Carolina first lady. Other exhibits include early modes of transportation, furnishings, pottery, textiles, and military artifacts. There is no admission charge. Hours are 10 a.m. to 5 p.m. Tuesday through Saturday and 2 to 5 p.m. on Sunday.

Six miles northwest of Greensboro on U.S. 220, a 220-acre park— **Guilford Courthouse National Military Park,** P.O. Box 9806, Greensboro,

NC 27429 (tel. 919/288-1776)—marks one of the closing battles of the Revolution, the Battle of Guilford Courthouse on March 15, 1781. Gen. Nathanael Greene (Greensboro was named for him) led a group of inexperienced troops against Lord Cornwallis, and although he was defeated, he inflicted severe losses on the British. Cornwallis hotfooted it out of this part of the country and headed for Yorktown, Virginia, where he surrendered his depleted forces just seven months later, on October 19. The visitor center is open from 8:30 a.m. to 5 p.m. daily, and has films, brochures, and displays about the historic battle. There are also wayside exhibits along the two-mile, self-guided auto-tour road that leads to some of the many monuments. No charge.

Six miles southwest of nearby Burlington, on N.C. 62, is where those upstart farmers marched against Royal Governor Tryon in 1771 to protest British taxes. Ill-trained and poorly equipped, they were soundly defeated—the battle lasted only two hours—but the stouthearted "Regulators" were among the first southern colonists to demonstrate their objection to royal rule. The **Alamance Battleground State Historic Site** has a visitor center (with an audiovisual presentation) that's open Monday through Saturday from 9 a.m. to 5 p.m. and on Sunday from 1 to 5 p.m., April through October; Tuesday through Saturday from 10 a.m. to 4 p.m. and on Sunday from 1 to 4 p.m., November through March. Admission is free.

Just south of Greensboro, **High Point** is one of the leading furniture-manufacturing centers in the country. High Point (which got its name because it was the highest point along the 1853 North Carolina and Midland Railroad from Salem to Fayetteville) has a very good museum at 1805 E. Lexington Ave. (at McGuinn Avenue, tel. 885-6859), with displays of Native American artifacts and Quaker history exhibits. Right next door there's a restored 1786 Flemish bond-pattern-brick stagecoach stop, the **John Haley House,** a Quaker home with a still-functioning blacksmith shop.

Just about halfway between Greensboro and Charlotte, a little off I-85 (near historic Salisbury), the little town of Spencer is a mecca for dyed-in-the-wool railway buffs who come here to wander through the **Spencer Shops,** 411 S. Salisbury Ave. (tel. 704/636-2889), which were established in 1896 as a major repair facility for the Southern Railway. Opened as a museum in 1983, the Master Mechanics Building is the focal point in the 57-acre site. Indeed, visitors are free to wander among the growing collection of transportation memorabilia (with emphasis, of course, on trains) and let their imagination people the railyards with those hardworking, hard-living railroad men who once (in the 1930s) built a locomotive in one day. It's a friendly, informal place, where the project director, Michael Wells, or any member of his staff is likely to jump in with anecdotes about the shops' history at your first show of enthusiasm. It's free, and hours are 9 a.m. to 5 p.m. Monday through Saturday, from 1 p.m. on Sunday April through October; and from 10 a.m. to 4 p.m. Tuesday through Saturday, from 1 to 4 p.m. on Sunday, November through March. Hours are subject to change. Rail rides are sometimes available, and a large museum shop offers unusual railroad items ranging from 15¢ maps to *Orient Express* crystal.

Note: Just across the street, stop in at **Krider's restaurant** (tel. 704/633-5219), where Evelyn Krider loves to recall the days when railroading was the hub of activity in Spencer—she also serves up *very* good home-cooked meals at unbelievably low prices.

3. Charlotte

One of the largest cities in the Piedmont is Charlotte. It was named for King George III's wife, Queen Charlotte, but evidently its residents didn't take their royal affiliation too seriously: when Lord Cornwallis occupied the town briefly in 1780, he was so annoyed by patriot activities that he called the town a "hornet's nest," a name that stuck and now proudly adorns the city seal. He should have known what to expect, because more than a year before the Declaration of Independence was signed in Philadelphia, the Mecklenburg document declaring independence from Britain was signed in Charlotte—on May 20, 1775, to be exact. Present-day citizens will tell you that Thomas Jefferson used *their* declaration as a model for the one he wrote. Charlotte was prominent in national history again in 1865, when Jefferson Davis convened his last full cabinet meeting here that year.

After the Confederacy fell and the local boys came home from war, the city set out on a course that would free it of dependence on slave labor and that would eventually lead it to a position of industrial leadership in the South. The Catawba River furnished a rich supply of water power for industrialization, and development of manufacturing plants and textile mills was rather rapid. There are now more than 600 textile plants within a 100-mile radius.

Charlotte is also the center of a region that was for years the major gold producer for the United States. In fact, a branch of the U.S. mint was located here from 1837 to 1913, although it was inoperative from 1861 to 1867 because of the Civil War. This exquisite original 1835 William Strickland structure is now the Mint Museum, and with its $7.5-million expansion, houses one of the Southern Atlantic region's major art collections.

In the last decade or so, Charlotte has sprouted skyscrapers at an amazing rate, and one of the most interesting punctuation points of its skyline is the 40-story, trapezoidal steel-and-glass tower of the North Carolina National Bank Plaza. Throughout the 1980s a new tall building has been started before its predecessor was finished. When it's completed by the early 1990s, a 50-story NCNB Charter Properties office tower will be the tallest structure between Philadelphia and Atlanta.

Suburban areas too have mushroomed, with landscaped housing developments and enormous shopping malls springing up in every direction. This is one of the Southern Atlantic region's most graphic examples of the "new" South building squarely on the foundation of that fabled Old South.

WHERE TO STAY

The **Radisson Plaza Hotel,** 2 NCNB Plaza, Charlotte, NC 28280 (tel. 704/377-0400, or toll free 800/228-9822), has a trapezoidal shape to blend harmoniously with the North Carolina National Bank Plaza of which it is a part. It's connected by a covered walkway above the street to Charlotte's new convention center. The 381 rooms are the ultimate in comfort and contemporary design. There's concierge service, a pool, a health club, and free covered parking. The hotel has a bright, airy coffeeshop and an elegant upscale restaurant, Reflections, where semi-à la carte dinners range from $11 to $22. One of the city's most popular Sunday brunches is held here from 11:30 a.m. to 2 p.m., and it's in the $12 to $15 range. Doubles begin at $100, on the Plaza Club concierge floor it's $113. This is one of the most convenient locations in town, at the corner of Trade and Tryon streets.

It's a pleasure just to check in at the sleek new downtown **Marriott–City Center,** 100 W. Trade St., Charlotte, NC 28202 (tel. 704/333-9000, or toll free 800/228-9290 except in North Carolina). The enthusiastic young front-desk staff is especially helpful and friendly without being overbouncy. And the rooms, tastefully decorated with period reproduction furnishings and fabrics, exude a warmly welcoming ambience. There's a coin laundry, heated pool, and health club, along with valet parking (for a fee). There are two excellent dining rooms, Sweetbay (entrees range from about $8 to $17), named for the area showcasing a fabulous dessert buffet, and the somewhat pricier Chardonnay, where entrees are about $12 to $25. The room is impeccably decorated in tones of rose and gray, and highlighted with fine oil portraits, landscapes, and Oriental porcelains. A pianist plays softly in the foyer, and the fresh seafood entrees are especially good. Doubles are $100, $115 on the concierge floor, and corporate rates and senior citizen discounts are available.

There's an all-suite **Guest Quarters** at 6300 Morrison Blvd., Charlotte, NC 28211 (tel. 704/364-2400, or toll free 800/424-2900), with a price range of $119, double occupancy, for a one-bedroom suite and $185 (one to four people) for two bedrooms. Highly recommended.

The Marriott folks have blanketed the Charlotte area with representatives of each of their rate levels.

There are two of the upscale **Residence by Marriott** facilities. Both have extended-stay rates that descend the longer you stay, barbecue and picnic facilities, microwaves in all suites, and good restaurants within easy reach. Addresses are as follows: 8503 U.S. 29, Charlotte, NC 28213 (tel. 704/547-1122 or toll free 800/331-3131), on the north side of town, with rates of $84 to $104 for studio suites, and $99 to $119 for penthouse suites; and 5800 Westpark Dr., Charlotte, NC 28210 (tel. 704/527-8110 or toll free 800/331-3131), in the Tyvola Executive Park area, with rates of $80 to $89 for studios, $95 to $104 for penthouse suites.

Two **Courtyard by Marriott** locations—with pools and built in the attractive courtyard style, and offering extended-stay (six nights or longer) and reduced weekend rates—follow: 800 Arrowood Rd., Charlotte, NC 28217 (tel. 704/527-5055 or toll free 800/321-2211), with rates of $64 to $78 Sunday through Thursday, $46 to $68 Friday and Saturday; and 6023 Park Rd., Charlotte, NC 28210 (tel. 704/552-7333 or toll free 800/321-2211), with weekday rates of $66 to $80, dropping to $46 to $70 on weekends.

The budget-priced **Fairfield Inn by Marriott** also has two Charlotte locations, both with rates starting at $39.95. You'll find them at I-85 at Billy Graham Parkway, Charlotte, NC 28208 (tel. 704/392-0600 or toll free 800/228-2800), near the airport; and 5415 North I-85 Service Rd., Charlotte, NC 28213 (tel. 704/596-2999 or toll free 800/228-2800), on the northeast side of town.

The dependable **Days Inn** people have three motels in Charlotte, and I especially like the one at 122 W. Woodlawn Rd., Charlotte, NC 28210 (tel. 704/527-1620 or toll free 800/325-2525), which is convenient to the airport and Carowinds. I've never yet run across a Days Inn with disappointing accommodations, and this was no exception. Rooms are always adequate in size, comfortable, and the decor is pleasing. This one has a pool, a restaurant, and one unit especially fitted for the handicapped. Doubles are $45 to $60.

The popular **Econo Lodge** system, with national headquarters in Charlotte, has five locations in the city. Its conveniently located Charlotte Airport facility, I-85 and Little Rock Road (P.O. Box 668203), Charlotte, NC 28266 (tel. 704/394-0172, or toll free 800/446-6900), is just four miles from downtown and offers free airport-limousine service. There's a pool, restaurant, free cribs, and color satellite TV. Doubles start at $36, and it's $4 each for additional guests sharing. Senior-citizen and family discounts are offered.

Motel 6, 3433 Mulberry Church Rd., Charlotte, NC 28208 (tel. 704/394-0899), has a very convenient location if you're driving in via I-85. Either north- or southbound, take exit 33 (Billy Graham Parkway–Mulberry Church Road) south one block, turn left across the divided parkway onto Mulberry Church Road; then turn left and it's one block to the motel. From I-77, exit onto Billy Graham Parkway and go north to Mulberry Church Road. This is one of the best buys in the area. Rates are $28 double; each additional person over 12 stays for $6, and it's free for those under 3. This is a very well-maintained, clean, and comfortable new inn. It has a pool, and you can have color TV for a modest extra charge. Restaurants are nearby.

WHERE TO EAT

For broiled live lobster, steak, or prime rib, you probably can't do better in the Charlotte area than the **Epicurean,** 1324 East Blvd. (tel. 704/377-4529), which has been in business more than a quarter of a century. This is a chef-owned establishment, which probably accounts for the excellence of its food and its popularity locally. It boasts one of the city's most extensive wine lists, and not surprisingly, there is a dress code. The semi–à la carte prices range from $12 to $20, but there are children's plates for about $10. It's advisable to call ahead to reserve for dinner, which is served from 6 to 10 p.m. Closed Sunday and the first two weeks in July.

La Tache, an award-winning dining room in the Registry Inn Motor Hotel, 321 W. Woodlawn Rd. at I-77 (tel. 704/525-4441), is one of Charlotte's prettiest—and priciest—places to eat. A series of airy, mirror-lined rooms open onto each other in a valentine-like setting enhanced by soft pink tablecloths topped with vases of pink and white flowers. Luminous Oriental vases are reflected in the mirrors. Dinner appetizers include smoked sliced Canadian salmon with horseradish-dill sauce, and there's an astounding soup—essence of wild duck with quail eggs, covered with puff pastry. Among the entrees are steak Diane with mushrooms and cream, prepared tableside; and sautéed veal and lobster with cognac, finished with cream. As I said, it's pricey ($17 to $26), but worthy of your attention for a special occasion. The adjoining lounge with its dramatic light-spattered black ceiling is a locally popular piano bar where you can enjoy complimentary hors d'oeuvres weekdays from 5 to 8 p.m. At lunch you'll find sandwiches, omelets, and other light dishes, which run $6 to $12, or you can opt for the $10 buffet. La Tache is open from 6:30 to 11 a.m., 11 a.m. to 2 p.m., and 6 to 11 p.m. daily.

Eli's on East, 311 East Blvd. (tel. 704/375-0756), is one of those delightful "in" places favored by locals. It's in a charming 1908 Victorian frame house, where author Carson McCullers lived briefly in the 1930s. 'Tis said she did her research while sipping sherry from a Thermos in the local library. There's a French menu with continental touches, featuring beef, veal, swordfish, and salmon, along with such lighter luncheon fare as salads, quiches, and burgers. One house specialty is an uncommonly delicious Indian mulligatawny soup. Save room for the chef's delightful cakes or peanut-butter pie with fudge sauce! Eli's is open from 11:30 a.m. to 2 p.m. and 5:30 to 10 p.m. Tuesday through Thursday, to 11 p.m. on Friday and Saturday. Also, Sunday brunch is served from 10:30 a.m. to 2:30 p.m. Lunch is in the $5 to $8 range, and a semi–à la carte dinner costs $11 to $19. Reservations are suggested.

For a special late-night treat, **Jonathan's Uptown,** 330 N. Tryon St. (tel. 704/332-3663), is a popular late-night rendezvous spot for upwardly mobile young Charlotteans who drop in for live jazz and fresh American cuisine after a Spirit Square performance. It's a sophisticated "big city" room with a dramatic black-and-white decor, where service is deft and friendly at the same time. The menu is anything but basic, highlighted by such entrees as broiled halibut topped with orange-pecan butter and boneless chicken breast sautéed in white wine and cream, topped with crabmeat, artichoke hearts, and parmesan. The carrot and chocolate-raspberry cakes melt in your mouth. Jonathan's boasts a climate-controlled wine cellar with 22,000-bottle capacity. Evenings there's a pianist, and occasionally one of the servers goes on stage to sing along. Lunch ranges from $6 to $10, and dinner from $12 to $18. Dress may be casual, but this definitely doesn't mean jeans, tennis shoes, or cutoffs. If you're staying in the uptown Radisson or Marriott, it's a short couple-of-blocks' stroll to Jonathan's, which is open from 11:30 a.m. to 2:30 p.m. Monday through Friday, from 6 to 10:30 p.m. Monday through Saturday, and from 6 to 9:30 p.m. on Sunday. The Jazz Lounge (with a small admission fee) is open from 9 p.m. to 1 a.m. Monday through Saturday. A limited menu is also served in the bar adjoining the dining room from 4:30 to 11:30 p.m. Monday through Saturday.

Whenever I visit friends in Charlotte, we always seem to wind up in their favorite neighborhood Chinese restaurant, the **Golden Palace,** 6437 Albemarle Rd., in Loehmann Plaza (tel. 704/568-3216 or 568-3217). It's about a half mile past the popular Eastland Mall shopping center, and it has become my favorite too for its wonderful range of Chinese dishes at moderate cost. It's hard to top the special dinner, which for under $10 will bring you a choice of wonton or egg-drop soup, egg roll or paper chicken, one of 15 entrees—including sweet-and-sour shrimp (marvelous huge prawns), beef with bean sprouts, or almond fried chicken—fortune or almond cookies, and a pot of tea, of course. A house specialty is sizzling Wor Bar—chunks of lobster, shrimp, chicken, roast pork, and fresh Chinese veggies, served sizzling tableside over crispy rice patties, for just $8. And although the owner-chefs come from southern China (the Canton area), that doesn't stop them from being expert in preparation of such spicy Szechuan delicacies as shredded beef with hot chile or kung-po chicken ding, with diced bamboo shoots, chiles, water chestnuts, peanuts, celery, mushrooms, and scallions. Service is continuous from 11:30 a.m. to 10 p.m. Monday through Friday, from 5 to 11 p.m. on Saturday, and from noon to 10 p.m. on Sunday. From 11:30 a.m. to 2:30 p.m. Monday through Friday, there are special luncheon plates or platters for $5 and under. You can come in as casually dressed as you please, settle down cozily in one of two dining rooms adorned with Chinese scroll paintings, and prepare for a culinary treat.

The Charlotte area is notable for its "fish camps"—homey, informal, family-style restaurants, which serve gargantuan portions of fresh seafood at moderate cost. The **Fish Farm,** 1200 Sam Newell Rd. in nearby Matthews (tel. 704/847-8578), is not as laid-back and rustic as some of the riverside "camps," but since 1975 this locally popular restaurant has had a wide following for its fresh broiled or fried seafoods. All-you-can-eat specials include Carolina flounder, steamed-in-the-shell shrimp, Calabash-style shrimp, and catfish, all for $10 or under. The Fish Farm is open from 4:30 to 9:30 p.m. Tuesday through Thursday, to 10 p.m. on Friday and Saturday, and to 9:30 p.m. on Sunday. To reach it from Charlotte, drive east on East Independence Boulevard, turn right on Sam Newell Road, and drive about half a mile.

Arthur's, in three Ivey's department stores—Uptown, 127 N. Tryon St. (tel. 704/333-4867); Eastland Mall, 5501 Central Ave. (tel. 704/588-0210); and Southpark Mall, 4400 Sharon Rd. (tel. 704/366-6456)—offers freshly made sandwiches, hoagies, quiches, soups, and salads in a comfortable café atmosphere. Each includes a wine shop. They're open from 10 a.m. to 8:30 p.m. Monday through Saturday, and from 12:30 to 5 p.m. on Sunday. You can have a very good repast for around $5.

You'll find one of the reliable **Morrison's Cafeterias** at 5633 Central Ave., in the Eastland Mall (tel. 704/568-7136). You can have breakfast for about $3, and there are daily Monday through Saturday $4 daily specials (Monday, it's baked, chopped steak with rice or potato; Tuesday, one-quarter broiled or fried chicken with vegetable and potato; other equally good stick-to-your-ribs specials are offered each day). Sunday dinner, served all day, is turkey and dressing, salad, vegetable, bread, and dessert, for $7. Morrison's is open daily, including major holidays, from 11 a.m. until 8:30 p.m.

THINGS TO SEE AND DO

For sightseeing in detail, contact: **Charlotte Convention & Visitors Bureau,** 229 N. Church St., Charlotte, NC 28232 (tel. 704/334-2282).

The **Mint Museum of Art,** 2730 Randolph Rd. (tel. 704/337-2000), with the recently added Dalton wing, displays fine European and American survey collections, the internationally recognized Delhom Collection of porcelain and pottery, pre-Columbian art, contemporary American prints, African objects, vast costume and antique maps collections, and gold coins originally minted at the facility. It's open from 10 a.m. to 10 p.m. on Tuesday, to 5 p.m. Wednesday through Saturday, and from 1 to 6 p.m. on Sunday. Admission is $2 for adults, $1 for students and senior citizens, free for ages 12 and under, with an extra charge for occasional special exhibits.

If you're in Charlotte during April and May, drive north on N.C. 49 to the **University of North Carolina at Charlotte** campus to see their rhododendron garden—spectacular! And if you're on campus at either 7:30 a.m. or 5:15 p.m., you'll get in on the carillon concerts (on Sunday, it's 3:30 p.m.).

Take the children to the **Charlotte Nature Museum and Planetarium** at 1658 Sterling Rd. (enter via East Boulevard)—exhibits are specially planned for developing an awareness and appreciation of nature through displays and programs designed especially for young children. There's also a planetarium, a puppet theater, and a nature trail. Admission to the museum is 75¢ (under 3, free with parents), and hours are 9 a.m. to 6 p.m. Monday through Saturday, 1 to 6 p.m. on Sunday. Planetarium shows are at 3 and 4 p.m. on Saturday and Sunday, and cost $1 for adults and 75¢ for students. Special children's shows at 2 p.m. on Saturday and Sunday, cost 75¢ for all ages.

Joining with the Nature Museum to form the combined Science Museums of Charlotte, Inc., is the **Discovery Place Science and Technology Center** at 301 N. Tryon St. in uptown Charlotte. Discovery Place takes you through eight major exhibit areas, including a tropical rain forest, an aquarium, and a life center, and stresses a hands-on approach to learning. There's a $3 admission for adults, $2 for students and senior citizens, and $1 for ages 3 to 5; and hours are 9 a.m. to 6 p.m. Monday through Saturday and 1 to 6 p.m. on Sunday.

One of Charlotte's most delightful attractions is absolutely free: **Wing Haven Gardens,** 248 Ridgewood Ave., Charlotte, NC 28209 (tel. 704/332-5770). They were the inspiration and longtime labor of love of Mrs. Elizabeth Clarkson, who is sometimes known as Charlotte's "bird lady" because of her deep love for the 142 winged species that have been sighted in the three-acre walled garden she created from a once-bare clay field. Bird-watchers will have a field day, as will garden-lovers, as they browse through the Upper, Lower, Main, Wild, and Herb gardens. Lovely any time of the year, it is in the spring, when birds are returning from their winter sojourn in warmer climes, that the gardens are perhaps their most splendid. They're open to the public all year on Sunday, Tuesday, and Wednesday from 3 to 5 p.m., and a bulletin board tells you which birds are around at the moment.

The 11th president of the United States was born in 1795 in Mecklenburg County, North Carolina, about 12 miles south of Charlotte on U.S. 521. Today, the birthplace is one of North Carolina's historic sites, the **James K. Polk Memorial,** P.O. Box 475, Pineville, NC 28134 (tel. 704/889-7145). In addition to reconstructed log buildings typical of the 19th century, like the log house with a separate kitchen that's authentically furnished, you'll find exhibits in the modern visitor center illustrating the life and times of this president. Featured is a 25-minute film, *Who is Polk?,* and guided tours are conducted through the log buildings. There's no admission, and hours are 9 a.m. to 5 p.m. Monday through Saturday, 1 to 5 p.m. Sunday, April through October; 10 a.m. to 4 p.m. Tuesday through Saturday and 1 to 4 p.m. Sunday, November through March.

The **Charlotte Hornets** of the National Basketball Association play from November to April at the Charlotte Coliseum on West Tyvola Road. Tickets range from $7 to $16 and can be obtained by calling the ticket information office (704/338-9662) or Teletron (800/543-3041).

The **Charlotte Motor Speedway,** 12 miles northeast of Charlotte on U.S. 29 (or just off I-85), is host in late May (Memorial Day Sunday) of each year to the **Coca-Cola 600 NASCAR Winston Cup Stock Car Race,** longest and richest such race in the U.S., which draws upward of 160,000 enthusiastic fans. If you're a devotee of the daredevil sport, you may want to plan your trip then or in early October, when the **Oakwood Homes 500 Winston Cup Stock Car Race** is run. You can get exact dates and full details of both events by writing Charlotte Motor Speedway, P.O. Box 600, Harrisburg, NC 28075 (tel. 704/455-2121).

If you're taking children along on your Charlotte trip, you undoubtedly already know about **Carowinds Theme Park,** I-77 at the North Carolina–South Carolina border (tel. 704/588-2600). But even without the kids, it's worth a day just for fun. The $40-million park straddles the North and South Carolina state line and has nine theme areas reflecting facets of the two states' past and present. The rides are entertaining and inventive, especially the flume and mine train rides, although I must confess my romantic favorite is the stern-wheeler that set me thinking of slower days. For the more adventurous, the Thunder Road and White Lightnin' roller coasters may beckon you. On the sightseeing side of things, look for a re-creation of the Old Charleston water-front, Pirate Island, and enjoy fast-paced revues at Midway Music Hall and Troubador's Roost Theatre. In Blue Ridge Junction, you'll enjoy the shops and crafts (from the days of British rule) at Queen's Colony; and you can tap your toes to bluegrass music in Harmony Hall. One cautionary word: They won't let you bring pets in; however, there is a kennel for stashing them. Admission, which includes all rides and most entertainments, is $14.50 for ages 7 and over, $7.25 for ages 4 to 6 and over 60, and free for children 3 and under; and there's a $2 parking fee. The park is open every day except Friday from 10 a.m. to 8 p.m. from the second week in June through mid-August; weekends only in mid-March, April, May, September, and early October. It's closed from mid-October through March.

VIII

THE SANDHILLS OF NORTH CAROLINA

The Sandhills' porous, sandy soil is a reminder that in prehistoric times Atlantic Ocean waves rolled over the land. It also provides an ideal drainage situation that is a big factor in the area's "Golf Capital of the World" standing, for no matter what the rainfall, no puddles accumulate on the rolling green golf courses (there are 27 within a 15-mile radius). And with mean temperatures that range between 78° and 44°, the games go on year round.

But golf hasn't always been king here. In fact, when Boston philanthropist James Walker Tufts bought up 5,000 acres of land in 1895 at $1 per, his main thought was to build the little resort village of Pinehurst as a retreat from harsher climes for wealthy Northerners. Recreation for guests back then consisted mainly of croquet on the grassy lawns, outdoor concerts, hayrides, or just quiet walks through the pines. The story goes that his attention first turned to golf, which had only recently arrived in the U.S. from Great Britain, when one of his dairy employees complained that guests were "hitting the cows with a little white ball." By 1900 Tufts had enlisted Donald Ross (whose skill had been gained at Scotland's St. Andrews) to come to Pinehurst and introduce golf. In time (he remained in the Sandhills the rest of his life) Ross designed courses here that drew some of the most distinguished golfers in the world: Ben Hogan, Walter Travis, Bobby Jones, Walter Hagen, Patty Berg, Sam Snead, Arnold Palmer, Gary Player, Jack Nicklaus—and that's only a partial list!

Golf is not, however, the only attraction of the Sandhills area. Over the years, this region has become a mecca for artists and craftspeople, and the pottery workshops here have gained national and international reputations. Scattered around the vicinity in rustic, pine-sheltered settings, the potters welcome visitors, and most are quite happy to have you watch them at their work.

PINEHURST, SOUTHERN PINES, AND VICINITY

For years, golf on the superb courses, beginning and ending at the Pinehurst Country Club's clubhouse, was by invitation only. The list of invitees was so exclusive that Walter Hagen is reported to have said (after finally receiving the treasured summons) on returning from his first game, "The place is so exclusive that, hell, the duke of Windsor would have trouble getting in!" Today, however, although the golf world's top players no doubt consider Pinehurst their own turf, you don't have to wait for an invitation, nor do you have to be a millionaire to play. Prices are certainly high enough at the Pinehurst Hotel, but they're not exorbitant by comparison with other luxury hotels around the country. And there is a profusion of other hotels and motels, something in almost any price range; and, expert or duffer, guests can always play the courses.

In 1973 the first World Open Championship was played in Pinehurst, replaced in 1977 by the Colgate–Hall of Fame Classic. In September of 1974 President Gerald Ford presided at the opening of the World Golf Hall of Fame, overlooking Ross's famous Number Two Course (one of the top 10 in the country), with all the living inductees there for the ceremonies.

Through all the hullabaloo over celebrity golf matches, Pinehurst has retained its New England village air, built by Frederick Law Olmstead (the architect-landscaper who also planned New York's Central Park), with a village green and shaded residential streets, many paved only by a carpet of pine needles. It hasn't changed, but continues to carry out the Tufts concept of a retreat here in the Sandhills. Year-round greenery is provided by pines (some with needles 15 inches long), stately magnolias, and hollies. Moderate temperatures account for color through all seasons—camellias, azaleas, wisteria, peach trees, dogwoods, and summer-blooming yard flowers. Shops, restaurants, hotels, and other business enterprises make it a complete, self-sufficient community, yet none intrude in an abrasive way, all adhering to the original style and preserving a leisurely graciousness that's as refreshing to the spirit as to the eye.

For those whose idea of a good time is *not* chasing around after that elusive little white ball (you can count me in that esteemed company), there are plenty of other things to do. There's a tennis club, any number of excellent courts, over 200 miles of riding trails and stables with good mounts for hire, boating on a 200-acre lake, trap and skeet ranges, archery, over 9,000 acres of woods to explore via meandering pathways, and shopping in the little boutiques that is out of this world.

Pinehurst's sister town, **Southern Pines,** is a delight, too. The short drive on Midland Road (N.C. 2), a double-lane highway divided by a strip of pines and bordered by lovely homes and lavish gardens, goes right past **Midland Crafters.** You'll see it on your right, and take my word for it, stop. The rambling white building is a virtual gallery of American crafts, ranging from beanbags to paintings to furniture, to candles, to pottery, to glassware, to . . . well, almost any handcraft you can think of.

Like those in Pinehurst, shops here are small, charming, and filled with interesting, often exquisite items. Outstanding among the offbeat shops is **Something Special,** on Pennsylvania Avenue (tel. 919/692-9602). Inside are collectors' dolls and dollhouses, miniature grandfather clocks that keep time, all kinds of materials to make your own dollhouse, and items so special (like the miniature dentures I saw there) that people come here from all over the Southern Atlantic region to have a look.

All this will give you some idea of what to expect when you come to this part of North Carolina's Piedmont, but I strongly recommend that you write ahead for detailed information on Pinehurst (Pinehurst Hotel and Country Club, P.O. Box 4000, Pinehurst, NC 28374; tel. 704/295-6811) and the entire Sandhills (**Sandhills Area Chamber of Commerce,** P.O. Box 458, Southern Pines, NC 28387; tel. 919/692-3926).

WHERE TO STAY

Both Pinehurst and Southern Pines are fairly broken out with places to stay.

In Pinehurst

Although the **Pinehurst Hotel and Country Club,** P.O. Box 4000, Pinehurst, NC 28374 (tel. 919/295-6811, or toll free 800/334-9560, 800/672-4644 in North Carolina), is still *the* place to stay in Pinehurst, as it has been from the beginning, there are several other hotels in the village that offer luxury on a smaller scale and graciousness on the same level at somewhat more moderate prices. And, of course, Southern Pines is close by, with numerous motels catering to Pinehurst visitors.

About that grand old Pinehurst Hotel: Now owned by Club Resorts, Inc., a subsidiary of Club Corporation of America, it proudly rears its head with all the splendid aristocracy of the past enhanced by the most modern improvements (for example, in the old days the only air conditioning came from open windows or fans). The white, four-story, 300-room building, with wings on each side sporting broad, columned porches lined with comfortable rocking chairs, was called the Carolina for years, and you'll still hear residents refer to it by that name. Whatever you call it, when you drive up to the columned portico and walk through its huge lobby furnished with a pleasing mixture of antique and contemporary fittings, you'll know this is a place where the art of gracious living is still practiced. Public rooms and guest rooms have undergone extensive renovation, and while bright, cheerful colors predominate in the spacious accommodations, there's an air of subdued elegance that newer establishments never seem quite able to achieve. And besides the main building, there are over 160 one-, two-, and three-bedroom condominiums.

The tennis complex, with some 28 courts (18 are clay), is presided over by a highly professional staff. Clinics and individual instruction are available to all guests in addition to a Tennis Advantage program.

For equestrians, saddle horses are available, and there are miles of riding trails, supervised and unsupervised riding, instructions, and, if you bring your own mount, boarding. The stables also offer carriage rides, a particularly charming way to see the village. There are nine trap-and-skeet fields (two of which are lighted), croquet and lawn bowls.

But, of course, the major attractions are those seven 18-hole golf courses, es-

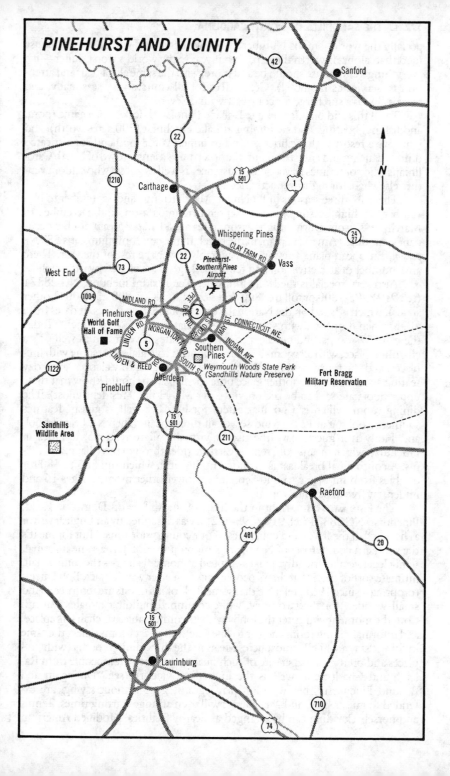

PINEHURST AND VICINITY

pecially the world-famous Number Two. Five begin and end at the clubhouse (and that, alone, is worth the trip, even if you're the world's worst duffer—it's everything a clubhouse should be and more, with the same elegant air and attention to service as the hotel). Greens fees for all courses vary seasonally, and there's always a surcharge for courses Two and Seven.

To all this add bicycles, a huge L-shaped pool and deck area, a game room, and fishing, boating, and swimming at Lake Pinehurst (200 acres worth), and you have a resort with facilities second to none. As for food and sophisticated dinner-dancing and entertainment, the hotel draws a large crowd of North Carolinians who sometimes travel quite a distance, as well as guests who seldom venture elsewhere for nighttime activities.

There are three seasons in Pinehurst: March to June and September to November are high season; June to September, midseason; and December to March, off-season. During high season, rates are $102 *per person* double occupancy, modified American plan, in the hotel. In the condominiums, it's $87 *per person,* European plan. They are considerably lower the rest of the year. There are a number of attractive golf and tennis package plans offered by the hotel.

Also very special is the **Holly Inn,** Cherokee Road, Pinehurst, NC 28374 (tel. 919/295-2300 or toll free 800/682-6901 in NC, 1-800/533-0041 other states), which is listed on the National Register of Historic Places. It dates from 1895, when it opened with some 45 rooms that went for $3 per night. Today there are 77 rooms, and needless to say, room rates have grown as well. It's a charming place, with all rooms and suites done in colonial style, some with fireplaces, and the fourth and fifth floors all sorts of angles, tiny alcoves, and cozy seating spots that lend another grace note (perhaps you should know that these upper floors are said to be the province of "Mr. Holly," resident ghost). The dining room, which is a popular eatery for locals as well as guests, features southern cooking at its best and serves all three meals. There's a heated pool, and Holly Inn guests have the use of virtually all recreational facilities in Pinehurst, which means golf, tennis, carriage rides through the village, and tennis. A continental breakfast is included in the rates, which run $65 to $80 for doubles from mid-June to mid-September, lower other months. Ages 16 and under stay free in parents' room.

The **Pine Crest Inn,** right in the heart of the Village on Dogwood Road, Pinehurst, NC 28374 (tel. 919/295-6121), was described by an English visitor as having "all the flavor and courtesies of our countryside inns." But for me it's the southern counterpart of New York's Algonquin Hotel: the same informal, semi-elegance and friendly, makes-you-feel-at-home feeling—the same small, intimate sort of place that draws people back year after year. In fact, Bob Barrett (proprietor since 1961) tells me that some 80% of his guests are returnees. And small wonder, for the two-story, white-columned building radiates warmth from the moment you enter the lobby with its comfortable armchairs, fireplace, and informal dining room and bar to one side; and guest rooms reflect the same inviting "stay a while" atmosphere. Meals in the three dining rooms (with fireplaces and pretty wallpaper) are of such quality that they draw people from Raleigh and Charlotte as well as the immediate vicinity (see "Dining in and Around Pinehurst," below). Golf privileges, it goes without saying, are extended to guests here, and Mr. Barrett will even arrange starting times. Tennis and horseback riding can be arranged at nearby facilities. Modified American plan (breakfast and dinner) rates *per person,* double occupancy, run $55 to $80, depending on the season. Golf and "all sports" packages are available.

In Southern Pines

While Southern Pines has a plethora of modern motels with exceptionally high standards, my personal favorite place to stay is an oldtimer. The **Jefferson Inn,** 150 W. New Hampshire Ave., Southern Pines, NC 28387 (tel. 919/692-6400), dates from 1902, when it was built as a private home, which perhaps explains the sense of "at homeness" you feel from the moment you walk into the lobby. On second thought, that warm, homey feeling undoubtedly stems from the graciousness of attractive Sylvia Bowles, who a few years ago brought her extensive hospitality experience to bear on the old inn, which had slipped more than a little in the years since it first welcomed guests. Sylvia and her son, Randy, as well as her lovely daughter Diana, have brought a luster back to the Jefferson that attracts both out-of-towners and locals. They come in regularly for good southern cooking in the inn's Diana's Restaurant and outdoor café, The Courtyard; or for a friendly drink or two in The Pub, a friendly, informal gathering place. Guests also find its central location a bonus.

The 20 rooms are all sizes, from very spacious to small and cozy, and each is individually decorated. All have private baths; bed sizes range from king to queen to double to twin; and several have connecting rooms for families. If it's space with a touch of elegance you're looking for, ask for #4, which has a sitting area, walk-in closet, and a queen-size, four-poster bed. Rates for doubles begin at $50; for singles, $45; and attractive golf packages as well as weekly rates are available. Recommended.

One of the leading resorts in this area is the **Mid Pines,** a Clarion Resort, on Midland Road, Southern Pines, NC 28387 (tel. 919/692-2114, 800/323-2114). It's a graceful, colonial-style building with wings stretching out on either side of the main entrance. That main entrance leads to a lobby rotunda that is strikingly beautiful, with twin white staircases. There are 63 rooms in the three-story hotel, and all are decorated with style. And if cottage living suits you best, there are several on the premises, some with fireplaces, accommodating up to 17. There's an 18-hole golf course, a putting green, a landscaped pool (set off by a charming split-rail fence), four tennis courts which are lighted at night, and a recreation room. Both the lovely formal dining room and the more informal Terrace (overlooking the fairways of the championship golf course) serve excellent meals—I especially liked the buffet lunch on the Terrace—at moderate to expensive prices. Double-room rates (full American plan) run $160 to $190 in season, lower other months, and cottages are $198.

The **Sheraton Inn,** on U.S. 1 at Morgantown Road (P.O. Box 1467), Southern Pines, NC 28387 (tel. 919/692-8585), has oversize beds in its cheerful, modern rooms. Two lounges provide entertainment and dancing, and there are tennis courts and a jogging trail. And, of course, golf privileges. Doubles here begin at $50 in season, lower other months.

The **Hyland Hills Resort,** 41110 U.S. 1 North, Southern Pines, NC 28387 (tel. 919/692-7615), has efficiencies as well as spacious guest rooms, all with patios. There's a pool and an 18-hole golf course right on the premises. Seasonal rates for doubles and efficiencies are in the $40 to $50 range; and golf packages are available.

The **Days Inn,** 1420 U.S. 1 South, Southern Pines, NC 28387 (tel. 919/692-7581 or toll free 800/325-2525), has comfortably furnished and tastefully decorated guest rooms, and a pool, Jacuzzi, restaurant, and lounge with entertainment are all on the premises. Double-room rates run $48 to $60, and golf packages are available.

There are picnic areas on the grounds of the **Econo Lodge,** U.S. 1 South, P.O. Box 150 Comfort Inn, 1214 Monroe Street, Southern Pines, NC 28677 (tel. 919/944-2324 or toll free 800/446-6900). Some of the comfortable guest rooms have king-size beds. There's a 24-hour restaurant, a lounge, a pool, and laundry and dry-cleaning service. Doubles start at $33.95, and golf packages are offered.

Campgrounds

The **Heritage,** Whispering Pines, NC 28327 (tel. 919/949-3433), is actually a 200-acre country estate, a peaceful and relaxing place for campers. With a spring-fed, 14-acre lake and sandy beach, it offers swimming, canoeing, pedal boats and fishing, a playground, shuffleboard, volleyball, basketball, croquet, a putting green, horseback riding, and horseshoes. A meeting room with a large deck overlooks the lake. The privacy and beautiful wooded setting give The Heritage special appeal, and it's only a few minutes away from restaurants and shopping. There are 50 sites with water and electric, 22 with full hookups, flush toilets, hot showers, laundry, ice, picnic tables, and firewood. Rates start at $16.

DINING IN AND AROUND PINEHURST

Almost all the inns, hotels, and motels in the Pinehurst area have very good dining rooms.

The **Carolina Room** at the Pinehurst Hotel (tel. 919/295-6811) is a formal dining room that serves dinner from 6:30 to 10 p.m. in candlelit elegance. The menu is extensive and a five-course meal will average $20 to $25. Needless to say, the service is impeccable. During the season, there's top-flight entertainment and dinner-dancing.

Although small, the **Pine Crest Inn** in Pinehurst (tel. 919/295-6121) has made such a name for itself in the food field that reservations are made from towns all over the state. Their prime beef, homemade pastries, and insistence on the freshest of vegetables are the reasons for that reputation. And as good as the food is, I'm firmly convinced people come back, too, for the warm hospitality that pervades this place. There's dancing in Mr. B's Lounge. Dinner prices range from $10 to $22 complete, and you really must reserve ahead here.

Diana's Restaurant, in the Jefferson Inn, 150 W. New Hampshire Ave., Southern Pines (tel. 919/692-6400), is a relaxed, friendly place to eat, with a menu that features seafood, beef, and chicken. Without doubt, the value-for-dollar star of that menu is the Wednesday night two-for-the-price-of-one prime rib special, when dinner for two will run under $20. The 9-oz. prime rib comes with soup or salad, baked potato, vegetable, homemade rolls and butter, and homemade apple pie. This popular spot also has lunch specials at around $5 to $6, and an excellent Sunday brunch. Lunch hours are 11:30 a.m. to 2:30 p.m. Monday through Friday; dinner, 5:30 to 9 p.m. Tuesday through Saturday, and Sunday brunch from 11:30 a.m. to 2:30 p.m. Be sure to reserve ahead for dinner and Sunday brunch.

Whiskey McNeill's, 181 N.E. Broad St., Southern Pines (tel. 919/692-5440), is a whimsical sort of place—it was once a service station, and leftover gas pumps have been retained inside the eatery. Its menu is a nice mixture of gourmet-quality sandwiches (many made with croissants), burgers, salads (including the standout seafood-salad plate, a mixture of whitefish, shrimp, and crabmeat), tasty homemade soups (don't miss the traditional southern-style Brunswick stew), and homemade desserts. Nothing is priced above $8, and most items are nearer to $5. Hours are 11:30 a.m. to 9 p.m., Tuesday through Saturday.

Combine lunch with a delightful shopping experience at the **Greenhouse Restaurant,** in Pinehurst Place, a mile and a half out Linden Road off Hwy. 5 North (tel. 919/295-1761). Shops, which are open 9:30 a.m. to 5:30 p.m. Monday through Saturday and until 4 p.m. on Sunday, offer a wide variety of gifts, brass, arts and crafts, baskets, sportsware, candles, and a host of other categories. As for lunch, the Greenhouse is a light, airy place with blonde bentwood chairs and, as you might expect, lots of hanging plants. The menu has such specialties as crab and seafood on a toasted English muffin, topped with cheddar cheese sauce, and specialty meatballs, provolone cheese in a zesty tomato sauce on toasted loaf bread. Soups are memorable, as are desserts like the Greenhouse mud pie and strawberry shortcake. They have a wide selection of beer and mixed drinks, as well as wine by the glass. Prices are under $5.

For prime steaks, lobster and other fresh seafood, and an excellent salad bar, one of the best places in the area is the **Lob Steer Inn,** U.S. 1 South in Southern Pines (tel. 919/692-3503). The menu includes steak-and-lobster combination plates, and so popular is this eatery with the locals that advance reservations are highly advisable. Prices are in the $11 to $25 range, and hours are 5 to 10:30 p.m., seven days a week.

If a yen for ethnic specialties strikes, you'll find fine French cuisine at **Antoine's,** 270 S.W. Broad St., Southern Pines (tel. 919/692-5622), which serves lunch and dinner Tuesday through Saturday.

Italian dishes, plus steaks and seafood, are the stars at **Raffaele's,** 1113 U.S. 1 South, Southern Pines (tel. 919/692-1952), with hours of 5 to 10 p.m., Monday through Saturday. Prices at both will run $12 to $22.

For a mid-day light snack, the folks hereabouts will steer you to **Morrie's Deli and Bakery,** 120 S.W. Broad St. in Southern Pines (tel. 919/692-5759). Everything here is homemade, with large sandwiches (including such filler-uppers as the hot meatball sandwich), quiche, pasta, burgers, and hot dogs. Salads are fresh, and homemade desserts are terrific. Hours are 9:30 a.m. to 3 p.m., and prices are in the $3 to $5 range. Incidentally, if you get the itch to do a bit of entertaining in your hotel room, they cater smashing lazy Susan trays.

AFTER DARK

Most of the major golf resorts have dancing and periodic evening entertainment. In addition, check the following for current goings-on.

Mannie's Dinner Theatre, West Pennsylvania Avenue in Southern Pines (tel. 919/692-8400), presents professional troupes in Broadway shows during the summer season, along with dinner in a relaxed atmosphere. Advance booking is a must.

Jazz music and other variety shows are staged at the **Sandhills Community**

College, Airport Road, Pinehurst (tel. 919/692-6185); and the **Performing Arts Center,** N.W. Broad Street in Southern Pines (tel. 919/692-4356), is home for the Sandhills Little Theater and a number of other local concert and entertainment groups.

During the summer season, there's usually live music in **The Pub** of the Jefferson Inn, 150 W. New Hampshire Ave., Southern Pines (tel. 919/692-6400).

THINGS TO SEE AND DO

For advance sightseeing information, you can contact **Resorts of Pinehurst, Inc.,** Pinehurst Hotel and Country Club, P.O. Box 4000, Pinehurst, NC 28374 (tel. 919/295-6811), and/or the Sand Hills Area **Chamber of Commerce,** P.O. Box 458, Southern Pines, NC 28387 (tel. 919/692-3926).

Golf, golf, and more golf—that's really why most people come to Pinehurst. And if there's a hotel or motel that doesn't arrange play for its guests, I didn't find it. Most can also set you up for tennis, cycling, or boat rentals on one of the many lakes around. For a complete list of golf courses, ask the Chamber of Commerce for their "Accommodations" brochure.

Horseback riders can arrange for mounts by calling the **Pinehurst Stables** (tel. 919/295-6811), where expert instruction is available for novices; or contact Mrs. Harold Sadler at **The Heritage** (tel. 919/949-3433).

Aside from recreation facilities, the Pinehurst area also offers the **World Golf Hall of Fame,** PGA Boulevard, Pinehurst (tel. 295-6651), and even nongolfers will be impressed by the white-columned porticoes and sparkling fountains of the Entrance Pavilion, which overlooks Pinehurst Country Club's Number Two course and the new Number Seven course. The Entrance Pavilion is centered by a pool and another fountain and leads to the main lobby of the museum. Even before you enter the lobby, you'll see a 10-foot statue of Bobby Jones through the glass doors. The north and south wings of the museum tell the story of the development of golf and people associated with it, like Henry VIII's first wife, Katherine, who loved it as much as Scotland's three kings James (II, III, and IV) hated it. And hundreds of golf items from the past are displayed (there are balls used from 1750 to 1850 made of tanned animal hides stuffed with leather). The Ryder Cup Room, Old Clubmakers Shop, and new Walter Hagen exhibit offer other fascinating insights into the grand old game.

The theater is the only one in the world devoted exclusively to golf, and it features films of major tournaments as well as instructional pictures. Behind the museum is the actual Hall of Fame with bronzes of the inductees, a shrine completely surrounded by water, approached by a covered walkway. It is open from 9 a.m. to 5 p.m. daily from mid-March through November, and admission is $3 for adults, $2 for ages 10 to 18, and free for those under 10.

In Southern Pines, the **Campbell House,** a handsome Georgian structure on East Connecticut Avenue that was once a family residence, now houses the Arts Council of Moore County. Its art galleries display the works of local artists.

On the Fort Bragg–Aberdeen Road, 1½ miles southeast of Southern Pines, you'll come to **Weymouth Woods–Sandhills Nature Preserve,** a beautiful nature spot with foot and bridle paths and some 600 acres of pine-covered "sandridges." There's also a natural history museum, free, that's open Monday through Saturday from 9 a.m. to 6 p.m., on Sunday from noon to 5 p.m.

There are a lot of fine horse farms in the Sandhills. Steeplechasers trained here show up regularly at tracks around the country. Trotters and pacers are also trained around here; and the late Del Cameron, renowned three-time winner of the Hambletonian, kept a winter training stable in this area for more than 30 years.

The **Mid-South Horse Show Association** holds schooling shows every Sunday afternoon from January to April; in early March there's the **Moore County Hounds Hunter Trials** at Scotts Corner, Southern Pines, with reserved parking spaces overlooking the course for spectators; and the **Stoneybrook Steeplechase Races** are held on a Saturday in early April on a farm near Southern Pines where race horses are bred and trained the rest of the year by owner Michael G. Walsh, an Irishman from County Cork. The Sandhills Area Chamber of Commerce, P.O. Box 458, Southern Pines, NC 28387, can furnish exact dates and full details on all these events, as well as others throughout the year.

About an hour's drive to the northwest is the little town of **Seagrove** (it's on U.S. 220), which has been turning out pottery for over 200 years. The red and gray clays of this section of the Piedmont were first used by settlers from Staffordshire, England, and the very first items they produced were jugs for transporting whisky. The art is practiced today just as it was then: clays are ground and mixed by machines turned by mules, simple designs are fashioned on kick wheels, and glazing is still done in wood-burning kilns. Many of the potters work in or behind their homes, with only a small sign outside to identify their trade, so if you have difficulty finding them, stop and ask—everybody does, so don't be shy. There are some sales rooms in the town, but the real fun is seeing the pottery actually being made. And while you're asking, inquire about **Jugtown,** a group of rustic, log-hewn buildings in a grove of pines where potters demonstrate their art with pride Monday through Saturday. Be sure to stop by **The Potter's Museum** to browse through items of long-ago vintage and a gift shop displaying today's wares.

There are some 28 potters operating in the Seagrove area, and two that have caught my fancy are **Walton's Pottery,** Rte. 2, Box 426, Seagrove, NC 27341 (tel. 919/879-3270), where Don Walton's potter's wheel turns out delicate cutout designs on candle holders as well as a full line of more traditional bowls, vases, teapots, casseroles, etc.; and **M. L. Owens Pottery,** Rte. 2, Seagrove, NC 27341 (tel. 919/462-3553), where Melvin Owens has been turning the wheel since 1937, following in the family tradition begun by his grandfather in 1895. Be assured that you'll hardly be disappointed, no matter with which potters you choose to stop and chat and shop, but I think these two are worth seeking out.

A little north of Seagrove (still on U.S. 220), you'll come to Asheboro, where you should turn onto U.S. 64 East, then head south on N.C. 159 to reach the **North Carolina Zoological Park,** Rte. 4, Box 83, Asheboro, NC 27203 (tel. 919/879-5606). The 300-acre Africa region is the first of seven continental-exhibit regions planned for the 1,448-acre park and features no less than 700 animals in barless natural habitats. In this still-developing, world-class zoo, gorillas and 200 rare animals such as meerkats inhabit the African Pavilion, while lions, elephants, and chimpanzees dwell in spacious outdoor habitats. A 37-acre African Plains exhibit is home to a dozen species of antelope, gazelles, and oryx. The R. J. Reynolds Forest Aviary holds 150 exotic birds flying free amid lush tropical trees and plants. There's a tram ride, picnic area, restaurants, and gift shops. The zoo is open 9 a.m. to 5 p.m. Monday through Friday, 10 a.m. to 6 p.m. weekends and holidays April through October 15; from October 16 through March, hours are 9 a.m. to 5 p.m. daily. Adults pay $3, seniors and ages 2 to 15, $1.

Also in the Seagrove area, the **Town Creek Indian Mound,** Rte. 3, Box 50, Mt. Gilead, NC 27306 (tel. 919/439-6802), gives you a fascinating glimpse into the lives of the Native Americans who established this religious, ceremonial, and burial center some 300 years ago on this bluff overlooking the junction of Little River and Town Creek. Followers of the Pee Dee culture, they left for us remnants of that culture that have now been excavated and/or reconstructed: a major temple, the dwelling place of priests, ceremonial grounds, and many, many artifacts. There's no charge for this trip back in time, but hours vary with the season and day of the week, so best call before stopping by.

North Carolina's frontier days spring to life when you visit the **Alston House,** more familiarly known as the **House in the Horseshoe** (for the horseshoe bend of the Deep River, which the house overlooks), Rte. 3, Box 924, Sanford, NC 27330 (tel. 919/947-2051). Built in the late 1770s, it was the "big house" of a plantation on what was then the fringe of colonization. The two-story frame house, with its central hall plan, is typical of plantation houses of that era, and its colorful history has left it with bullet holes put there in 1781 when Whigs and Tories battled it out on the grounds. "Miss Ruby" Newton, who takes visitors through the house, will fill you in with other anecdotes about the historic house and its owners down through the years. A bit of all that history is reenacted the first weekend of every August, when a Revolutionary War battle takes place here; and in early December there's a cheery open house and candlelighting celebration. Admission is free, and hours are 9 a.m. to 5 p.m. Monday through Saturday, 1 to 5 p.m. on Sunday most of the year, although it's a good idea to call ahead, since hours sometimes vary.

The entire little town of **Cameron,** about 10 miles north of Southern Pines (off U.S. 1), has been designated a historic district, with some 19 historical sites and buildings within walking distance. More than 60 antiques dealers are housed in shops here, and there's an annual antiques street fair the first Saturday in May and again in October. Among things to look for are the **Greenwood Inn** of 1874, the **Muse Brothers' store** of 1880, and the fine Queen Anne–style **Rodwell House** of 1890. Most shops open from 10 a.m. to 5 p.m. Wednesday through Saturday, and you really should top off a morning of delightful sightseeing and shopping with lunch at **Miss Bell's Antique and Tea Room** (served from 11 a.m. to 2 p.m.).

IX

INTRODUCTION TO SOUTH CAROLINA

1. BY WAY OF BACKGROUND
2. TRAVELING TO SOUTH CAROLINA
3. TRAVELING WITHIN SOUTH CAROLINA

There are really two South Carolinas, with differences between the coastal "low country" and the "up country" (including the rolling midlands) so distinct I sometimes feel there should be a state line between the two. South Carolinians, however, seem able to hold on to those divisions and at the same time take great pride in presenting a united front to the rest of the world.

1. By Way of Background

1526 TO 1990

It isn't only the topography of the state that makes for the distinctiveness of each section, although like most states along the Atlantic, South Carolina has its coastal plain, piedmont, and mountains. The differences really spring from a history of settlement and development that saw aristocratic rice and indigo planters build one lifestyle along the coast and German, Scottish-Irish, and Welsh immigrants gravitate farther inland to build another. The first attempts to settle along the coast were as early as 1526 and 1562, but nothing came of them. It wasn't until Charles II of England granted both the Carolinas to eight noblemen, the lords proprietors, that colonists arrived to stay. Charles Towne was established at Albemarle Point in 1670, then moved 10 years later to the peninsula formed by the Ashley and Cooper rivers.

That low, marshy country proved ideal for large rice and indigo plantations, and Charles Towne's harbor was perfect for shipping these crops around the world. Successful planters maintained huge homes on outlying farms, and most built sumptuous mansions in town as well. A life of formal ease and graciousness developed that has never entirely disappeared, even though the low country has seen great fortunes come and go with the changes of time.

Away from the coast, those hardy frontiersmen—who set up small farms, built up a brisk trade in pelts, and fought Indians, often with no help from their British landlords—had little time or inclination for the social goings-on in Charles Towne. And a sore point was the issue of taxation—but with a local twist: in spite of the fact that everyone paid taxes, only the low country had any say in how things were run. And that remained the case until 1770, even though there had been popular representation in the colonial government as early as 1693. The rift between the two groups would be a long time healing, and even during the Revolution (although the first decisive American victory was won here at Fort Moultrie in June 1776), South Carolina suffered about equally from British troops and local loyalists, mostly from the low country.

When Charles Towne was finally occupied by the British in 1780, it was supposed to be the jumping-off point for a spearhead drive to join forces in the north that would crush Washington's troops. But thanks to the efforts of Continental troops under Gen. Nathanael Greene and South Carolina natives who followed "the Swamp Fox" (Frances Marion) and "the Game-cock" (Thomas Sumter) in a very effective sort of guerrilla warfare, the royal soldiers were more or less confined to Charles Towne (renamed Charleston in 1783). There are some historians who contend that the battles of Kings Mountain (in 1780) and Cowpens (1781) were *the* decisive encounters of the Revolution. When independence was finally achieved, South Carolina was the eighth state to ratify the Federal Constitution, in 1788.

By 1790 those cantankerous up-country citizens made such a fuss about the state's capital remaining in low-country Charleston, when four-fifths of the white population lived inland, that the state government was moved to neutral ground, centrally located Columbia. Not to be outdone, the low-country population (which controlled four-fifths of the *wealth*) continued to maintain state offices, and the supreme court actually met in both cities to hear appeals until 1865.

When tensions between the North and South reached the breaking point in 1860, fiery John C. Calhoun led the state legislature to pass an Ordinance of Secession in December that made South Carolina the first state to secede from the Union. And in *that* step, citizens seemed united. In fact their first military action was to take Fort Sumter from the Federal troops garrisoned there, and they continued to hold it until 1865. Altogether, the state lost 22% of its population in the bitter Civil War; and General Sherman, in his "march to the sea," saw to it that just about the entire state was left in shambles.

If there's one thing *all* South Carolinians—low- or up-country—have in abundance, it's pride. And that pride suffered greatly, along with the economy, as carpetbaggers and scalawags moved in during Reconstruction. I always feel, when traveling in this state, that "Yankee" and "Rebel" distinctions are more alive here today than in any other single place in the South. That's not really surprising, however, when you remember that not until World War II did South Carolina begin to get back on its feet economically. Ironically, it was "Yankee" industry, moving to a location of enormous waterpowered energy and supply and a ready labor market, that led the state's booming industrialization. And just in the last 20 or 30 years the Civil War scars have faded more quickly than before.

As a place to visit, the state is a tourist's gold mine—more than 280 miles

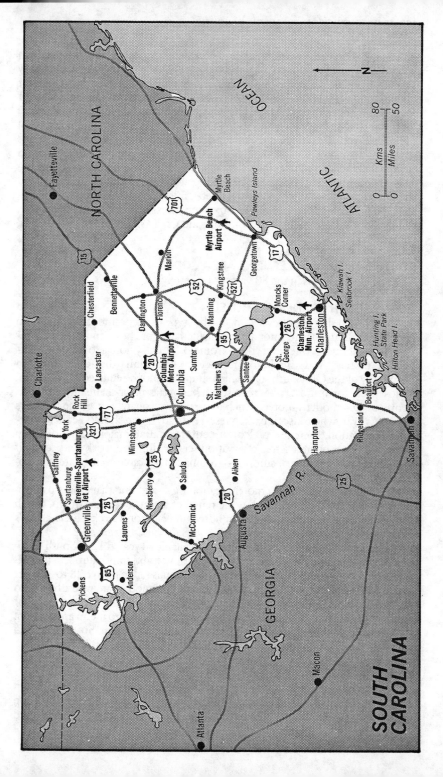

of seashore, with lovely white-sand beaches shaded by palms, resort islands like Hilton Head that are a world apart, and Charleston's gracious Old South charm still intact. The area around Columbia reflects both the "New South" of vitality and some of the Old in the university campus, which has served, with its great old oaks and early 1800s buildings, as the background for several movies about antebellum life. Sportsmen, drawn to coastal and inland fishing, also come here for the unusually long hunting season (Thanksgiving, more or less, to March 1) for such game as deer, wild turkey, quail, fox, and many more. Equestrians come for horse shows, polo, the Carolina Cup Steeplechase (in early April) and Colonial Cup Steeplechase (in mid-November) at Camden, and harness racing and other horse events in Aiken (beginning about the middle of March). And the Darlington Raceway features the "Rebel 500" (in mid-April) and "Southern 500" (Labor Day) late-model stock-car races. History buffs, of course, can retrace all those colonial, Revolution, and Civil War events to their hearts' content.

SOUTH CAROLINA TELEPHONE AREA CODE
The entire state is in the 803 area code zone.

ABOUT SOUTH CAROLINA'S HOTELS
You'll find just about every imaginable type of accommodation in South Carolina, although there's not always a wide range of choice in a specific location. Coastal resorts offer everything from posh luxury hotels to modest, inexpensive motels. And Charleston has several small inns that offer southern hospitality of the Old South style which simply cannot be equaled. In between, almost every town and city has representatives of the major chains and independently owned modern motels which more than adequately meet the traveler's needs. As everywhere else, it pays to reserve ahead. If you should get here *without* a reservation, there are **welcome centers** at nine major points of entry whose hostesses operate a free reservation service. But that's risky, especially if you come during spring or summer—rooms can be scarce even as late as October along the coast.

An alternative to hotel/motel vacationing—and one that works particularly well for families, I think—is the rental of a cottage or apartment. South Carolina's resort areas have literally hundreds available on a weekly basis, and it's a fairly simple matter to engage one *if you plan far enough in advance.*

There are also cabin accommodations available all year in 12 of South Carolina's state parks. All are heated and air-conditioned and fully equipped, including cooking utensils, tableware, and linens. Rentals range from $28 to $80 per night, $126 to $480 per week, and the cabins accommodate anywhere from 4 to 12 people. Here again, however, advance planning is absolutely necessary for summer reservations. For full details on these cabins, how to file an application, rates, and accommodations at the 31 other state parks, write: **South Carolina State Parks,** 1205 Pendleton St., Columbia, SC 29201 (tel. 803/734-0156).

AS FOR FOOD
South Carolina menus vary across the state in a reflection of its population mix. Low-country seafood ragoûts and Charleston's famous she-crab soup dominate coastal cooking, while country ham and grits served up with "red

eye" gravy are prominent on inland tables. The best meals are undoubtedly served in private homes, for as in most southern states, cooking is an art lovingly transferred from one generation to another. But restaurants, too, seem to take particular pride in their kitchens, and I've had some exquisite meals in small, unpretentious establishments where the management would be embarrassed if you called their food "gourmet," but where that term nevertheless fits. And there are many fine restaurants that would no doubt be embarrassed if you *didn't* use "gourmet" in describing their cuisine—and most of it is. All in all, South Carolina is a good place to eat, with plenty of dining places handy for the traveler.

You'll be able to buy alcoholic beverages in many restaurants. Some are licensed to serve only beer and wine, but a great many serve those plus liquor (which is served in mini-bottles to be added to cocktail mixes). And if you think you'll want a drink on Sunday, stock up: there's no alcohol sold in the state on the Sabbath. The minimum drinking age is 18 for beer and wine, 21 for liquor.

SOUTH CAROLINA CLIMATE

Although parts of South Carolina can be very hot and steamy in summer, temperatures are never extreme, as is shown in the average highs and lows noted below.

	High	Low
Charleston	88	44
Columbia	93	35

VISITOR INFORMATION

In order to do a good job with your homework before coming to South Carolina, write or call ahead for any specific information on sports (fishing, hunting, beaches, etc.) and sightseeing to: **South Carolina Dept. of Parks, Recreation & Tourism,** P.O. Box 71, Columbia, SC 29202 (tel. 803/734-0122).

2. Traveling to South Carolina

BY AIR

You can fly into Charleston's International Airport on Delta, USAir (Piedmont), and American; and all also serve Columbia. USAir (Piedmont) and Northwest reach the Greenville-Spartanburg region, and USAir (Piedmont) goes to Florence, Hilton Head Island, and Myrtle Beach.

BY TRAIN

Amtrak reaches Camden, Charleston, Clemson, Columbia, Denmark, Dillon, Florence, Greenville, Kingstree, Spartanburg, and Yemassee. Amtrak also has tour packages that include hotel, breakfasts, and historic site tours in Charleston at bargain rates.

BY BUS

Greyhound reaches almost any destination in South Carolina.

BY CAR

The many-laned, divided I-95 superhighway enters South Carolina from the north near Dillon and runs straight through the state to Hardeeville on the Georgia border. The major east-west highway artery is I-26, from Charleston northwest through Columbia and on up to Hendersonville, North Carolina. Along the coast, U.S. 17 stretches from Georgia to North Carolina. In the western region I-85 crosses from Georgia to North Carolina. The state does a beautiful job of furnishing travel information to motorists, and there are well-equipped, efficiently staffed **visitor welcome centers** at the northern entrances on U.S. 17, I-95, I-85, and I-26, as well as the southern ends of I-85, I-20, and U.S. 301.

---

3. Traveling Within South Carolina

BY AIR

Delta and USAir (Piedmont) airlines both have connecting flights to South Carolina airports, although schedules are sometimes awkward for connections.

BY TRAIN

See above for Amtrak destinations.

BY BUS

Greyhound operates intrastate routes to most South Carolina towns.

BY CAR

Those marvelous interstate and U.S. highways listed in the above section give South Carolina a network of exceptionally good roadways. However, even when you leave the highways for the state-maintained byways, driving is easy on well-maintained roads. South Carolina used to be one of those notorious "speedtrap" states for visitors, and while the setups and rigged stoplights have been gone for a while now, it *does* pay to watch the speed limits: they still keep an eye on out-of-state drivers (and in-state as well, I suspect).

You will find **Thrifty Car Rentals** locations in Charleston, Columbia, Summerville, and Hilton Head Island, with their usual good service and rates.

X

COASTAL SOUTH CAROLINA

1. MYRTLE BEACH AND THE GRAND STRAND
2. CHARLESTON
3. HILTON HEAD ISLAND

All the romance, beauty, and graciousness of the Old South manage to survive along South Carolina's lovely coast. Well, maybe it isn't all that evident visually along the Grand Strand up around Myrtle Beach, which looks pretty much like most other beach resort areas—although even this section exudes southern charm in its slow-paced vacation outlook and the warm hospitality of the locals. A little farther south, however, at Georgetown, then Charleston, and all the way to Beaufort at the bottom of the state's coastline, automobiles and modern dress seem almost out of place when you drive through old, cobblestone streets under trees draped with the mysterious Spanish moss and past antebellum homes built in the early days of this country. Oh, they've been outfitted with all the conveniences of today, but I often think they could revert easily to their original state and keep occupants comfortable even in the face of an oil crisis that forced the return of wood-burning fireplaces and kerosene lamps or candles. As for the people who live in them, you'll find they possess for the most part an appreciation of up-to-date, sophisticated lifestyles (very few, if any, rednecks in *this* part of the South!), as well as an active memory of things as they once were—a happy mixture, indeed.

Physically, the coastline, from the Grand Strand in the north all the way south to Charleston and the "low country," is almost breathtakingly beautiful. Its broad, white-sand beaches are warmed by the Gulf Stream just a few miles offshore and fringed with palm trees and rolling dunes. Palms mingle with live oaks, dogwood, and pines all along the coast, and everywhere you'll see the silver-gray something called Spanish moss that drapes airily from tree branches, lending a dream-like softness to the landscape. I call it "something" because even scientists can't quite figure out what it is—it isn't *really* a moss, because that grows on the ground; it isn't a parasite, because it doesn't feed on sap from the trees; and it has no roots, seeming to extract nourishment somehow from the air. They call it an epiphyte (air plant), but as yet they aren't sure—even after exhaustive tests—just how it manages to keep alive and grow. My favorite quotation about Spanish moss is the answer given northern tourists by a South Carolina publication to all those questions about the lovely mystery: "Yes, it does grow on trees; no, it isn't a parasite; no, they *don't* take it in at night and put it out in the morning."

Speaking of native plants: Whatever you do, don't pull the graceful sea oats that grow on sand-dune stretches along the beaches—it's against the law, and an infraction carries a stiff fine. The hardy plant (it grows from Cape Charles, Virginia, to the Gulf Coast of Mexico and is officially named *Uniola paniculato)* not only acts as a natural anchor for the dunes, but also serves as a plentiful food supply for shore birds. Actually, it is also instrumental in the forming of new or higher dunes, since it catches and holds blowing sands. So look, enjoy their spare beauty, but don't touch.

As I've said, low-country South Carolina is full of memories, but it's also a place to *make* memories—whether of the recreation, sightseeing, or just plain relaxing genre. The subtropical climate, where spring arrives early and summer lingers until late October, permits golf, tennis, fishing (public piers, at Cherry Grove Beach, Tilghman Beach, Crescent Beach, Windy Hill, Myrtle Beach, Isle of Palms, and Folly Beach; and charter boats for deep-sea fishing), sightseeing in that grand old lady of the low country, Charleston, or sitting on an uncrowded beach (as I did once for an entire October week at Hilton Head). There are islands that don't even require a boat for a visit (South Carolina has provided marvelous double-laned causeways), like Pawleys, Seabrook, Edisto, and Hilton Island.

1. Myrtle Beach and the Grand Strand

Myrtle Beach, with a permanent population of about 20,000 is at the center of the Grand Strand, a 55-mile string of beaches that includes Little River, Cherry Grove, Crescent Beach, Ocean Drive, Atlantic Beach, Surfside Beach, Garden City, Murrells Inlet, Litchfield Beach, and Pawleys Island. And besides the beaches, there are amusement parks, stock-car races, nightspots with top entertainment, an internationally known sculpture garden, some of the best seafood restaurants on the Atlantic coast, and all those golf courses. Named for all the myrtle trees in this area, Myrtle Beach itself is an ideal base for a Grand Strand vacation. Maybe I should say here that my personal feeling about this resort is that if you're looking for a wild, swinging kind of beach resort, this isn't it—there's plenty to do, of course, and it certainly isn't dull, but the whole tone is that of a *family* resort, with almost as much attention paid at the various hotels and motels to children's needs as to those of adults. Many provide activity programs and playgrounds with supervision, and nearly all have babysitter lists for parents who like a little nightlife. It's a nice sort of place and one that looks out for all members of the family.

WHERE TO STAY

The Grand Strand is literally lined with hotels, motels, condominiums, and cottages. The **Myrtle Beach Area Chamber of Commerce,** 1301 N. Kings

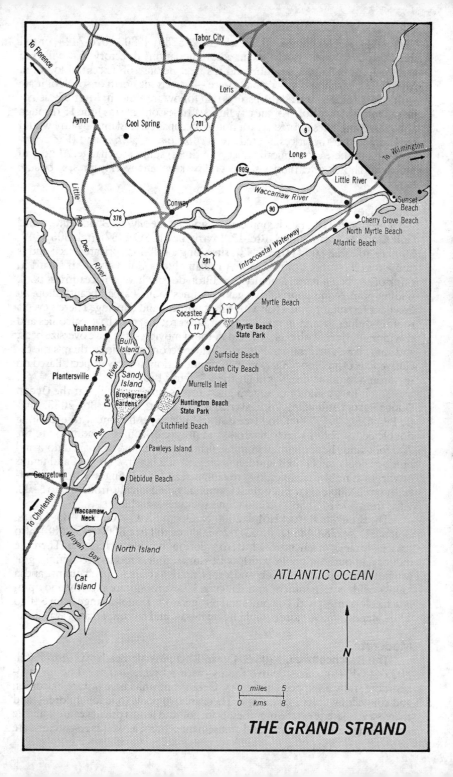

THE GRAND STRAND

Hwy. (P.O. Box 2115), Myrtle Beach, SC 29578 (tel. 803/626-7444, or toll free 800/626-7444), publishes an accommodations directory that will be a great help in making a selection and it's free. Because of its central location, Myrtle Beach itself is my personal choice—attractions north or south of it are within easy reach—and all the listings that follow are either in Myrtle Beach or just a short distance north of the city limits. "In season" means June 15 through Labor Day, and rates quoted are for double occupancy. And once again I would remind you that the prices quoted are *as of the time of writing* and (like everything else in these economically uncertain times) subject to change. Almost all motels and hotels offer money-saving golf packages and weekly rates, so be sure to check.

Expensive

Catering to both beachcombers and golfers, the **Myrtle Beach Hilton and Golf Club,** Arcadian Shores, Rte. 17, Myrtle Beach, SC 29577 (tel. 803/449-5000 or toll free 800/HILTONS), sits along a 600-foot private beach and is just across the street from its own Arcadian Shores Golf Course. It's hard to think of any beach-resort amenity the Hilton doesn't have: an oceanfront pool, wading pool, tennis courts, lawn games, games room, barber, beauty shop, an excellent restaurant, and a bar with entertainment and dancing. There's even a rooftop dinner theater in season. As for guest rooms, they have balconies and spacious interiors, with cable TV and in-room movies; some have oversize beds, and some have refrigerators. For extra deluxe accommodations, there's the exclusive Executive Floor. A superior accommodation in every respect. Based on season and location, doubles range from $50 to $170.

You'll have a choice of superb guest rooms, suites, or villas at the **Ocean Dunes Resort and Villas,** 74th Avenue North, Dept. 90, P.O. Box 2035, Myrtle Beach, SC 29577 (tel. toll free 800/845-0635). All come with extra-long double beds, cable TV, refrigerators, and private balconies. In addition to the 700-foot sandy beach, with swimming, fishing, and sailing, there are indoor and outdoor pools, supervised children's programs, a health club, golf and tennis privileges at nearby facilities, two restaurants, and two lounges with live entertainment. Double occupancy guest rooms range, seasonally, from $75 to $100; villas from $98 to $180; golf and tennis packages available.

The **Breakers Resort Hotel,** 2006 N. Ocean Blvd., P.O. Box 485, Myrtle Beach, SC 29578-0485 (tel. 803/626-5000 or toll free 800/845-0688), also has a wide range of amenities added to a glorious beachfront location. There are indoor and outdoor pools, whirlpools, saunas, fitness rooms, free tennis, golf privileges at the Dunes Club and other nearby courses, a restaurant, and a lounge with entertainment and dancing. Guest rooms are nicely done up in beach colors, most with balconies and refrigerators. Doubles range from $40 to $114, depending on season. Golf, honeymoon, and family packages available.

Moderate

The **Beachcomber,** 1705 S. Ocean Blvd., Myrtle Beach, SC 29577 (tel. 803/448-4345), offers deluxe rooms (with refrigerators) and one- or two-bedroom, fully equipped efficiencies. Oceanfront units have private balconies, and connecting units are available. There are two pools (one for children), and there's a washerette on the premises. Both golf and tennis privileges are available at nearby facilities. Shopping and amusement centers, as well as restaurants, are close at hand. In-season rates start at $50. After Labor Day, the same accommodations drop considerably. Open all year, and weekly rates are available.

The Jamaican, 3006 N. Ocean Blvd., Myrtle Beach, SC 29577 (tel. 803/448-4321), is an inviting, five-story motel at the edge of Myrtle Beach's north-end residential section. Its rooms, efficiencies, and suites are bright and airy, each with a private balcony and ocean view, and I found the staff here exceptionally pleasant and helpful. The beach is less crowded here, and right next door is one of the area's top restaurants, the Sea Captain's House (see "Where to Eat," below). The boardwalk, Pavilion, and amusement area are 20 rather short blocks to the south—a very long stroll or a short drive away. There's an oceanfront pool (a kiddie pool is also on the ocean), and both golf and tennis facilities are close by. This is, in my opinion, one of the best motels on the beach in the moderate price range. In season, rooms begin at $60, efficiencies at $65, with varying lower rates the rest of the year. Weekly rates are available.

Not just a motel, but a complete resort, the **Sea Mist,** 1200 S. Ocean Blvd., Myrtle Beach, SC 29577 (tel. 803/448-1551, or toll free 800/732-6478), has nine pools (one is enclosed for year-round use), Jacuzzis, a tennis court, supervised children's programs, playgrounds, a recreation room, ice-cream parlor, gift cove, and guest privileges at 40 golf courses. The 666 units consist of large rooms, apartments, suites, and even a penthouse and villas. There are special package plans for honeymooners, tennis players, and golfers. The elegant dining room, softly lit by candles, has old-world charm, and the Prime Rib Room features entertainment most of the year, along with prime beef and fresh seafood. Rates during the season range from $65 to $81, but there's a special low rate between September and May (and don't forget that swimming is good here until late October).

For luxury rooms, efficiencies, and suites at moderate prices, the **St. John's Inn,** 6801 N. Ocean Blvd., Myrtle Beach, SC 29577 (tel. 803/449-5251, or toll free 800/845-0624), is one of the best. All rooms have balconies, the swimming pool is heated on cool days, and golf and tennis packages are available. There's a restaurant and coffeeshop. Rates are in the $70 to $80 range in season for doubles, lower other times. Open year round.

Myrtle Shores, 1902-1904 N. Ocean Blvd. (P.O. Box 335), Myrtle Beach, SC 29578 (tel. 803/448-1434), is an apartment motel in a pleasant oceanfront setting, and is very popular with families. It has a dozen spacious and attractive two-bedroom units and 26 efficiencies with refrigerators. Most units have private balconies, and all have free cable color TV. There's a heated pool, and golf and tennis privileges are available. Daily maid service is offered, and there are coin-operated washers and dryers. Rates range from $60 to $70 for doubles June through August, and can drop as low as $35 off-season. Ask, too, about special long-term winter rates.

Inexpensive

The **Teakwood Motel,** 7201 N. Ocean Blvd., Myrtle Beach, SC 29577 (tel. 803/449-5653), is a most attractive and welcoming family inn across from the ocean. Walt and Karen Fisher, the owners-managers, are cordial, caring hosts who make guests feel right at home. The 25 rooms are attractively furnished, some in Polynesian decor, and 12 of them are efficiencies with refrigerators. There's a social lobby with free coffee, a heated pool, a playground, and a pleasant cookout area. Airport transportation is offered, along with golf privileges. From May through September, doubles are $49 to $55 and can drop to $30 off-season. Weekly rates are offered, too. A reservation deposit is required.

The **Ocean Front Motel,** 510 N. Ocean Blvd., Myrtle Beach, SC 29577 (tel. 803/626-9473), is a family-owned 30-unit establishment that caters to families. It's a pleasant place right on the ocean, just two blocks from the pavilion, and there are restaurants nearby. You can have your choice of single rooms, a two-bedroom unit, or an efficiency; all have refrigerators and free color TV. There are adult and kiddie pools, both heated, along with on-premises laundry facilities. You can also have daily maid service. Doubles for two people, one bed, begin at $45 from late May through August, and can drop to under $30 at other times. A reservation deposit is required.

Days Inn Central, 601 S. Ocean Blvd., Myrtle Beach, SC 29577 (tel. 803/448-1491 or toll free 800/325-2525) is, as its name implies, centrally located. There are one-room efficiencies, two-room apartments, suites, and penthouses, all with cooking facilities that include a microwave. Some have in-room whirlpools; and there are two outdoor pools and an indoor Olympic-size pool in addition to a whirlpool and a pool for the small fry; playground; and coin laundry. There's a good restaurant within walking distance, and guests enjoy golf privileges at nearby courses. Doubles range from $25 to $75, depending on the season and type of accommodation. Golf packages and weekly rates available.

Nonsmokers will find smoke-free rooms at the **Comfort Inn,** 2801 S. Kings Hwy., Myrtle Beach, SC 29577 (tel. 803/626-444 or toll free 800/228-5150). In addition to exceptionally nice guest rooms, there are suites and efficiencies, a few with in-room whirlpools. Amenities include a pool, whirlpool, health club, and sauna, and there's a restaurant close by. Doubles range from $33 to $99, based on season and accommodations, with a discount for seniors.

Bed and Breakfast

Ellen and Cos Ficarra are hosts at the **Serendipity Inn,** 407 71st Ave. N., Myrtle Beach, SC 29577 (tel. 803/449-5268). Located on a quiet side street a block and a half from the beach, the Spanish mission–style inn has a dozen guest rooms. All are decorated and furnished in individual style (wicker, oak, pine, Oriental, art deco, etc.), and there are lovely suites ideal for honeymooners, and just as ideal for anyone who wants a little pampering. The Ficarras, who moved south from New York City some 12 years ago, put out a marvelous breakfast buffet that includes fresh fruit, hard-boiled eggs, hot breads, and more. Hospitality at the Serendipity is as warm as the climate, and per-room rates of $58 to $82 in season, $50 to $60 other months, represent true value for dollar.

Campgrounds

There is a generous supply of campsites along the Grand Strand, many on the oceanfront. Rates drop considerably after Labor Day. Most will accept families only—no singles. The following is located about halfway between Myrtle Beach and North Myrtle Beach, and it is on the ocean.

There are 760 sites at the **Apache Family Campground,** 9700 Kings Rd., Myrtle Beach, SC 29577 (tel. 803/449-7323). Here the amenities include a free swimming pool and recreation pavilion, water, electricity, shade shelters, modern bathhouses with hot water, sewer hookups, carpet golf, a laundry, trading post, playground, public telephones, ice, beach umbrellas, floats for rent, and golf privileges. You can reserve here year round except for the week of July 4th. Rates are $12 to $20.

READER'S BEACH ACCOMMODATIONS SUGGESTION : "About 15 miles northeast of Myrtle Beach, halfway between there and Wilmington, N.C., we found beautiful oceanfront accommodations within 10 minutes of 12 golf courses at the **Winds Beach and Golf Resort,** 310 E. First St., Ocean Isle Beach, NC 28459 (tel. 919/579-6275 or toll free 800/334-3581). They have motel units, studio efficiencies, suites, and villa units at rates we thought were very reasonable for this quiet, get-away-from-it-all bit of beach paradise. Daily rates aren't always available for all types of accommodations, but we can't imagine not wanting to spend a week" (S. Ramsauer, Orangeburg, S.C.).

WHERE TO EAT

You may be tempted to eat more than three meals a day just to sample the many restaurants along the Grand Strand. My own weakness for fresh seafood well prepared always produces a noticeable expansion of the waistline during my stay. And price should by no means be a measure of quality, for prices are unexpectedly moderate at even the best of the lot.

Not to Be Missed

Treat yourself to at least one dinner at the **Rice Planter's,** 6707 Kings Hwy. North, which is another name for Hwy. 17 (tel. 803/449-3456). The present large, old-brick building replaces the original, which burned in 1975, resulting in a loss of irreplaceable artifacts and antiques from rice plantations in the area. Not lost, however, was the charm of the place, which is as much alive in the new as it was in the old. The high-ceilinged main dining room, warmed by a fire in the brick hearth on cool nights, is overlooked by an open balcony reached by a graceful stairway and divided into alcoves for individual parties of six or eight. Exposed-brick walls, copper kettles at the fireplace, dark-stained woodwork and beams, old-fashioned ceiling fans and frosted-glass chandeliers, red-checkered tablecloths, and candlelight add up to a perfect setting for dining that can only be described as sumptuous. And the personable manager, David Gilbert, seems to be everywhere at once with a warm welcome and a watchful eye on the service, which matches the food in excellence. Seafood is featured, and a favorite is the Rice Planter's Dinner, which begins with shrimp, followed by clam chowder, fried shrimp, filet of fish, oysters, baked crabmeat, and deep-sea scallops. It comes with a crisp salad of greens, potato, tartar sauce, and home-baked bread. And—would you believe it?—the price is just $16. If you're not a seafood lover, try one of their low-country specialties: Carolina cured ham or southern fried chicken, both served with rice and gravy, salad, and that same good home-baked bread. It's open for dinner only, from 5 to 10 p.m., with prices ranging from $9.50 to $18.

Over on the beach, David Brittain presides over the **Sea Captain's House,** 3002 N. Ocean Blvd. (tel. 803/448-8082), in an old beach home. The restaurant has been family run since 1963 and is known and loved by a host of South

Carolinians, as well as "outsider" regulars who vacation at Myrtle Beach year after year. There's a fireplace in the paneled inner dining room and its glow adds to the informal, friendly atmosphere on cool nights. A many-windowed porch room affords a superb ocean view. She-crab soup is on the menu; the seafood platter includes five different fish, served with slaw, potatoes, and hush puppies; and there's a selection of flame-broiled steaks, lamb chops, and country ham steak at prices from $8 to $18. Lunch is served from 11:30 a.m. to 2:30 p.m., and dinner from 5 to 10 p.m. seven days a week (except for January, when it's closed).

Tony's Italian Restaurant, 1407 U.S. 17, across from Robber's Roost golf course (tel. 803/249-1314), offers a welcome respite when you seek a change from all that wonderful fresh seafood. The oldest Italian restaurant on the Grand Strand, Tony's is about a 20-minute drive north from the heart of Myrtle Beach. It's a casual, cozy, welcoming place with such perfectly scrumptious specialties as fresh veal dishes and homemade pastas. There'll usually be fresh clams on the menu, too. Children's plates are available, and the youngsters can even have a burger if they're not into Italian fare. The semi–à la carte meals range from $7 to $20, and Tony's is open daily from 5 to 10 p.m. in peak season; it closes Sunday from September through May and December through January. Reservations recommended.

Hotel and Motel Dining Rooms

The **Sidewalk Vendor Café** at The Breakers Resort Hotel, Oceanfront at 21st Avenue North, Myrtle Beach (tel. 803/626-5000, ext. 7139), serves an excellent all-you-can-eat breakfast buffet daily from 7 to 11 a.m. for just $4.50. At dinner, specialties include flounder stuffed with crabmeat, sautéed shrimp, prime rib, sirloin, and veal, at prices of $10 to $18. On Friday nights, there's a seafood buffet for just $13.95. Dinner hours are 6 to 10 p.m.

At the **Ocean Dunes,** 74th Avenue North (tel. 803/449-7441), there's dancing and entertainment year round in the Brass Anchor lounge and restaurant. Particularly noteworthy is the seafood buffet on Tuesday and Friday, one of the best in the area. Wednesday and Sunday, prime rib (served buffet style, all you can eat) are featured. Moderate prices are for complete dinners and include a trip to the very good salad bar. Dinner hours are 6 to 10 p.m., but the lounge is active from 4 p.m. to 1:30 a.m.

Right next door to the Ocean Dunes, and under the same management, the **Sand Dunes** (tel. 803/449-3313) also has dancing and live entertainment. The unique decor of the dining room and lounge carries out an aviation theme —very attractive—and both food and entertainment are tops. Breakfast, lunch, and dinner are served in the dining room at surprisingly moderate prices, lounge hours are 4 p.m. to 1:30 a.m.

It is possible to eat quite well without spending a fortune at Myrtle Beach, and here's a quick rundown on just two of the many budget eateries in town.

All three meals are served at **Bojangle's Famous Chicken & Biscuits,** 2301 S. Kings Hwy., Myrtle Beach, SC (tel. 803/626-9051), with breakfast served from 6 to 9:30 a.m., lunch and dinner menus available continuously until 10 p.m. Specialties are (guess what?) chicken, homemade biscuits, and sandwiches. A meal here will run well below $5.

The dependable **Morrison's Cafeteria** is in Myrtle Square Mall (tel. 803/

448-4302), and dishes up wholesome, home-cooked meals seven days a week from 11 a.m. to 8:30 p.m. Lunches and dinners will run under $5, and there's a children's menu.

North on the Strand

Little River, a fishing village on the Intracoastal Waterway at the northern tip of the Grand Strand, has several good restaurants that feature just-caught fish. The best known is **Captain Juel's Hurricane** (tel. 803/249-2211), which began back in 1945 as a tiny waterfront restaurant nestled in a grove of 300-year-old, moss-draped live oaks and has grown to become one of the largest seafood restaurants in the area. Pana Robertson and Helen Kaltsunis, the present owners, see to it, however, that the small-restaurant atmosphere is maintained. There are six separate rooms, each with an individual character (my favorite is the glass-enclosed porch where you can watch boats traveling past), and there's music most nights. Prices are moderate, the salad bar (each dinner includes as many trips as you wish) is really spectacular, and the seafood platter is a bargain.

At Murrell's Inlet

Way back when, low-country families used to entertain and dine on the wide porches that ran between the main house and the summer kitchen out back. One of the finest restaurants along the Strand takes its name from that custom, and it's a "must" for good eating in a garden atmosphere that re-creates the graciousness of the old days. **The Planters Back Porch,** 6707 U.S. 17 North (tel. 803/651-5263 or 651-5544), is in an old farmhouse built before the turn of the century, and photos hanging just inside the entrance show it as it used to be. The new interior is bright and cheerful, done in garden colors accented by lots of white—white chairs, white latticework partitions, etc. You can dine on enclosed porches that run down each side, but my favorite is the main room with its cathedral ceiling and fireplace at one end. The Spring House lounge is all done up in keeping with the rest of the house and features frozen cocktails that have become legendary. Since it's operated by the Rice Planter's people, I don't have to tell you that the food is superb (and similarly priced), but I *should* tell you about the Back Porch Inlet Dinner, a seafood feast that goes on and on. Hours here are 5 to 10 p.m., seven days a week, with a price range of $8 to $19.

NIGHTLIFE

Most of the nightlife along the Grand Strand is centered in hotel or motel lounges, some in leading restaurants. Music may vary from country and western to jazz to nostalgia to rock and roll to disco.

THINGS TO SEE AND DO

There are **two publications** just filled with specific information on what, where, when, and how much along the Grand Strand, and either or both will be helpful in planning your vacation here. *Coast* is distributed free by most hotels and motels and is also on counters in many retail establishments and restaurants. The Myrtle Beach Area Chamber of Commerce puts out *See & Do,* and they'll send you a copy if you write them at P.O. Box 2115, Myrtle Beach, SC 29578 (tel. 803/626-7444, or toll free 800/722-3224), or drop by their 1301 N. Kings Hwy. office.

Of course, the big attraction is the **beach**—and sunbathing, swimming, boating, and all the other water sports rank first among things to do. **Fishing** is right up there with them, and whether you cast your line from the surf, a public pier, or a charter boat, you'll probably wind up with a pretty good catch. Surf fishing is permitted all along the beach, and there are fishing piers at Garden City, Surfside, Second Avenue, State Park, Windy Hill, Kits, Crescent Beach, Tilghman Beach, Cherry Grove, and Springmaid.

Charter boats (if you want to sound like a native, call them "head boats") are available at marinas up and down the Strand. In Little River, Vance Kinlaw helps operate daily half-day and longer day trips from Little River Inlet (tel. 803/249-1824). Capt. Everett Ayers operates half-day trips aboard the *New Inlet Princess* from Capt. Dick's Marina at Murrel's Inlet (tel. 803/651-3676); *The Flying Fisher* will take you out for six hours from the Anchor Marina at Murrells Inlet (tel. 803/651-0028); and Capt. Frank Juel's *Hurricane* is available for charter at Little River (tel. 803/249-3571). These are just a few, but they're typical, and even at the height of the season you'll be able to book a trip without much difficulty. Depending on the season, your catch may include croaker, bluefish, flounder, spot, pompano, black seabass, or whiting.

If you're not swimming or fishing, chances are you'll be out on the links swinging a club in one of the three dozen or so championship golf courses. Most, if not all, of the motels and hotels hold memberships in more than one club and will issue guest cards (which entitle you to reduced greens fees). Fees may run anywhere from $8 to $25, depending on the club and the time of the year. It really doesn't matter much which course you play—they're all well laid out and maintained. As for the time of year, the "season" is virtually year round, extending from February through November. Play is heaviest, however, from early February until late April. A golfer friend tells me that if you're planning to spend much time on the Grand Strand courses, you should practice your long shots from the sand; not being a devotee of the game, I'm not quite sure what that means, but it probably has something to do with the sandy roughs I hear mentioned in golfing conversations. At any rate, for what it's worth, I pass it along.

Your **tennis** racquet will get a workout if you bring it along, for there are more than 150 public and private courts in the Grand Strand area. A typical tennis facility is the **Dunes Golf and Beach Club** in the Dunes section of Myrtle Beach (tel. 803/449-5914), which has asphalt courts and charges about $8 per person per hour for singles.

And when you get tired of all that sports activity, there's the boardwalk, just chockablock with amusements and shops.

Myrtle Beach is a good touring center when you tire of the beach, and if you'd rather leave the driving to someone else, **Leisure Time Unlimited** has an excellent schedule of historic tours, both north and south of the Grand Strand. They use a 15-passenger touring van, furnish lunch, and visit such places as Georgetown, Charleston, Orton Plantation, and Historic Wilmington (N.C.), and low-country, privately owned plantations. For current schedules, fees, and reservations, call them at 803/448-9483.

If you'd rather do it yourself, **Georgetown** is a short drive south on U.S. 17, but an incredibly long step back in time. The pre-Revolutionary houses, churches, and public buildings are best seen on a train tour that runs daily at 10 and 11 a.m. and 1, 2, and 3 p.m. with an excellent commentary. For reservations and fare information, contact the **Georgetown Chamber of Commerce,** 600 Front St. P.O. Box 1776, Georgetown, SC 29440 (tel. 803/546-8436). They will also set you out on self-guided tours armed with maps and brochures.

Highlights to look for on your tour of Georgetown include the following:

At the **Prince George Winyah Church,** Broad and Highmarket streets, which dates to about 1750, services have been interrupted only by the Revolution and the Civil War. That stained-glass window behind the altar was once part of the slaves' chapel on a nearby plantation. There's no admission charge.

The **Rice Museum,** in the 1842 Market Building, Front and Screven streets, is the repository of maps, artifacts, dioramas, and other exhibits that trace the development of rice cultivation that was for so long Georgetown's primary economic base.

The **Harold Kaminski House,** 1003 Front St., is a pre-Revolutionary home (1760 or thereabouts), and is furnished with antiques. There's a small admission fee.

On your way to or from Georgetown, you'll pass the charming old fishing village of **Murrell's Inlet** (home of terrific seafood restaurants—see above) and **Pawleys Island,** which has been a resort for over 200 years and is a great place to shop for handcrafts, like the famous Pawleys Island rope hammock. In fact, look for the **Hammock Shop,** which is in a sort of village of handcraft shops called **Plantation Stores,** where you'll find wicker, pewter, miniature doll furniture, brass, china, and all sorts of goodies.

Halfway between Myrtle Beach and Georgetown on U.S. 17 (near Litchfield Beach) is a unique sculpture garden and wildlife park on the grounds of a colonial rice plantation. **Brookgreen Gardens** (tel. 803/237-4218) was begun in 1931 as a setting for representative American garden sculpture from mid-19th century to the present. Archer Milton and Anna Hyatt Huntington planned the garden walks in the shape of a butterfly with outspread wings, all leading back to the central space which was the site of the plantation house. On opposite sides of this space are the Small Sculpture Gallery and the original plantation kitchen. In the wildlife park, an outstanding feature is the Cypress Bird Sanctuary, a 90-foot-tall aviary housing species of wading birds within half an acre of cypress swamp. The gardens are open daily except Christmas from 9:30 a.m. to 4:45 p.m., and admission is $5 for adults, $2 for children 6 to 12, free to those under 6. Tape tours are available for $1.

READER'S SIGHTSEEING SUGGESTION:"We found golf on **Kiawah Island** (not far from Myrtle Beach) to be absolutely superb, and the place itself is an ecological wonderland. The peace and quiet and chance to see so much of nature left unspoiled were a real treat—this is one place man has managed to make room for his own pleasures without displacing the natural inhabitants" (T. Gleason, Bogota, N.J.).

2. Charleston

If the Old South still lives all through South Carolina's low country, it positively thrives in Charleston. And that's just as it should be, for all our romantic notions of antebellum days—stately homes, courtly manners, gracious hospitality, and, above all, gentle dignity—are facts of everyday life in the old city. Oh, it's kept pace with the times, all right—in fact, many "firsts" in its history mark it as a leader in changing trends. Just a few examples: The first indigo crop in the U.S. was grown here in 1690 and proved the basis, along with rice, for many a Charleston family fortune; America's first fire insurance company, "The Friendly Society for the Mutual Insurance of Houses Against Fire," was established in 1736 in Charleston (but was wiped out financially when a disastrous fire in 1740 burned down half the city); the first "weather man" in America, Dr. John Lening, began recording daily temperatures in 1738 to study the effect of weather on the human body; the first shipment of American cotton abroad (seven bags exported to England, at a value of about $873) was from Charleston in 1748; its chamber of commerce, organized in 1773, was the first in America; a British flag was pulled down in Charleston and replaced by the Stars and Stripes in 1775, the first time it happened in the colonies; the country's first "fireproof" building was constructed here in 1826, designed by Robert Mills (designer of the Washington Monument, among other landmarks); the first steam locomotive hauling passengers in America ran from Charleston to Hamberg, S.C., in 1831, as one newspaper reported, "on the wings of the wind, annihilating space and leaving all the world behind at the fantastic speed of 15 m.p.h."; the first shot in the "War for Southern Independence" was fired here in 1861; and, more recently, Charleston was the first port in the world to approve the transport of atomic material. From this impressive *partial* list of leadership, you can see that this "grand old southern belle" has always been—and still is—quite a dame!

Her history clearly shows Charleston to have been a spirited lady right from the start. It all began when King Charles of England magnanimously gave eight of his royal friends a strip of land that included the area between the 29th and 36th parallels of latitude and westward to the Pacific (somehow overlooking the fact that France and Spain already claimed much of that land). Anyway, the lords proprietors sent out colonists who first settled at Albemarle Point, then moved to the peninsula as a location more easily defensible against surprise attack. By the mid-1770s Charleston (originally named Charles Towne) was an important seaport. As the mood for independence grew, Charlestonians threw out the last royal governor, built a palmetto-log and sand fort on Sullivan's Island (that was Fort Moultrie, and it stayed a working fort right on through World War II), repulsed a British fleet on June 28, 1776, then sent couriers to Philadelphia to tell of the victory just in time to convince the Continental Congress that it could be done. The British returned, in 1780 however, with a large land force and took the city, holding it (with the support of loyal Tories) until December of 1782, when it took more than 300 ships to move them out—soldiers, Tories, slaves, and tons of loot.

Then, in 1797, Charleston's spirit reared its head again when a native son, Charles Cotesworth Pinckney, then minister to the French Republic, spoke the supremely American words, "Millions for defense, but not one damned penny for tribute!"—and very nearly got us into war with France.

That first Ordinance of Secession, passed in Columbia in 1860, was actually signed here in Charleston when an epidemic caused the legislature to move, and that fateful shot from Fort Johnson against the Union-held Fort Sumter set the Civil War off and running. The city remained a Confederate stronghold until February of 1865, although it was attacked again and again during the war.

During all those tumultuous years, Charleston was essentially a center of gentility and culture, of wealthy rice and indigo planters who pleasured themselves with imported luxuries, built magnificent town houses (to which they regularly repaired for the summer on May 10 of each year to escape backcountry mosquitoes and malaria), supported the first theater in America, held glittering "socials," originated the "Planters Punch" drink, and ran the state government with an iron hand (in the classic silk glove, of course) until upcountry people forced a new capital in 1790.

Many of those families still own and live in the homes their planter ancestors built, and they still take pride in beautiful, walled gardens, a cultured lifestyle, and a gracious welcome to visitors. Despite the ups and downs of family fortunes, Charlestonians manage to maintain a way of life that, in many respects, has little to do with wealth. I lived here a while during World War II, when there wasn't much socializing, yet the simplest encounter with Charleston natives—even in such ordinary activities as grocery shopping—seemed invested with a "social" air, as though I were a valued guest to be pleased. And I've met with that same treatment on each return trip. Now, I've met those who feel a certain snobbishness in Charlestonians, and, in truth, I think you'd have to live here a few hundred years to be considered an "insider"—but I'll settle for this kind of "outsider" (I prefer to think it's really "guest") acceptance anytime!

Walk along the palmetto-lined Battery or through narrow, crooked streets (some are called "alleys"—but they're not your usual ashcan alleys), or down Cabbage Row (which you will know as Catfish Row of *Porgy and Bess* fame), or drive out to the famous Middleton or Magnolia plantation gardens, and by all means get to know Charlestonians in restaurants or simply on the street, and you'll leave the city as much a "Charleston lover" as everyone else who visits here.

WHERE TO STAY

Charleston's hotels and motels are priced in direct ratio to their proximity to the 789-acre historic district, but if the tariffs close in are too high for your budget, it's really no great problem to drive in from "west of the Ashley," where rates are lower.

Unique

This gracious old city boasts several charming small inns. One of my favorites, an elegant restoration of 18th-century Charleston, is the **Indigo Inn,** 1 Maiden Lane, Charleston, SC 29401 (tel. 803/577-5900, or toll free 800/845-7639). Located in the historic district, it has 40 lovely rooms, all of which face the inner courtyard and are furnished with antiques and reproductions. There's a scrumptious buffet hunt breakfast served from a 1700s Sheraton sideboard every morning, and it's within easy walking distance of major sightseeing attractions. Doubles run about $105 to $115.

The **Elliott House Inn,** 78 Queen St., Charleston, SC 29401 (tel. 803/723-1855), survived the Civil War, earthquakes, and hurricanes to become transformed into one of Charleston's most elegant small inns. Its 26 rooms are appointed with canopied beds, period furnishings, and Oriental rugs. Mornings begin with a sumptuous breakfast of Benedict cheesecake and ham croissants presented in your room on a silver service; each afternoon you'll find a complimentary bottle of imported wine in your room. There's afternoon tea in the landscaped courtyard, and after a complimentary bicycle ride, you'll surely want to relax in the heated courtyard Jacuzzi. Doubles range from $85 to $120, and the numerous seasonal packages and senior citizen discounts can bring that down considerably.

The **Lodge Alley Inn**, 195 E. Bay St., Charleston, SC 29401 (tel. 803/722-1611, or toll free 800/845-1004 outside South Carolina), offers 34 luxurious rooms, each with a fireplace; 37 one- and two-bedroom suites; and a two-bedroom penthouse. All are luxuriously decorated with Charleston period reproduction furnishings and Oriental carpets. You'll find your refrigerator stocked with refreshments, including a complimentary bottle of wine. The French Quarter, one of Charleston's most imaginative new dining rooms, features a grand rôtisserie where the chef prepares roast squab, saddle of lamb, and other house specialties. A la carte entrees are in the $13 to $25 range. And the Charleston Tea Party Lounge, with its ornate bar, is a favorite local watering spot. There's a valet parking lot. Doubles range from $108 to $140, and drop somewhat from mid-November to early February.

The elegant **Planters Inn,** Market at Meeting Street, Charleston, SC 29401 (tel. 803/722-2345, or toll free 800/845-7082 outside South Carolina), near the fine Old City Market, combines the warmth and graciousness of an intimate inn with the amenities of a truly grand hotel. Its 41 guest rooms are impeccably decorated with four-poster beds, and there has been a faithful use of Charleston fabrics and colors. Large travertine marble baths are complete with French milled soap and plush towels, and pamperings continue with nightly turndown service and Italian chocolates on the pillows. The Planters Inn is home to the excellent Robert's of Charleston (see "Where To Eat"). Doubles begin at $100 and drop December through February and from mid-June to mid-September.

The **Middleton Inn & Conference Center,** at Middleton Place, U.S. 61 (Ashley River Road), Charleston, SC 29407 (tel. 803/556-0500, or toll free 800/334-9098, 800/827-5650 in South Carolina), is one of Charleston's newer inns—and surely one of the most appealing you'll find anywhere! High on a secluded bluff, linked to the famed Middleton Gardens by a winding footpath, it is made up of a cluster of four separate, architecturally simple contemporary buildings which blend in with the colors and textures of the surrounding woodlands. The 55 spacious rooms (including 8 parlor suites and a master suite) are decorated with understated elegance. Floor-to-ceiling windows with louvered wooden shutters open to views of the woods and river, and all rooms have a working fireplace with ironwork forged by the plantation's blacksmith. Large European-style bathrooms have hand-laid tile tubs and floors of gray Carrara marble. There's remote-control television in recessed wall niches, in-room movies are offered, and all rooms and suites have refrigerators. There are three restaurants on the premises, and guests have full access to the Middleton Place house, gardens, and stableyards. There's riding from Middleton Stables, miles of jogging trails and scenic walks, lighted tennis courts, and a heated swimming pool. Complimentary golfing and spa privileges are available. All in all, it's the perfect hideaway you owe yourself at least once! Doubles begin at $95 March through June and drop to $80 to $90 at other times. There are also discounts for senior citizens.

A Touch of Luxury

The **Mills House Hotel,** 115 Meeting St., Charleston, SC 29401 (tel. 803/577-2400, or toll free 800/465-4329), was widely heralded as one of the city's finest reconstructions when it opened on the site of an earlier historic hostelry. With its painstaking attention to period decor and ambience amid the expected 20th-century amenities, it's a heartening example of how past and present can blend beautifully. All 214 spacious rooms and suites are beautifully furnished in period, and public areas are enhanced with antiques and Oriental porcelains. There's a pool, concierge service, and valet parking (for a fee), plus carriage rides are available to tour the historic district. Doubles range from $110 to $130 mid-March to mid-June and mid-September to mid-November. Children under 19 stay free in a room with their parents. Rates drop at other times of the year. The Mills House boasts one of Charleston's finest dining rooms (see "Dining in Charleston").

The **Omni Hotel at Charleston Place,** 130 Market St., Charleston, SC 29401 (tel. 803/722-4900, or toll free 800/228-2121), opened late in 1986, bringing Charleston its first world-class hostelry. Adjoining the Old City Market, it so mirrors the ambience of its 18th- and 19th-century surroundings that it almost seems to have been there all along. The lobby welcomes you with a pristine expanse of Italian marble, and whitewashed Georgian pillars frame a stately double staircase. In 450 guest rooms and suites, period furnishings include poster beds, an armoire, and a ceiling fan, along with such modern conveniences as a wet bar. There's a complete health club with a pool, gymnasium, sauna, steambath, and Jacuzzi. There's dining in the Palmetto Café and the Shaftesbury Room, which features regional and historical recipes. Doubles range from $120 to $150, and the top two floors are Omni Clubs, with full concierge service, complimentary cocktails and continental breakfast, and upgraded guest-room decor. The hotel is part of the block-square, $78-million Charleston Place revitalization, which includes 40 upscale shops such as Gucci, Godiva, Laura Ashley, and Banana Republic.

The Best of the Rest

The **Francis Marion–Radisson Hotel,** 387 King St., Charleston, SC 29403 (tel. 803/722-8831, or toll free 800/333-3333), is a landmark hotel that has been a meeting place for Charlestonians for generations, and its loyal following will be delighted to know it has been beautifully renovated and restored. Its location in the historic district opposite Marion Square is delightful, the spacious lobby is replete with marble and antiques, and there's concierge service, along with complimentary evening cocktails and hors d'oeuvres at the piano bar and a morning paper delivered to your door. There's a coffeeshop and dining room where entrees are in the $5 to $13 range. Doubles range from $50 to $70 April through mid-June and mid-September through October, and drop considerably at other times. Teens under 16 stay free in their parents' room. Altogether this is a most cheery and welcoming "home away from home."

Across the Ashley River Bridge on U.S. 17S at 1501 Savannah Hwy., Charleston, SC 29407 (tel. 803/766-1611), the 48-unit **Lord Ashley** is a well-run, pleasant place to stay. Golf privileges are extended and babysitters can be arranged. There is a pool, though no dining room (restaurants are not far away). Rates are in the $34 to $40 range.

The **Best Western King Charles Inn,** 237 Meeting St., Charleston, SC 29401 (tel. 803/723-7451, or toll free 800/528-1234), just one block from the historic district's market area, has bright, comfortable rooms, a pool, a restaurant that serves breakfast only, and a lounge. Doubles here range from $75 to $90, depending on season.

The circular, 13-story **Holiday Inn–Riverview,** U.S. 17 at Ashley River, Charleston, SC 29407 (tel. 803/556-7100, or toll free 800/465-4329), overlooks the river and the city on the opposite bank. It's just two miles from the center of town, not at all inconvenient. Rooms have balconies; there's a pool, a dining room that serves all meals, and a lounge that features entertainment and dancing. Some rooms have been fitted for the handicapped. Doubles begin at $64.

If Charleston's famous gardens are on your "must see" lists, the **Econo Lodge,** 2237 Savannah Hwy., Charleston, SC 29407 (tel. 803/571-1880, or toll free 800/446-6900), offers budget prices combined with convenience. Both Magnolia and Middleton Gardens are close by, as is Charlestowne Landing. Several golf courses are also in the vicinity. As is true of all members of this chain, there is no pool and no restaurant (Perkins Pancake House is just down the road, however). Rooms are more than adequate, and the price of a double is only $38 to $40.

La Quinta Motor Inn, 2499 La Quinta Lane, North Charleston, SC 29405 (tel. 803/797-8181, or toll free 800/531-5900), is near the handsome new Charleston International Airport, and there's a direct line in the baggage claim area to call for free pickup service; if you're driving in off I-26, take exit 209. This fast-growing Texas-based system now has a number of moderately priced inns in the Southern Atlantic region, and I have always found them clean, comfortable, well run, and a good buy. This one is no exception. Rooms are attractively furnished, the beds are extra-long, and there's free cable color TV along with free local phone calls. You can also request a nonsmoking room. There's a pool, and a Shoney's restaurant is next door; you can even call them for room service from 6 a.m. to 11 p.m. Double rate is $41, and a 20% senior citizen discount is available. Cribs are free, and children under 18 stay free in their parents' room. Fido is welcome, too!

Motel 6, 2058 Savannah Hwy., Charleston, SC 29407 (tel. 803/571-0560), offers the clean, comfortable accommodations I have come to expect from this fast-growing system, and I applaud its efforts to keep rates economical, as some others continue to escalate. It has a pool, offers color TV for a modest charge, and there's a restaurant nearby. Rates are $34 to $36 double; each additional person over 12 stays for $2, children 3 to 11 stay for $1 each, and it's free for those under 3.

Bed and Breakfast

There are two organizations that can help you locate exactly the kind of bed-and-breakfast home for your stay in Charleston. The range extends from historic homes to carriage houses to simple cottages, and they're found in virtually every section of the city. For full details and booking, contact: **Historic Charleston Bed and Breakfast,** 43 Legare St., Charleston, SC 29402 (tel. 803/722-6606); and the **Charleston Society Bed and Breakfast,** 84 Murray Blvd., Charleston, SC 29401 (tel. 803/723-4948).

Two typical Charleston bed-and-breakfast homes are: **Brasington House,** 328 East Bay St., Charleston, SC 29401 (tel. 803/722-1274), a 1790s home with wide verandas and three guest rooms with private baths, furnished with antiques ($71 to $90); and **The Coach House,** 39 East Battery, Charleston, SC 29401 (tel. 803/722-8145), with two nicely appointed guest rooms ($65 to $90).

READER'S GUESTHOUSE SELECTIONS: "In Charleston, we made a special find. We stayed at the **Battery Carriage House,** 20 South Battery (tel. 803/723-9881, or toll free 800/845-7638, 800/922-7638 in South Carolina), a ten-room carriage house which had just been restored to a guesthouse (we were there the first month). The rooms were most attractive, the owners pleasant and helpful, and the service elegant (a butler served a continental breakfast on a silver tray). Also in Charleston, we had a delicious meal at the lovely **Mills Hyatt House Hotel**" (J. Prince, Pottstown, Penna.).

"Not enough recommendations can be given Charleston's **Sweet Grass Inn,** 23 Vendue Range, Charleston, SC 29401. It is superbly managed by a minister and his charming wife. What a find! Full southern breakfast is included, either in a quaint and tastefully decorated dining room, in your own room, or on the roof terrace with its views of the river and the city. The room, which was quite large, was beautifully furnished with antiques" (M. Ryan, New York, N.Y.) [*Author's Note:* Near the colorful waterfront, it's now part of the adjacent Vendue Inn, and both are indeed delightful places to stay. For reservations or information at both, phone 803/723-9980, or toll free 800/845-7900, 800/922-7900 in South Carolina.

Campgrounds

The **Charleston KOA** (write Ladson, SC 29456; tel. 803/797-1045) is about 15 miles northwest on U.S. 78, 1 mile west of its junction with I-26. There are shaded (and some open), level sites, a disposal station, laundry, store, propane gas, pool, recreation room, and playground. Sightseeing tours depart the campgrounds daily. You'll need to send a deposit to hold your reservation. Rates are $16 and up.

DINING IN CHARLESTON

There's good eating everywhere you turn in Charleston, so I've made the arbitrary decision to list a very personal selection of restaurants, most of them in the historic old market area—the character of the city is most reflected here, I think. To compile your own selective list, pick up the "Official Dining Guide" from the visitors center.

In or Near the Market

Robert Dickson, owner, chef, and star attraction of **Robert's of Charleston,** 112 N. Market St. (at Meeting St., in the Plantus Inn (see "Where To Stay"), (tel. 803/577-7565), asked me to explain to readers that because the elegant but small restaurant seats only 56, reservations for weekend evenings must be made two months or more in advance. Since the place has received rave reviews in popular publications, this young man has had to disappoint hundreds of travelers who simply don't understand the space limitations. Well, now that you're forewarned, I'll tell you what you're likely to miss unless you can plan to come during the week. Robert and his wife, Pam, are displaced Yankees now firmly entrenched in the South who serve a six-course, prix-fixe dinner, with one sitting at 8 p.m. every night except Sunday and Monday. The entree is confined to a single item each evening, and is always a masterpiece of perfection, as are the fish course, salad, duck course, fresh fruits, fresh vegetables, grilled tenderloin, and dessert. Robert introduces each course with song, either show music or opera, in a rich bass baritone, and dinner becomes an event. The cost is $60 and cheap at the price (includes dinner, wine, and gratuities). So call in advance for a reservation or a place on the waiting list, and keep your fingers crossed.

Just a few blocks away on the waterfront, the **Colony House,** 35 Prioleau St. (tel. 803/723-3424), occupies a historic old warehouse, but there's nothing in its present appearance that even remotely suggests that lowly past. "Elegant" is the only word for the sparkling white exterior with black shutters framing windows adorned inside with rich draperies. The Colony House features murals of Charleston's famous Cypress, Middleton, and Magnolia gardens, and offers seafood, beef, fowl, and veal dishes; while the Wine Cellar (tel. 803/723-9463)—a charming room you really have to see to appreciate—offers luscious French delicacies like escalope de veau aux chanterelles and is open for dinner only: 6:30 to 9:30 p.m. Monday through Saturday. The delightful Sam Prioleau's Tavern serves creative drinks. Prices in the main dining rooms are also expensive by Charleston standards ($5 to $10 at lunch, $10 to $21 for à la carte dinners), but both food and atmosphere are memorable. There are also children's menus. Lunch is served here from 11:30 a.m. to 3 p.m. Monday through Saturday, dinner from 5:30 to 10:30 p.m. Monday through Saturday, to 9:30 p.m. on Sunday. Reservations are advisable, and there is an evening dress code.

The **Barbadoes Room,** in the Mills House Hotel, Queen and Meeting streets (tel. 803/577-2400), is in an elegantly appointed formal setting overlooking a garden courtyard with a gently splashing fountain. Its notable low-country dinner specialties include shrimp Middleton, sautéed with garlic and Dijon mustard, flamed with white wine and blended with cream ($15), and snapper Dorchester, poached with white wine and mushrooms ($13). This is the perfect spot to sample sherry-dolloped she-crab soup, so named because the crab roe offers a unique flavor. And don't miss the famous Mills House mud pie, mocha ice cream in a chocolate-cookie crust, topped with fudge, whipped cream, and pecans! There's a varied luncheon menu of sandwiches, omelets, seafoods, and other entrees in the $4.75 to $6.50 range. The Sunday brunch buffet, from 11 a.m. to 3 p.m., is a Charleston institution. The Barbadoes (that's the original spelling of the island) Room is open for breakfast from 7 a.m. to 11 a.m. (to 10:30 a.m. on Sunday), from 11 a.m. to 3 p.m. for lunch, and from 5:30 to 10:30 p.m. for dinner. Reservations are required for brunch and dinner, and jackets are a must, as they should be in this elegant room, after 7 p.m.

82 Queen, at 82 Queen St. (tel. 803/723-7591), one of Charleston's most popular restaurants, offers both outdoor and indoor dining in a handsomely restored 19th-century townhouse. Specialties include Carolina crab

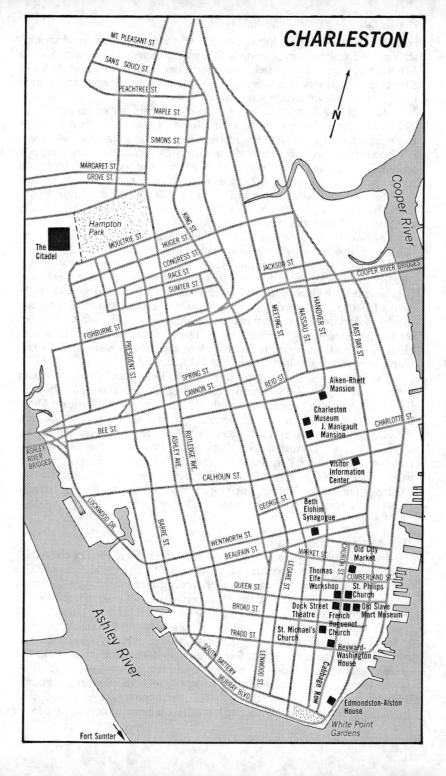

cakes, broiled whole Maine lobster, sautéed veal and mushrooms, and shrimp, scallops and crabmeat over spinach fettuccine. Entrees range from $13 to $18.95, and there's always a fresh catch of the day. Luncheons are in the $6 to $10 range, and are served daily from 11:30 a.m. to 2 p.m.; dinner is daily from 6 to 10 p.m. It's a good idea to make reservations.

The **East Bay Trading Company,** Queen and East Bay streets (tel. 803/722-0722), keeps drawing me back both for its wonderful ambience and its menu selections. In this former warehouse, antiques, artifacts, and lush greenery decorate three stunning levels which encompass a dramatic, skylight-topped atrium. Entrees range from Carolina quail and fresh seafoods to beef, lamb, and some continental preparations. Lunches range from $5 to $10, and dinners average $10 to $16. It's open from 11:30 a.m. to 2:30 p.m. Monday through Saturday, from 5:30 to 10:30 p.m. Monday through Thursday, to 11 p.m. Friday and Saturday. Parties of six or more should call for reservations.

Le Midi, 337 King St. (tel. 803/577-5571), is one of the fine French restaurants that add another dimension to the Charleston dining experience. Behind the unpretentious storefront façade of this locally popular café you'll discover a wide selection of French wines and superb French country cooking: boneless breast of chicken sautéed in champagne sauce with cream and mushrooms ($10.95), scalloped veal sautéed in a lemon-butter sauce ($12), lamb shanks cooked in white wine, tomatoes, and spices ($11.95), and the list goes on from there, tempting me even now to hop on the next plane for Charleston. Hours are 11:30 a.m. to 2 p.m. for lunch Monday through Friday, 6 to 10 p.m. for dinner Monday through Saturday, and closed Sunday.

The Trawler, four miles southeast on U.S. 17 at Shem Creek, in Mount Pleasant (tel. 803/884-2560), is an excellent choice to stop at for a hearty seafood lunch or dinner if you're visiting the Patriots Point Naval-Maritime Museum. Local, freshly caught seafood, broiled or fried, is the order of the day, and there's a good salad bar. Specialties include fish stew, and shrimp à la Newberg. There's a pleasantly casual nautical ambience, and you'll need to make reservations only in the somewhat fancier Captain's Table Room, which is open only from 5 to 9 p.m. Dinners are $9 to $20, lunches somewhat less, and there's a children's menu. The Trawler is open from 5 to 10:30 p.m. Monday through Friday, noon to 10:30 p.m. on Saturday, and from noon to 9 p.m. on Sunday.

The Best for the Budget

In an unpainted wooden house on stilts right at the edge of the Ashley River, next to the municipal marina, the **Variety Store** (tel. 803/723-6325) is a good place to feed an entire family on appetizing dishes without serious injury to the pocketbook. The restaurant occupies one side of a store that sells fishing supplies and souvenirs. You can enjoy okra soup (I'll bet you've never tasted it—do, it's delicious!) or chili, a variety of sandwiches, or fried fish dinners, all at budget prices. Breakfast is served anytime: two eggs, bacon or sausage, toast, and, of course, grits, cost about $4. Picture windows frame the comings and goings of all sorts of boats—I even saw a Chinese junk sail past. Orders are placed at the counter and waitresses bring the food to comfortable booths. There's a relaxed atmosphere that I, for one, thoroughly enjoyed. Mike Altine, Jr., manager and son of the owner, tells me that the store has been serving locals and boat owners who put in to the adjacent dock for more than 25 years. Hours are 6:30 a.m. to 3 p.m. and 5 to 10 p.m. Monday through Saturday, 7 a.m. to 3 p.m.

THINGS TO SEE AND DO

The **visitor information center** at 85 Calhoun St. (tel. 803/722-8338, across from the Gaillard Municipal Auditorium) should be your first destination. They have brochures, self-guided walking and driving tour maps, up-to-the-minute information on cultural events, and a staff that exemplifies Charleston charm. You might want to write ahead, in fact, for their *Charleston Area Visitor's Guide* (P.O. Box 975, Charleston, SC 29402; tel. 803/722-5225). The center stays open from 8:30 a.m. to 5:30 p.m. Monday through Friday, to 5 p.m. on Saturday and Sunday.

Located in the information center, the **Adventure Theatre** presents a multi-image look at Charleston called *The Charleston Adventure*. On a 40-foot-wide screen, color panoramas and an interesting narrative give you a 30-minute preview of what lies in store during your visit. Check with the information center for exact show times and admission charges (minimal).

A Charlestonian once told me that in 1860 "South Carolina seceded from the Union, Charleston seceded from South Carolina, and South of Broad Street seceded from Charleston." Well, I don't know about *that,* but I *do* know that "south of Broad Street" is the heart of Old Charleston and the place to walk or cycle back to another world.

I always head for the **Battery** (if you want to be official about it, the **White Point Gardens**) to get back into the feel of this city. It's right on the end of the peninsula, facing the Cooper River and the harbor. There's a lovely park, shaded by palmettos and live oaks and filled with walkways that pass old monuments, cannon, and other war relics, and that view of the harbor looks out to Fort Sumter. I like to walk along the sea wall on East Battery and Murray Boulevard (where a blue marlin or some such large ocean fish entertained me with acrobatics one afternoon for nearly an hour) and sink slowly into the history of Charleston. Turning your back to the water, you'll face a row of large, graceful houses that line South Battery, so that when you walk away from the park, it's as though you're going through a sort of gateway into the rest of the town.

Once off South Battery, almost every home is of historic or architectural interest, and I'd need an entire book to tell you about them all. But some you really shouldn't miss are: the **Edmondston-Alston House,** 21 East Battery, built in 1828 by a wealthy merchant and wharf owner and later bought by a Colonel Alston, whose son redid it in the Greek Revival style. Guided tours run from 10 a.m. to 5 p.m. Monday through Saturday, and 2 to 5 p.m. on Sunday and holidays and cost $3.50. You can purchase combination tickets that include this and the Russell House for $5. The **Nathaniel Russell House,** 51 Meeting St., was built before 1809 and has a lovely, unusual, free-flying staircase. Hours and prices are the same as above. The 1803 **Joseph Manigault House,** 350 Meeting St., is an Adams-style structure and also has a notable staircase. It's open every day from 10 a.m. to 5 p.m.; adults pay $3, and children 3 to 12 $1.50. There is a combination ticket ($5) that includes the **Heyward-Washington House,** 87 Church St., which was built in 1772 and was the home of a signer of the Declaration of Independence. Open every day from 10 a.m. to 4:30 p.m.; admission is $3 for adults, $1.50 for ages 6 to 18. Combination tickets available (see above). The **Thomas Elfe Workshop,** 54 Queen St., built prior to 1760 by Charleston's most famous cabinetmaker, is a charming small version of a Charleston "single house," and its collections of cabinetmaking tools and artifacts add to its appeal. An adjoining gift shop showcases 18th-century reproductions and accessories, low-country gift items. Tours are offered at 10 and 11 a.m., noon, and 2:30, 3:30, and 4:30 p.m. Monday through Friday, and at 10 and 11 a.m. and noon on Saturday. Admission is $3. The **Aiken-Rhett Mansion,** 48 Elizabeth St., home of Gov. William Aiken, displays some original furnishings, paint, and wallpaper. It's under restoration by the Charleston Museum and is open from 10 a.m. to 5 p.m. Wednesday through Saturday and 1 to 5 p.m. Sunday. Guided tours are $3 for adults, $1.50 for juniors; combination tickets are offered with the Heyward-Washington and Joseph Manigault houses.

And don't miss the **Dock Street Theatre,** at the corner of Church and Queen streets (tel. 723-5648). When it opened in 1736, it was the first building in the colonies planned just for theater. The first building burned, and in the early 1800s the Planters Hotel, a very popular local drinking spot, was built around its ruins (that's where "Planters Punch" came from, they say). The theater's back now (since 1936), remodeled and still doing business, with plays, ballet performances, concerts, and other events (it's the longtime home of the Footlight Players, Charleston's resident theater company, and opera and drama here are a part of the annual Spoleto Festival U.S.A. in May and June). You can visit the theater Monday through Friday from noon to 6 p.m. There are guided tours on Saturday at a cost of $1 for adults, 50¢ for children. Call for hours.

Charleston has been a church town from the start, and there are several worth a visit: **St. Michael's Episcopal Church,** Meeting and Broad streets, is the oldest in the city, dating back to 1761. Its eight bells (imported in 1764) are historic and well traveled: they were taken as a British prize of war in the Revolution and sent back to England, then burned during the Civil War, having to cross the Atlantic again for recasting. The chandelier, installed in 1803, has been lighted by candles, gas, and electricity. Washington worshipped here during his 1791 southern tour.

At 136 Church St., the present **French Huguenot Church** (1844–1845) is the fourth version on this site, the first being built in 1687. In the early days, so many of the congregation came downriver by boat that services were planned so they could arrive on the ebb tide and go home on the flood. It's the only French Huguenot church in the U.S. that still uses the French liturgy.

Congregation Beth Elohim, 90 Hassel St., is the oldest synagogue in continuous use in the U.S., and the second oldest in the country, dating from 1840. This is a replacement for the original, built in 1794, which burned in 1838, and its Greek Revival architecture is considered one of America's finest examples of that style.

The mother church of the Roman Catholic dioceses of South Carolina, North Carolina, and Georgia is **St. Mary's,** at 89 Hasell St. It's another replacement (in 1839) for an earlier church (1789), which burned in 1838.

Now, about **Catfish Row**—its real name is **Cabbage Row** (because of the vegetables that used to be sold on the sidewalk), and it's a row of connected buildings from 89 to 91 Church St. that surround a courtyard. DuBose Heyward changed its name in his novel *Porgy,* and when he and George Gershwin collaborated on the *Porgy and Bess* opera, its fame spread all over the world.

The **Old City Market,** at East Bay and Market streets, still functions, its open stalls under brick sheds with tile roofs that stretch for roughly three blocks. All sorts of things are sold at the stalls, one of the most interesting being Sea Island vegetables brought in daily by owners of small outlying farms. On either side of the open sheds, old market buildings have been leased to small boutiques filled with marvelous linens, cookware, clothing, gifts, etc. Some of the best restaurants (and some of the oldest) are here also (see "Dining in Charleston," above). A few blocks away from the market, at the corner of Meeting and Broad streets, look for the **"Flower Ladies"** who sell colorful bunches of blooms from the nearby islands.

The **Citadel,** Moultrie Street and Elmwood Avenue, was established in 1842 on the site of a fortress originally built as an arsenal to suppress any slave uprising (and as a refuge for whites if it came to that). In 1922, it moved to its present location. The campus of this military college, with its buildings of Moorish design, including crenelated battlements and sentry towers, is especially interesting when the college is in session; and the public is invited to a precision drill parade on the quadrangle at 3:45 p.m. every Friday. There's also an interesting World War II photomural of Europe, with narration, among the Gen. Mark Clark archives (he was president of the college from 1954 to 1965) at the **Citadel Memorial Archives Museum,** (tel. 792-6846; free; open Sunday through Friday from 2 to 5 p.m., on Saturday from 9 a.m.)

I sometimes get the feeling that the whole city is a museum, but then I remember its several outstanding museums of the "standard" sort. For instance, there's the **Charleston Museum,** founded in 1773, making it the oldest in the country. It's at 360 Meeting St., in a $6-million complex at the corner of Meeting and John streets (tel. 803/722-2996). There are more than a million items in the museum's collection, including a full-scale replica of the famed Confederate submarine *Hunley,* and those on display include early crafts of the area (look for the massive collection of Charleston silver), natural history relics, anthropological exhibits, and a children's Discovery Room. It's open from 9 a.m. to 5 p.m. Monday through Saturday, and 1 to 5 p.m. on Sunday. Admission is $3 for adults, $1.50 for children.

The **Old Slave Mart Museum,** 6 Chalmers St., in the National Register of Historic Places, is the oldest museum in the country (1938) devoted exclusively to the contributions of blacks to American culture. It is poetic justice, indeed, that this building, once used to auction slaves, now exhibits African arts and crafts as well as those of American blacks both before and after the days of slavery. Open Monday through Saturday from 10 a.m. to 4:30 p.m. Adults pay $3, children, $1.

Kids will love the **aircraft carrier** U.S.S. *Yorktown* at Patriot's Point (on the Mount Pleasant Side of the Cooper River Bridge), and I suspect all navy veterans will, too. The World War II, Korea, and Vietnam exploits of "the Fighting Lady" are, as you'd expect, well documented, and in addition naval history is illustrated through models of ships, planes, and weapons. You can wander through the bridge, wheelhouse, flight and hangar decks, chapel, sick bay, and several other areas, and view the film, *The Fighting Lady,* depicting life aboard the carrier. The *Yorktown* is the nucleus of the world's largest naval and maritime museum. Also at Patriots Point, and welcoming visitors aboard, are the nuclear ship *Savannah,* the world's first nuclear-powered merchant ship; the World War II destroyer *Laffey;* the World War II submarine *Clamagore;* and the cutter *Comanche.* Patriot's Point is open from 9 a.m. to 6 p.m. daily April through October, to 5 p.m. November through March. Admission is $7.50 for adults, $6.50 for those over 62 and military personnel in uniform, and $4 for children ages 6 to 11. Adjoining is the fine 18-hole public Patriot's Point golf course. For further information, telephone 803/884-2727.

Charles Towne Landing, on the site of that first 1670 settlement, is a 663-acre park on S.C. 171 at 1500 Old Town Rd., between U.S. 17 and I-126 (tel. 803/556-4450). An open-air, rather modernistic interpretive center has underground exhibits that show the colony's history, and there's a re-creation of a small village, a full-scale replica of a 17th-century trading ship, and a tram tour for $1 (or you can rent a bike for $1.50 an hour). Best of all, there's no flashy "theme park" atmosphere: what you see as you walk under huge old oaks, past freshwater lagoons, and through the Animal Forest (which has animals of the same species that lived here in 1670) is what those early settlers saw. The park is open every day, all year, from 9 a.m. to 5 p.m. Adults pay $4; children 6 to 14, $1; senior citizens, $2; free for the handicapped.

A lot of people come to Charleston just for the "gardens"—and they are lovely. Of course, there are gardens everywhere you look in the city, but when natives use the word, they're referring to Middleton Place, Magnolia Plantation, Cypress Gardens, Charles Towne Landing's 85-acre English Park Garden, and Boone Hall Plantation.

Middleton Place, 14 miles northwest of Charleston on Hwy. 61 (tel. 803/556-6020), was the home of Henry Middleton, president of the First Continental Congress, and his son, Arthur, a signer of the Declaration of Independence. Today, the national historic landmark includes this country's oldest landscaped gardens, the Middleton Place House, and the Plantation Stableyards. The gardens, begun in 1741, reflect the elegant symmetry of European gardens of the period. Ornamental lakes, terraces, and plantings of camellias, azaleas, magnolias, and crepe myrtle accent the grand design. The Middleton Place House was built in 1755, and in 1865 all but the south flank was ransacked and burned by Union troops. It was restored in the 1870s as a family residence, and today it mirrors the family's important role in American history, with collections of fine silver, furniture, rare first editions by Catesby and Audubon, and portraits by Benjamin West and Thomas Sully. Children, as well as adults, will be enthralled by the stableyards, where craftspeople demonstrate life on the largely self-sufficient plantation of yesteryear when rice and cotton were its economic rulers. There are horses and mules, hogs, milk cows, sheep, and goats. A morning spent exploring this beautiful and fascinating place is best ended with a plantation lunch at the **Middleton Place Restaurant,** where dishes like okra gumbo, plantation, chicken, and ham biscuits will cost between $4 and $8. Admission to the gardens and stableyards is $9 for adults from mid-March to mid-June, $8 other months; $4.50 for ages 6 to 12 (plus $4 extra to tour the house), and those under age 5 are free. Guided tours of the house are $5 in the high season, $4 other months, and hours are 9 a.m. to 5 p.m. daily year round.

Ten generations of the Drayton family have lived continuously at **Magnolia Plantation** (10 miles northwest of S.C. 61; tel. 803/571-1266) since the 1670s. They haven't had much luck keeping a roof over their heads: the first mansion burned just after the Revolution and its replacement was burned by Sherman. But you can't call *its* replacement "modern" (or even Victorian)—a simple, pre-Revolutionary house was barged down from Summerville and set on the basement foundations of its unfortunate predecessors. The magnificent gardens of camellias and azaleas, however, have been among the most beautiful in America down through the years. They reach their height of bloom in March and April, but the gardens are colorful year round. You can tour the house, the gardens (which include an herb garden, horticultural maze, topiary garden, and biblical garden), and a petting zoo; stroll down the Audubon swamp board-walk; ride canoes through a 125-acre waterfowl refuge; or walk or cycle through wildlife trails. It's open daily from 8 a.m. to 6:30 p.m., and costs $7 for adults, $6 for senior citizens, (over 65), $5 for ages 13 to 19, and $3 for ages 4 to 12 (under 4, free).

There are footpaths and boats to take you through flower-filled **Cypress Gardens,** 23 miles from Charleston on S.C. 52 (look for turnoff signs). The swamp garden was used as a freshwater reserve for Dean Hall, a huge Cooper River rice plantation, and was given to the city in 1963. Hours are 8 a.m. to 5 p.m. daily and admission is $5 for adults, $2 for children 6 to 16, and $4 for senior citizens. Boat rides are extra. Open year round.

Boone Hall Plantation, six miles north on U.S. 17 (tel. 803/884-4371), is approached by a famous "Avenue of Oaks," huge old moss-draped trees planted in 1743 by one Capt. Thomas Boone. The first floor of the beautiful plantation house is elegantly furnished and open to the public. Hours are 8:30 a.m. to 6:30 p.m. Monday through Saturday and 1 to 5 p.m. on Sunday, April through Labor Day; 9 a.m. to 5 p.m. Monday through Saturday and 1 to 4 p.m. on Sunday in other months. The guided tour is $5 for adults, $4.50 for seniors (over 60), and $1 for ages 6 to 12.

Nine miles from Charleston, on the Ashley River Road (S.C. 61; tel. 803/766-0188), **Drayton Hall** is one of the oldest surviving plantations. Built in 1738, it was owned by the Drayton family until 1974. Framed by majestic live oaks, the lovely old Georgian-Palladian house is now a property of the National Trust for Historic Preservation (and if you're a member of the Trust, you get in free with your membership card). It's open from 10 a.m. to 4 p.m. daily March through October, with tours on the hour (last one at 3 p.m.), 10 a.m. to 3 p.m. other months. Rates are $6 for adults and $3 for school-age children. Closed Thanksgiving, Christmas, and New Year's days.

Both **Fort Moultrie,** on Sullivan's Island, West Middle Street, 10 miles east of the city (tel. 803/833-3123), and **Fort Sumter** (in the harbor) are open to visitors. There's no charge at Fort Moultrie, which is open from 9 a.m. to 6 p.m. in summer and 9 a.m. to 5 p.m. in winter, and there's a visitor center. To reach Fort Sumter, the U.S. Coast Guard supervises sightseeing yachts operated by **Fort Sumter Tours** (see below).

One last "thing to do": In May of 1977 Charleston inaugurated an annual **Spoleto Festival U.S.A.,** a 17-day culture explosion that brought 600 performers and over 100 events (opera, theater, ballet, jazz, symphony, choral concerts, and art exhibits) directed by Gian Carlo Menotti, who orchestrates the Spoleto,

Italy, festival each summer. The first festival was a rousing success, fun for everybody, and it gets better every year. Write Spoleto U.S.A., P.O. Box 157, Charleston, SC 29402 (tel. 803/722-2764), for future dates if you're interested.

Tours

The **Harbor and Naval Base Tour,** operated from the city marina by Ft. Sumter Tours, Inc., 205 King St., Suite 204 (tel. 803/722-1691), is a 2 ¼-hour narrated cruise covering some 85 points of interest within 30 miles. Highlight of the cruise is a one-hour stopover on Fort Sumter, with free access to the Civil War Museum and a commentary/lecture by National Park Service historians. Other points of interest are the U.S. Coast Guard Base (on the site of an old rice mill), Fort Johnson (the one that fired on Fort Sumter to start the Civil War), Fort Moultrie, the Cooper River bridges (two of the largest in the world), and historic Battery homes. Fares are $7.50 for adults, $3.75 for children. Call for current schedules, since they vary seasonally.

Gray Line Water Tours, City Municipal Marina, Lockwood Blvd. (tel. 803/722-1112 or 723-5858), conducts 2 ½-hour cruises with an itinerary much like that above. Adults pay $7.50; seniors, $5.50; ages 6 to 11, $3.50.

Charleston Trolley Tours leave the visitor information center, 85 Calhoun St. (tel. 803/577-0042), for one-hour trolley tours of the historic district. Fares are $7 for adults, $3.50 for ages 3 to 12.

Other tours include: **Charleston Carriage Company,** 96 N. Market St. (tel. 803/577-0042), horse-drawn carriage tours (narrated) depart from that address from 9 a.m. until dusk at $10 for adults, $4.50 ages 3 to 12 (call to reserve); **Palmetto Carriage Tours,** 40 N. Market St. Guignard St. (tel. 803/723-8145) $10 for adults, $4 for ages 4 to 11; cassette walking or driving tours from **Charles Towne Tours,** P.O. Box 1118, Charleston, SC 29402 (tel. 803/723-5133), available at the Mills Hyatt House gift shop, the Days Inn Downtown, and Quality Inn Downtown, which cost $10; **Gray Line Bus Tours** (leave from information center and all downtown hotels; tel. 803/722-4444), for city and surroundings tours.

IN THE EVENING

Most of the larger hotels in Charleston have lounges with live music and/or entertainment, and there are several lively bars. Check local papers for current goings-on.

The **Young Charleston Theatre Company,** 133 Church St. (tel. 803/577-5967), produces a wide variety of plays and musicals from October to June at the Dock Street Theatre at extremely moderate prices. The **Charleston Symphony Orchestra,** 14 George St. (tel. 723-7528), presents classical, chamber music, and pop concerts from September through May. During the same season, the **Charleston Civic Ballet** and **Charleston Opera Company** perform at Gaillard Municipal Auditorium, 77 Calhoun St. (tel. 803/577-4500 or 577-4502).

One of the most enjoyable ways I can think of to spend a Charleston evening is aboard the *Spirit of Charleston* for a three-hour dinner cruise. Cocktails are followed by a four-course prime rib dinner, and there's dancing to the music of a live band. For schedules, fares, and bookings, contact Ft. Sumter Tours, Inc., 205 King St., Suite 204, Charleston, SC 29401 (tel. 803/722-1691).

3. Hilton Head Island

Colonization efforts and squabbling over ownership of Hilton Head—the largest sea island between New Jersey and Florida—went on among Spain, France, and England from the early 1600s until the mid-1700s. Native Americans, certain of their claim to the land, harassed them all. But by the end of the 18th century, things had quieted down enough for large plantations to flourish, and a leisurely island lifestyle evolved. Today's "plantations" (most resort areas define their boundaries by the term) hold on to that leisure—indeed, offer it to all comers—and modern "crops" come in the form of tourism instead of rice. Some 450,000 to 500,000 resort guests visit the island annually, and that's some "harvest" for a permanent population of about 7,500 (most of whom are engaged in attracting or servicing the visitors).

Although only 42 square miles in area (12 miles long and 5 miles at its widest), Hilton Head has a feeling of spaciousness, due to judicious planning from the start of its development in 1952. The only "city" (of sorts) is Harbour Town at Sea Pines Plantation. The broad beaches on its ocean side, beautiful sea marshes over on the sound, natural wooded areas of live and water oak, pine, bay, and palmetto trees have all been carefully preserved amid the commercial enterprise that has created over 2,000 hotel rooms (mostly oceanfront) and some 4,000 vacation villas, condominiums, and retirement homes. It's an environmental paradise that regularly attracts artists, writers, musicians (jazz, classical, and even rock), theater groups, and craftsmen.

Recreation, Hilton Head's economic base, goes on year round in a subtropical climate that ranges from the low 50s in winter to mid-80s in summer. There are 23 golf courses (18 are championship caliber—the Heritage Gold Classic and Women's International Professional are annual events), over 300 tennis courts (which are settings for the World Invitational Tennis Classic, Avon Futures Tennis Championship, and the Family Circle Cup), eight marinas that can dock yachts up to 100 feet long, a sailing club, all sorts of rental boats, charter fishing boats for hire (there's an annual billfishing tournament). You'll also find miles and miles of beach (some up to 600 feet wide at low tide), rental bicycles and 25 miles of rambling bike paths, four riding stables (with boarding facilities for those who bring their own mounts), 15 shopping centers (with exquisite craft shops and elegant resort-apparel boutiques), some 100 restaurants that range from gourmet to fast food, and . . . well, you name it and it's probably here. Nightlife is found chiefly in hotel or shopping-center lounges, which can be quiet, intimate rendezvous spots or lively entertainment centers with sophisticated bands for dancing and top performers doing their thing.

GETTING THERE

Even though Hilton Head is an island, you get there over a bridge (about 40 miles east of I-95, 30 miles north of Savannah, Georgia). USAir (Piedmont) flies directly to Hilton Head, and American, USAir (Piedmont), and Delta Airlines all fly into Savannah, where there's limousine service. Of course, if you fly your own, you'll land directly at the island's airport, a 3,700-foot paved runway that can handle most nonjet private planes. For boat owners, getting there is simple, since it's directly on the Intracoastal Waterway. Amtrak and Greyhound take train and bus riders to Savannah.

Incidentally, the **Hilton Head Island Chamber of Commerce,** P.O. Box 5647, Hilton Head Island, SC 29938 (tel. 803/785-3673), is especially helpful in planning a visit, either before or after your arrival.

WHERE TO STAY

There is really no such thing as "budget" on Hilton Head Island. However, it *is* possible these days to spend time here for a *reasonable* cost. Of course, the older resort establishments (called plantations) are the very embodiment of luxury, with prices to match. When booking, be sure to ask about golf, tennis, or family package rates.

There is, however, a central reservation service which can book you into various rooms and villas almost anywhere on the island, and there's no booking fee. Write or call: **Hilton Head Central Reservation Service,** P.O. Box 5312, Hilton Head Island, SC 29938 (tel. 803/785-9050, or toll free 800/845-7018).

Another suggestion is the rental of private homes, and for up-to-date availability, rates, and bookings, you can contact **Island Rentals and Real Estate, Inc.,** P.O. Box 5915, Hilton Head Island, SC 29938 (tel. 803/785-3813, or toll free 800/845-6134).

The Luxury Level

Sea Pines Plantation (write Sea Pines Resort, Hilton Head Island, SC 29938; tel. 803/785-3333, or toll free 800/845-6131) was Hilton Head's first resort and has a faithful following who would not stay anywhere else. Spread over more than 5,000 acres, it has 4 miles of ocean beach, 14 miles of bike trails, three championship golf courses, 80 lighted tennis courts, an outstanding children's summer recreation program, and over a dozen restaurants and entertainment spots within its boundaries. You can eat, shop, or enjoy nightlife without being a Sea Pines guest, but there's a small fee to enter the grounds if you're not. Double rooms at the oceanfront Hilton Head Inn rent for $90 and up per night in season (late March to December), and there are over 500 rental villas, completely furnished, which rent for $115 to $250 per day and range from one to five bedrooms. Prices vary by season, location, view, and number of bedrooms. There are package plans for golf, tennis, families, and honeymooners, and the best way to get full details is to write for their free "Sea Pines Vacation Guide" and package brochure.

Palmetto Dunes Resort, P.O. Box 5606, Hilton Head Island, SC 29938 (tel. 803/785-1161 or toll free 800/845-6130), is located midway along the island's coastline and is one of its finest resorts. It's a family-oriented vacation spot, with 3 miles of beach, 3 golf courses, 24 pools, an excellent tennis center with 25 courts, rental bikes, sailboats, canoes, playground, supervised children's programs, a multitude of shops, and no less than 13 restaurants. The 500 villas vary in size and style, some with fireplaces and balconies. Rates are in the $100 to $195 range during season, much lower other months, and attract-

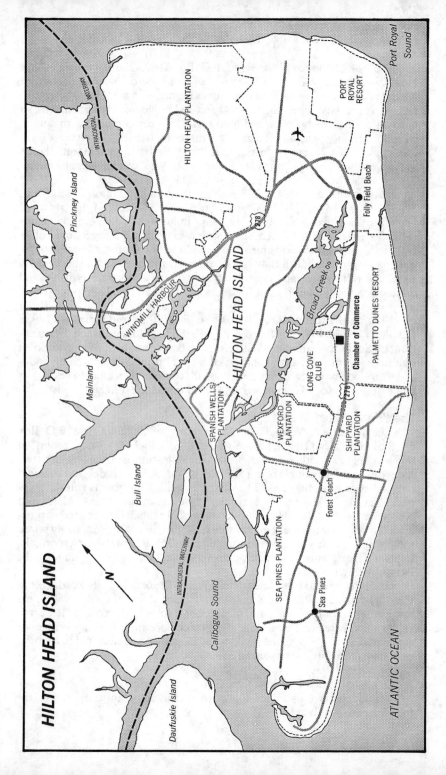

HILTON HEAD ISLAND

ive package deals are available. Call or write for a colorful brochure giving full details.

The **Hyatt Regency Hilton Head,** P.O. Box 6167, One Hyatt Cir., Hilton Head Island, SC 29938 (tel. 803/785-1234), is a 505-room deluxe oceanfront hotel on the grounds of the Palmetto Dunes Resort, with complete resort facilities. There are three restaurants, a pool bar, two lounges with entertainment, an outdoor pool and whirlpool, and health-club facilities complete with saunas, whirlpool, indoor pool, and exercise/weight room. In addition, there are 3 18-hole golf courses, 25 tennis courts, and sailboats. In the summer months there's a good children's program available. Luxuriously appointed guest rooms all have private balconies, and rates range from $115 to $190.

Hotel Inter-Continental, 135 South Port Royal Dr., Hilton Head Island, SC 29928 (tel. 803/681-4000 or toll free 800/33-AGAIN), has a sort of beachfront elegance with a slight continental influence. Guest rooms are luxuriously decorated and furnished, some with oversize beds, refrigerators, balconies, and/or patios. Guest amenities include a superb private beach, tennis, golf, putting green, health club, games room, lawn games, barber shop, beauty shop, and recreational programs. Golf and tennis packages are available, and double-occupancy rates during high season run $150 to $180, lower rest of the year.

Marriott's Vacation Villas, P.O. Box 6959 Hilton Head Island, SC 29938 (tel. 803/785-2040 or toll free 800/527-3490), are located along the oceanfront on Sea Pines Plantation. Villas have two bedrooms, each with private bath (whirlpool in master bath). Landscaped tropical plantings, swimming pools, and whirlpools are features of the various villa complexes. Seasonal weekly rates range from a low of $425 to a high of $1,100 (mid-June through August).

The "Reasonable" Level

The **Sea Crest Motel,** Avocet Street, north of Coligny Circle (P.O. Box 5818), Hilton Head Island, SC 29938 (tel. 803/785-2121), has 92 rooms, all of which overlook either pool or ocean. The exceptionally large and attractive rooms all have two double beds ($85 oceanfront, $75 poolside), and there are two-bedroom apartments ($720 and $660 weekly) and rooms with kitchenettes ($540 and $480 weekly) available. These are seasonal rates—March 1 to November 1—and they drop considerably at other times. Golf and tennis privileges can be arranged here. This is, I think, the prettiest of the reasonably priced motels, and it's the site of two fine restaurants. The gourmet dining room, the Captain's Table, is unquestionably one of the island's finest (see "Dining on the Island," below).

The **Hilton Head Island Beach and Tennis Resort,** 40 Folly Road, Hilton Head Island, SC 29928 (tel. 803/842-4402 or toll free 800/845-9508), has some 300 villas, all with private balconies, and some will accommodate up to six people. There are 2 pools, one right on the oceanfront, 10 lighted tennis courts and a pro shop, rental bicycles, and a golf course nearby. High-season rates start at $69, in low season, $42.

As Close to Budget as You Can Get

If budget concerns are more important than an oceanfront location, the following are your best bets:

The **Days Inn,** 2 Tanglewood Dr., Hilton Head Island, SC 29928, (tel. 803/842-3297 or toll free 800/322-2525), has a pool, water slides, miniature golf, and a moderately priced restaurant. Doubles run from $45 to $82 depending on season, and there's a discount for seniors.

Knights Inn, 1 Marina Side Dr., Hilton Head Island, SC 29928 (tel. 803/785-2700), has some efficiencies in addition to standard guest rooms. There's a pool, and free coffee. No restaurant, but one next door. Doubles start at $49 in high season, $42 in low.

The **Red Roof Inn,** William Hilton Parkway (U.S. 278), Hilton Head Island, SC 29928 (tel. 803/686-6808), offers some rooms with oversize beds, free coffee for guests, and in-room movies. There's a restaurant close by. Double-occupancy rates run $42 to $48.

Campgrounds

Outdoor Resorts RV Resort & Yacht Club, 43 Jenkins Rd., Hilton Head Island, SC 29928 (tel. 803/681-3256 or toll free 800/845-9560), has some 200 RV sites situated on the Intracoastal Waterway. Amenities on the premises include two pools, saunas and whirlpools, lighted tennis courts, charter-fishing arrangements, marina and ramp, grocery shop, coin laundry, restaurant, and lounge. Rates for up to four people range from $18 to $22, depending on the season.

DINING ON THE ISLAND

I counted some 75 eating spots on Hilton Head—and I may have missed a few. So, whatever else you have in mind, rest assured that a restaurant—and a good one—will never be far away during your stay. Needless to say, every one of the hotels offers food, and most of the dining rooms are pretty good. I am listing only one such here, and that only because it's superior to most others on the island; but mostly, I want to tell you about those places *other* than hotels where you'll find good food and atmosphere.

Hudson's Seafood House on the Docks, One Hudson Rd., on the water between Intracoastal Waterway markers 13 and 14 (tel. 803/681-2772), was built as a seafood processing factory in 1912 and still processes fish, clams, and oysters for local distribution—so there's no need to mention freshness. Service is on a first-come, first-served basis, and if you're seated in the north dining room, you'll be eating in the original oyster factory. A few "drydock" courses show up on the menu (a 12-ounce rib-eye steak, for example), but I strongly recommend that you opt for seafood, such as stuffed prawns or blackened redfish. Everything is cooked to order and very, very good. Before and after dinner (6 to 10 p.m. daily; closed Wednesday September 1 to April 1), you're welcome to stroll on the docks past shrimp boats and enjoy the view of the mainland and nearby Parris Island. Sunsets here are always spectacular and are accompanied by live entertainment.

Over at Harbor Town, a former artist's studio has been turned into a delightful restaurant and lounge that serves lunch from 11:30 a.m. to 3 p.m. and dinner from 6 to 10 p.m. Monday through Saturday. The glassed-in porch area at **CQ's,** Area 4, Lighthouse Road, Harbour Town, Sea Pines Plantation (tel. 803/671-2779), is shaded by huge oaks and pines, and the decor is reminiscent of a New York pub. Quiches, crêpes, seafood, and beef specialties are excellent

—as well as quite moderate in price. The staff here is one of the friendliest and most helpful anywhere, which helps account for CQ's popularity (you may have a short wait to be seated, but *do* stay).

The attractive owners of CQ's also operate another restaurant located in Palmetto Dunes Resort. **Alexander's,** Area 2, Queen's Folly Road, Palmetto Dunes Resort (tel. 803/785-4999), features high ceilings, lots of glass, and is on a picturesque lagoon close to the Hyatt Hotel. Lunch is served from noon to 3 p.m., dinner from 6:30 to 10 p.m., Monday through Saturday (dinner only on Sunday).

For excellent charbroiled seafood, you'll fare well at **The Landing,** One Hudson Rd. (tel. 803/681-3363). It's adjacent to Hudson's (see above), and has the same waterfront view. During the high season, there's periodic entertainment at night. Lunch, from noon to 3 p.m., runs $5 to $10, dinner $12 to $15, and there's a children's menu at both meals.

The menu is French at the **Gaslight Restaurant,** 303 Market Place (tel. 803/785-5814), and you'll find the owner most often in the kitchen, since he's also the chef. Hours are 6 to 10 p.m., seven days a week, and reservations are definitely in order at this popular place.

When you've begun to feel a little "finny" from all that seafood, try the barbecue ribs, chicken, steaks, or prime rib at **Damon's Restaurant,** Village at Wexford (tel. 803/785-6677). They also do a terrific onion loaf. Service is continuous from 11:30 a.m. to 10 p.m., and lunch will run between $3 and $6, dinner between $5 and $17.

For dependable budget meals, **Fuddruckers,** 32 Shelter Cove Lane (tel. 803/686-5161), dishes up burgers, hot dogs, steaks, chicken, salads, and a long list of snacks. Their brownies are also held in high esteem hereabouts. Prices fall in the $2 to $6 range, and service is continuous from 11 a.m. to 10 p.m. Sunday through Thursday, 'til 11 p.m. Friday and Saturday.

THINGS TO SEE AND DO

Your first order of business should be to contact the helpful staff at the **Hilton Head Island Chamber of Commerce,** P.O. Box 5647, Hilton Head Island, SC 29938 (tel. 803/785-3673), either in advance or upon arrival. They are happy to fill you in on every aspect of Hilton Head Island, and if you'd like an advance look, you can order their 10-minute VHS video "Hilton Head Island: Simply Better," which gives a great rundown on activities, dining, and shopping. Send $20 check or money order (postage and handling included in that price).

Recreational facilities abound on Hilton Head: there are no less than 23 golf courses, 300 tennis courts, and more than 25 miles of biking, jogging, and hiking trails. Bird-watchers will have a field day, since more than 250 species of birds have been counted here by the Audubon Society.

Golf and tennis compete with miles of beaches for first place on the "what to do" list, and facilities for all three come with most hotel reservations. Sailing and fishing devotees have only to hie themselves down to the **Harbour Town Marina,** and cyclists will find rental bikes readily available at hotels and shopping centers. Nine marinas cater to boat owners and boat lovers, and more than 30 shopping centers await the avid shopper.

To explore Hilton Head's surrounding waters, contact **Adventure**

Cruises, Inc., Box A, 32 Indian Trail, Hilton Head Island, SC 19929 (tel. 803/785-4558) for a brochure outlining their sightseeing and dinner cruises. If you'd like to see the island from above, **Hilton Head Helicopters** (tel. 803/681-9120) has a variety of sightseeing flights, and they also furnish shuttle service to and from the Savannah airport. Sightseeing on the ground level is a specialty with **Low Country Adventures, Ltd.** (tel. toll free 800/845-5582), which can arrange special-interest tours, as well as furnish airport transportation.

Day Trips from Hilton Head

At some point in your Hilton Head Island stay, your imagination is quite likely to take flight back to an earlier age, before the arrival of all these sophisticated "plantations" and holiday resorts. If that should happen, indulge yourself and make arrangements for a day trip to nearby **Daufuskie Island.** Inhabited now by less than a hundred residents, Daufuskie is hauntingly alive with the rhythms of a history and lifestyle that date from 2,000 B.C., when this was the province of the Muskogee Indians. It stretches through the 1500s, when the Spanish appeared; the 1600s, when English settlers established thriving indigo plantations; both the Revolutionary (when natives remained loyal Tories) and Civil wars (by which time cotton was king until it was toppled by the boll weevil); the mid-1900s (which saw oystering come and go, done in by industrial pollution from the Savannah River); and continues right up to the present day, when the population consists almost entirely of descendants of slaves from the plantation days. Their inbred Gullah culture comes to the fore as they greet and pass the time of day with visitors in accents left over from 17th- and 18th-century West African dialects adapted to English when their forebears arrived to work in the fields here.

You'll arrive at Haig Point, and you'll want to stop by the **Strachan Mansion,** which was brought by barge from Sea Island, Georgia, and holds a reception center and restaurant. Take a look at the 1872 lighthouse, the ruins of Haig Point plantation house, and a nearby group of slave cabins. Cars have not as yet invaded Daufuskie, so sightseeing consists mainly of rambling down dirt roads shaded by live oaks, with occasional stops to chat with residents. It makes for a relaxing, oddly comforting sort of day that puts the stresses of our modern-day life into proper perspective. And, since there are now two developments under way on the island—one a community of private holiday homes, the other a private country-club affair—who knows how much longer you'll have the privilege.

To arrange such an outing, with transportation by private ferry, contact either **Haig Point,** P.O. Box 7319, Hilton Head Island, SC 29938 (tel. 800/992-3635) or the **Melrose Company,** P.O. Box 6779, Hilton Head Island, SC 29938 (tel. 803/681-6173).

An interesting do-it-yourself tour is a half-day drive to **Beaufort** (low-country pronunciation is "*Bew*-fort"), the picturesque old seaport just a few miles away on S.C. 170. "Quaint" is the only way to describe its narrow streets shaded by huge old live oaks and homes that have survived from the 1700s (the oldest was built in 1717 and is at Port Republic and New streets). This was the second area in North America discovered by the Spanish (1520), the site of the first fort (1525) and of the first attempted settlement (1562), and several forts have been excavated which date from 1566 and 1577. The **Beaufort Chamber of Commerce** on Freedom Mall, 1006 Bay St. (P.O. Box 910), Beaufort, SC 29901 (tel. 803/524-3163), has self-guided tours and lots of other information about the historic town. And if your trip plans are for early to mid-October, write the **Historic Beaufort Foundation,** P.O. Box 11, Beaufort, SC 29901, for specific dates and detailed information on their two days of antebellum houses and gardens tours.

READERS' GUESTHOUSE AND RESTAURANT SUGGESTIONS—BEAUFORT: "It's terrific to stay in a real antebellum home in Beaufort, like the **Bay Street Inn** at 601 Bay St., Beaufort, SC 29902 (tel. 803/524-7720). All five of their third-floor rooms have marvelous river views and a fireplace. Also, private baths. Breakfast can be either in your room or the garden, and they furnish bicycles for touring" (M. Lee, Savannah, GA.). . . . "Two really fine restaurants are the **Anchorage,** on Bay Street in Beaufort, and the **White Hall Inn,** across the river from Beaufort" (P. Brown, New York, N.Y.).

XI

CENTRAL SOUTH CAROLINA AND THE CAPITAL CITY

1. COLUMBIA
2. HORSE FLESH AND LAKES TO THE SOUTH
3. HISTORY AND FAST CARS TO THE NORTH

Moving inland from the coast, today's visitor comes face to face with vivid reminders of South Carolina's colorful past, as well as the "New South," which is reflected all across this part of the state.

Industries such as textiles, chemicals, precision-tool making, and metalworks, making full use of the abundant waterpower, thrive happily alongside large dairy farms and others that produce tobacco, soybeans, peaches, wheat, and cotton as money crops, and still others with large stands of pine trees for an ever-growing paper industry. There's a vitality which springs no doubt from those early settlers who scorned the leisurely "low-country" pace from the start—yet there's certainly no lack of warmth and hospitality throughout the region. Traditional southern customs are very much alive and well, but they mingle without friction with those of the modern world.

1. Columbia

Columbia, unlike many of our older cities, has the orderly look of a planned community, with streets laid out in an almost unbroken checkerboard pattern, and broad boulevards giving it a particularly graceful beauty. All of that is not surprising, since it was in fact created back in 1786 as a compromise capital to satisfy both "low-" and "up-country" factions, since it is just three miles from the exact geographical center of the state. George Washington paid a visit to Columbia in 1791, just one year after the first general assembly convened in the brand-new city.

It was here that things came to a head in the North/South dispute that eventually became the Civil War. The trouble that had been brewing for years erupted in a convention held in the First Baptist Church here, which passed the first Ordinance of Secession in the southern states on December 17, 1860. (Because of a local smallpox epidemic, however, it was actually signed in Charleston.) The city itself was little touched by battle until General Sherman arrived with his Union troops on February 17, 1865, and virtually wiped out the town by fire: an 84-block area and some 1,386 buildings were left in ashes, although the new state house (still under construction), the university, and the home of the French consul on Main Street were spared.

Although recovery during Reconstruction was slow, the city that emerged from almost complete devastation is one of stately homes and public buildings, with government and education (there are seven colleges located here) playing leading roles in its economy, followed closely by a wide diversity of industry. Fort Jackson, a U.S. Army basic training post on the southeast edge of town, adds another element to the economic mix.

WHERE TO STAY

The **Radisson Hotel Columbia,** 937 Assembly St., Columbia, SC 29201 (tel. 803/799-8200, or toll free 800/228-9822), is a 14-story highrise, with some 240 rooms, located within walking distance of the state house, the University of South Carolina, the coliseum, the Columbia Museum of Art, and downtown shopping, theaters, and restaurants. Spacious rooms are tastefully furnished in a traditional decor, and many have oversize beds. There's an Olympic-size pool, and Beau's Lounge, which features a "no cover, no minimum" policy and popular, beach, and dance music. The dining room on the first floor is a great favorite of local businesspeople and politicians and is open for breakfast and lunch from 7 a.m. to 2:30 p.m., for dinner from 6 to 11 p.m. (prices in the $12 to $20 range). Doubles start at $85.

The **Columbia Marriott,** 1200 Hampton St., Columbia, SC 29201 (tel. 803/771-7000 or toll free 800/228-9290), is one of the capital's leading deluxe hotels. The luxury quality guest rooms have cable TV and in-room movies, some have oversize beds, balconies, and refrigerators. Other facilities include an indoor pool, sauna, whirlpool, restaurant, and a lounge with entertainment. Doubles start at $95.

Another centrally located, very popular hotel is the **Town House,** 1615 Gervais St., at Henderson Street, Columbia, SC 29201 (tel. 803/771-8711). Maybe it was that convenient location that led General Sherman to pick the site as his headquarters in February of 1865—but you won't find any evidence there today of that gentleman's brief encampment on the spot. The hotel is heavily patronized by government personnel, and local industrial firms often quarter important visitors here. Recent renovations have upgraded the lobby, Mimnaugh's café, bar, and restaurant, and the guest rooms, which are larger than most and decorated in contemporary fabrics and white pine furniture. There's an outdoor pool available almost year round in the warm climate. Also, the staff here is especially friendly and helpful. How much you pay for a double- or king-bedded room depends on where your room is situated, although there's little difference in the quality among the rooms themselves. Rooms in the Tower Section (facing Gervais Street) start at $65, and rooms in the Courtyard Section begin at $60. There's no charge for children up to 18 in the same room with their parents.

Claussen's Inn, 2003 Green St., Columbia, SC 29205 (tel. 803/765-0440 or toll free 800/622-3382), is a charming hostelry in a converted bakery that dates to 1928. Rooms are tastefully decorated, and some have private patios. A continental breakfast is included in the rates, and there are complimentary drinks in the evening. Doubles run $75 to $90.

The **Residence Inn by Marriott,** 150 Stoneridge Dr., Columbia, SC 29221 (tel. 803/779-700 or toll free 800/331-3131), is a lovely example of these moderately priced, upscale accommodations (see Introduction for full description). Located quite close to the Riverbank Zoo, it has one- and two-bedroom suites, most of which have fireplaces. There's a pool, whirlpool, barbeque facilities, health club, and coin laundry. Complimentary drinks are served in the evening Monday through Thursday. Studio suites run $72 to $89, and penthouse suites go for $92 to $110; as always, there are lower rates for stays beyond six nights.

In Cayce (that's really Columbia, and just a mile from the state house), the **Tremont Motor Inn,** 111 Knox Abbott Dr., Cayce, SC 29033 (tel. 803/796-6240), is set back from the road in wooded, landscaped grounds. Not only is the staff at the Tremont extremely helpful and friendly, the list of extras is also impressive. To begin with, beds are oversize in the cheerfully decorated rooms. Then there are irons and ironing boards available, a swimming pool, coin laundry, valet service, room service (unusual in a motel), babysitting service, children's playground, and complimentary coffee in the lobby. There's a 24-hour restaurant and a lounge that's open until the wee hours. Rates for doubles range from $38 to $47.

At the Broad River Road exit on I-20, the **Quality Inn,** 1029 Briargate Circle, Columbia, SC 29210 (tel. 803/772-0270), is also out of the downtown area, a convenient location for getting to the lovely Riverbanks Park. Rooms are large (some have kitchens), there's a heated pool, they'll let you bring Fido along, and the office keeps an up-to-date babysitter list—all of which makes this a good family vacation headquarters. The dining room is open from 6:30 a.m. to 2 p.m. and 5 to 10 p.m., the bar from 5 p.m. to 1 a.m. They also arrange golf privileges at one of Columbia's private golf courses. Double rooms start at $48; those with kitchens cost an additional $5.

Economy-minded travelers will find the **Days Inn,** 7128 Parklane Rd. (two blocks off I-20), Columbia, SC 29204 (tel. 803/736-0000 or toll free 800/325-2525), a comfortable, budget-priced place to stay, with a restaurant on the premises. Double rooms here cost a mere $38. The **Days Inn, Governor's House,** 1301 Main St., Columbia, SC 29201 (tel. 803/779-7790 or toll free 800/325-2525), is centrally located, just one block from the capitol building, and also has a restaurant. Doubles run $38 to $49. Both locations offer discounts to seniors.

There are also two locations for the budget-priced **Red Roof Inns: Red Roof Inn East,** 7580 Two Notch Rd., Columbia, SC 29223 (tel. 803/736-0850), with complimentary coffee and a good restaurant nearby; and **Red Roof Inn West,** 10 Berryhill Rd., Columbia, SC 29210 (tel. 803/798-9220). Toll-free telephone for both is 800/843-7663. Rates for doubles at both are $33 to $37, and both offer discounts to seniors.

WHERE TO EAT

Le Petit Château, 4423 Devine St. (tel. 803/782-7231), on U.S. 76 at Fort Jackson Boulevard, is a lovely French restaurant serving such delicacies as roast duckling and veal in various guises. There's also a good wine list at reasonable prices. So popular is this place that you'd best reserve on Friday or Saturday, when locals are in attendance in large numbers. Dinner from the semi–à la carte menu will run between $10 and $18, and hours are 6 to 11 p.m. Tuesday through Saturday; closed Sunday and most holidays.

Hennessey's, 1649 Main St. (tel. 803/799-8280), is an atmospheric restaurant set in an old hardware store that's been converted into one of Columbia's most interesting restaurants. Emphasis here is on seafood, and the Maryland crab cakes take top billing, in my opinion. They do their own baking so save room for desserts, and for the lighter-minded diner, there's a good salad bar at lunch. Prices on the semi–à la carte menu at lunch are in the $5 to $8 range, while dinner will average about $9 to $18. Hours are 11:30 a.m. to 3 p.m. and 6 to 10 p.m. Monday through Friday, until 11 p.m. on Saturday.

Set in a restored turn-of-the-century railway station, **California Dreaming,** 401 South Main St. (tel. 803/254-6767), is a large eatery, very popular with both locals and visitors. Large as it is, you'll usually find this lively place filled to capacity, and on Friday and Saturday nights, it's downright packed. Specialties are prime rib and seafood, with especially good salads. Lunch will run $5 or under, dinner no more than $12. Hours are 11 a.m. to 3 p.m. and 5 to 10 p.m. weekdays, later hours on weekends, with continuous service from 11 a.m. to 11 p.m. Saturday, 'til 10 p.m. Sunday.

Garibaldi's, 2013 Green St. (tel. 803/771-8888), is popular with locals for good Italian dishes surrounded by an art deco decor. In addition to pasta, specialties include seafood, beef, and chicken. It's open daily from 11:30 a.m. to 2:30 p.m. and 6 to 10:30 p.m. (to 11 p.m. Friday and Saturday); lunch prices are in the $4 to $7 range, dinner $5 to $17. Best reserve ahead, especially at dinner.

Timothy's Restaurant and Piano Lounge, 741 Saluda Ave. (tel. 803/ 799-6303), is in the Five Points section, and its menu stars seafood and veal dishes. There's entertainment in the evening, when a dress code is in effect (gentlemen, wear a jacket). Lunch prices average $4 to $7, and you'll pay $11 to $17 at dinner. Hours are 11:45 a.m. to 2 p.m. Monday through Friday and 6 to 10 p.m. Monday through Thursday, 'til 11 p.m. Friday and Saturday. Closed Sunday. Advance reservations are advised.

If you've a weakness for Greek food, **Zorba's,** 2628 Decker Blvd. (tel. 803/736-5200), is the place to go, although they also include a goodly number of Italian selections on the menu. Prices are moderate—$4 to $15—and it's open from 11 a.m. to 11 p.m. every day except Sunday. A second **Zorba's** is in the 7 Oaks Shopping Center (tel. 772-4617), with a similar menu, hours, and prices.

When you're in the mood for truly exceptional light lunches, pick-me-up snacks, and refreshing Italian gelato, **Adriana's,** 721 Saluda Ave. (tel. 803/ 799-7595), is a delightful place to find them. Soups, sandwiches, salads, homemade cookies, cappuccino and espresso are also on offer, and nothing runs over $5. Hours are 11 a.m. to midnight every day except Sunday, when they close at 11 p.m.

THINGS TO SEE AND DO

Even before you leave home, it's a good idea to contact the **Greater Columbia Convention and Visitors Bureau,** 301 Gervais St., Columbia, SC 29201 (tel. 803/254-0479), for in-depth information on the capital city and its surroundings. The **Greater Columbia Visitors Center,** with the same address and telephone number, is well worth a stop once you've arrived.

The **state house,** Main and Gervais streets, was begun in 1855 and was only half-finished when General Sherman bombarded Columbia in 1865. The west and south walls are marked with bronze stars where shells struck. In the fire that wiped out so much of the city, the state house escaped destruction, but the architect's plans were burned, with the result that the dome is not the one originally envisioned. Despite that, the building, with its Corinthian granite columns, is considered one of the most beautiful state capitols in the country. It is always interesting to visit—the landscaped grounds hold memorial tablets and monuments, and inside are portraits and statues of South Carolina greats—but especially so when the legislature is in session from mid-January through May. The building is open every weekday from 9 a.m. to 5 p.m.

The **governor's mansion,** 800 Richland St. at Gadsden Street, was originally built as officers' quarters for Arsenal Academy. When Sherman swept through the town, this was the only building on the academy grounds left standing. South Carolina governors have lived here since 1868. For a free, 30-minute guided tour (Tuesday through Thursday), call 803/737-1710 for an appointment.

Located on the corner of Senate and Bull streets, the **Columbia Museum of Art,** 1112 Bull St. (tel. 803/799-2810), has an impressive permanent collection of more than 5,000 items that run the gamut from baroque and Renaissance art to the only Vietnam art collection in the country. Galleries change constantly with new exhibitions representing art from all over the world. A "don't miss" is the hands-on gallery. The **Gibbes Planetarium,** located within the museum, is a sight-and-sound extravaganza the entire family will enjoy. Hours are 10 a.m. to 5 p.m. Tuesday through Friday, noon to 9 p.m. on Wednesday, 1 to 5 p.m. Saturday and Sunday. Adults pay $2, ages 6 to 12, $1; free admission to all on Wednesday.

The **South Carolina State Museum,** 301 Gervais St. (tel. 803/737-4595), is housed in the world's first all-electric textile mill, which has been renovated to suit the needs of this quite different tenant. There are four floors, each dedicated to one of four important areas: art, history, natural history, and science and technology. Lots of hands-on exhibits, realistic dioramas, and laser displays make for exciting browsing through South Carolina's past, from prehistory through the present and even into the future. Hours are 10 a.m. to 5 p.m. Monday through Saturday, 1 to 5 p.m. Sunday. Adults pay $3; seniors, military personnel, and college students, $2; ages 6 through 17, $1.25. Unaccompanied children under the age of 13 are not admitted.

The 218-acre **University of South Carolina campus** is bounded by Gregg, Pendleton, and Main streets. The grounds are really lovely—so beautiful, in fact, that Hollywood has several times filmed antebellum story background shots on the Horseshoe, lined with buildings dating from the early 1800s (the university was founded in 1801) and filled with ancient oaks and magnolias. While you're there, it's worth half an hour or so to go by the **McKissick**

Museum, located in a fine old building at the head of the historic Horseshoe at the corner of Pendleton and Sumter streets. The museum features changing exhibitions on regional folk art, history, natural science, and fine art, as well as presentations based on the university's collection of historic 20th Century Fox Movietone newsreels. Admission is free, and hours are 9 a.m. to 4 p.m. Monday through Friday, 10 a.m. to 5 p.m. Saturday, and 1 to 5 p.m. on Sunday.

Look for **Woodrow Wilson's boyhood home** at 1705 Hampton St., the restored 1820 **Hampton-Preston House** at 1615 Blanding St., and the **Robert Mills Historic House and Park** at 1616 Blanding St. Woodrow Wilson you know; Wade Hampton was a South Carolina hero from a family of state leaders; and Robert Mills served seven presidents as our first federal architect, designing such landmarks as the Washington Monument, the U.S. Treasury Building, and the Old Patent Office in Washington. All three houses are furnished with originals, and the Mills House has some outstanding mantels and chandeliers of the Regency period. They're open from 10 a.m. to 4 p.m. Tuesday through Saturday and 2 to 5 p.m. on Sunday; closed Thanksgiving, Christmas, and New Year's Day. Admission to each is $2 for adults, $1 for ages 6 to 18.

If you're a lover of church architecture, be sure to visit **Trinity Church,** 1100 Sumter St. between Senate and Gervais streets. It's an exquisite example of English Gothic, modeled after York Cathedral in England. It's open Monday through Friday from 9 a.m. to 4 p.m., on Saturday from 9 a.m. to noon.

Whatever else you plan to do in Columbia, save time to drive out to the **Riverbanks Zoological Gardens** at the intersection of Greystone Boulevard and I-126 (tel. 803/779-8717 or 779-8730). In a relatively small space, something of a miracle has been accomplished in establishing a refuge for many endangered species (such as the American bald eagle). The animals and birds (more than 700!) here are the healthiest, liveliest I've ever seen in a zoo—for instance, rather than simply standing around, two young elephants I saw were playing as naturally and delightfully as if they were in their native habitat. Penguins are kept happy in an environmental duplicate of the bacteria-free Antarctic ice shelf. Botanically significant trees and plants are labeled throughout the park. Don't miss the **Farm and the Aquarium Reptile Complex.** All kinds of domestic animals can be petted at the farm, which also has an automated milking parlor in action for the education of city-bred folk. The aquarium reptile area is a spectacular facility that introduces the aquatic and reptilian creatures of South Carolina—the large saltwater tank (55,000 gallons) in "the Ocean" is a real eye popper. It's open seven days a week (except Christmas Day) from 9 a.m. to 5 p.m., with a $3.25 charge for adults, $1.25 for children 6 to 12 (under 6, free). The last tickets are sold one hour before closing.

I don't know if the back of a commercial building can really be called a "sightseeing" item, but there's one in Columbia that I found absolutely intriguing. The **Farm Credit Bank Building,** on Marion Street where it intersects with Hampton Street, has turned its parking lot into a sort of "event" by commissioning a local artist with the interesting name of Blue Sky to paint a 50- by 75-foot mural on the back of the bank building. Now, outdoor paintings aren't that unusual, but this one, to quote a local publication, could literally drive you "up a wall." Named *Tunnelvision,* it pictures a highway tunnel opening onto a mountain sunrise so realistically that it looks as if you could drive right into it! And, indeed, you *can* drive through the lot and up to the wall itself, which is even spookier if you park at the "tunnel's" entrance. If you're in this part of town, even at night (when it's floodlit), swing by and take a look—it's really something.

2. Horse Flesh and Lakes to the South

South Carolina south of the capital is a virtual supermarket of attractions for sports-minded people. The horsey set hangs out in the country around Aiken; those with fishing, boating, or other water sports on their minds head for the Santee Cooper Lakes; and golf courses and tennis courts freckle the face of this sun-blessed region.

WHERE TO STAY

Distances lend themselves to easy day trips from a base in Columbia; however, so beguiling is this part of the state that you may find yourself wanting to settle in for a day or so. Accommodations in either Aiken or the lake country bring sightseeing attractions within easy driving distance. You should be aware that when special events are on (horse races, the Masters Golf Tournament in neighboring Augusta, Georgia, etc.), rates in the Aiken area often carry a surcharge—always inquire when booking. Be sure, too, to ask about golf, honeymoon, or family package rates at all the establishments listed below.

In Aiken

Top honors go to the **Willcox Inn,** 100 Colleton Ave., Aiken, SC 29801 (tel. 803/649-1377), today's reincarnation of an 1897 inn (Winston Churchill, as well as the likes of the Astors and Vanderbilts were guests here in days gone by). Guest rooms (some of which have a fridge and/or a fireplace) are individually decorated, and the lobby has the distinctive air of an English country home. Antique furnishings are used liberally throughout. Its dining room serves all three meals, as well as an excellent Sunday brunch. Doubles start at $82, suites at $108, and weekly rates are available.

The **Holly Inn,** 235 Richland Ave., Aiken, SC 29801 (tel. 803/648-4265), sits around a courtyard and pool in the very center of Aiken's Historic District. The inn dates from 1929, and the tastefully decorated guest rooms have high ceilings typical of that era. Some have fireplaces. Double rooms start at $80.

The **Aiken Inn,** 1204 Richland Ave. West, Aiken, SC 29801 (tel. 803/ 649-5524), also has attractive guest rooms, and there's a small pool. No restaurant, but there is a cocktail lounge. Rates for doubles begin at $35.

Two miles west of Aiken on U.S. 1, the **Best Western Executive Inn,** 3560 Augusta Rd., Aiken, SC 29801 (tel. 803/649-3968), has in-room movies, an exercise room, indoor pool, whirlpool, and a nice cocktail lounge. Doubles start at $46.

The **Comfort Inn,** 2660 Columbia Hwy., Aiken, SC 29801 (tel. 803/ 642-5692), is at the junction of I-20 and U.S. 1. Guest rooms are standard for this chain (which means more than just acceptable), and while there's no restaurant, there's one within easy distance; and there *is* a pool. Doubles are in the $38 to $44 range.

Around the Lakes

Accommodations around the Santee Cooper Lakes come in all shapes and sizes, from tent and RV camping sites to houseboat rentals to vacation cabins to good-quality motels. If you don't see what you're looking for below, contact the **Santee-Cooper Counties Promotion Commission,** Drawer 40, Santee, SC 29142 (tel. 803/854-2131 or toll free 800/227-8510 outside S.C.) for a list of other possibilities. For details on camping and lakefront vacation cabins on Lake Marion, contact the Superintendent, Santee State Park, Rte. 1, Box 79, Santee, SC 29142 (tel. 803/854-2408). In all cases, be sure to inquire about fishing or golf package deals.

The **Ramada Inn,** P.O. Box 501, Santee, SC 29142 (tel. 803/854-2191), provides a pool and wading pool, mini-driving range, putting green, coin laundry, golf and tennis privileges for guests, dining room, and a lounge with entertainment and dancing. Guest rooms are spacious and well appointed. Doubles start at $55, but there are several attractive golf and fishing packages, as well as lower weekly rates.

To reach **Clark's,** P.O. Box 36, Santee, SC 29142 (tel. 803/854-2141), a member of the Quality Inn chain, leave I-95 at Exit 98. There are 100 attractive and comfortable guest rooms, including two-bedroom units and an efficiency, as well as a pool; and youngsters can work off excess energy in the play area. The family-style dining room serves home-cooked meals, and there's also a coffeeshop. Double rooms start at $37.

The **Santee Economy Inn,** P.O. Box 125, Santee, SC 29142 (tel. 803/854-2107), has both one- and two-bedroom units, and while there's no restaurant, there is one just opposite. On-premises amenities include a pool and playground. Double-room rates are in the $30 to $40 range.

WHERE TO EAT

In Aiken, **The Wilcox Inn,** 100 Colleton Ave. (tel. 803/649-1377), is your best bet. The cuisine is a pleasing mixture of American, southern, and French, and their southern breakfasts are a standout. Prices at lunch are well below $10; dinner runs $9 to $24. Hours are 7 to 10 a.m. for breakfast, 11:30 a.m. to 2 p.m. for lunch, and 6 to 9:30 p.m. for dinner except Sunday, when it's 6 to 8 p.m. Jackets are required.

Italian dishes, veal, steaks, and fresh seafood are the specialties at **West Side Bowery,** 151 Bee Lane (tel. 803/648-2900). Prices are moderate (lunch around $6, dinner about $10), and there's a full range of alcoholic-beverage service. Hours are 11:30 a.m. to 10 p.m., Monday through Saturday. Closed Sunday.

In Santee, the **Ramada Inn's Garden Dining Room** (tel. 803/854-2191), noted above, is good value for tasty meals. The menu features family-style prime rib and seafood buffets, and there's also a children's menu. Prices are in the moderate range (around $6 for lunch, $18 and under for dinner), and hours are 6 to 11 a.m. for breakfast, 11 a.m. to 4 p.m. for lunch, and 5 to 10 p.m. for dinner.

The **Shrimper Seafood Restaurant,** I-95 and S.C. 6, Santee (tel. 803/854-2962), features fish and shrimp, and they make the extra effort to use premium all-vegetable oil that meets the recommendations of the American Heart

Association for reducing saturated fat and cholesterol. Prices are moderate; call for current hours.

For moderately priced steaks, it's **Western Steer,** S.C. Hwy. 6 (tel. 803/854-3269). They also have good salads and a hot vegetable bar. Hours are 11 a.m. to 9 p.m., seven days a week.

THINGS TO SEE AND DO

When heading south from Columbia, nature-lovers may want to stop by the **Congaree Swamp National Monument,** 200 Caroline Sims Rd., Hopkins, SC 29061 (tel. 803/776-4396). Located just 20 miles from the capital city, this 15,000-acre nature preserve is actually an alluvial floodplain. Its designation as a national monument assures the protection of perhaps the last significant old-growth river-bottom forest in the country, and it is not rare to see ancient trees whose trunks measure more than 20 feet in circumference. There are some 22 miles of walking trails, self-guided canoe trails, and a boardwalk overlooks Weston Lake. If you come on a Saturday, there are guided nature walks beginning at 1:30 p.m. A three-quarter-mile boardwalk gives the handicapped access to the preserve. Open daily, and it's free.

To visit beautiful **Edisto Gardens,** drive southeast from Columbia to **Orangeburg.** The 110-acre city park located on U.S. 301, along the banks of the North Edisto River, is a wonderland of moss-draped oaks, camellias, and azaleas (which bloom from mid-March to mid-April), flowering crabapple, day lilies, dogwoods, and over 9,500 roses which bloom from the middle of April until early October. It's one of the loveliest truly "southern" gardens anywhere. There are also tennis courts and picnic areas, and it's free (open every day).

Incidentally, a little north of the Edisto Gardens entrance, on the righthand side of U.S. 301, there's a marvelous restaurant you're likely to ride right by because of its rather misleading name. It's the **House of Pizza,** 910 Calhoun Dr. (U.S. 301), Orangeburg, SC 29115 (tel. 803/531-4000). Well, they *do* serve pizza, all right—16 versions, in fact—as well as sandwiches, burgers, and salads. But the real specialties in this superb eatery are the Greek dishes like moussaka, or biftekia, or the Greek-style stuffed peppers and tomatoes, or—my own weakness—the honey-sweet baklava. Their Greek salad is nothing short of spectacular. And there's beer and wine to accompany whatever you choose. Surprising to find this cuisine in a South Carolina setting, but it seems that the Dimopoulos brothers, after leaving Greece and living for several years in Massachusetts, tired of the climate in the North and simply headed south with their families. Orangeburg is where they settled, and their House of Pizza quickly became a favorite with locals as well as travelers. Prices are budget to moderate; the place has a bright, cheerful atmosphere, with Greek music playing softly in the background, and they have a take-out service if you should want to picnic in the gardens. Hours are 11 a.m. to 10:30 p.m. Monday to Thursday, 11 a.m. to 11:30 p.m. on Friday and Saturday, and 4 to 10:30 p.m. on Sunday. I strongly suggest that you stop, whether your tastes run to pizza or the Greek specialties.

Thoroughbred Country

Farther south, horse training and racing are the preoccupations of the folks around Aiken, and it's a fairly common driving experience to share the road with a horse and its mount (there's even a stoplight just for horses on Whiskey Road!). Nearly a thousand horses winter and train in this area, and Aiken sports two racetracks, as well as polo grounds. Without doubt the three weekends of horse racing in March that make up the Aiken Triple Crown are the highlight of the year. Even nonhorsey folks, however, will delight in the lovely old homes in the town's historic district. By contacting **Thoroughbred Country,** P.O. Box 850, Aiken, SC 29801 (tel. 803/649-7981), before you come, you may be able to arrange visits to some of the private stables around Aiken. For self-guided walking and driving tours, go by the **Aiken Chamber of Commerce,** 400 Laurens St. NW (tel. 803/648-0485).

The **Aiken County Historical Museum,** 433 Newberry St. SW (tel. 803/642-2015), occupies part of a former millionaire's estate. Items of special interest are Indian artifacts, an oldtime drug store from a little South Carolina town that no longer exists, and several rooms whose furnishings depict life in Aiken County during the late-18th and early-19th century. There's no charge, and hours are 9:30 a.m. to 4:30 p.m. Tuesday through Friday. Open on weekends only on the first Sunday of each month from 2 to 5 p.m.

One of Aiken's loveliest attractions is the **Hopelands Gardens,** 149 Dupree Place (tel. 803/648-5461); the grounds also hold the Thoroughbred Racing Hall of Fame in a restored carriage house. The gardens have one trail, dubbed the "touch and scent" trail, which has plaques in braille to identify the plants and to lead the blind, as well as the sighted, to a performing arts stage. There, open-air concerts are performed during summer months on Monday evenings. Outdoor theatrical productions as well are offered periodically. There's no charge to visit either the gardens or the hall of fame, and hours are 10 a.m. to dusk daily for the gardens, 2 to 5 p.m. for the hall of fame Tuesday through Sunday.

The Santee Cooper Lakes

Lake Marion and Lake Moultrie, known collectively as the Santee Cooper Lakes, cover more than 171,000 acres, and their waters are an angler's dream come true. Three world-record and eight state-record catches have been recorded here, and anglers flock to try their luck with the striped, largemouth, hybrid, and white bass, catfish, and assorted panfish that stock these waters. The lakes are lined with fish camps, marinas, and campgrounds, and modern motels provide more of the comforts of home for vacationers. You don't have to be a fisherperson to enjoy this beautiful region: there are numerous golf courses, tennis courts, and wildlife sanctuaries to be enjoyed.

The **Santee-Cooper Counties Promotion Commission,** Drawer 40, Santee, SC 29142 (tel. 803/854-2131 or toll free 800/227-8510 outside S.C.), can furnish full details on recreational facilities, accommodations, etc.

3. History and Fast Cars to the North

America's battle for freedom from Britain is very much a part of north-central South Carolina's history, for the state was the scene of several significant engagements in the Revolution. Indeed, Camden was actually Lord

Cornwallis's most important garrison for quite some time, and the turning point of the war is believed by many to have been the battle at Kings Mountain. Battles of another sort are regularly waged these days on Darlington's raceway, as stock cars engage in fierce competition.

WHERE TO STAY

While many of the attractions in this part of the state lend themselves to day trips from a Columbia base (albeit a long day, except for Camden), you may well want to plan at least an overnight to take in stock-car races or to explore in depth the historic country around York and the Kings Mountain national and state parks. The best accommodations for the Darlington area are found in Florence, and Rock Hill or York is the best base for Revolutionary War historical sightseeing.

In Florence

The **Ramada Inn,** 2038 W. Lucas St., Florence, SC 29501 (tel. 803/669-4241) has nicely appointed guest rooms, some with extra-large beds, and amenities include a pool and wading pool, health club, playground, restaurant, and lounge with entertainment. Doubles start at $55, and those under 18 stay free in room with parents.

In a central location, the **Quality Inn Downtown,** 121 Palmetto St., Florence, SC 29503 (tel. 803/662-6341 or toll free 800/228-5151), furnishes free transportation to the airport, bus depot, and railway station. Rooms are large, and some have oversize beds. There's a pool, restaurant, and cocktail lounge on the premises. Rates for double rooms run $40 to $52.

The **Comfort Inn,** P.O. Box 5688, Florence, SC 29502 (tel. 803/665-4558 or toll free 800/228-5150), is located at the junction of I-95 and U.S. 52. Rooms are available with outsize beds, and there's a pool and whirlpool, as well as a health club. No restaurant, but one is close by. Doubles go for $37 to $45, and a continental breakfast is included in the rates.

The **Red Roof Inn,** 2690 David McLeod Blvd., Florence, SC 29501 (tel. 803/678-9000 or toll free 800/843-7663), has economy-priced guest rooms that are attractive and comfortable. If you're traveling with a beloved pet (of reasonable size and temperament), you'll both be welcome here. Doubles cost $35 to $38, and there's a discount for seniors.

The **Travelers Inn,** 1914 W. Lucas St., Florence, SC 29502 (tel. 803/665-2575), has guest rooms with extra-large beds. There's a 24-hour restaurant, as well as a lounge with entertainment and dancing (except Sunday). Other amenities include a pool and wading pool.

In Rock Hill and York

Before considering motel accommodations in this area, I think you should know about three rather special places that will immerse you in the historical atmosphere up here.

The **Oakland Inn,** 326 Oakland Ave., Rock Hill, SC 29730 (tel. 803/329-8147), is a 1910, Queen Ann–style home between downtown Rock Hill and Winthrop College, just off I-77. Innkeeper Cathy Fairey and her husband have lavished love and attention on the old home, providing private baths for all three guest rooms, and furnishing all with southern antiques or reproductions they've actually made themselves. Two rooms have queen-size beds, and the third has twins. The grounds are handsomely landscaped, and guests are free to sit and rock on the large porch. Highlights of the breakfast included in the rates are Cathy's homemade breads and an ample supply of fresh fruits. Rates are $45 to $50 for doubles.

Also in Rock Hill, **Brook Bend,** 2871 Oak Park Rd., Rock Hill, SC 29730 (tel. 803/327-2224), is a charming country home with a guest cottage that can be yours for $50 per night, double occupancy.

In York, you can settle into a one-bedroom apartment in a historic home in the downtown area, **Brandon House,** 36 N. Congress St., York, SC 29745 (tel. 803/684-2353). The apartment goes for $170 per night, or you might opt for only the bedroom at $100 per night.

As for motels, there's the **Ramada Inn,** I-77 and U.S. 21 North, Rock Hill, SC 29730 (tel. 803/329-1122), which provides in-room movies in the attractive guest rooms and has a good, moderately priced restaurant, plus a cocktail lounge. Doubles are in the $50 to $58 range, and seniors get a discount.

The **Days Inn,** 914 Riverview Rd., Rock Hill, SC 29730 (tel. 803/329-6581 or toll free 800/325-2525), has exceptionally nice guest rooms, a pool, and a coffeeshop. Doubles are in the $40 to $48 range, less for seniors.

WHERE TO EAT

In Florence, **Bonneaus,** 231 Irby St. (tel. 803/665-2409), is a beautifully restored southern mansion with intimate dining spaces, so you feel more like a guest at a private dinner party than a paying customer. Dinner runs $25 and under, and hours are 6 to 11 p.m., Tuesday through Saturday. Best book ahead.

For steaks, try the inexpensive (under $10 for dinner) **Quincy's,** 704 S. Irby St., Florence (tel. 803/667-8435). Hours are 11 a.m. to 10 p.m. Sunday through Thursday, till 11 p.m. Friday and Saturday.

Night owls should know about the 24-hour **Waffle House,** 1817 Lucus St., Florence (tel. 803/667-0736).

Rock Hill, York and Environs

This is fish-camp country—very often you'll run across terrific fish dinners (all you can eat for practically nothing) in rustic cafés down unpaved side roads. If that whets your appetite, stop at a gas station, grocery store, or some other local establishment, and just ask—everybody has a favorite, and believe me, it's worth an exploratory detour to find the hospitable fish-camp eateries if you like this sort of thing. (Incidentally, I've picked up some classic fish stories in these surroundings.) To get you started, here are three fish camps in the area that have been highly recommended, although I haven't yet managed a visit to these particular eateries. It's a good idea to call ahead both for hours and for specific driving directions: **Shell Inn Fish Camp,** Rte. 6, Porter Road, Rock Hill (tel. 803/324-3823); **Catawba Fish Camp,** S.C. 9, Fort Lawn (tel. 803/872-4477); and **Moss Fish Camp,** Box 184, Hickory Grove (tel. 803/925-2603).

For steaks and fresh seafood, look for **The Branding Iron,** 3040 Cherry Rd., Rock Hill (tel. 803/366-9692). Dinner runs between $10 and $17, and service begins at 6 p.m. nightly. Closed Sunday.

The **Homeplace,** 4821 Old York Rd. (Hwy. 161), Rock Hill (tel. 803/

366-2143), is a century-old house in which hickory-smoked barbecue and chicken are the stars of an all-you-can-eat buffet at both lunch and dinner.

THINGS TO SEE AND DO

An easy day trip from Columbia that will take you straight back to this country's beginnings as a nation is the drive to Camden. The town was founded by Irish Quakers back in 1751, and it's the state's oldest inland town. During the Revolution, some 14 battles raged within a 30-mile radius. General Cornwallis took the town and made it his command post for the British campaign throughout the South. Despite all the military engagements in the area, Camden remained in British hands until they moved out in 1781, burning the town behind them. During the Civil War, another invader, General Sherman, brought his Union troops to burn the town once more, since it had served the Confederate cause as a storehouse and as a hospital for the wounded.

Relics of all that history are everywhere you look, but these days Camden is equally well known for the training of fine thoroughbred horses; the internationally known Colonial Cup steeplechase at nearby Springdale Course draws huge crowds of devoted followers.

Make your first stop the **Kershaw County Chamber of Commerce,** 700 W. DeKalb St. (tel. 803/432-2525), to pick up a guidebook and a self-guided driving tour to point you to some 63 historic sites in the area. Look for these highlights:

Historic Camden, South Broad Street (tel. 803/432-9841), is a Revolutionary War park administered by the National Park Service. Based on archeological studies, there are restored log houses, fortifications, the Cornwallis House, powder magazine, a model of the original town of some 80 buildings, and miniature dioramas depicting military action between 1780 and 1781. There's also a narrated slide presentation and picnic facilities. From June through Labor Day, hours are 10 a.m. to 4 p.m. Tuesday through Saturday, 1 to 5 p.m. Sunday; shorter hours other months. Adults pay a $1.50 admission; students, $1; under six, free.

At nearby **Goodale State Park,** two miles north of Camden on Old Wire Road (off U.S. 1), you'll find lake swimming and fishing, with pedal and fishing boats for rent. Bring along a picnic, and take time to wander the nature trail.

Darlington and Vicinity

Stock-car fans in the thousands invade Darlington in early April for **NASCAR's TransSouth 500 race,** and again on Labor Day weekend for the **Southern 500.** The Darlington Chamber of Commerce, 120 Orange St., P.O. Box 274, Darlington, SC 29532 (tel. 803/393-2641), can furnish detailed information on racing activity, as well as sightseeing in this area.

If you arrive between the year's two main races, hie yourself over to the **Stock Car Hall of Fame** (tel. 803/393-2103), at the Darlington International Raceway a mile outside town to the west on S.C. 34. It holds the world's largest collection of race cars, including those of such racing greats as Richard Petty, Fireball Roberts, and Bill Elliott. There's also a simulated two-lap ride over the raceway. Hours are 9 a.m. to 5 p.m. daily, and admission is $2.

Take a stroll through **Darlington's Historic District** (the chamber of commerce can furnish a self-guided walking tour), and do take a look at the marvelous mural painted by Blue Sky that shows the town square in days gone by (it's on North Main Street).

Nearby Florence is a railroad town, the home of large railroad yards and shops. For detailed sightseeing information, contact the **Greater Florence Chamber of Commerce,** P.O. Box 948, Florence, SC 29503 (tel. 803/665-0515). Stop by the **Florence Museum,** 558 Spruce St. at Graham Street (tel. 803/662-3351), to see the African and Oriental art and American Indian pottery collections. It also has the interesting Hall of South Carolina History. There's no charge, and hours are 10 a.m. to 5 p.m. Tuesday through Saturday, 2 to 5 p.m. on Sunday.

The **Florence Air & Missile Museum,** P.O. Box 1326, Florence, SC 29503 (tel. 803/665-5118), is near the airport and is well signposted from I-95 (take Exit 170), U.S. 76, and U.S. 301. During World War II, this was a fighter-pilot training base, and it now holds more than 38 aircraft, missiles, and rockets. Jet fighters, bombers, tanks, and ground-to-ground rockets are represented. The space suit worn by Alan Shepard on the Apollo flight is there, as are Apollo-launch computers and many other space-age items. It's open 9 a.m. to 6 p.m. daily, and admission is $4 for adults, $3 for ages 4 to 16.

Historic York and Kings Mountain

You'll be ahead of the game if you come armed with detailed information on this historically rich region, from the **Greater York Chamber of Commerce,** P.O. Box 97, York, SC 29745 (tel. 803/684-2590). If that is not the case, however, stop by the city hall in York for self-guided walking-tour maps of the 340-acre York Historic District. The more than 180 structures and landmarks include beautifully preserved and restored homes.

Nearby historic Brattonsville, Rte. 1, McConnells, SC 29327 (tel. 803/684-2327), is a restored southern village of 18th- and 19th-century buildings. To reach it, take U.S. 321 from York, S.C. 322 from Rock Hill. There's the dirt-floor "Backwoodsman" cabin, replica of a 1750s frontier home; and an authentic antebellum plantation home; hand-hewn log storage buildings; split rail fences; a brick slave cabin; a medical museum, and many other restorations. Hours are 10 a.m. to 4 p.m. Tuesday through Thursday, 2 to 5 p.m. Saturday and Sunday. Guided tours begin on the hour, the last one hour before closing. Adults pay $2, students $1.

Rock Hill has many preserved historic homes and neighborhoods, and the **Rock Hill Area Chamber of Commerce,** 115 Dave Lyle Blvd., P.O. Box 590, Rock Hill, SC 29731 (tel. 803/324-7500), has an easy-to-follow walking-tour map for visitors. Look for the Hampton-Marion-Moore streets and the Main-Reid-Confederate avenues areas for interesting old homes in what were the "in" residential neighborhoods around the turn of this century.

Take Exit 82A off I-77 to reach the **Museum of York County,** 4621 Mt. Gallant Rd., Rock Hill, SC 29730 (tel. 803/329-2121). This modern structure holds an astounding collection—the largest in the world—of mounted hooved African mammals. Art galleries, a planetarium, Hall of Electricity, and Hall of Yesteryear make this an intriguing spot that invites lingering. Hours are 10 a.m. to 5 p.m. Tuesday through Saturday, 1 to 5 p.m. Sunday. Admission for adults is $2, for children, students, and seniors, $1.

On I-85 just across the border from North Carolina, the **Kings Mountain**

National Military Park marks the site of a Revolutionary battle that some historians label crucial to the eventual American victory. The southern Appalachians had been almost totally undisturbed by the war until 1780, when British Maj. Patrick Ferguson, who had threatened to "lay the country waste with fire and sword," set up camp here with a large Loyalist force. Well, local backwoodsmen recruited Whigs from Virginia and North Carolina to form a largely untrained, but very determined, army to throw the invaders out. The colonists were not only ill-trained, they were outnumbered, but they converged on Kings Mountain and simply kept on advancing on Ferguson's men—in spite of wave after wave of bayonet charges—until they took the summit. Ferguson himself was killed in the battle, and the Appalachians were once more under colonial control. You can see the battle re-created in a diorama at the visitor center, along with other relics. It's open every day of the year except Thanksgiving, Christmas, and New Year's Day, from 9 a.m. to 5 p.m., and it's free.

XII

SOUTH CAROLINA'S "UP COUNTRY" AND THE WEST

1. BATTLEFIELDS AND PLANTATIONS
2. A SCENIC DRIVE TO THE PAST

South Carolina's northwest, her beloved "up country," is a land of scenic wonders: miles and miles of soaring mountain peaks, unspoiled forests, splendid waterfalls, and small mountain hamlets. The magnificent, rugged terrain has more than once felt the tides of this country's history, and it was in this region that American patriots trounced vastly superior British forces in one of the most decisive battles of their southern campaign during the Revolution.

To wander through this part of South Carolina today is to visit the sites of historical happenings and marvel at the hardiness of those valiant "mountainy men" who overcame such odds in their determination to win freedom; to drink in the richness of Mother Nature's bounty, stopping awhile for a hike down lovely wooded trails, engaging in white-water rafting that makes the blood race with excitement, or fishing a little. For the visitor who takes the time to wander, rather than race, the reward will surely be a soul refreshed.

1. Battlefields and Plantations

That important Revolutionary War battle was at **The Cowpens,** now a national battlefield, and a visit there is a not-to-be-missed experience when traveling in this part of the state. The several surviving plantation and other historic homes in the area are windows to the way early settlers lived in this region.

WHERE TO STAY

From a Spartanburg base, it's easy driving to attractions in the "Up Country," and the city is only a short distance off the Cherokee Foothills Scenic Highway.

A Plantation Guesthouse

A 10-minute drive from Spartanburg will bring you to the **Nicholls-Crook Plantation,** Plantation Drive, P.O. Box 5812, Spartanburg, SC 29304 (tel. 803/583-7337). This lovely Georgian style plantation house dates from the early 1800s, and its furnishings are typical of the era and the location. Now listed on the National Register of Historic Places, the house opens three rooms, all beautifully appointed, to guests. Rates for doubles run $70 to $90, and best reserve as far in advance as possible.

Other Accommodations

The **Residence Inn by Marriott,** 9011 Fairforest Rd., P.O. Box 4156, Spartanburg, SC 29305 (tel. 803/576-3333 or toll free 800/331-3131), is an upscale hostelry, with studio suites and two-story penthouse suites. All have separate living and sleeping quarters and kitchens (they even have a grocery-shopping service). Other facilities include a pool, whirlpool, health club, sports court, barbecue and picnic facilities, coin laundry, and a complimentary hospitality hour Monday through Thursday. Nonsmoking suites are available. Studios go for $75 to $90, penthouses for $95 to $110, and rates drop for stays of six or more nights.

The **Ramada Inn,** 1000 Hearon Circle, Spartanburg, SC 29303 (tel. 803/578-7170), is at the junction of I-85 and I-585. Some rooms have whirlpool baths and/or extra-large beds, and free coffee is dispensed in the lobby. There's a pool, whirlpool, sauna, health club, and playground, as well as a good restaurant and a cocktail lounge with dancing and entertainment every day except Sunday. Rates for doubles run $55 to $65.

The **Quality Inn,** 578 N. Church St., Spartanburg, SC 29303 (tel. 803/585-4311 or toll free 800/228-5151), has in-room cable TV and movies, a pool, and a coffeeshop. Doubles start at $42, and there's a discount for seniors.

The **Hampton Inn,** 4930 College Dr., Spartanburg, SC 29301 (tel. 803/576-6080), is at Exit 69 on I-85. There's a pool, and a continental breakfast is included in the rates, which run $40 to $45 for doubles.

Campgrounds

The **Spartanburg Cunningham KOA Campground,** 600 Campground Rd., Spartanburg, SC 29303 (tel. 803/576-0970), is signposted from Exit 69 on I-85 and Exit 17 on I-26. There are 125 sites on exceptionally well maintained grounds. Both shaded and open locations are available. There are groceries and propane, a coin laundry, pool, recreation room, playground, and a nature trail for end-of-the-day walks. Pets are OK. Rates are $15 to $21 for two, $4 each additional person.

In wooded grounds set back from the highway, **Pine Ridge Campground,** 199 Pine Ridge Campground Rd., Roebuck, SC 29376 (tel. 803/576-0302), has 45 shaded sites. There's a pool, recreation room, playground, and fishing. Pets are accepted. Rates run $9 to $14 for up to four people, $2 each additional person.

WHERE TO EAT

All restaurants listed below are in Spartanburg, but you will have no trouble finding a place to eat as you meander through the countryside. And don't be afraid to try the small, off-the-beaten-path place that looks so inviting—you just may run into a real "home cookin" find.

Annie Oaks Restaurant, 464 Main St. (tel. 803/583-8021), is a good stop for either lunch or dinner. Terrific specialty sandwiches and homemade desserts start at lunchtime, and the dinner menu features steaks, fresh seafood, and veal. Lunch will average $4 to $10, dinner $9 to $20. Hours are 11:30 a.m. to 2:30 p.m., and 5:30 to 10 p.m. Monday through Thursday, till 10:30 on Friday and Saturday. Best reserve ahead at this popular place in the Town Square Mall.

In the Pinewood Shopping Center, **Wades Restaurant,** 964 Pine St. (tel. 803/582-3800), specializes in home-cooked meals (try the fried chicken), fresh vegetables, and homemade yeast rolls. Prices are downright cheap—$6 and less for either lunch or dinner—and there's service from 10:45 a.m. to 9 p.m. seven days a week.

The **Red Lobster Restaurant,** 1811 E. Main St., (tel. 803/582-3444), specializes in good seafood dishes at moderate prices. You'll pay $3 to $7 at lunch, $7 to $17 at dinner. Hours are 11 a.m. to 10 p.m. weekdays, till 11 p.m. Friday and Saturday.

Quincy's, 1045 Fernwood-Glendale Rd. (tel. 803/582-7847), features steaks and both salad and hot-vegetable bars, as well as fresh yeast rolls. Prices at both lunch and dinner are in the $3.50 to $9 range, and hours are 11 a.m. to 10 p.m. Sunday through Thursday, 'til 11 p.m. Friday and Saturday.

THINGS TO SEE AND DO

Drive north from Spartanburg, or west if you're coming from Kings Mountain, to begin your "Up Country" sightseeing just a short distance from the North Carolina border.

Cowpens National Battlefield

Eleven miles northwest of Gaffney at the junction of S.C. 11 and 110, a decisive colonial victory was won at **The Cowpens** in January of 1781. Gen. Nathanael Greene, who headed the American forces in the South, sent one Daniel Morgan to divert Cornwallis (who was still in South Carolina with a large British force) from his reorganization of colonial troops. When General Morgan threatened the British fort at Ninety Six, Cornwallis dispatched a large number of infantry and dragoons to repulse the backwoods army, and the two forces met at The Cowpens (named for a nearby winter cattle enclosure). Morgan was brilliant in his use of guerrilla tactics, and when the British were at last defeated, they had suffered 110 men killed, 200 wounded, and another 550 captured—while Morgan lost 12 men and counted 60 wounded! This defeat of a corps of professional British Regulars was not only important militarily; it also spurred some patriots into action who had previously doubted an American victory and probably swung over a good many wavering Loyalists. Make your first stop the visitors center to watch "Daybreak at the Cowpens," a multi-image slide presentation about the battle. The battlefield is open daily from 8:30 a.m. to 8:30 p.m. May to September (when there's a small admission), 9 a.m. to 5 p.m. other months.

Plantations

A short drive from Spartanburg, you'll find a really superb example of a colonial plantation house—although it won't fit most people's image of that term: it's simply a large farmhouse typical of landowners' homes in this region, not the stately, columned sort found in the low country. **Walnut Grove Plantation,** 1200 Ott's Shoal Rd., Roebuck, SC 29376 (tel. 803/576-6546) is 9½ miles south of I-85 on I-26, just 1 mile from its intersection with U.S. 221. It was built in 1765 on a land grant from King George III when this was the western frontier. The house itself is fascinating, with its authentic furnishings (I love the separate kitchen filled with early vintage gadgets), and the outbuildings include a barn which holds a Conestoga-type wagon. Walnut Grove is open April to October from 11 a.m. to 5 p.m. Tuesday through Saturday, and on Sunday from 2 to 5 p.m. all year; closed on major holidays. Adults pay $3 for a tour; students, $1.50.

The **Thomas Price House,** 1200 Oak View Farms Rd., Woodruff, SC 29388 (tel. 803/476-2483), is an imposing house that dates from about 1795 and is built from bricks made right on the premises. They were laid in a distinctive Flemish bond, which—along with its inside end chimneys and steep gambrel roof—gives the house a style seldom seen in these parts. Its builder was a gentleman farmer, but an enterprising one: he ran a general store, the post office, and even had a license to feed and bed stagecoach travelers in his home, licensed as a "house of entertainment." Furnishings, while not the originals, are all authentic items of the period. The Price House is open from 11 a.m. to 5 p.m. Tuesday through Saturday, 2 to 5 p.m. Sundays, April through October, with Sunday hours only the rest of the year. Adults pay $2.50, students and seniors $1.50.

In Spartanburg

The **Regional Museum of Spartanburg County,** 501 Otis Blvd. (tel. 803/596-3501), features a permanent collection of exhibits depicting the Battle of Cowpens and the founding of the city of Spartanburg, as well as an extensive doll collection. Periodic exhibits deal with upcountry life in South Carolina. The museum (behind the library) is open from 9 a.m. to 1 p.m. and 3 to 5 p.m. Tuesday through Saturday, 2 to 5 p.m. Sunday (closed Sunday, June through Labor Day), and there's no admission.

The interesting **Jammie Seay House,** 106 Darby Rd. (tel. 803/576-6546), dates back to 1790. The oldest part of the house is a hand-hewn log cabin with a fieldstone foundation and fieldstone "pipestem" chimney. Furnishings, though not yet complete, are all either originals, donated by descendants of Jammie Seay (who owned the house until 1974), or are of the period. There's no admission, but you'll have to call for an appointment to see the interior.

---

2. A Scenic Drive to the Past

It's known as the **Cherokee Foothills Scenic Highway,** and it curves some 130 miles through the heart of South Carolina's Blue Ridge Mountain foothills. Officially, it's S.C. 11, and it stretches from I-85 at Gaffney, near the North Carolina border, almost to the Georgia border at Lake Hartwell State Park, where it links up once more with I-85. For travelers, it is a lovely alternative to the throughway driving that so often takes us from place to place. Most important of all, it spreads a lavish buffet of scenic and historic treats from which to choose.

The drive would be a beautiful one if you did nothing but stick to S.C. 11, but rewards are plentiful for those who veer off the highway. For example, there are no less than 10 state parks and 5 recreational areas along the way, as well as many county-operated parks. And anglers should bring along the gear—fish are just waiting for the bait in sparkling streams and lakes. Historians will be happy to find South Carolina's only covered bridge, an Native American museum, and the Pendleton Historic District, one of the nation's largest.

Your enjoyment of the drive will be enhanced tenfold if you contact the **South Carolina Department of Parks, Recreation and Tourism,** P.O. Box 71, Columbia, SC 29202 (tel. 803/734-0122), for their brochure detailing the drive. If you'd like to take advantage of all those state parks, some of which allow camping, contact the **South Carolina Division of State Parks,** 1205 Pendleton St., Columbia, SC 29201 (tel. 803/734-0159), and ask for details.

If you join the highway at Gaffney, take a look (actually, you can't really miss it!) at the town's huge water tower that is dubbed the **Peachoid** because it looks just like a gigantic peach. As you travel south, look for signs leading to a turnoff for Campbell's Bridge, which dates to 1909 and is the only covered bridge still standing in the state. The bridge is south of the highway; north, at about the same turnpoint, detour to see the thousand-foot, sheer rock face cliff of Glassy Mountain.

There are numerous overlooks that afford spectacular, literally breathtaking, views. One of these, on **Caesar's Head Mountain,** is in Caesar's Head State Park, with an easy-to-walk, two-mile trail. At **Raven Cliff Falls,** you can view the spectacle from a wood deck. **Sassafras Mountain,** north of the highway in Table Rock State Park (Rte. 3, Pickens, SC 29671, tel. 803/878-9813), near the little town of Rocky Bottom, is the highest in South Carolina, with an elevation of 3,548 feet. At the park's nature center, look for exhibits on rare plant species that have been identified within its borders, as well as other flora and fauna and the geology of the park. The park opens at 6 a.m. daily, with seasonal closing hours.

Plan a stop at the **Keowee-Toxaway State Park,** on the shores of Lake Keowee (S.C. 11, Sunset, SC 29685, tel. 803/868-2605), to spend some time at the interesting Cherokee Indian museum. Be sure to walk the short interpretive trail along which exhibit kiosks depict Cherokee lifestyles. The park is open daily from 9 a.m. to sunset, the museum until 5 p.m., with no admission. The interesting "World of Energy" audiovisual presentation, which tells the story of electricity is also at Lake Keowee (follow signs off S.C. 11 to the intersection of S.C. 130 and S.C. 183).

You may well want to linger a few days at **Lake Hartwell State Park,** the southern terminus of the Cherokee Foothills Scenic Highway. It's a good base for several interesting day trips, and the park itself offers a host of recreational activities (contact the Division of State Parks at the address shown above).

The little town of Pendleton, a short drive from Lake Hartwell, is headquarters for the **Pendleton Historical and Recreational District,** which covers three adjoining counties. You can learn about the area in advance of your trip by contacting the Pendleton District Historical and Recreational Commission, 125 E. Queen St., P.O. Box 565, Pendleton, SC 29670 (tel. 803/646-3782). If you're planning to visit during 1990, inquire about special events planned in celebration of Pendleton's 200th birthday; it begins on April 17, 1990, with the **Historic Pendleton Spring Jubilee.** Across from Pendleton's village green (a restoration delight in itself), stop by **Hunter's Store,** an 1850s restoration that now serves as a visitors center. They can furnish cassette-tape tours of the town and maps and information for the entire district. Allow time to browse through the Foothills Arts and Crafts shop inside the store, which stocks handmade items from the locality.

Note: If you'd like to stay in Pendleton, the **Liberty Hall Inn,** Pendleton, SC 29670 (tel. 803/646-7500), is a charming 1840s building that began life as a private home. Guest rooms are individually decorated and furnished with antiques. All have TVs and private baths, as well as ceiling fans. There are two dining rooms, and wide verandas (where the complimentary breakfast is often served). Rates for doubles range from $50 to $65.

Farther afield, the **Ninety Six National Historic Site** (on S.C. 248 two miles south of Ninety Six) was a frontier trading post, and served as a fort during the French and Indian War before South Carolina's first Revolutionary War battle erupted here. The visitors center is operated by the National Park Service, with loads of information on the archeological digs and the restoration work now afoot. It's open daily from 8 a.m. to 5 p.m., and there's no admission. For further details, call 803/543-4068.

INTRODUCTION TO GEORGIA

Georgia is not only the largest state east of the Mississippi—it is also one of the most varied and complex. Its public image is all too often an antebellum one, full of Tara-like plantations, a slow-moving social life, and a warm southern climate that encourages drowsiness. Well, all of that is there, but from the beginning there has been an energetic bustle about Georgia's commerce that marked even those early planters and was the very basis of much interior settlement. Savannah, surrounded by cotton and rice plantations, was always an enterprising seaport, with its plantation owners as much involved in shipping and the course of trade as in overseeing their large land holdings. Atlanta began as a railroad terminal; and Columbus came into being because of the waterpower of the Chattahoochee and its nine-foot-deep channel (navigable all the way to the Gulf of Mexico) that provided easy access to the world's markets for industrial products. Unlike many other southern states, industry and agriculture, social graciousness, and business activity have not been sharply defined by either the state's geography or its citizens' interests—all those element shave been intertwined into a Georgia that very often comes as a surprise to a first-time visitor.

1. By Way of Background

FROM HERNANDO DE SOTO TO JIMMY CARTER

As is always the case, Georgia's present (and most probably her future) is explained by and built solidly on her past. That past reaches back to 1540 and Hernando de Soto's first European exploration of the Southeast. Spanish missions had settled in by 1566 (but not to stay, as it turned out), and by 1733 the English had arrived in the person of Gen. James Oglethorpe and his small band of settlers (whose personal motives for colonization were several degrees loftier than those of King George II, who was keeping a wary eye on the Spanish in Florida and along the Georgia coast). But it was not until a back-and-forth, four-year struggle called the War of Jenkins Ear (1739–1743) was settled by Oglethorpe's decisive victory at the Battle of Bloody Marsh that the future course of the colony could be determined. From 1745, when Oglethorpe and his trustees surrendered their charter to the king, until 1788, when Georgia became the fourth of the original 13 states, the region was a royal province.

As news of Georgia's wealth of natural resources spread, it drew new settlers from the north and from all over Europe; Germans, Scottish Highlanders, Swiss, Welsh, French, and Irish all arrived with varying dreams and aspirations, but perhaps most important, with a driving industriousness. They followed the rivers inland, explored and settled the rolling piedmont, and pushed on into the western mountains. As the Revolution approached, those from the north spread their burning zeal for freedom from the British and were in bitter conflict with the entrenched Loyalists along the coast—until they managed to convince most of the 50,000 residents that the troubles of the northern colonies were the troubles of all colonies, and Georgia unanimously joined in the fight for independence.

There was division and conflict among Georgians again just prior to the Civil War over the issue of slavery, a conflict that was finally settled when the state seceded from the Union in 1861 and joined the Confederacy. The war was a complete disaster for the state. Its manufacturing plants lay in ruins, plantations and small farms alike were burned over, and most of the young men were either killed or suffered lifelong wounds. It remained for the older leaders to rebuild a shattered economy, and they did it (with the help of youngsters not old enough to go off to war) in a surprisingly short time span. What had been large plantations, useless without slave labor, became small, privately owned farms. Out of the ashes of Atlanta rose an even greater metropolis, still based on transportation (railroads then, airlines today); manufacturing plants sprouted all over the state; the textile industry became important as a means of converting one of the state's most important crops into finished products; Jimmy Carter went from peanut farming to the governor's chair, then on to the U.S. presidency; and all the native industriousness and emotional intensity Georgians had inherited from their forebears led them to create present-day Georgia, a state that cherishes its past but does not dwell on it, looking instead to the future.

The same diversity that characterizes Georgia in everything else extends to recreation and sightseeing. The beaches and creature comforts of the Golden Isles would probably claim first place on my own list of where to go and what to do. But that's most likely because Brunswick and Savannah, with history enough to fill any vacation, aren't that far away. And then, the big-city excitement of Atlanta has its own special lure. If you're looking for that antebellum Old South, Thomasville's plantation country is perfect (and the chamber of commerce there aids and abets any such quest with lots of maps and information). Outdoorsmen can fish and hunt, white-water enthusiasts will have no trouble finding canoe trails down the state's rushing rivers, golfers bump into excellent courses all over the state (or can simply gape at the world's finest players in the Masters Golf Tournament in April every year at Augusta), and—well, I just can't think of any vacation activity you *won't* find in Georgia. Which accounts, I suppose, for the fact that tourism is high among its principal industries, with close to $2 billion a year coming into the state in the form of tourist dollars.

GEORGIA AREA CODES

Savannah, 912; Brunswick and the Golden Isles, 912; Atlanta, 404; Columbus and Pine Mountain, 404.

GEORGIA'S HOTELS

These range from the beachfront luxury of the Cloisters on Sea Island to the skyscraper luxury of Atlanta's soaring Peachtree Plaza to a multitude of Holiday Inns and other moderately priced motels to one of the best budget-priced chains in the country, Days Inn, with headquarters in Atlanta and a good distribution of locations around the state. As always, advance reservations will spare you a lot of grief.

CAMPING IN GEORGIA

There are 41 state parks in Georgia that welcome campers to sites that rent for $6 and up per night. Some 25 parks have vacation cottages that rent for $35 (one bedroom), $42 (two bedrooms), and $55 (three bedrooms) per night. In addition, Unicoi State Park rents lodge rooms for $44 single, $50 double. All rates are in-season, and drop other months. Reservations must be made at each park. For more information on these and other park facilities and programs, contact the **Georgia Department of Natural Resources,** Communications Office, 205 Butler St. SE, Suite 1258, Atlanta, GA 30334 (tel. toll free 800/ 5GA-PARK, 800/3GA-PARK in Georgia).

GEORGIA'S RESTAURANTS

Eating out in Georgia can mean having southern-style meals in a rustic setting; spicy, low-country cuisine in Savannah's elegant and historic restaurants; or sophisticated continental dishes in Atlanta's cosmopolitan dining rooms. As for price, except for a few "ultra-elegant" restaurants in Atlanta, even the costliest meals are in the lower register of "expensive." And all across the state, you'll find quite good food at surprisingly modest prices.

As for alcoholic beverages, you can buy them at retail package stores between 8 a.m. and 11:45 p.m. (except on Sunday, election days, Thanksgiving, and Christmas); and whether or not you'll be able to buy mixed drinks in lounges and restaurants depends on which county you're in—that's a local option, although beer and wines are available everywhere. Of course, you have to be 21 to indulge.

GEORGIA CLIMATE

The average high and low temperatures at coastal Savannah and central Atlanta show that "low-country" locations are somewhat warmer year round than those further inland.

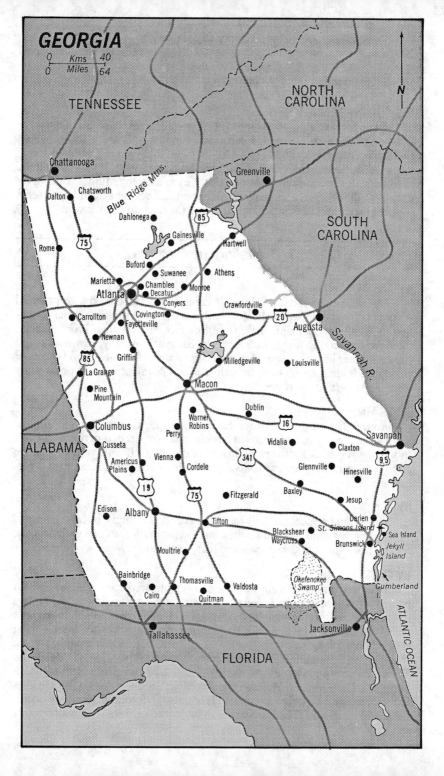

	High	Low
Savannah	91	40
Atlanta	88	36
Columbus	92	37

VISITOR INFORMATION

For advance reading and planning before you come to Georgia, contact the **Division of Tourism,** Georgia Department of Industry, Trade & Tourism, P.O. Box 1776, Atlanta, GA 30301 (tel. 404/656-3590). Be sure to ask for information on specific interests such as fishing, golfing, beach resorts, etc., but inquire as well about the comprehensive booklet "Georgia on my Mind," which gives details on all regions within the state. Ask them, as well, for a calendar of events —some pretty special things happen around the state during the year.

---

2. Traveling to Georgia

BY AIR

Home base for Delta Air Lines, Atlanta's busy **Hartsfield International Airport** is the world's second busiest, with more than 41 million annual passengers. Virtually every major national airline flies into Atlanta. From Atlanta, there are connecting flights into Augusta, Savannah, Albany, Brunswick, and (on commuter line) into several smaller cities around the state. Travel agents or any of the leading airlines can furnish specific information about possibilities through Atlanta's airport.

BY TRAIN

Amtrak has stops in Atlanta, Savannah, Jesup, Gainesville, and Toccoa. Amtrak frequently has real bargain fares in effect for limited periods, and you should always check for the most economical way to schedule your trip. As we go to press, attractive Amtrak tours are available to Atlanta and Savannah at bargain prices.

BY BUS

Greyhound reaches not only the major points in Georgia, but also goes into almost any smaller town you might want to visit in the state. As with Amtrak, the bus line runs periodic special rates that are real money-savers, so check.

BY CAR

I can remember driving in Georgia over unpaved red-clay roads, which turned into slippery obstacle courses that not infrequently slid you right into a roadside ditch. But that was a long time ago, and today the state's highways are a real pleasure to travel. Several interstate highways crisscross the state, giving easy access to major points: from west to east, I-16 goes through Macon, Dublin, and Savannah; and I-20 reaches Atlanta, Decatur, Conyers, Madison, Thomson, and Augusta. From north to south, I-75 runs from Dalton to Calhoun, Marietta, Atlanta, Macon, Perry, Cordele, Tifton, Valdosta; I-85 reaches Lavonia, Atlanta, La Grange, and West Point; and I-95 goes to Savannah, Brunswick, and Kingsland. There are state-run **welcome centers** at all major points of entry, staffed with knowledgeable, helpful Georgians who can often give you local tips as to time-saving routes.

You will find **Thrifty Car Rental** offices in Atlanta, Augusta, Brunswick, and Savannah.

---

3. Traveling Within Georgia

BY AIR

USAir (Piedmont) and Commuter airlines both have connecting service within the state. (For other possibilities from Atlanta, see "Traveling to Georgia," above.)

BY TRAIN

Amtrak runs from Toccoa to Gainesville and Atlanta, as well as from Savannah to Jesup, and Georgia Railroad operates between Atlanta and Augusta.

BY BUS

Besides Greyhound, Southeastern Motor Lines, Inc., operates to intrastate cities and smaller towns.

BY CAR

In addition to the interstates that make it easy to get around the state, U.S. 84 crosses from the Alabama state line southeast to Macon and Valdosta and on south to Florida; and U.S. 441 runs from the North Carolina border south to Athens, Dublin, and the Florida state line.

GEORGIA'S COAST

No more than 150 miles long, Georgia's coastline is everything you'd imagine a semitropical, wildly romantic, richly historic stretch of waterfront to be. There are moss-draped live oaks and palmettos (some of the prettiest driving in the South is along Georgia's portion of U.S. 17), broad beaches, creeks and rivers, the remains of early-day plantations, offshore islands with resort accommodations that make you feel like an instant member of the "millionaires' club" that first developed them, that lady-like queen of Atlantic seaports, Savannah, and the newest national seashore, still under development. Since 1540 (when Hernando de Soto became the first European to set foot on what would one day be Georgia), it has sheltered Native Americans, Spanish missionaries, British colonists, pirates, cotton growers and shippers, English troops, an infamous (to the southern way of thinking; "ruthless" to Northerners) Union general during the Civil War, wealthy Yankees seeking an unspoiled retreat—and most recently, a former president of the United States.

Spanish missions had gained a foothold on St. Simons and Jekyll islands as early as 1566, but civilization came to stay on this part of the Atlantic coast with Gen. James Oglethorpe and a tiny band of settlers in 1733, who looked to the New World for a new beginning that would win respectability for former inmates of England's debtor prisons and nonconformist Protestants (both groups held in the same contempt back home). The Revolution brought bitter conflict between prosperous, "status quo" Loyalists and those who sympathized with the cause of American independence, with Savannah changing hands with the tide of battle.

The Civil War brought almost complete devastation to the area, since Sherman ended his "march to the sea" here in Savannah (which, however, escaped almost unscathed). But a Yankee invasion of another sort has since blossomed into the prosperity of tourism, and today's visitor will find the coast a real delight, from Savannah all the way down to Brunswick and those offshore "golden isles."

1. Savannah

When Gen. James Oglethorpe landed at Yamacraw Bluff on February 12, 1733, with his 125 English settlers, his idealism went beyond a new future for those unfortunates he'd brought with him, and extended to a town plan that would assure spaciousness, beauty, and comfort for every resident of the colony. A sketch in Robert Castell's *Village of the Ancients* inspired him to lay out a settlement of houses, each with its own garden plot, town squares (there were 24 in the original plan), and an orderly mercantile section. Thus Savannah was America's very first "planned city," and it is still studied by modern urban planners.

The natural deep-water harbor very soon attracted Spanish, Portuguese, German, Scottish, and Irish immigrants, and as wharves sprang up along the bustling waterfront, a lively sea trade brought seafarers from all over the world —along with hordes of pirates who put into the port from time to time. The town never lost its atmosphere of gentility, but rowdyism was rampant along the docks and in seamen's inns and taverns.

When Savannah got word of the colonial victory at Lexington, there was jubilation, a "liberty pole," and a hastily formed patriot battalion, all of which led the royal governor to ship out for Nova Scotia. He came back, however, in December of 1778 and stayed until 1782, when "Mad Anthony" Wayne was finally successful in recapturing the city. There had been an unsuccessful attempt by American and French troops to take the city in the fall of 1779, with disastrous defeat for "our" side—some 800 men were lost, including the Polish hero, Count Casimir Pulaski. Savannah, which had been named the state capital following the 1776 Declaration of Independence, remained so until 1807, when proslavers managed to have it moved to Milledgeville.

The years between the Revolutionary and Civil wars were a period of great prosperity for Savannah, and many of the Classic Revival, Regency, and Georgian colonial homes you'll see restored today were built at that time. It was the day of "King Cotton" and great tobacco farms. Cotton "factors" (brokers) kept track of huge fortunes along River Street on what came to be known as Factors' Row. And always, builders, merchants, and shippers kept to Oglethorpe's master plan for the city, preserving the parks and squares in the midst of all that commercial hubbub.

When secession rumblings reached fever pitch in 1861, Georgia's Governor Brown ordered state troops to seize Fort Pulaski, 15 miles east of Savannah, even though the state did not withdraw from the Union until 16 days later. So in a sense, the Civil War could be said to have begun here. And it certainly ended for Georgia in Savannah, when Sherman marched in more quietly than was his usual custom, since Confederate General Hardee had evacuated his troops to prevent the destruction Sherman had left in his wake all across the state. In spite of Reconstruction difficulties, Savannah's port was soon humming again, with cotton once more ruling the economy, closely followed by a developing lumber and resin trade based on its surrounding pine forests. Manufacturing began to take hold, and by the early 1900s there were infant industries that would grow to a total of 200 by the outbreak of World War II. Shipbuilding was a natural here and led the list during both world wars.

Today the economy and much of city life still revolve around port activity. But for the visitor, it's Old Savannah, in a beautifully restored and maintained historic area, that draws the most attention. And for that we can thank seven Savannah ladies who literally snatched the first restoration from the wrecker's ball in 1954. They had watched mansion after mansion go down in the name of "progress" and managed to raise funds to buy the Isaiah Davenport house (which had deteriorated into a virtual slum) just hours before it was slated for demolition to make way for a funeral parlor's parking lot. What has grown from that first determined effort to preserve Savannah's history is an inspiration to other American cities, which seem headed more and more toward the facelessness of "no-character" glass and steel. They banded together as the Historic Savannah Foundation, then went to work buying up architecturally valuable buildings and (herein lies the sheer genius of their plan) reselling them to private owners *who would promise to restore them.* As a result of the foresight and dedication of those ladies and others who joined them, more than 800 of the 1,100 historic buildings of Old Savannah have been restored (they're even painted in the original colors of the town, after volunteers chipped away layers of paint to disclose the pinks and reds and blues and greens first used). The "living museum" they've created is now the largest urban National Historic Landmark District in the country—some 2½ square miles, including 20 one-acre squares that still survive from Oglethorpe's dream of a gracious city.

An entire book could be written about this charming and lively city—I'll do my best to tell you about it in our limited space.

WHERE TO STAY

Savannah can deliver virtually any type of "home away from home" that suits your fancy. There are posh luxury hotels, major national motel chains, and —the undisputed stars of Savannah's accommodations firmament—small, charming historic inns that provide a very special regional atmosphere.

In the Old South Tradition

Back in the 1920s, a group of Savannah's wealthiest citizens banded together to build an elegant and exclusive resort hotel of the country-club variety just outside the city on Wilmington Island. Their efforts and investment were such that today when you drive up to the **Sheraton Savannah Resort and Country Club,** 612 Wilmington Island Rd., Savannah, GA 31410 (tel. 912/897-1612), there's a sense of driving back in time to an era when such establishments were of a classic and enduring nature. Just across the Wilmington River Bridge, a short drive from town, the resort is set in more than 200 lush coastal acres, with the 18-hole, Donald Ross—designed championship golf course on the premises (this is the scene of the annual Michelob Georgia Open), as well as facilities for tennis, fishing, sailing, boating, jogging (along scenic trails), bicycling, and sunning on a man-made beach (there's an Olympic-size pool for swimming).

Accommodations here have always been posh, but a renovation program to the tune of some $4.1 million has seen every guest room in the beautiful main building, as well as the Country Club Villas, refurbished with fine period reproductions (and most have one king-size or two double beds). The splendid public rooms are graciously furnished, with the warm glow of carved wood reflecting in the shimmer of crystal chandeliers. Aunnie Belle's Café is an ideal place for casual breakfasting and lunching; the 19th Hole Lounge serves cocktails from 11 a.m. until 7 p.m. (after which H.P.'s Lounge takes over and adds entertainment until 1 a.m.); and H.P.'s Restaurant, which overlooks the water, serves some of the best seafood dishes around (as well as beef, chicken, and veal entrees), and throws in spectacular sunset views.

Double-room rates at this very special place range from $105 to $120, and the villas are about $300. They offer many attractive golf packages, as well as a very good honeymoon special (and I, personally, cannot think of a better place in which to begin married life!).

Deluxe in the Historic District

Located on the site of the historic DeSoto Hotel (gone many years now), the **DeSoto Hilton,** 15 E. Liberty St. (P.O. Box 8207), Savannah, GA 31412 (tel. 912/232-9000, or toll free 800/445-8667), is in the very heart of downtown Savannah, within easy walking distance of the riverfront, almost all major historical attractions, shopping, and some of the finest restaurants in town. There's a tour service located right in the lobby, as well as some airline reservation services. Rooms are definitely in the deluxe class, there's top-notch entertainment in the Red Lion Lounge, and the Pavilion Restaurant is excellent. An outdoor pool is on the premises, and the lounge offers entertainment nightly. Rates vary according to location within the hotel, and run from $85 up, with no charge for children staying in the same room with their parents.

Also in the historic district and right on the riverfront is the spectacular **Hyatt Regency Savannah,** 2 W. Bay St., Savannah, GA 31401 (tel. 912/238-1234, or toll free 800/228-9000). Its style is strikingly contemporary, yet blends surprisingly well into Riverfront Plaza restorations. There's a seven-story, open-atrium lobby (complete with concierge to give personalized attention to guests), which features a cocktail lounge named, appropriately, the Landing; a delightful, casual Patrick's Porch restaurant, which serves all three meals at moderate prices (from 6:30 a.m. to 11 p.m., with dinner prices in the $9 to $19 range) and Sunday brunch from 10:30 a.m. to 3 p.m.; and M.D.'s Lounge for cocktails and live entertainment. Guest rooms are lovely, definitely in the luxury class, and there's an indoor pool and sundeck. Doubles range from $99 up.

Lovely, Historic Small Inns

If you want to experience Savannah graciousness firsthand, then by all means book into one of the small inns springing up in the historic district, most in lovely old homes that have been brought up to date with the most modern conveniences, while retaining every bit of their original charm. One of my personal favorites is the **Ballastone Inn,** 14 E. Oglethorpe Ave., Savannah, GA 31401 (tel. 912/236-1484). It's right next door to the Juliette Gordon Low Girl Scout shrine, and convenient to everything in the historic district. The 18 rooms are all superbly decorated with antiques or authentic reproductions, ceiling fans (air conditioning is also provided), and Scalamandré wallpapers, and each has a distinctive decorative theme. Many regulars have become attached to "their" particular room, and the friendly staff here do their best to cater to such personal tastes. Incidentally, if your tastes happen to run to low-ceilinged coziness rather than the more formal elegance of 14-foot ceilings, ask for one of the garden-level rooms, which are in the original servants' quarters and have a more rustic appearance, with brick walls, exposed beams, and more casual furnishings. Even more gracious than furnishings at the Ballastone is the pampering each guest receives—that friendly staff has seen to it that fresh fruit and flowers are in your room on arrival, that shoes left outside the door will be polished overnight, and that your bed is turned down, with a chocolate on your pillow and a brandy on the bedside table when it's time to retire. A continental breakfast is included in the rate, and you can have it in the privacy of your room or in the lovely little courtyard with other guests. A feature I especially enjoy is the inviting parlor, where there is always coffee or tea available, as well as almost any liquid refreshment you could wish for, from fresh fruit juice to a cocktail. It's especially pleasant to end the day here (by an open fire on cool evenings) in the company of other guests. Rates begin at $95 for standard rooms, $150 to $175 for Master Rooms, which are especially large and have a separate dressing room and wet bar. Incidentally, it's a good idea to book well in advance.

Unlike the two inns above, the **Mulberry Inn,** 601 E. Bay St., Savannah, GA 31401 (tel. 912/238-1200 or toll free 800/554-5544), is located in what was built as a livery stable, and became a warehouse back in the 1860s. It then became the area's first Coca-Cola bottling factory, and when it began life as a small inn, in the fall of 1982, its size had been doubled with new construction designed to blend nicely with the original structure. In 1988 the Mulberry underwent a million-dollar refurbishing, making it a real standout among Savannah's small luxury inns. Adding to its charm is the courtyard, with gas lights, a fountain, and plantings of blooming plants. The lobby (which has the air of and is called the Living Room) is beautifully appointed with overstuffed sofas and armchairs in the manner of an elegant country home. This is where complimentary afternoon tea is served guests every afternoon (open also to the paying public), as well as after-dinner coffee, dessert, and liqueurs. The adjoining library sports an elegant fireplace and a good selection of books for relaxed vacation reading. The bar is a handsome room with lots of mahogany, ship models, and leather.

The tastefully decorated guest rooms have twin or queen-size beds, antique reproduction furnishings, and plush terrycloth robes. Suites come with a fridge and wet bar. The elegant dining room features Regency decor and southern specialties, and meals are also served in the delightful grass-enclosed garden café in the courtyard. There's a pool and Jacuzzi, and complimentary bicycles are provided for guests to explore the historic district. Rates also include complimentary membership in the Downtown Athletic Club.

Singles at the Mulberry run $115 to $150; doubles, $125 to $150; and excellent three-day packages are available.

Magnolia Place, 503 Whitaker St., Savannah, GA 31401 (tel. 912/236-7674 or toll free 800/238-7674 outside Georgia), dates from the late 1800s and was built as a private home for one of Savannah's most distinguished families. A wide, two-story piazza (veranda) overlooks Whitaker Street; and inside, both the grand staircase and elegant back parlor—where afternoon tea and wine are served to guests—reflect an elegance hard to come by these days. The house is filled with antiques, and each of the 13 guest rooms has a private bath, queen- or king-size poster bed; and 6 have whirlpool baths, 11 have fireplaces. Breakfast

SAVANNAH

Savannah River

RIVER STREET

RIVER STREET

Ships of the Sea Museum

FACTORS WALK

Cotton Exchange

Old Harbor Light

BAY ST.

City Hall

BAY ST.

Emmet Park

BRYAN ST.

EAST BROAD ST.

Franklin Sq.

Ellis Sq.

Johnson Sq.

Reynolds Sq.

Warren Sq.

Washington Sq.

CONGRESS ST.

BULL ST.

Christ Episcopal Church

BROUGHTON ST.

STATE ST.

Lutheran Church of the Ascension

Owens-Thomas House

Davenport House

WEST BROAD ST.

Liberty Sq.

Telfair Sq.

Wright Sq.

Oglethorpe Sq.

Columbia Sq.

Greene Sq.

YORK ST.

BARNARD ST.

Old Courthouse

LINCOLN ST.

HABERSHAM ST.

PRICE ST.

MONTGOMERY ST.

JEFFERSON ST.

OGLETHORPE AVE.

HULL ST.

HULL ST.

First Baptist Church

Orleans Sq.

Chippewa Sq.

McDONOUGH ST.

Colonial Park Cemetery

Crawford Sq.

WHITAKER ST.

PERRY ST.

ABERCORN ST.

Civic Center

LIBERTY ST.

DRAYTON ST.

Green-Meldrim Mansion

HARRIS ST.

JEFFERSON ST.

TATNALL ST.

Pulaski Sq.

Madison Sq.

Lafayette Sq.

Troup Sq.

MACON ST.

BARNARD ST.

St. John's Episc. Church

Colonial Dames House

BULL ST.

JONES ST.

LINCOLN ST.

JONES ST.

TAYLOR ST.

TAYLOR ST.

WAYNE ST.

Chatham Sq.

Monterey Sq.

WAYNE ST.

Calhoun Sq.

Whitefield Sq.

GORDON ST.

Mikve Israel Synagogue

Wesley Mon. Meth. Church

GASTON ST.

GASTON ST.

HARTRIDGE ST.

HUNTINGDON ST.

HUNTINGDON ST.

HUNTINGDON ST.

LORCH ST.

Forsyth Park

HALL ST.

PRICE ST.

NICOLL ST.

HALL ST.

HALL ST.

GOODWIN ST.

ABERCORN ST.

HABERSHAM ST.

EAST BROAD ST.

GWINNETT ST.

GWINNETT ST.

is served on the veranda when weather permits. Rates for singles or doubles range from $80 to $140. They also have a money-saving three-day package rate.

The **Gastonian,** 220 E. Gaston St., Savannah, GA 31401 (tel. 912/232-2869), is presided over by owners Hugh and Roberta Lineberger, Californians who fell in love with the city on a visit in 1984. They bought the two, four-story Italianate brick town houses that now make up the Gastonian. The two are now connected by an elevated walkway. The 13 guest rooms and suites are individually decorated (French, English, Victorian, Italianate, etc.), most have Jacuzzis, and all have operating fireplaces and central air conditioning. A charming carriage house is now a honeymoon suite. The $87 to $200 rates include a full breakfast, a fruit-and-wine basket on arrival, and turndown service with cordials and sweets.

Other Accommodations

The **Courtyard by Marriott,** 6703 Abercorn St., Savannah, GA 31405 (tel. 912/354-7878 or toll free 800/321-2211), is built around a landscaped courtyard: the attractive guest rooms have separate seating areas, oversize work desks, and private patios or balconies. There's a pool, whirlpool, health club, coin laundry, restaurant, and bar. Doubles are $58 Sunday through Thursday, $48 Friday and Saturday; suites run $75 and $65.

The **Best Western Riverfront Inn,** 412 W. Bay Rd., Savannah, GA 31401 (tel. 912/233-1011), is a moderately priced hostelry in a convenient location. Rooms are well appointed, with in-room movies, and there's a pool, restaurant, and bar. Doubles are in the $55 to $60 range.

Savannah, or rather Tybee Island, saw the beginning of that dependable budget motel chain, Days Inn, because its founder, the late Cecil B. Day, spent so many summers there in his younger days. Well, now there's a Days Inn that deserves special mention, and it's smack in the middle of the historic district. When a new building was constructed here for the **Days Inn** at 201 W. Bay St., Savannah, GA 31401 (tel. 912/236-4440), in 1981, it was cited by the Historic Savannah Foundation "for their sensitive design of a new hotel within Savannah's historic market district," and indeed you would be forgiven for taking the new structure for one of the area's original warehouses that had been lovingly restored. The 196 rooms are all up to the usual Days Inn high standards, and there's a 24-hour restaurant right on the premises, parking facilities, and a tour service. Rates for doubles run $45 to $68. Adjacent to the new building is the Executive Center Suite Building, which would justify another award for its renovation of a building that really is a part of the city's history. Much care has been taken in creating some 57 suites (each with a kitchen complete right down to a dishwasher, living room, bedroom, and bath, and views of either the river, one block away, or the historic city center) not to violate the exterior, but to keep the four-story brick building's façade much as it was when it was a part of the active market district. Holding to its usual budget rate structure, Days Inn charges rates of $59 to $79 for these choice accommodations in a choice location.

The **Knights Inn,** 5711 Abercorn St., Savannah, GA 31402 (tel. 912/354-0434), has exceptionally nice guest rooms and some efficiencies. There's a pool, and pets are acceptable. Doubles run $38, efficiencies $40 to $55, and there's a discount for seniors.

Campground

The **Safari Bellaire Woods Campground,** Ga., 204, 2½ miles west of I-95, 4½ miles west of U.S. 17—write Rte. 4, Box 451-B, Savannah, GA 31419 (tel. 912/748-4000)—is 12 miles from the Savannah Historic District on the banks of the Ogeechee River. There are full hookups, LP gas service, a store, self-service gas and diesel fuel, dump station, hot showers, laundry, swimming pool, and recreation hall. Boat and canoe rentals with a boat ramp are also available. Rates start at $14.50, and reservations are accepted with a $10 deposit.

THAT GOOD SAVANNAH EATING

Savannah cuisine is a happy combination of coastal and low-country cooking with a special dish of its own added to hearty okra and vegetable soups. If you're asked "One or two?" when soup comes to the tables in a steaming tureen, your host is inquiring how many little green hot peppers you want mashed in the plate before soup is poured. Your answer should depend, of course, on your personal taste, but even if you have a cast-iron stomach, don't fail to remove the pepper itself, for as one native puts it, "a touch of the pepper is purgatory undiluted!"

A Savannah Institution

Remember the days of the boarding houses, when everybody sat together and food was served in big dishes placed in the center of the table? Well, **Mrs. Sema Wilkes** has been serving locals and travelers in just that manner since the 1940s, and for some of the region's best home-cooking, practice up that "boarding house reach" and head for 107 W. Jones St., between 11:30 a.m. and 3 p.m. any weekday. You won't find a sign ("it would look so commercial, not at all like home," according to Mrs. Wilkes), but what you're likely to find is a long line of people patiently waiting for a seat at one of the six tables in the basement dining room of an 1870 gray brick house with curving steps and cast-iron trim. If you take your place and wait it out (as Kate Smith, Richard Chamberlain, and scores of other celebrities have in the past), you'll be rewarded with a tasty, well-balanced lunch cooked to perfection with whatever fresh foods are available. Mrs. Wilkes believes in freshness and plans her daily menu around the seasons. She also believes in people getting enough to eat, and $10 buys all you can put down. Rest assured your food will be a true reflection of the cuisine Savannah residents have enjoyed for generations.

The Best of the Rest

I'd heard about the **Boar's Head,** 1 N. Lincoln St. (tel. 912/232-3196), in Atlanta, New Orleans, and Miami; and truthfully, I was inclined to doubt that it could live up to all the accolades. Well, it can, and I can now be counted a loyal member of its widespread fan club. Situated on the waterfront (Lincoln Street is one of those that dead-ends into River Street) in a 200-year-old warehouse, the Boar's Head has a sophistication in atmosphere and service and an excellence in cuisine that would make it outstanding in any setting. First of all, there's that marvelous river view, and every table is placed to take advantage of it. Then, fresh flowers on every table, hanging baskets of greenery, and soft candlelight make for a cozy, intimate atmosphere that creates just the right mood for the professionalism that comes from the kitchen. Most of this is directly due to Heinz Lindeman, the owner-manager, but credit must also go to the staff he has assembled. From the handsome host to the waiter who began things by introducing himself, there was no snag in providing a memorable meal. The menu is continental and American, with superb seafood, veal, and steaks. My selection was a bouillabaisse that turned out to be perfect, but others in my party sampled dishes such as a seafood casserole au gratin and pepper steak. All were excellent, with prices of $10 to $18. It's open daily for lunch from 11:30 a.m. to 2:30 p.m. and dinner from 6 to 10:30 p.m. or later, and reservations are strongly suggested, since it's been a favorite with locals for years, as well as with tourists.

The **Pirates' House,** 20 E. Broad St. (tel. 912/233-5757), holds a restaurant, a rain-forest bar, gift shop, and museum. The 1754 inn was a rendezvous for pirates and rough-and-tumble sailors who put into the port of Savannah way back when. There are legends galore associated with the place, and Robert Louis Stevenson used it as part of the setting of *Treasure Island*. It's listed as an authentic house museum by the American Museum Society, and you'll want to set aside time to explore every one of the 23 fascinating dining rooms. There are seafood specialties, of course, like oysters Savannah or sherry-flavored shrimp and crabmeat Newburg, as well as chicken Cordon Bleu, duck à l'orange, and a variety of flaming entrees and some 36 desserts. If you come during summer months without a reservation, you're likely to have a wait. But that's not all that bad—if there isn't room at the bar, a cocktail waitress will come down the line and take your order (but do try for the rain-forest bar—it's entertaining and lively). And bring the children: the friendly staff here will give them special attention, and they'll each leave with a pirate's mask as a souvenir. The food here is very good, and more than that, it's a fun place to dine. Prices range from $12 to $20 at dinner, $4.75 to $10 at lunch. This winner of the National Restaurant Association's Great Menu Award is open seven days a week from 11:30 a.m. to 3 p.m. and 5 to 10 p.m.

Elizabeth and Michael Terry have added a real charmer to the Savannah restaurant scene with their **Elizabeth on 37th Restaurant and Dessert Café,** 105 E. 37th St. (tel. 912/236-5547). Michael, an attorney who turned his back on the legal profession, welcomes diners and serves as wine steward, while Elizabeth presides over the kitchen in a charming turn-of-the-century mansion. There's a full menu, specializing in fresh seafood from local waters. For nonseafood-lovers there are outstanding lamb, steak, veal, and chicken dishes, and Elizabeth even caters to vegetarian tastes with several entrees. There's an excellent wine list, and on Thursday all wines are sold by the glass. As you might guess from its name, desserts are something to write home about, so bear that in mind when perusing the entrees. Prices are $14 to $25 at dinner (special children's plates are less) on the semi–à la carte menu. Hours are 6 to 10:30 p.m. Monday through Saturday. Best reserve.

Decor at the **Shrimp Factory,** 313 River St. (tel. 912/236-4229), reflects the whimsical mind of Janie Harris, a lively lady who (with her husband, Frank) is determined to set a table truly representative of this region. In an 1826 cotton warehouse setting of exposed old brick, wooden plank walls, and a marvelous salad bar resting next to a miniature shrimp boat, the Harrises serve the freshest seafoods from local waters (their Savannah shrimp Créole is without peer), salads that are real creations, and steak and chicken dishes for those who can pass up seafood. Prices at dinner range from $12 to $20 and include salad bar and after-dinner cordial. Now, while seafood may be a bit old hat along the coast, you aren't likely to find pine-bark stew many places other than the Shrimp Factory. It's a terrific seafood stew, served in a little iron pot with a bottle of sherry on the side, that's been simmered with a delicate herb seasoning and comes with French bread and a whipped cheese spread. You won't have to ask how it came by its peculiar name—the legend is printed right on the menu. Janie is almost always on hand. The large bar is a popular hangout for Savannahians both before and after dinner, and there's live music in the bar most nights. Hours are 11 a.m. to 10 p.m. Monday through Thursday, to 11 p.m. on Friday and Saturday, and 12 to 10 p.m. on Sunday. Oh, be sure to ask about their Chatham Artillery Punch, and, if you dare, try one—delicious (also, potent).

The **Olde Pink House Restaurant and Planters' Tavern,** 23 Abercorn St. (tel. 912/232-4286), is another dining spot that will send you spinning back in time. Built in 1771, the old house has been a private residence, a bank, headquarters for one of Sherman's generals, and a tea room. Now restored and containing an antique shop as well as the restaurant, it's an ideal spot for lunch Monday through Saturday from 11:30 a.m. to 3:30 p.m. in a lovely colonial room or in front of the Planters' Tavern's large open fireplaces. Lunch prices run $5 to $7. Dinner is by candlelight and quite elegant (5:30 to 11 p.m. daily). Prices start at $15 to $25 for complete dinners, which include such dishes as riverfront gumbo, black turtle bean soup, baby flounder stuffed with crab, Old Savannah trifle, and the like, all delicious!

You'll find **The River's End,** 3122 River Dr., (tel. 912/354-2973), at Tassie's Pier next door to the Thunderbolt Marina on the Intracoastal Waterway. It's wonderfully relaxing to watch the shrimp-boat and pleasure-boat traffic pass just outside, and the fresh seafood (much of it from those same boats) comes in a marvelous array of culinary creations. For landlubbers, there are choice steaks. Desserts are homemade and absolutely luscious. Hours are 11:30 a.m. to 2:30 p.m. Monday through Saturday, and 5 to 10 p.m. Monday through Thursday, till 11 p.m. Friday and Saturday, closed Sunday.

River House, 125 W. River St. (tel. 912/234-1900), in a converted cotton warehouse on the riverfront, excells in fresh seafood creations. Hours are 11 a.m. to 10 p.m., till 11 p.m. on Saturday, from noon on Sunday. Lunch prices are in the $7 to $10 range, dinner, $12 to $20.

The **Crystal Beer Parlor,** 301 W. Jones St. (tel. 912/232-1153), has been a favorite of just about everybody in Savannah since it opened its doors in the depression days of 1933 and sold huge sandwiches for a dime. Prices may have gone up since then, but the affection for this plain, unpretentious place has diminished not one whit. So popular is it that my best advice is to try to go earlier or later than peak lunch or dinner hours (if you get there at noon, you'll be in for a lengthy wait). Inside, things haven't changed all that much since its opening —you can order draft beer in a frosted mug, and owner Conrad Thomson still serves up great fried oyster and shrimp salad sandwiches, crab stew and chili, but you really shouldn't miss the seafood gumbo, one of the best in the Southern Atlantic region, in my personal opinion. Hours are 11 a.m. to 9 p.m., prices are in the modest range (no item on the menu runs over $8), and there's ample parking in the lot off Jones Street. This is a "don't miss" for me.

The **Chart House,** 202 W. Bay St. (tel. 912/233-6686), is a snug and very nautical seafood restaurant overlooking Riverfront Plaza and the big ships on the Savannah River. Oysters, shrimp, crab, and other local catches are excellent, and the bar is a cozy meeting place. Dinners range from about $12 to $30. Hours are 5 to 10 p.m. Sunday through Thursday, to 11 p.m. on Friday and Saturday.

The **Exchange Tavern,** 201 E. River St. (tel. 912/234-9311), has a great selection of sandwiches, an interesting clock collection, and is open Monday through Saturday from 10:30 a.m. to 2 a.m., on Sunday from noon to 6 p.m. Beer and cocktails are served in this tavern that really *looks* like a tavern, and it proved to be one of my favorite "drop in" places, for food, atmosphere, and relaxation.

A WORD ABOUT NIGHTLIFE

As is true in so many southern cities, Savannah's nightlife is largely to be found in motel or hotel lounges or restaurants that offer dinner-dancing. But for my money, hotel lounges are hotel lounges the world over, and the night-time Savannah *I* like best is in the taverns over on the waterfront. **Spanky's Pizza Galley & Saloon,** 317 E. River St. (tel. 912/236-3009), is a fun place, where the food is both good and inexpensive. **Emma's,** 224 W. Bay St. (tel. 912/232-1223), near the Hyatt Regency, stars the wonderful Emma Kelly, a chanteuse and pianist who has delighted Savannah for many a year. If you request an old favorite, don't be surprised to find yourself at the piano singing it along with her. Open 6 p.m. to midnight Monday through Saturday. **Kevin Barry's,** 117 W. River St. (tel. 912/233-9626), is a typical Irish pub, open seven days a week from 11:30 a.m. to 3 a.m., with both food and music (the music is live Wednesday through Sunday). There's entertainment Monday through Saturday at the **Long Branch Saloon,** 215 E. River St. (tel. 912/236-9350), along with soups, salads, and sandwiches. **Shucker's,** 225 W. River St. (tel. 912/236-1427), is always a lively place after dark. Nightspots come and go along the waterfront, but I'm sure you'll find your own favorites—just walk along River Street and join the other nightlifers who've discovered this strip of Old Savannah that invites tavern hopping.

In the city market, both **Sweet Georgia Brown's,** 312 W. St. Julian St. (tel. 912/232-7464) and **Mikki's Piano and Jazz Bar,** 219 W. St. Julian St. (tel. 912/233-3015 or 238-9025), have great music and are good fun.

More sedate dance music can be found out at the Savannah Resort's **H.P.'s Lounge** and in **Johnny Harris's** popular restaurant on Victory Drive.

SAVANNAH SIGHTS

Savannah's **visitor center** *is* one of the city's sights. It's in the restored Central of Georgia Railroad passenger station dating from the late 1850s, part of a 35-acre railroad-yard complex that once bustled with train traffic. The mid-Victorian building is decorated with "Savannah colors" (the Factors red, Tabby white, and Geechee teal, among others, unearthed by all those determined, chisel-wielding citizens who chipped away at building exteriors until they revealed original 18th- and 19th-century paints), and the train shed out back houses the Great Savannah Exposition (see below). The extremely friendly and efficient staff can tell you anything you want to know about Georgia's "mother city," give you a free orientation slide show, help you join an organized tour (several originate here), or send you off on self-guided walking, driving, or bike (very popular) tours with excellent maps, cassette tapes, and brochures. From I-16, you reach the center by taking the "Downtown" exit and turning left at the first traffic light. The route is well marked, and there's plenty of free parking. The address is 301 W. Broad St., Savannah, GA 31499 (tel. 912/944-0456 or toll free 800/444-2427), and it's open from 8:30 a.m. to 5 p.m. Monday through Friday, from 9 a.m. to 5 p.m. on Saturday, Sunday, and holidays.

As a prelude to *any* sightseeing, walk out back of the visitor center and take in the **Spirit of the South Museum,** 303 W. Broad St., Savannah, GA 31499 (tel. 912/238-1778 or 238-1779). Housed in the restored train shed of the old Central of Georgia Railway station, it's a smashing introduction to this charming city, its history, and its present. There are two theaters, each of which uses film, computer-controlled figures, and stereophonic sound to present outstanding performances. In the Spirit of the South theater, you're witness to such historic milestones as Oglethorpe's meeting with the Yamacraw Indian chief Tomochichi, secret revolutionary meetings in Tondee's Tavern, the coming of the cotton gin, the sailing of the first steamship to cross the Atlantic (the S.S. *Savannah,* in 1819), and a host of other events that bring you right up to today's city. In the second theater, the Siege of Savannah during the Revolution is played out before your eyes in a way that will change forever the way in which you view this city. In addition to the theatrics, there's an exhibition hall displaying all manner of memorabilia from every era of Savannah's history, from the early Native Americans to the first colonists to the cotton industry to the city's varying architectural styles, ethnic groups, and commercial enterprises. There's food service aboard two beautifully restored train cars and at the Crossings Restaurant. Hours are 9 a.m. to 5 p.m. April through September, till 4 p.m. October through March; admission is $4 for adults, $2.50 for children 12 and under —money well spent!

Savannah's history comes full circle around Ellis and Franklin squares. Back in 1954, the demolition of the century-old city market outraged Savannahians and sparked the "restoration rebellion." Now, the unsightly garage has come down for an exciting **New City Market.** The four-block market is filled with interesting little eateries, shops, and antique dealers.

You will surely want to pick up a copy of *Sojourn in Savannah,* which was approved before it went to press by both the Savannah Area Chamber of Commerce and the Historic Savannah Foundation. It is such an interesting, informative guide to this city and the surrounding area that I think it may be underpriced at $4. It's on sale at the center, or you can order by sending $5 (including postage and handling) to *Sojourn in Savannah,* 708 E. 46th St., Savannah, GA 31405. It's a beautifully printed book and a lasting souvenir of your visit.

There's so much to see in Savannah that it's really hard to say where to start. Personally, I like a stroll along the **waterfront**—it's unlike any you'll find elsewhere. Like the rest of the city's restored and preserved historic district, the old buildings that line Factors Row are in actual use, not set aside as sterile museums. It's as lively a commercial center today as it was in its rowdier days, the only difference being that now there are charming boutiques, restaurants, and taverns in what used to be brokers' offices and warehouses. Strung along the river's edge alongside a high bluff, the brick buildings rise three (sometimes more) stories above River Street and date from the early 1800s. Each level has its own street—River Street, Lower Factors Walk, Upper Factors Walk—and there are bridgeways connecting each level to streets along the bluff. The entrance ramps, from Bay Street down to River Street, are paved with cobblestones that crossed the Atlantic as ballast in sailing ships. It's a fasacinating, fun sort of place that (perhaps even more than those lovely homes that border Savannah's wide streets) gives you a feeling of the *continuing* history of this town. And if you happen to be there on the first Saturday of any month, you'll be swept up in a River Street festival, with live entertainment, street vendors, and sidewalk artists and craftspeople, that is something special.

Incidentally, that statue at the foot of the East Broad Street ramp, of a young girl waving toward the harbor, is in memory of Florence Martus, who (so they say) fell in love with a sailor. She promised to greet every ship until he returned to marry her, so henceforth for 44 years, she waved a white cloth by day and a lantern by night to every ship entering the harbor past the Elba Island Light, where she lived with her brother who tended the light. She was greatly loved by seamen and was looked for eagerly, never missing a ship (she said she could "feel" one approaching) and assisting in at least one heroic rescue of sailors from a sinking ship. Sadly, her own sailor never returned for the wedding. Her story is the subject of a ballet, *The Legend of the Waving Girl,* choreographed by the Savannah Ballet's artistic director, Bojan Spassoff, presented for the first time in January of 1977.

Then there's **Bull Street,** stretching south from the river and marking the division between east and west on streets that cross it. It was named for Col. William Bull, an aide to General Oglethorpe, and it holds five of those lovely squares, coming at last to Forsyth Park. Revolutionary War hero Nathanael Greene is buried in **Johnson Square,** the first of the five, between Bay and Congress streets. **Wright Square,** between York and State, holds a large memorial honoring Tomochichi, the Yamacraw Indian chief without whose friendship the Oglethorpe settlement might have perished. A bronze figure of Oglethorpe himself stands in **Chippewa Square** (between Perry and Hull); and **Madison Square** (between Harris and Charlton) and **Monterey Square** (between Taylor and Gordon) each have monuments and statues commemorating people important to Savannah's history. The people of Savannah love their squares, and they are wonderfully relaxed "people-watching" stations.

The white, cast-iron fountain in **Forsyth Park** is one focal point for Savannah residents, who sit on its railing, feed pigeons, listen to strolling musicians, and generally take a break from the rigors of modern-day life. But aside from the squares and parks, just strolling the streets is an escape from today into yesterday. **Gordon Row,** for example, has town houses with graceful curving stair rails made from ornate ironwork, and the handsome brick homes on **Marshall Row** face a broad avenue with grass and trees down its center. Indeed, to my way of thinking, sightseeing in Savannah should either begin or end with a day of walking—along the waterfront, through the squares, and along the streets—in order to get an overall picture of what the city is all about.

Old Savannah

To see where those seven determined ladies started the whole restoration thing, see the **Davenport House** at 324 E. State St. (on Columbia Square), built between 1815 and 1820 by master builder Isaiah Davenport. It's one of the truly great Federal-style houses in this country, and has lovely, delicate iron-work and a handsome elliptical stairway. The house is open Monday to Saturday from 10 a.m. to 3:30 p.m., on Sundays from 1:30 to 3:30 p.m. (it closes Thanksgiving, Christmas, and New Year's days), and admission is $2.50 for adults, $1.25 for ages 10 and under.

The Gothic-style **Green-Meldrim Home,** 14 W. Macon St., is where General Sherman headquartered when his troops occupied Savannah in 1864. In fact, it was from this house that the general sent his famous (in Savannah, at least) telegram to President Lincoln offering him the city as a Christmas gift. The house now belongs to St. John's Church, which uses the former kitchen, servants' quarters, and stable as its rectory. The rest of the premises is open to visitors on Tuesday through Saturday from 1 to 4 p.m. (adults pay $2; students, $1; under 6, free).

Girl Scouts will be especially interested in **Juliette Gordon Low's birth-place** at 142 Bull and Oglethorpe Avenue (so will non–Girl Scouts). The founder of Girl Scouting lived in a Regency-style house that is maintained both as a memorial to her and as a National Program Center. The Victorian additions to the 1818 house were made in 1886, just before Juliette (called "Daisy" by her family) married William Mackay Low. It's open daily, except Wednesday, from 10 a.m. to 4 p.m., on Sunday from 12:30 a.m. to 4:30 p.m. (closed Sunday in January and December and major holidays). Admission is $2.50 for adults, $1.75 for students.

After her marriage, Juliette lived at what is now the **Andrew Low House** (built in 1848) at 329 Abercorn St., facing Lafayette Square, and it was here that she actually founded the Girl Scouts. She died here in 1927. The classic mid-19th-century house is of stucco over brick with elaborate ironwork outside, jalousied porches, carved woodwork, and crystal chandeliers. William Makepeace Thackeray visited here twice (the desk at which he worked is in one bedroom), as did Robert E. Lee, in 1870, who was entertained at a gala reception in the double parlors. In 1928 the house was bought by the Georgia Colonial Dames as their headquarters, and the carriage house is now headquarters for the local Girl Scout council. Visiting hours are 10:30 a.m. to 4 p.m. every day (except Thursday and national holidays), with a donation of $2.50 for adults, $1.75 for ages 6 to 10.

The **William Scarbrough Mansion and Garden,** 41 W. Broad St., is the home of the Historic Savannah Foundation and features a living-history program five times daily on Monday, Wednesday, and Friday. Local actresses portray the home's original mistress, Julia Scarbrough, in the 20-minute program. Hours are 10 a.m. to 4 p.m. Monday through Friday; admission $2.50 for adults, $1.50 for ages 10 to 17.

Museums

The **Savannah Science Museum,** 4405 Paulsen St. (tel. 912/355-6705), has hands-on exhibits in natural history, astronomy, and science. Reptiles and amphibians of Georgia are featured. Planetarium shows realistically re-create night skies every Sunday at 3 p.m. (admission $1.50). Hours are 10 a.m. to 5 p.m. Tuesday through Saturday, 2 to 5 p.m. Sunday; closed major holidays. There's a small admission.

Located in a renovated waterfront building, the **Ships of the Sea Maritime Museum**, 503 E. River St. (tel. 912/232-1511), with another entrance at 504 E. Bay St., is dedicated to the history of the seas and those who sail them. Beautifully constructed ship models depict seagoing vessels from Viking warships right up to today's nuclear-powered ships. There's also a marvelous collection of ships in a bottle. Admission is $2 for adults, 75/ for ages 7 to 12, under 7 free. Hours are 10 a.m. to 5 p.m. daily except major holidays.

Operated under the auspices of the Association for the Study of Afro-American Life and History, the **King-Tisdell Cottage**, 514 E. Huntingdon St. (tel. 912/234-8000), holds documents relating to black history, furniture typical of a coastal black residence in the late 1800s, and art objects. The cottage, with its intricate gingerbread ornamentation, narrowly escaped demolition in a program of urban redevelopment in the Ott Street area, but was saved at the last moment and moved to this location. Call for hours.

Tours

The river has always been a focal point for Savannah, and one of the best ways to see the city is from the water, aboard the *Cap'n Sam*, the *Harbor Queen*, or the *Waving Girl*, under the able hand of Capt. Sam Stevens. Cap'n Sam has been on the river for most of his lifetime and shares with his passengers a knowledge that comes from long (about 60 years) association with Savannah's growth. **Cap'n Sam's Riverboat Cruises** leave seven days a week at noon from a dock on River Street at the foot of Bull Street, behind city hall. The two-hour narrated trip includes all historic and shipping sites along the harbor (about 20 miles). There's also a twilight cocktail cruise, as well as moonlight supper cruises. The two-hour harbor cruise costs $6.50 for adults, $3.50 for children under 12. Call 912/234-7248 for information and reservations.

Another delightful way to see Savannah (and save your feet) is by **horse-drawn carriage.** Authentic antique carriages, painstakingly restored, carry you over cobblestone streets as the coachman spins a tale of the town's history. The one-hour tours cover 15 of the 20 squares. Rates are $8.50 for adults, $4 for children. Reservations are required—contact Savannah Carriage Co., P.O. Box 2402, Savannah, GA 31401 (tel. 912/236-6756), to reserve and for departure times.

Colonial Tours, P.O. Box 9704, Savannah, GA 31412 (tel. 912/233-0083), operates Old Time Trolley tours of the historic district, with pickup at most downtown inns and hotels. Adults pay $9, children under 12, $5. They also run a Lowcountry Tour that includes the fishing village of Thunderbolt, a plantation, a historic fort, and other points of interest. Rates are $13 for adults, $6 for children. Call to reserve for all tours.

Historic Savannah Foundation Tours, 41 W. Broad St. (tel. 912/233-7703), conducts narrated bus tours of the historic district, the lowcountry, and the Victorian district. There's also a 2½-hour breakfast walking tour of the historic district, and you have the bonus of knowing that your admission fees are channeled into nonprofit efforts to continue the preservation of Savannah's heritage.

Gray Line Savannah Landmark Tours, Inc., 215 W. Boundary St., and **Historic Savannah Foundations Tours** (tel. 912/236-9604) have narrated bus tours of museums, squares, parks, and homes. Reservations must be made for all tours, and most have starting points at the visitor center and pickup points at various hotels and motels.

There are tours on tape for self-guided driving, walking, or bike excursions at costs ranging from $6 to $12 (including a tape player and maps) available at the visitors center, the DeSoto Hilton, Hyatt Regency, and Pirate's House restaurant.

In late March or early April, the **Homes and Gardens Tour** shows off more than 30 homes, gardens, and museums in four days of daylight and candlelight tours. For specific dates, hours, and charges, write Savannah Tour of Homes and Gardens, 18 Abercorn St., Savannah, GA 31401 (tel. 912/233-7703).

Outside the City

About 2½ miles from downtown Savannah via U.S. 80, there's a fort with a nine-foot-deep tidal moat around its brick walls. It's **Fort Jackson,** which was built by the U.S. Corps of Engineers between 1809 and 1879 at a strategic point on the Savannah River. This is the fort that Georgia troops occupied before the outbreak of the Civil War and held until Sherman arrived in 1864. Its arched rooms (designed to support the weight of heavy cannon mounted above, which commanded the harbor entrance) hold 13 exhibit areas. Call 912/232-3945 for additional information and admission charges.

Fort McAllister is 10 miles east of U.S. 17 at Richmond Hill, on the banks of the Great Ogeechee River, and was a Confederate earthenwork fortification. There's a visitor center with historic exhibits, and there's a $1 fee for adults, 50¢ for children. Open Tuesday to Saturday from 9 a.m. to 5 p.m. and on Sunday from 2 to 5:30 p.m.

Fort Pulaski, a national monument, is 15 miles east of Savannah off U.S. 80 on Cockspur and McQueens islands at the very mouth of the Savannah River. It took 18 years to complete the massive, pentagonally shaped fort, with its casemate galleries and drawbridges crossing the moat. It was captured by Union troops in 1862 after a 30-hour bombardment, and you can still see shells from that battle embedded in the walls. There are exhibits on the fort's history in the visitor center, which is open every day except Christmas and New Year's days from 8:30 a.m. to 5:30 p.m. (to 7 p.m. in summer), and admission is $1 per person, free to those 16 and under and 62 and over, with a $3 maximum per car. (For complete information, write: Superintendent, Fort Pulaski, P.O. Box 30757, Savannah, GA 31410-0757 (tel. 912/248-4232).

There's a quiet little beach over on **Tybee Island,** a short drive from Savannah on U.S. 80. Oglethorpe built a lighthouse here in 1736, which was destroyed by a storm and replaced in 1773 by a structure you can visit and even climb. Pirates sought haven on Tybee Island, and it was a favorite place for duels between Savannah gentlemen—but today it's a relaxing memorial park playground, with a fishing pier, boat-launching ramp, marina, and a museum featuring historical dioramas, documents, relics, and artwork. For details, contact the Tybee Island Chamber of Commerce, P.O. Box 491, Tybee Island, GA 31328 (tel. 912/786-5444).

If you opt for a few days at this friendly, very casual beach settlement, the very first **Days Inn,** 1402 Butler Ave. (P.O. Box 1820), Tybee Island, GA 31328 (tel. 912/786-4576 or toll free 800/325-2525), is still here—it was built in 1970, and is a plain, two-story building just off the oceanfront. Rates are seasonal, with doubles running from $40 to $50. Directly behind it, on the waterfront, the pleasant Veranda Restaurant serves everything from snacks to full meals (home-cooked and delicious) at very moderate prices.

Some Very Special Events

On the third Sunday of June every year, shrimp boats in and around Savannah gather at Thunderbolt (just over the bridge) for the annual **Blessing of the Fleet.** But if you'd like to see this traditional ceremony and the colorful religious pageant that accompanies it, by all means plan to get there at least three days in advance. There are all sorts of gala activities before the big day itself, and the dances, street fairs, art exhibits, and a general air of celebration create a sort of carnival atmosphere.

They say in New York that "there's a little of Irish in every New Yorker on St. Paddy's Day." Well, in Savannah the same thing goes—their **St. Patrick's Day Parade** on March 17 is second in size only to New York's, and everybody gets into the act, even the Savannah River, which they tell me is dyed green for the day (can't really vouch for *that,* but I can tell you it's a great time to be in the city).

No matter what your ethnic background, you'll fit right in at the annual **Night in Old Savannah,** which celebrates all this country's cultural groups. Blocks are set aside for what amounts to a massive street fair. For three enchanted days there's ethnic food and entertainment outside the visitor center. The date is usually in late April, and for specific dates and details, write or call Night in Old Savannah, P.O. Box 14147, Savannah, GA 31416 (tel. 912/355-2422).

Christmas in Savannah is a time of warm sociability, and if you plan to be there during that season, be sure to book for the **Christmas Tour of Homes** sponsored by the Downtown Neighborhood Association. Seven homes are shown on one day of the weekend event, with another seven the next, and there's a candlelight tour included in your ticket. Carriage rides, complete with hand-bell ringers and carolers, are a part of the experience too. For dates, prices, and reservations, contact: Savannah Hospitality Association, P.O. Box 9841, Savannah, GA 31412 (tel. 912/964-1421).

2. Brunswick and the Golden Isles

Brunswick is just 81 miles south of Savannah (I-95 is quicker; U.S. 17 more beautiful, although a little longer in mileage). A stopover at Midway, some 30 miles south of Savannah, is worthwhile if only to see the **Midway Church,** which dates back to 1792 (an earlier one burned—this is the "new" church), with its large slave gallery, high pulpit, and colonial-era headstones in the tiny graveyard.

The Colonial Council of the Royal Province of Georgia laid out Brunswick's streets back in 1771, making it another of early Georgia's planned cities. It has always been an important port, with a natural harbor that can handle oceangoing ships. Over the years it has also developed into quite a manufacturing and food-processing center (principally seafood), but there are still several vestiges of its colonial past. It is also a very pretty town, with palms, flowering shrubs, and moss-draped live oaks all over the place. And watching the large fleet of shrimp boats (Brunswick calls itself "Shrimp Capital of the World") put in on a sunny afternoon is a favorite pasttime for both locals and visitors.

In addition, Brunswick is the gateway to Georgia's "Golden Isles" (a local appellation), the three best known of that string of lush, semitropical islands that runs the length of the state's coastline. **Sea Island** and **St. Simons** are just across the Torras Causeway (which passes over the famous "Marshes of Glynn" immortalized by poet Sidney Lanier, who came from these parts), and **Jekyll Island** is south of town across the Lanier Bridge, then south on Ga. 50 (don't bother looking for highway numbers, though—large signs point the way). Together, they form one of the loveliest resort areas along the entire Atlantic coast.

The islands haven't always been dedicated to fun in the sun, however. The Spanish had missions on them as early as 1566, and there were peaceful Creek Indians fishing, hunting, and farming here from 2500 B.C., say anthropologists who've studied the evidence. And St. Simons was the scene of the small but important "Battle of Bloody Marsh" in 1742 that probably determined once and for all the southern part of the country would remain under British, not Spanish, domination. General Oglethorpe had built Fort Frederica on the west side of St. Simons and a smaller battery, Fort St. Simons, on the south end as a defense against the Spanish, who were entrenched in nearby Florida and had a greedy eye on the lands to their north. He didn't have nearly enough troops to repulse any serious Spanish attack, but after the British victory at Bloody Marsh, and some brilliant strategy that included parading the same seven horsemen up and down a faraway beach during one whole day of negotiations to give the illusion of a full complement of cavalry, the Spanish finally were convinced that his position was much stronger than it really was and withdrew from the territory for good.

After the Revolution, the islands were world famous for their Sea Island cotton, grown on huge plantations supported mainly by slave labor. So important was slavery to their economy, in fact, that the last slaver, the *Wanderer*, landed its cargo of Africans on Jekyll Island as late as 1858, with the world looking on: the importing of slaves was by that time illegal, and its crew was promptly arrested. After the Civil War, without their large labor force, the plantations languished and finally disappeared. There was a brief period of prosperity based on a lumber mill on St. Simons (from the 1870s to 1903), and the first daily postal service began in 1876.

It was in the late 1880s, however, that the Golden Isles got into the resort business, when a group of Yankee millionaires "discovered" Jekyll Island and decided it was the ideal retreat from shivery northern weather during January, February, and March. They bought the island for $125,000 and built "cottages" with anywhere from 15 to 25 rooms (remember, these were men with names like J. P. Morgan, P. Lorillard, Vanderbilt, Goodyear, etc.) and a club house large enough to accommodate up to 100 members. From then until 1947, when second-generation members of the Jekyll Island Club found the island life less glamorous than other "jet set" resorts and sold Jekyll to the state of Georgia for $675,000, the "Millionaires' Village" was so exclusive that no uninvited guest *ever* set foot on the place, and even invited guests were limited to visits of no more than two weeks if they stayed in the club house. Many of those cottages are open to visitors today, and all the attractions that drew those men of wealth and their families are public property, with plenty of accommodations to take care of us "ordinary" folk. One of the not-so-ordinary people to look for relaxation on St. Simons is former President Jimmy Carter, who headed straight there following his election.

As for Sea Island, it was purchased back in 1927 by Howard Coffin (he already owned another "golden isle," Sapelo Island), who built a causeway from St. Simons to reach the five-mile-long barrier island, then set about developing what has become a world-famous resort, the Cloister, which opened in October 1928.

Incidentally, no matter how you approach Brunswick, I strongly recommend a trip to the **Brunswick–Golden Isles Welcome Center,** on I-95 southbound between exits 8 and 9 (mail address: Rte. 10, Box I-95, Brunswick, GA 31520; tel. 912/264-0202). The attractive center rivals any state welcome center I've ever seen. The friendly staff can give you any kind of area information you want (and some you may not have even known you wanted); and if you should happen to land here without reservations (God forbid!), they have an electronic reservations board for more than 20 hotels and motels with up-to-the-minute vacancy data and can book a room for you right there. There's also a welcome center at 2000 Glynn Ave., Brunswick, GA 31520 (tel. 912/264-5337).

Other useful sources for helpful information in advance are: **Jekyll Island Convention and Visitors Bureau,** Jekyll Island, GA 31520 (tel. 912/635-3400) and **St. Simons Chamber of Commerce,** St. Simons, GA 31522 (tel. 912/638-9014).

WHERE TO STAY

Where you stay will probably depend on how you plan to visit the islands. If this is only a way station for you, with just a quick look around, then your best bet is to stop at one of the motels clustered at the U.S. 341/I-95 interchange, where restaurants, service stations, stores, gift shops, and easy access to the islands causeway add up to real convenience. It's a different story, of course, if a few days' escape from the cares of civilization in an island setting is what you're after.

Sea Island

Sea Island (northernmost of the Golden Isles) *means* the world-famous **Cloister Hotel,** Sea Island, GA 31561 (tel. 912/638-3611 or toll free 800/SEA ISLAND in Georgia). Operating on full American plan (which means three superb meals a day are included), the Cloister, a Spanish-Moorish–style complex roofed with red tile, has 264 rooms in the main building and its newer, adjacent low-rise hotel structures (separately sited, with garden-like surroundings), all complete with the ultimate in luxury, convenience, and comfort. Hotel guests and occupants of some 450 privately owned homes (often available for rental) enjoy the Sea Island Beach Club, with a diving pool, heated swimming pool, wading pool, sundecks for acquiring that island tan, health and fitness facilities, luxurious dining rooms right at the ocean's edge, and the particularly charming Spanish Lounge, with three cloister windows, high wooden ceilings, wood-burning fireplaces, and oversize armchairs. Facilities also include golf (54 holes), tennis (17 all-weather courts), riding stables, skeet and trap shooting, fishing and boating docks, bicycles (the best way of all to get around, in my humble opinion), and lawn sports like croquet, shuffleboard, and chip and putt. There's dancing every night and special events feature plantation suppers, cookouts, musical happenings, and all fresco dinner-dances. This elegant place has been family owned since it opened in 1928, and with a staff ratio of three employees to every two guests, you'll begin to get that pampered feeling the minute you register. Rates change with the seasons and vary according to room type and location. From March 15 to May 31, doubles run about $237 to $357 plus tax and service, but drop drastically other months. And remember, *rates include all meals*. Golf, tennis, and honeymoon (and what a perfect honeymoon spot!) package plans are available.

St. Simons

The **King and Prince Beach Resort,** Arnold Road, St. Simons Island, GA 31522 (tel. 912/638-3631 or toll free 800/342-0212), is more an experience than just a hotel. The 124-room inn is directly on the ocean, and from the moment you step into the elegant and long verandas and patios, shaded by ancient oaks and lots and lots of palm trees, you feel an open invitation to sit and unwind. The food in the elegant Delegal Dining Room is legendary and includes a chicken with wine sauce and a "Mile High Pie" that's out of this world. For more casual dining, it's the Tavern Lounge. When you're tired of sitting, there's a pool (and the beach, of course), tennis, golf, fishing, sailing, horseback riding, and bikes for exploring the island. Oceanfront doubles range from $89 to $129, with rates descending for ocean view, courtyard view (charming), and studio rooms. Two- and three-bedroom villas run $159 to $319.

Sea Palms Golf and Tennis Resort, Frederica Road, St. Simons Island, GA 31522 (tel. 912/638-3351, or toll free 800/841-6268), covers some 800 acres that accommodate both permanent residents and vacationers. Thus holidayers become part of an entire community, rather than simply a resort development. There are fully furnished one-, two-, and three-bedroom villas overlooking the golf course and the Marshes of Glynn, as well as the newer, very posh Sea Marsh Villas. A championship golf course and the wooded, secluded Sea Palms Racquet Club with 12 all-weather, lighted courts are highlights. Other amenities include pools, a playground, health center, sauna and whirlpool, and the delightful Oglethorpe's Restaurant. Rates for hotel rooms range from $78 to $96; villas are $120 to $237. Best buys, however, are the large range of tennis and golf plans, and off-season lower rates.

The less expensive **Sea Gate Inn,** 1014 Ocean Blvd., St. Simons Island, GA 31522 (tel. 912/638-8661), has 49 rooms. All are bright and colorful and some have kitchens, private patios, or balconies. There's free coffee and doughnuts for all, and although there is no dining room, restaurants are only three blocks away. Rates range from $40 to $98 for rooms, $70 to $220 for one- or two-bedroom condos.

Queen's Court Motel, 437 Kings Way, St. Simons Island, GA 31522 (tel. 912/638-8459), is a complex of two-story buildings surrounding a shaded, grassy lawn. Rooms come with one double bed or two single beds, and there are suites with two double beds and a large sitting room, as well as kitchenette units. Rates for doubles range from $40 to $55, depending on the type of accommodation. No pets allowed.

Private cottages are available for weekly or monthly rental on St. Simons, and you can get an illustrated brochure with rates and availability information from: **Parker-Kaufman Realtors,** 1699 Frederica Rd., St. Simons Island, GA 31522 (tel. 912/638-3368).

Jekyll Island

The undisputed star of Jekyll Island is the **Jekyll Island Club Hotel,** 371 Riverview Dr., Jekyll Island, GA 31520 (tel. 912/635-2600, or toll free 800/333-3333). In the heyday of Jekyll's millionaires, the rambling, turreted Club was the center of social activities, and deluxe lodgings for privileged guests such as the Morgans, Vanderbilts, and Rockefellers. In 1987 the Club reopened as a Radisson Hotels Resort, with 136 gorgeous guest rooms, pool, tennis, shopping, and access to the island's 63 holes of golf and 10 miles of beaches. Doubles are $79 to $109; suites, $119 to $199.

The **Quality Inn Buccaneer,** 85 Beachview Dr., Jekyll Island, GA 31520 (tel. 912/635-2261, or toll free 800/228-5151), is a 213-room ocean front resort in a setting of lush foliage. Rooms all have a private balcony or terrace and border on the luxurious. For families, there are kitchenettes available, children's playground, year-round recreation program, and bike rentals come in handy. Golfers and tennis buffs will find a home here, and there's a pool and oceanfront hot tub in addition to that gorgeous beach. The ocean-view restaurant features very good regional cooking. Rates March through mid-August are $56 to $97 for double rooms, with lower rates the rest of the year and attractive discount packages available year round.

The **Comfort Inn Island Suites,** 711 Beachview Dr., Jekyll Island, GA 31520 (tel. 912/635-2211 or toll free 800/228-5150), is a 179-suite ocean-front resort on beautifully landscaped grounds. Included in the rates are a complimentary breakfast buffet and social hour. Suites include double or king-size beds, and some have kitchenettes or private whirlpools overlooking the ocean. There are two outdoor hot tubs, pool, playground, and an arbor area for outdoor dining. There's also a good moderately priced restaurant next door. Suites range from $55 to $115 from March through mid-August, lower other months. There are attractive package discounts, as well as weekly and monthly rates.

Jekyll Island cottage rental rates and availability can be obtained through **Parker-Kaufman Realtors,** Beachview Drive (P.O. Box 3126), Jekyll Island, GA 31520 (tel. 912/635-2512).

Camping

The **Jekyll Island Campground,** North Beachview Drive, Jekyll Island, GA 31520 (tel. 912/635-3021), is managed by the Jekyll Island Authority and is the only island campground in the Golden Isles. Its 18 wooded acres have more than 200 sites nestled among live oaks and pines. Facilities include bathhouses, showers, laundry, camping equipment, pure tap water, grocery store, garbage pickup, LP gas, and bike rentals. Tent sites cost $10; regular sites are $12; and full hookup sites are $14.

EATING ON THE ISLANDS

Gourmet dining reigns supreme at most of the hotels listed for all three islands, but be sure to reserve for dinner at places like the **Cloister** (use the telephone numbers shown for the hotels, above). However, excellent dining at less expensive prices is also available on St. Simons.

Blanche's Courtyard, 440 Kings Way, St. Simons Island (tel. 912/638-8892), serves mostly seafood in a Victorian atmosphere, with lots of old brickwork, antiques, and a private patio. On Friday and Saturday, there's entertainment (dress is casual). Dinner hours are 5:30 to 10 p.m., and prices range from $10 to $16.

Altogether different is the rustic decor of the **Crab Trap,** 1209 Ocean Blvd., St. Simons (tel. 912/638-3552). No fancy trappings, but the seafood is superb. Fresh local shrimp, oysters, and scallops come with coleslaw and hush puppies, at prices that range from $6 to $12. Dinner is served Monday through Saturday from 5 to 10 p.m.

Emmeline and Hessie, 100 Marina Dr., St. Simons (tel. 912/638-9084), was named after two ferries that once plied the waters between Brunswick and St. Simons, a fitting appellation for this unique restaurant overlooking the Intracoastal Waterway and St. Simons Bay. So well does it fit into its setting that raccoons come right up to the picture windows, begging to be fed. Inside, its ship decor is cozied up by plants and more plants. As you'd expect, seafood tops the menu here, with a live-lobster tank, specialty shrimp dishes, and an excellent oyster bar. They do their own baking and dish up homemade soup and sauces. Hours are 7 a.m. to 10 p.m. with a raw bar open til midnight. Lunch is under $10, dinner under $18.

A warm, rustic interior with lots of exposed beams greets you at **Frederica House,** 3611 Frederica Rd. (tel. 912/638-6789). It's right in the center of St. Simons, and serves regional seafood specialties, as well as beef dishes, at dinner only. Hours are 6 to 10 p.m., and reservations are definitely in order (casual dress is also in order).

At **Poor Stephen's,** on Frederica Road (tel. 912/638-7316), they serve burgers, chowder, salads, and *great* sandwiches from noon until ? (that usually means about 11 p.m., but they refuse to post a quitting time). There's a lounge, very popular with islanders, that stays open from noon until 2 a.m. Prices run from under a dollar to about $5, dress is casual, and this place is a real find.

On Jekyll Island, look for the small, rustic **café** at the end of the pier at the Marina, where fresh-caught seafood is sold at remarkably low prices.

READER'S DINING SUGGESTION: "A nice stop for us at St. Simons was **Dana's,** near the St. Simons pier—good chili and other snacks, very reasonable, in a woody, barn-like building" (M. Ryan, New York, N.Y.).

ISLAND ACTIVITIES

Well, there are the **beaches**—and they're absolutely gorgeous on all three islands. Sunning or splashing, you'll find the fine-sand strand and the gentle-surfed ocean ideal. There are beachfront bathhouses on Jekyll's east shore.

Golfers can pretend they're Jekyll Island millionaires and play the Ocean-side Nine holes those gentlemen patterned after the "olde" course at St. Andrews, Scotland. Or the three 18-hole **golf** courses on the island: **Oleander,**

Pine Lakes, and **Indian Mound.** Fees are $9 a day for nine holes, $14.50 for unlimited, all-day play.

Also on Jekyll Island are eight outdoor **tennis** courts and one indoor, **bicycle** rentals and bike paths, pier **fishing** (at no charge), and charter boats for offshore and inlet fishing. No license is required for saltwater fishing; freshwater licenses cost $6 for five days and can be obtained at most hardware or sporting goods stores or at the **Howard Coffin Recreational Park** in Brunswick (freshwater fish around here include bream, red breast, crappie or white perch, shad, bass, and trout). Deep-sea fishing can be arranged by calling the **Troupe Creek Marina** (it's on Yacht Road, east of U.S. 17N) at 912/264-3862.

The **Aquarama,** on Beachview Drive and Parkway, is a modernistic structure with a circular ballroom for dancing and an Olympic-size outdoor swimming pool overlooking the ocean. Check when you get there about dancing times and charges.

You can visit the Jekyll Island Club Historical District and the **Millionaires' Village "cottages"** (translate "mansions") on a 1½-hour interpretive tour. The tour originates at the museum orientation center on Stable Road (tel. 635-2762 or 635-2727). Highlights include a stained-glass window that Louis Comfort Tiffany personally installed in Faith Chapel in 1904 and several of the buildings themselves (all others may be seen only from the outside). Adults pay $6; students 6 to 18 years, $4; and children under 6, free.

Jekyll is also the site of Georgia's first **brewery** (on the northwest end of the island), started by General Oglethorpe, who evidently knew how to "put first things first" for his settlers. Very near the brewery stand the ruins of a home built in 1738 by William Horton, one of Oglethorpe's captains. It was constructed of "tabby," a mortar made of lime, sand, oyster shells, and water, and much used in coastal areas during colonial times.

St. Simons Island is real sightseeing territory. No sightseer worthy of the name would miss **Fort Frederica National Monument** on the northwest end of the island. About all that's left of the original construction is a small portion of the king's magazine and the barracks tower, but archeological excavations have unearthed many foundations, and the visitor center has a film on the history of the fort and the town, which once had a population of 1,000. There's a donation box, with a $1.50 admission, and it's open every day from 8 a.m. to 5 p.m., later during the summer.

I guess my personal favorite on St. Simons is the **Museum of Coastal History,** in the restored lighthouse keeper's house next to the St. Simons Light at 600 Beachview Dr. There are six rooms of artifacts, books, letters, photos, and a Victorian parlor that sets my romantic mind dreaming. Hardy souls will want to climb the lighthouse's 129 steps for a spectacular view of the Golden Isles. There are changing exhibits, and the $1.50 admission for adults, $1 for ages 6 to 12, includes the museum and the lighthouse. Hours are 10 a.m. to 5 p.m. Tuesday through Saturday and 1:30 to 5 p.m. on Sunday, from Memorial Day to Labor Day; 1 to 4 p.m. Tuesday through Saturday and 1:30 to 4 p.m. on Sunday, in other months.

Then there's the **Coastal Center for the Arts,** on Demere Road near the airport, where local and "traveling" art and craft exhibits are displayed, and there are lectures, classes, and demonstrations. It is open from 11 a.m. to 5 p.m. Monday through Saturday year round, and there's no admission.

Scattered from end to end of St. Simons are ruins of the plantation era: **Hampton Plantation** (where Aaron Burr spent a month after his duel with Alexander Hamilton), and **Cannon's Point** on the north; **West Point, Pines Bluff,** and **Hamilton Plantations** on the west along the Frederica River; **Harrington Hall** and **Mulberry Grove** in the interior; **Lawrence, St. Clair, Black Banks, The Village,** and **Kelvyn Grove** on the east; and **Retreat Plantation** on the south end. Ruins are about all you'll see today, but there's a restored chapel on the West Point Plantation (made of tabby, the mortar turned pink because of an unusual lichen; natives say it reflected blood on the hands of Dr. Thomas Hazzard, who killed a neighbor in a land dispute and built the chapel after being so ostracized by island society that he would not attend Christ Church) and tabby slave cabins, which have been restored and put to use (one is an activity center of the Methodist-run Epworth-by-the-Sea; another is home of the Island Garden Club on Gascoigne Bluff).

Christ Church, 6329 Frederica Rd. at the north end of the island, was built first in 1820, on ground where John and Charles Wesley had preached under the oaks in 1736. It was virtually destroyed when Union troops camped here during the Civil War, burning pews for firewood and butchering cattle in the chapel. Then, in 1886, Anson Greene Phelps Dodge, Jr., restored it as a memorial to his first wife, who had died on their honeymoon. It's a serene, white wooden building nestled under huge old oaks and looks exactly as an island church should. The doors are open every day from 2 to 5 p.m. during Daylight Saving Time months, 1 to 4 p.m. other times, and there is no charge, of course, to go inside.

NIGHTLIFE

After dark, social life centers around motel lounges, like the Buccaneer's **Leeward Lounge** or the Wanderer's **Pirates Cove,** with more elegant entertainment at the **Cloister.** There's entertainment also at **Misty's Lounge** in the Hilton Inn. Check with the information center on Jekyll Island to see what's going on when you're there.

EXCURSIONS FROM THE GOLDEN ISLES

There are several day and half-day trips from the islands. **Brunswick,** for example, has some sights to see: the **James Oglethorpe Monument** (a statue of Georgia's founder) in Queens Square on the east side of Newcastle Street; the **Lover's Oak,** a giant, 900-year-old oak at Albany and Prince streets; **Lanier's Oak** (honoring the poet), half a mile south of town on U.S. 17; and **Bay Street** (between Third and Gloucester), lined with seafood-processing plants, where you can watch the shrimp boats dock beginning about 3 p.m.—a lively, interesting spectacle.

A longer trip is the one inland to Waycross to visit the **Okefenokee Swamp** (mailing address: Fargo, GA 31631 (tel. 912/637-5274). This is the largest freshwater swamp still preserved in the U.S., some 700 square miles, and it really presents a picture of nature in the raw. The best entrance is about eight miles south of Waycross on U.S. 1, U.S. 23, and Ga. 177, where there are cypress boardwalks out over the swamp, an observation tower, serpentarium, picnic area, and interpretive centers. The admission charge ($7 for adults, $5 for children under 12) includes a two-mile boat trip along waterways lined with thickly tangled growth and alive with snakes, alligators, and lovely white blossoms of water plants. The swamp is a fantastic "other world," but it may not be for you if you're squeamish when it comes to reptiles, spiders (they come in giant sizes), and the like. If you're squeamish but still interested, a better place to visit is the **Okefenokee Heritage Center,** two miles west of Waycross on U.S. 82 (tel. 912/285-4260). There are a restored 1912 steam locomotive and depot, an "operating" 1890 print shop, the restored 1840 Gen. Thomas Hilliard House, and general exhibits on local history, the arts, sciences, and special studies. There's a small admission fee, and hours are 10 a.m. to 5 p.m. Tuesday through Saturday, and 2 to 4 p.m. on Sunday.

At that same site, there's no charge to visit the **Southern Forest World** (tel. 912/285-4056), a museum depicting the development and history of the forest industry in the South. The collection includes a logging train, tools, and other forestry-related artifacts, as well as a variety of audio visuals to expound on the subject. Hours are the same as at the Heritage Center.

---

3. Cumberland Island

If the semisophistication and wide variety of things to do at the above islands are what you're looking for on Georgia's coast, you're not likely to want to come to Cumberland Island. If, on the other hand, total peace, unspoiled natural surroundings, and a sense of what these islands were like from the beginning of time up until man started "developing" them, have special meaning for you, then Cumberland will draw you like a magnet! Nowhere else on the East Coast are those island qualities so perfectly preserved.

On this little bit of offshore land (just 16 miles long and 3 miles across at its widest point), people have been in residence as far back as 4,000 years ago; but rather than "develop" the resources here, they have lived in harmony with all manner of wildlife and spectacular tree and plant life, using only those necessary for survival and moving in rhythm with nature's patterns. True, timber was harvested here at one time to supply shipbuilders. True, also, cotton was once cultivated on the island as a commercial crop. But neither was undertaken on a destructive, industrial basis, and nothing was done to upset the balance struck by natural forces as they piled up sand and marshes to create this little bit of paradise that one writer describes as existing "somewhere between Atlantis, Bali Hai, and the Garden of Eden."

To step onto Cumberland Island is to step into a wilderness of maritime forest (with tunnel-like roads canopied by live oaks, cabbage palms, magnolia, holly, red cedar, and pine), salt marshes alive with waving grasses, sand dunes arranged by wind and tide into a double line of defense against destruction by those very forces, and gleaming sand beaches that measure a few hundred yards at low tide. It is to enter a breathtaking world of animal life, where alligators wallow in marshes, whitetailed deer bound through the trees or graze peacefully at dusk, wild pigs snuffle the undergrowth for food, armadillos move their armored-tank shapes about freely, wild turkeys roam unmolested, over 300 species of birds wheel overhead, and wild horses canter in herds or pick their way peacefully to watering holes.

It's enchanted, this island.

WHERE TO STAY

There's only one place *to* stay on Cumberland, and it's no less enchanted than the island itself. The only commercial building (if you can call it that), **Greyfield Inn** (Drawer B, Fernandina Beach, FL 32034; tel. 904/261-6408) is a three-story plantation mansion with a wide, inviting veranda set in a grove of live oaks. Built shortly after the turn of the century as a summer retreat by Thomas Carnegie (Andrew's brother and partner), Greyfield has remained family property ever since. Guests today are treated very much like family visitors were in years past: the extensive and very valuable library is open for your perusal; furnishings are those the family has always used; the bar is an open one, operated on an honor system (you simply pour your own and note it on a pad); meals are served buffet style from a mahogany sideboard, and you dine at the long family table, adorned with heirloom silver candlesticks. And you're at liberty to browse through old family photo albums, scrapbooks, and other memorabilia scattered about the large, paneled living room (if the weather is cool, there'll be a fire in the oversize fireplace). Soft chimes announce meals (dinnertime means "dress"—informal dresses and jackets, no shorts or jeans). And what meals! Seafood is likely to have been caught that very morning, and cooked to perfection. It's roast beef on Saturday night, and a fun-for-all oyster roast every Sunday night. Breakfasts are also sumptuous, and if beachcombing or exploring is what you have in mind for the day, the inn will pack a picnic lunch to carry along. As for the upstairs rooms, they vary in size from the large suite once used by the mother of Lucy Carnegie Ferguson (Thomas's granddaughter and the present owner) to less spacious ones. Bathrooms are shared and still hold the original, old-fashioned massive fittings.

In short, you will, as I said before, feel exactly like a family guest at Greyfield. Best of all, the friendly staff will *treat* you like family. The inn is staffed by Mrs. Ferguson's grandchildren. They're all on a first-name basis with guests and full of knowledge about Cumberland and how to enjoy it.

Rates at this unique inn, which include all three meals, are $90 to $100 per person daily (10% discount for children under 10). Since there are accommodations for only 18 guests, reservations must be made well in advance. A 50% deposit is required, and a 15% gratuity will be added to your bill, as well as a 5% tax.

How to Get There

There's an airstrip near the inn, and air-taxi arrangements can be made from Jacksonville or St. Simons Island (call the inn for details). But the best way to reach Greyfield is by its own ferry, the *Robert W. Ferguson,* which maintains a regular schedule to Fernandina Beach, Florida (a few miles east of I-95 on Ga. 40). Reservations are necessary on the *R.W.,* as it is affectionately known, and must be made through the inn. Round trip for passengers is $15. For cars, there's a $35 one-way fare. I strongly urge that you take your car or a bicycle, since there's no transportation on the island. If you don't wish to do so, however, you can leave your car with complete safety in the Fernandina Beach parking lot (across from the police station) until you return.

THINGS TO SEE AND DO

Don't look for a swimming pool, tennis courts, or a golf course—Cumberland's attractions are a different sort. The inn is just a short walk from those high sand dunes and a wild, undeveloped beach that had me looking for Long John Silver's longboat coming through the swells. Beachcombing, swimming, shelling, and fishing are high on the list of activities, but exploring the island and drinking in its long history offer stiff competition.

There are no signs left of the Native Americans who lived here some 4,000 years ago, unless you count the base of shells that underlies almost all roadways on the island. Nor can you find traces of Franciscan missionaries who came to convert the Indians during the 1500s. No ruins exist of the fort built at each end by Gen. James Oglethorpe in the 1700s as protection against Spanish invaders. The only thing that remains of Oglethorpe's hunting lodge is its name, Dungeness, a name that has clung to Gen. Nathanael Greene's post-Revolutionary mansion built of tabby (which burned to the ground after the Civil War) and its successor, a massive Carnegie mansion built on the same site.

What you *can* find as you poke around this fascinating place are: the ruins of Carnegie's Dungeness (which burned in 1959) and the still-standing recreation building, which housed spacious guest rooms, an indoor swimming pool, squash court, gymnasium, and billiard room; the Greene-Miller (Phineas Miller was Mrs. Greene's second husband) cemetery that first held the remains of Henry "Lighthorse Harry" Lee before they were removed to Virginia and still evokes ghosts of its inhabitants from Revolutionary times right through the Civil War era; Stafford plantation house and, down the lane a bit, "the chimneys," a melancholy ruin of post–Civil War drama (ask at the inn for the full story); Plum Orchard, a magnificent Carnegie mansion, fully furnished but unoccupied and now the property of the National Park Service; and most of all, the hushed solemnity of island roads, pathways, and fields being reclaimed by native plants and wildlife. In a very real sense, the past lives vividly in today's unchanged island environment.

SPECIAL NOTE

Since 1972, most of Cumberland Island has been a national seashore administered by the National Park Service. Passenger-ferry service is available from St. Marys, Ga., by reservation—no vehicles (write: Superintendent, P.O. Box 806, St. Marys, GA 31558; tel. 912/882-4335. Monday through Friday, 10 a.m. to 2 p.m.). There are usually two trips in each direction daily from Memorial Day to Labor Day; The ferry does not run Tuesday and Wednesday the rest of the year. For information only, tel. 912/882-4336.

Along with Cumberland, you can savor the wild beauty of Georgia's coast on **Little St. Simons Island.** Reached by boat from St. Simons, Little St. Simons, P.O. Box 1078, St. Simons Island, GA 31522 (tel. 912/638-7472), is a 10,000-acre privately owned sanctuary that offers you the uncrowded run of six miles of undeveloped beaches, fishing, swimming, horseback riding, and bird-watching for 200 species. Accommodations are rustic but comfortable lodges, some built before 1920, and newer ones opened in the past few years. Meals, served family style, feature locally caught seafoods and southern staples like fried chicken and barbecue. Rates range from $175 to $375, depending on accommodation, including all meals and facilities.

XV

GEORGIA'S CAPITAL CITY

Atlanta, the state's capital since 1868, typifies the economic vigor of inland Georgia, having recovered from almost total destruction to become the leading manufacturing and commercial center in the entire South. Agriculture, which has always been important, is now practiced on a grand scale, with tobacco, watermelons, sugarcane, okra, and pimiento peppers following close behind peaches, pecans, and peanuts in importance. And the region is rich in commercial clays and limestone, marble, granite, bauxite, talc, and feldspar, all of which are mined profitably.

ATLANTA

Georgia's capital is literally a railroad city. In fact, for a long time it had no name except "The Terminus," since it was the southern end of a Western and Atlantic Railroad spur linking the state with Tennessee and points west. A civil engineer who had surveyed the rail route is said to have predicted that it would "be a good location for one tavern, a blacksmith shop, a grocery store, and nothing else." That was back in 1837 (the first run on the line did not come until 1842), and the little settlement of dirt-floored shacks and wide-open bars kept its "work camp" atmosphere through two name changes (first to Marthasville, then Atlanta—a female form of the "Atlantic" in the railroad's name) and a municipal charter in 1847 that made it a legitimate town.

But as more and more rail lines met at the junction, life became more civilized, and businessmen arrived to attend to the warehousing, distributing, and wholesaling of freight coming in by rail. When the Confederacy came into being, Atlanta was an important supply and arms center, a role for which it paid dearly when Gen. William T. Sherman fought a long, bitter battle to win the city for the Union, kept it under harsh military rule from September to November of 1864 (most civilians were evacuated during this period), then burned all but 400 of its 3,600 homes and destroyed its railroads before setting out on his "march to the sea."

Only four years later, however, Atlanta had recovered to the point that it could be named the state capital (partly because of its location and the accessibility through rebuilt railroads to all parts of the state). The collapse of a slavery-based plantation economy proved a boon to this trade-oriented city, and its growth hasn't faltered since those Reconstruction recovery days. It has enlarged its rail transportation system, brought in six interstate highways (the trucking industry is now an important part of the local scene), and acquired an airport second only to Chicago's O'Hare in traffic. Its standing in the business world is such that 450 of the "Fortune 500" national corporations have offices here, and many have moved their home offices to the city.

The effect on Atlantans of all this commerce with the outside world has been to breed a cosmopolitanism and sort of acquired sophistication that keeps them constantly working to bring culture (whether it be in the form of the classical arts or entertainment of the "popular" genre) to their city. Although it never has been one of those legendary "sleepy southern towns," Atlanta today almost wiggles visibly with cultural activity. There are concerts and cabarets, ballets and bar-lounges, art galleries and avant-garde "happenings"—and the influx of European-cuisine restaurants has made it harder and harder to find fried chicken, country ham, hot biscuits, and grits. Today's Atlantans will tell you that their town is the "New York of the South"—and then proceed to take you by the hand and prove it.

GETTING AROUND ATLANTA

I'd like to offer one vital bit of advice to Atlanta visitors—if a native offers to show you around, by all means go! Otherwise, park your car and take advantage of the city's excellent bus and rapid rail system.

Marta (Metropolitan Atlanta Rapid Transit System, 401 W. Peachtree St. NE, Atlanta, GA 30308) operates some 124 bus routes, which connect with 29 rapid-rail stations. You must have exact change for the 85-cent fare (token vending machines are at all rapid-rail stations) and transfers are free. The rapid-rail system now extends to the airport, and east-west and north-south lines intersect at the Five Points station in midtown. Hours are 5:30 a.m. to 12:30 p.m.; for exact schedule and route information, call 848-4711 between 6 a.m. and 10 p.m. weekdays, 8 a.m. and 4 p.m. Saturday and Sunday.

Atlanta's **taxis** are a major *caveat emptor*. Many are unclean, mechanically suspect, and manned by drivers not familiar with the city. Be sure your driver has a lock on your destination, and that the fare is settled before setting off. One of the most reliable is **Checker Cab Company** (tel. 525-5466). Taxis usually cannot be flagged down on the streets, but must be called, or met at major hotels.

I can tell you from a long history of turning around and going back that Atlanta is one of the hardest cities on the face of the earth to get around in if you weren't born and raised in its street "system"—which isn't a system at all, just a perplexing maze of streets (at least to a stranger) that seem to have no particular plan. I don't think I've ever been in the city behind a wheel without being lost at least once. On the other hand, the buses or the monorail go everywhere, taxis are plentiful (although you usually have to get them at a hotel stand or by telephoning; see above), and even if you get lost while driving, some helpful local will set you straight with a friendly smile.

Having said all that, for what it's worth here are a few tips about Atlanta's streets. In the center of the downtown area, Peachtree, Marietta, Decatur, Edgewood, and Whitehall streets come together at **Five Points Intersection;** and all those NE, NW, SE, and SW addresses stem from this point. Peachtree runs north and south through the city, North Avenue and Ponce de Leon run east and west, and I-75 and I-85 (Northeast Expressway) run through downtown. I-20 (the East and West expressways) runs through the city center. And don't be misled by "expressway": at rush hours, they're as clogged as city streets, so plan accordingly. Another thing to remember is that "Peachtree" doesn't always mean Peachtree *Street* (which is the *real* main street in Atlanta); there are 26 "Peachtrees"—if it's followed by Drive, View, Circle, Avenue, or anything else, it isn't *the* Peachtree Street!

WHERE TO STAY

Two of Atlanta's splashiest hotels are in large complexes. The Peachtree Plaza is surrounded by a forest of shops, and the Omni International Hotel is neighbor to shops, movie theaters, discos, restaurants, and a three-block-long convention center. Both are in the heart of town, and both are terribly expensive (see below). But luxury hotels are nothing new to Atlanta, and although I have tried throughout this book to stress moderately priced accommodations (and will do so here, as well), there are hotels which fall into the expensive category that simply cannot be omitted in any discussion of this city. More than that, Atlanta now has an exquisite old-world hotel in a downtown location that would top any traveler's list for pure charm.

Old-World Elegance

While Atlanta has for years had a plentiful supply of glittering high-rise hotels that offer the ultimate in luxury, the **Ritz-Carlton, Atlanta,** 181 Peachtree St. NE, Atlanta, GA 30303 (tel. 404/659-0400, or toll free 800/241-3333), is the welcome addition of a small, personal-service hotel. Located right in the heart of the business district on the corner of Peachtree and Ellis streets, the Ritz-Carlton is a 25-story, rose-marble structure whose interior projects an old-world graciousness and charm very rare in modern hotels. The sunken lobby features Oriental rugs, paneled walls, touches of bronze, and fine antique furnishings interspersed with comfortable seating. Up the dramatic stairway there's one of the most club-like, intimate lounges I've come across, beyond which is the elegant dining room called simply The Restaurant. Even the elevators exude elegance, with the same paneling and bronze as in the lobby. Guest rooms are restful refuges of traditional furnishings, bay windows, an honor bar, fresh flowers, and marble bathrooms. If there's an "extra" they've omitted, *I* couldn't think of it! And both the 24th and 25th floors have been set apart as The Club, where guests enjoy a private lounge with complimentary refreshments and the services of a personal concierge. Personal service, however, is not limited to those floors: under the watchful eye of the personable head concierge,

Ronald Beattie (a Scotsman with long years of service at Glen Eagles behind him), every guest has access to a bevy of friendly, efficient assistants who happily arrange for limousine airport pickup, business services, tickets to local events, personal shopping, and almost any whim your fancy can whip up. Lunch and dinners in The Restaurant are both gourmet quality and accompanied by sophisticated piano music; The Café, just off the lobby, serves lighter fare from 6:30 a.m. to midnight; and the small lobby lounge offers continental breakfasts, afternoon tea, and cocktails. This is truly a gem of a hotel in one of the city's most convenient locations. Double rates range from $155 to $210.

If an "uptown" Buckhead location suits your purposes better, there's the **Ritz-Carlton, Buckhead,** 3434 Peachtree Rd. NE, Atlanta, GA 30326 (tel. 404/237-2700, or toll free 800/241-3333). The hotel completed an extensive rejuvenation in early 1987, and now is more splendid than ever. Public areas and dining rooms are rich with Italian marble, mahogany, crystal, and rare African woods. A museum's worth of 18th- and 19th-century English and French paintings and artworks further add to the luster of this magnificent hotel. With its dark-wood paneling, cheery fireplaces, and artworks, the new Ritz-Carlton Bar is reminiscent of Claridge's in London. It also has a fitness center, pool, and whirlpool. The hotel is 1 of only 2 in Georgia, and 45 in the U.S., Canada, and Mexico, to receive AAA's Five Diamond Award. Doubles run $165 to $220.

Expensive

The **Westin Peachtree Plaza,** 210 Peachtree St. NE, Atlanta, GA 30303 (tel. 404/659-1400, or toll free 800/228-3000), is that circular tower you'll notice soaring over Atlanta's skyline. It's 73 stories high, North America's tallest hotel, designed by Atlanta architect John Portman, who helped set the trend to atrium-lobby hotels with the Hyatt Regency a few years back. There's a Tivoli Gardens look to the newly renovated lobby, and glass elevators climb all the way to the top on the outside of the building. Rooms are plush, to say the least, with vibrant, modern furnishings. Needless to say, nothing has been overlooked in the way of guest facilities: there's a heated pool, several bars and restaurants, a health club and sauna, and a revolving rooftop bar and Sun Dial Restaurant (which also has a stationary level just in case you don't *want* to revolve). If big, innovative, and opulent is your thing, this is certainly the place to find it! Double rooms start at $130 and go up—and if you're really a big spender, you can get a two-floor "super-suite" for $1,100!

The **Omni International,** 1 CNN Center, Atlanta, GA 30335 (tel. 404/659-0000 or toll free 800/843-6664), anchors a modernistic megastructure that's now home of Ted Turner's Cable News Network. The marble lobby and tastefully luxurious guest rooms are very European. Doubles are in the $100 to $150 range. The hotel is across the street from the Georgia World's Congress Center and the Omni coliseum.

The **Hyatt Regency,** 265 Peachtree St. NE, Atlanta, GA 30303 (tel. 404/577-1234 or toll free 800/223-1234), was the first of Atlanta's "super hotels," and I confess to preferring it over many of the others. Its 23-story atrium lobby is somewhat more subdued, although it definitely is striking, with a gold and silver aluminum and stainless-steel sculpture that extends from the 2nd level to the 12th, much greenery, and glass elevators that go all the way to the blue-domed, revolving restaurant and cocktail lounge. This hotel, with 1,279 rooms and suites, has undergone a major renovation of all facilities. There's an outdoor pool, hot tub, several lounges, and four restaurants. Rates range from $100 to $375 for deluxe suites, with reduced $69 weekend rates and seasonal special rates.

The **Atlanta Hilton & Towers,** 255 Courtland St., at Harris Street, Atlanta, GA 30043 (tel. 404/659-2000, or toll free 800/445-8667), is downtown Atlanta's only resort hotel. Located just off I-75/85, in the heart of the business and entertainment district, the Hilton features lighted tennis courts, a jogging track, swimming pool, and a health club with an exercise room, whirlpool, and sauna. Seven restaurants and lounges include the four-star Nikolai's Roof, Café de la Paix, and Trader Vic's restaurants, a 24-hour coffeeshop, and Another World, the exotic nightclub atop the hotel. The International Shopping Mall houses gift and variety shops along with a hi-tech business support center. Double rooms run $119 to $159.

All-Suites

The **Guest Quarters-Perimeter Center,** 111 Perimeter Center West, Atlanta, GA 30346 (tel. 404/396-6800, or toll free 800/424-2900), is just off I-285, and furnishes courtesy transportation for nearby tennis and golf facilities. There are some 242 suites, surrounded by landscaped grounds, and the Perimeter Mall shopping center is just across the highway. Double-occupancy rates here are $145 for a one-bedroom suite, $170 for two bedrooms.

The Atlanta area has five **Residence Inns by Marriott,** which feature townhouse studio and penthouse suites in landscaped surroundings, as well as pools, whirlpools, fitness centers, a complimentary breakfast buffet, free grocery-shopping service, and complimentary hospitality hour on week nights. Rates fall in the $78 to $108 range for studios, $98 to $128 for penthouses (price decreases for stays of more than six nights). Toll-free telephone for all locations is 800/331-3131, and specific addresses are: Midtown, 1041 W. Peachtree St., Atlanta, GA 30309 (tel. 404/872-8885); Perimeter East, 1901 Savoy Dr., Atlanta, GA 30341 (tel. 404/455-4446); Perimeter West, 6096 Barfield Rd., Atlanta, GA 30328 (tel. 404/252-5066); Buckhead, 2960 Piedmont Rd. NE, Atlanta, GA 30305 (tel. 404/239-0677); Smyrna, 2771 Hargrove Rd., Smyrna, GA 30080 (tel. 404/433-8877).

Moderate

The Marriott Corporation has located six of its moderately priced **Courtyard By Marriott Hotels** in the metro Atlanta suburbs. Rooms are spacious, attractively furnished, and offer guests the use of swimming pools, restaurants, and lounges at rates in the $60 to $70 range for doubles on weekdays, lower rates on weekends. Area locations include: Atlanta Airport, 2050 Sullivan Rd., College Park, GA 30337 (tel. 404/997-2220); Northlake, 4083 Lavista Rd., at I-285, Tucker, GA 30329 (tel. 404/938-1200); Peachtree Corners, 3209 Holcomb Bridge Rd., Norcross, GA 30071 (tel. 404/446-3777); Peachtree-Dunwoody, 5601 Peachtree-Dunwoody Rd., Atlanta, GA 30346 (tel. 404/343-2300); Windy Hill Road, 2045 S. Park Pl., Smyrna, GA 30080 (tel. 404/955-3838); and Executive Park, 1236 Executive Park Dr., at I-85 North, Atlanta, GA 30329 (tel. 404/728-0708). Other locations are planned. For reservations nationwide phone toll free 800/321-2211.

In the downtown hotel and convention district, the spiffy new **Hotel Ibis,** 101 International Blvd., Atlanta, GA 30303 (tel. 404/524-5555), with doubles in the $59 to $89 range, including a complimentary buffet breakfast, has made a hit with budget travelers and people doing business at the nearby Atlanta Merchandise Mart and Apparel Mart. Rooms have a delightful French panache, and there's a good restaurant and bar.

The **Comfort Inn of Atlanta,** 120 North Ave., at I-75/85, Atlanta, GA 30313 (tel. 404/441-6788, or toll free 800/228-5150), is a small, well-kept chain motor hotel, convenient to Georgia Tech, Coca-Cola headquarters, and downtown Atlanta. Doubles are about $50.

The **Quality Inn Habersham Hotel,** 330 Peachtree St. NE, Atlanta, GA 30308 (tel. collect 404/577-1980, or toll free 800/241-4288), is a small, well-run hotel in downtown Atlanta which wears a charming European air. All guest rooms in this nine-story gem are spacious and recently redecorated, most with king-size beds, all with wet bar and fridge and comfortably elegant furnishings. A tastefully decorated sitting room leads to the Habersham Club, where a complimentary continental breakfast and a limited-menu dinner are served. Rates for doubles are $90, and there's free parking on the hotel premises (a money-saver in Atlanta!).

The conveniently located **Best Western Midtown,** 1470 Spring St. NW, Atlanta, GA 30309 (tel. 404/872-5821 or toll free 800/873-5820), also has free parking facilities, as well as a complimentary shuttle within the business district. Guest rooms have either two double beds or king-size beds, as well as in-room movies, and there's a pool and fitness room. Doubles are in the $75 to $95 range.

There is little to distinguish the chains from one another except location, although facilities do vary slightly. Those listed here can be assumed to have the standard, motel-quality rooms and decor, and I've added some of the nicer locally owned hostelries.

The **Holiday Inn–Downtown,** 175 Piedmont Ave. NE, Atlanta, GA 30303 (tel. 404/659-2727, or toll free 800/HOLIDAY), is within walking distance of Peachtree Street, the Civic Center, and several shopping plazas. The 470 rooms, most with 2 double beds, are available at an average rate of $90, and children under 18 stay free with their parents. An outdoor swimming pool, dining room (open from 6 a.m. to 10 p.m.), and two lounges, one with live entertainment, offer a choice of relaxed or active atmosphere. It's very much the same out at the **Holiday Inn–Airport,** 1380 Virginia Ave., Atlanta, GA 30344 (tel. 404/762-8411, or toll free 800/HOLIDAY), which is about seven miles from the city center. There's free shuttle-bus service to and from the airport, lighted tennis courts, sauna, pool, disco, and live entertainment in the lounges, and two restaurants. Doubles start at $70, and children under 18 stay free in the room with their parents.

The **Lanier Plaza Hotel,** I-85 at Monroe Drive, 418 Armour Dr., Atlanta, GA 30324 (tel. 404/873-4661, or toll free 800/554-8444), has a pool, restaurant, and lounge with entertainment. Double rooms, which are very attractively decorated, are in the $75 to $85 range, with no charge for children under 17 in the same room with their parents.

Stone Mountain Inn, Jefferson Davis Road, inside Stone Mountain Park, P.O. Box 775, Stone Mountain, GA 30086 (tel. 404/469-3311), is 16 miles east of the city, but there's public transportation on city buses from Stone Mountain Park, and it's a good location for avoiding city traffic. Rooms are especially comfortable and nicely decorated in 18th-century style. There's a heated pool (with a wading section for the kids and beverage service for the grown-ups). Rates are seasonal: $90 for double rooms from June 1 through Labor Day, a little lower other months.

Directly across from the Atlanta Merchandise Mart, only four blocks from the World Congress Center, a mile from the state capitol, and a half mile from the civic center, the **Days Inn Downtown Atlanta,** Spring Street at Baker Street, Atlanta, GA 30303 (tel. 404/523-1144, or toll free 800/325-2525), offers doubles for $70 to $80 and there's a restaurant and a pool.

Marriott's budget chain, the **Fairfield Inn,** has five locations in the Atlanta area. Guest rooms feature well-lit work desks, separate vanity areas, and either two double or one king-size bed. Rates run from $32 to $38, there's a discount for seniors, and the toll-free number for all locations is 800/228-2800. Locations: Airport, 2451 Old National Parkway, College Park, GA 30349; Gwinnett Mall, I-85 at Pleasant Hill Road, Duluth, GA 30136; Northlake, 2155 Ranchwood Dr., Northlake, GA 30345; Northwest, 2191 Northwest Parkway, Marietta, GA 30067; and Peachtree Corners, Peachtree Ind. Boulevard at Jones Mill Road, Norcross, GA 30092.

Bed and Breakfast

B&Bs are available in Atlanta in grand style—host homes range from modest, middle-class houses to some of the city's finest residences. And they're located in the downtown area, suburban neighborhoods, and even in Stone Mountain. So if this is your favorite way to get to know an area, you're sure to find one convenient to your personal interests. As a bonus, you'll probably effect even greater savings as local hosts clue you in to shopping bargains, entertainment, etc. As far in advance as possible, contact **Bed & Breakfast Atlanta,** 1801 Piedmont Ave., Suite 208, Atlanta, GA 30324 (tel. 404/875-0525). They carefully screen all host homes and will place you as near as possible to the section of the city you prefer. Rates run $32 to $60, with some exceptional lodgings in the $48 to $100 range. And that includes a continental breakfast.

Campgrounds

To the east of the city about 16 miles, the **Stone Mountain Campground** has 500 sites, full hookups, LP gas, showers, a laundry, supply store, restaurant, mini-golf, swimming, boating, and fishing. Rates begin at $10. To reach it, take I-285 to the Stone Mountain exit, then drive 7 ½ miles east on Ga. 78 to Stone Mountain Park and then follow the signs. For full details, write Stone Mountain Campground, P.O. Box 778, Stone Mountain, GA 30086 (tel. 404/498-5600).

ATLANTA'S RESTAURANTS

It's a point of pride among Atlantans that their town has more fine restaurants than any other major southern city (excluding, of course, New Orleans and Miami, each in a class by itself). Another point that should be made is that *real* southern cooking is surprisingly hard to come by in Atlanta's restaurants. What there is tends to be overdone, soggy, and far from the cuisine of southern homes (if you can wangle a dinner invitation "at home," you'll taste the real thing). There are two establishments that do a good job in this department, however, and because I've tried to emphasize regional cuisine throughout this book, these top my list of places to eat, even though neither is expensive or flashy —the important thing is that both are "southern."

To "Eat Southern"

Atlanta's best southern restaurant isn't in Atlanta at all, but in nearby Smyrna. I remember fondly the delicious meals and entertaining evenings I had at **Aunt Fanny's Cabin,** 2155 Campbell Rd., Smyrna (tel. 404/436-5218), when my home was in this area, but it's more than nostalgia—Aunt Fanny's is always the same when I return. Be forewarned, however, that the restaurant, in a former slave cabin, has a decided "plantation days" atmosphere in both the cuisine and its presentation. There really was an "Aunt Fanny" Williams, and this was her home (and some of the employees have worked here over 30 years). It's more than 130 years old and Aunt Fanny was in her 70s when she first began serving meals to the public in 1941. She bustled around the kitchen as long as she was able, then took to a rocking chair to personally greet guests. The fireplaces, the antique furniture, the old copper cookware hanging about, and the soft glow of candlelight in an essentially rustic setting all combine to re-create the world in which Aunt Fanny grew up (she died in 1949); and people from 59 countries have dined here over the years, including foreign ministers, cabinet members, state governors, senators, and countless entertainment personalities.

In all, it's a thoroughly delightful, very friendly place, and the food, too, is straight out of the Old South (in fact, many of the recipes were Aunt Fanny's). The menu is limited—fried chicken, Smithfield ham, charcoal-broiled steak, and fresh rainbow trout—and all entrees except fried chicken and steak are under $16. Vegetables are fresh, with a true home-cooked flavor—their baked squash belongs in a culinary hall of fame, as far as I'm concerned! All dishes are served family style, coming to the table in large dishes; and if there's chicken, for instance, left on the platter at the end of a meal, brown bags appear for you to take the remains home. Both beer and wine are served, and there's a bar that serves mint juleps along with other cocktails. Aunt Fanny's is open from 11:30 a.m. to 2 p.m. and 6 to 10 p.m. Monday through Friday, to 10:30 p.m. on Saturday, and from 1 to 10 p.m. on Sunday, and it's worth the drive for the experience.

On the northern edge of the downtown section, **Mary Mac's Tea Room,** 224 Ponce de Leon (tel. 404/875-4337), has been operated for more than a quarter of a century by Mrs. Margaret Lupo, now assisted by two of her six offspring. She advertises "southern hospitality with damyankee efficiency." With some 2,000 people served daily, they *have* to be efficient, but that doesn't seem to diminish either the hospitality or the quality of food. Fried chicken and country ham are really good here, and they—like Aunt Fanny's—do an especially good job with fresh vegetables and hot breads. Mary Mac's is open from 11 a.m. to 4 p.m. for lunch, 5 to 8 p.m. for dinner, and prices are very moderate: most dinners (meat, three vegetables, bread, and beverage) run $6 to $9, with a 10% discount to college students who show an ID card. Look for **Mary Mac's To Go** at 5674 Roswell Rd. (tel. 404/252-4819).

Expensive

The Dining Room of the **Ritz-Carlton Buckhead Hotel**, 3434 Peachtree Rd. NE (tel. 404/237-2700). Atlanta's most fashionable hotel boasts one of its loveliest dining rooms. Much-awarded chef Guenther Seeger creates nouvelle cuisine with celestial finesse and style in this beautiful, darkly romantic room, with its fresh flowers and English hunting portraits. Sauces, even Seeger's luscious-looking desserts, are so light you may sample several dishes and still leave feeling comfortably happy. Lunch is served Monday through Friday from 11:30 a.m. to 2:30 p.m., and dinner is Monday through Saturday from 6 to 10 p.m. A full dinner for two with wine will cost about $80 to $100.

The **Abbey,** 163 Ponce de Leon Ave. NE (tel. 404/876-8532), has won more culinary awards than perhaps any other Atlanta restaurant. Located in a renovated (converted?) church, the restaurant is lovely, with lots of stained glass, waiters in monks' robes, and candlelight giving a soft glow to the whole scene. Essentially French country cuisine dominates the menu, with specialties such as feuillêté d'agneau (roasted stuffed lamb in pastry), tournedos Provençale and saumon aux truffes. The wine cellar is outstanding. Prices are in the $18 to $30 range, and hours are 6 to 11 p.m. daily, except for major holidays.

For sheer elegance, I don't believe any Atlanta restaurant outdoes **Nikolai's Roof Restaurant,** Courtland and Harris streets, on the 30th floor of the Atlanta Hilton and Towers (tel. 404/659-2000). And that elegance extends to decor, cuisine, and service—all are well nigh perfect. Prices are high, but they represent, in the best sense of the phrase, value for dollar. Cuisine varies according to season, but it's basically continental, with Russian specialties. The wine list is one of the best in the city. The prix fixe, five-course dinner is $55, hours are 6:30 to 9:30 p.m. daily, and reservations are a must.

Hedgerose Heights Inn, 490 E. Paces Ferry Rd., Buckhead (tel. 404/233-7673). Old-world grandeur, attentive service, and imaginative American, Swiss, and French cuisine by owner Heinz Schwab make Hedgerose a memorable dining experience. Dinner is served from 6:30 to 10 p.m. Tuesday through Saturday, and a meal for two with wine runs about $85 to $120.

LaGrotta Ristorante Italiano, 2637 Peachtree Rd. NE (tel. 404/231-1368). Northern Italian pastas, seafood, veal, and chicken dishes are at their absolute finest in this lively subterranean dining room that crackles with self-confidence and good cheer. Dinner is served Monday through Saturday 6 to 10:30 p.m. Dinner for two with wine costs about $75 to $90.

Ruth Chris Steak House, 950 E. Paces Ferry Rd., Buckland (tel. 404/365-0660), with a stunning contemporary dining room, has taken Atlanta beef lovers by storm. Aged prime strips, filets, and rib eyes, served on sizzling hot platters, are the hallmark. The large menu also features seafood, excellent side dishes, a large wine list, and super desserts like blueberry cheesecake and New Orleans–style praline freezes. Hours are Monday through Friday from 11 a.m. to 11 p.m., and on Saturday and Sunday from 4 to 11 p.m. Dinner for two, with wine, will run about $70 to $80.

Moderate

Two blocks south of Atlanta's famous Fox Theater, the **Pleasant Peasant,** 555 Peachtree St. (tel. 404/874-3223), is in what used to be a Victorian ice-cream parlor, which, although renovated, retains much of that old style. Live plants and antiques scattered about give it an almost intimate atmosphere. They don't accept reservations, and it's always crowded, but the service is consistently good. There is a daily special (might be veal paprikash, a specialty), and other menu items include scallops parisienne and pork piquant at prices ranging from $10 to $20. There is full bar service and a respectable wine list. Dinner hours are 5:30 p.m. to midnight every day except Friday and Saturday, when they serve until 1 a.m.

Those of us who find Greek food irresistible will want to return again and again to **Niko's Greek Restaurant,** 1789 Cheshire Bridge Rd. (tel. 404/872-1254). Nikos Letsos, his wife, Anna, and their three daughters run this marvelous place in northeast Atlanta, creating an atmosphere which is both relaxing and zestful at the same time, something that seems to come naturally to Greeks. Begin with specialties like the saganaki appetizer, which is flamed at your table with accompanying shouts of "Opa" from waiters and other diners. And the Zorba Special—a combination plate of moussaka, pastitsio, and dolmades served with Greek beans and Greek salad—will bring you to your feet with "Opas" of your own. Then there are those luscious Greek desserts like baklava and rizogalo. All to the accompaniment of Greek music. Makes me hungry just remembering my last feast at this friendly and lively place! Prices are extremely moderate, in the $8 to $14 range, and there's a "Menu for Little Greeks." Hours are 11 a.m. to 11 p.m. Monday through Thursday, to 11:30 p.m. on Friday, from noon to 11:30 p.m. on Saturday.

Camille's, 1186 N. Highland Ave. (tel. 404/872-7203), is straight out of Italian New York. The perpetually busy little place does a land-office business in such temptations as stuffed artichokes; linguine pie; mussels, clams, shrimp, and squid in rich red sauces; and chicken and pastas of all sorts. Save room for ricotta cheesecake and espresso. In warm weather, find places at the red-checkered picnic tables outside. Lunch and dinner are on from 11 a.m. to 11 p.m. daily. Dishes start at about $6, and go up to $15 for some specials. Camille's is three blocks north of the lively Virginia/Highland corner.

Looking for a good steak at moderate prices? Head for one of the seven **Longhorn Steak Restaurant & Saloons** around town. There's one at 2151 Peachtree Rd. (tel. 404/351-6086), about halfway between downtown and Buckhead. They're open daily from 11:30 a.m. to 11 p.m. Two of you can dine very well, with drinks and side dishes for $35 or less.

Budget

"Budget" doesn't have to mean "fast food" in Atlanta. Consider the following: **Aunt Charley's,** 3107 Peachtree Rd. NE (tel. 404/231-8503), where a satisfying meal of homemade soups, daily specials, outstanding salads, entrees, and sandwiches will cost no more than $3 to $8 (open from 11:30 a.m. to 2 a.m. every day).

The Colonnade, 1879 Cheshire Bridge Rd. NE (tel. 404/874-5642), has been an Atlanta favorite for more than 30 years. Like a cheerful American restaurant of the 1950s, this friendly place serves delicious breakfasts, and moderately, even cheaply, priced steaks, chops, seafoods, southern fried chicken, and vegetables every day. Breakfast is from 7 to 10 a.m.; lunch, 11 a.m. to 2:30 p.m.; and dinner, 5 to 9 p.m.

Touch of India, 970 Peachtree St. (tel. 404/876-7777), serves spicy Indian curries, tandooris, vegetarian creations, and breads to appreciative intown adventurers at very modest prices. Lunch is served Monday through Friday from 11:30 a.m. to 2:30 p.m.; dinner, daily from 5 to 11 p.m.

If you're a born shopper and plan to spend a lot of time in Atlanta's fabulous malls, eating won't break the budget. At Lenox Square shopping center, there are simply too many to name—just look around when your feet begin to hurt and you're sure to spot one.

There are 11 locations of the **Old Hickory House** around Atlanta, all serving barbecued pork, beef, chicken, and ribs at prices that range from budget to moderate. If southern barbecue is a weakness, keep an eye out for their sign— I've had better in the South, but the Hickory House brand is above average. All locations feature a rustic decor and prices that range from $4 to $10. Hours vary, but most are open from 11 a.m. to 10:30 p.m., some until 11 p.m.

Just a couple of blocks from the Georgia Tech campus (alongside I-75 and I-85 where North Avenue crosses over the highway) is an Atlanta institution— the **Varsity Drive-In.** Now, maybe a drive-in doesn't qualify as a "restaurant," but for budget eating, you just can't beat the Varsity, and some 16,000 people a day agree with me. The food is good, service (both carside and inside, where they have seats and stand-up eating counters) is excellent and very fast, and prices are definitely budget for the hot-dog, hamburger, french-fries fare. They're open 24 hours daily.

There are an even dozen **Morrison's cafeterias** around town. Locations include 1025 Virginia Ave., near Hartsfield International Airport (tel. 404/761-8066); and Ansley Mall shopping center, Piedmont Avenue and Monroe Drive (tel. 404/872-8091). Open seven days, with continuous service from lunch through dinner.

For Cheese-Lovers

It's hard to know just *where* to list the two locations of **Dante's Down the Hatch,** 3380 Peachtree Road, across the street from Lenox Square (tel. 404/266-1600) and Underground Atlanta (tel. 404/577-1800). Because both menus are made up largely of cheese trays, cheese and beef fondues, and four complete fondue dinners, I'm not sure these establishments qualify as restaurants. On the other hand, if you are a dedicated cheese-lover, as I am, Dante's should top all other eating spots on your Atlanta list. Never mind the unique settings, service by people who know and care about cheeses, and superb entertainment (more about that in the nightlife section)—it's the *cheeses* under discussion here. As every cheese-lover knows, ordering brie in a restaurant is chancy, to say the least. It has to be the most temperamental of them all, and I've nibbled at underripe, "green" brie, spooned up runny, overripe brie, and just walked away from brie impossible to eat for whatever mysterious reason. Not so at Dante's. The cheese board that arrives at my table always holds a brie worthy of a poetic hymn of praise, and I have it on good authority (Atlanta friends who are regulars, backed up by Jerry Margolis, longtime manager here) that this is no accident—when the unpredictable delicacy doesn't measure up, it comes off the menu. For my money, that speaks volumes for these two places. Fondues are prepared with imported cheeses and loving care, and if you're in the mood for meat, the quality of beef is just as good as that brie. Restaurant, nightspot, or whatnot, Dante's Down the Hatch is a cheese-lover's haven. It's open seven days a week from 4 p.m. to 1 a.m., and prices are in the $10 to $20 range. Reservations are urged at both locations.

READER'S DINING SELECTION:"We had the most outstanding meal on our trip at **Pano's and Paul's,** 1232 W. Paces Ferry Rd. (tel. 404/261-4739). It's not cheap but if you stay away from the wine and the coffee Diablo, I would guess a couple could dine sumptuously for under $40. This is a top-drawer place" (G. Reeves, Philadelphia, Pa.).

ATLANTA NIGHTLIFE

If there is one thing Atlanta is rich in, it's nightlife—of all kinds! There is a dinner-theater, symphony, ballet, nightclub, lounge music (country-and-western, jazz, and rock-and-roll), cabaret, and almost any other kind of nocturnal entertainment you could name. Most hotels and motels distribute free the publications *Where, Key—This Week in Atlanta,* or *After Hours,* all good guides for where to find what. And for a complete rundown on what's going on while you're there, pick up the Saturday edition of the *Atlanta Constitution* (the local morning newspaper) with its "Weekend" amusement section. Depending on the time of year, you'll see listed performances by the Atlanta Symphony Orchestra and Chamber Chorus, the Atlanta Ballet (the country's oldest regional company), the Southern Ballet of Atlanta, the Ruth Mitchell Dance Company, the Academy Theatre, Alliance Theatre, and scores of other concerts or other cultural events. And no matter when you come to town, you'll find entertainment at the following:

Theater, Nightclubs, Cabarets, Etc.

The **Alliance Theatre** 1280 Peachtree St. (tel. 404/892-2414), which presents some 12 productions each season (September through May) by its resident troupe of performers on its two stages, plus the Atlanta Symphony Orchestra in a full season of orchestral and choral concerts.

My own longtime favorite after-dark has been **Dante's Down the Hatch,** across the street from Lenox Square (3380 Peachtree Road; tel. 404/266-1600), with entertainment, and those cheeses I carried on so about earlier. There's a second location in Atlanta Underground. Let me tell you about that decor: Dante has created the illusion of a pirate ship tied up to an old Mediterranean wharf, and the result is an engaging spot that combines fun with sophistication. In the "wharf" section, there is jazz, classical and flamenco guitar until 8 p.m. nightly. The Paul Mitchell Trio is on hand in the "ship" section. Paul is a jazz pianist who ranks with the greats, and his sidemen match his brilliant artistry. As for the "crew," most have been aboard for a long time, and all really make you feel cared for. Then, of course, there are those cheeses, fondues, special drinks, and an excellent wine list. Add to this the fact that Dante himself is always on hand to see that you have a good time, and you have a truly outstanding place to spend an evening. It's so popular that reservations are really a "must," and there's an entertainment charge of $4 per person after 8 p.m. on the ship ($5 on Friday and Saturday).

Dante's Buckhead neighborhood is the liveliest entertainment zone in town. Much of the fun is conveniently clustered around the triangular junction of Peachtree, Roswell, and East and West Paces Ferry roads. **Blues Harbor,**

3179 Peachtree Rd. (tel. 404/261-6717), features a revolving lineup of Chicago-style blues and jazz artists. Across the way at 3166 Peachtree Rd. (tel. 404/231-8666), **Tom Foolery** is one of the city's best-loved little clubs. Once the show starts, the magic pranks and surprises fly nonstop. The Foolery is just around a literal corner from Olde England and Ireland. The **Churchill Arms Pub,** 3223 Cains Hill Pl. (tel. 404/233-5633), lures local anglophiles with Bass ale, darts, a sing-along piano, and big pictures of Charles and Di; across the street at 56 E. Andrews Dr. (tel. 404/262-2227), the **County Cork Pub** headlines Guinness stout, Harp ale, and balladeers from Ireland.

The affluent yuppie set currently favors the bar and outdoor patio of **Peachtree Café,** 268 E. Paces Ferry Rd. (tel. 404/233-4402). Also in vogue is **Rio Bravo Cantina,** a campy Tex-Mex eatery and bar with delicious fajitas and margaritas and live mariachi music at 3172 Roswell Rd. (tel. 404/262-7431). **Jerry Farber's Club,** 54 Pharr Rd. (tel. 404/237-5181) is an intimate bistro with top-notch jazz.

The **Punch Line,** 80 Hildebrand Ave., Sandy Springs (tel. 404/252-5233), keeps 'em laughing with locally and nationally known comedians at this location and at 3250 Northlake Pkwy., Northlake.

Limelight, 3330 Piedmont Rd. (tel. 404/231-3520), is Atlanta's best-known nightclub. The cavernous complex of bars and a vast disco floor are equipped with the latest hi-tech sound and light effects, and attract a gaudy crowd of locals and visiting firemen. It's about the best place in town to spot movie, TV, and sports celebrities.

ATLANTA SHOPPING

There's no doubt about it, Atlanta is undoubtedly the best shopping city in the Southern Atlantic region, with regional shopping centers on or near every one of the metropolitan freeways. Downtown Atlanta is far from being a depressed shopping area drained off by these outlying malls, however, and there are two outstanding places to spend your money right at its heart.

Macy's Department Store (formerly Davison's), at 180 Peachtree St., at Ellis Street (tel. 404/221-7500), has received a major glamorization during the past few years, and is truly dazzling. Macy's Cellar is a fun place to browse for gourmet cookware and fancy foods, and to enjoy a pub-style lunch.

The **Peachtree Center Shopping Gallery,** two blocks north of Macy's, has also put on a chic new face. Numerous small shops and eateries are tucked into the three-level gallery, which connects via covered bridge with the Hyatt Regency and Marriott Marquis hotels. There's also a MARTA rapid-rail station.

Buckhead, a little north of the downtown area, has **Lenox Square,** with more than 130 stores in its enclosed mall, and **Phipps Plaza,** diagonally across the intersection, with branches of New York stores such as Saks Fifth Avenue, Lord & Taylor, and Tiffany & Co.

SPORTS

When I lived near Atlanta (about two decades ago), the city was as sports-happy as it is today. The only difference is that then it was concerned primarily with collegiate events, and now (while college competitions *still* keep alumni glued to TV sets and the bookies busy) it has added professional teams that elicit the same sort of loyalty.

Depending on which season finds you in Atlanta, call the following number for sports information: **Braves** baseball, 404/522-7630; **Falcons** football, 404/261-5400; **Hawks** basketball, 404/681-3600; **International Raceway** (auto), 404/946-4211.

SIGHTSEEING IN ATLANTA

Before you start out sightseeing, contact the **Atlanta Convention and Visitors Bureau,** Harris Tower, Suite 200P, 233 Peachtree St. NE, Atlanta, GA 30303 (tel. 404/521-6688), or go by the welcome center at Peachtree Center Mall, Lenox Square Mall, or at the airport.

The **Carter Presidential Center,** at North Highland and Cleburne avenues (tel. 404/331-3942), is a "must-see" for every visitor. Two miles east of downtown, with the skyline as dramatic backdrop, the center's four contemporary circular buildings are set among 30 acres of trees, gardens, lakes, and waterfalls. Inside are thousands of documents, photos, gifts, and memorabilia of Jimmy Carter's White House years. The center is also a tribute to all who have held our nation's highest office. You may walk into a full-scale reproduction of the Oval Office. On a keyboard and video monitor, choose your response to a terrorist crisis, and watch as President Carter spells out the consequences. Photos follow Carter from his boyhood in Plains, through his navy career, state politics, and the presidency. Gifts range from splendid silver, ivory, and crystal from heads of state, to paintings and peanut carving from admirers around the world. *Presidents,* a 30-minute film, looks at the crises and triumphs that hallmarked past administrations. You may have a light lunch, with a view of the gardens, in the center's restaurant. It's open daily from 9 a.m. to 5 p.m. Adults pay $2.50 admission; under age 16, no charge.

If you come looking for Margaret Mitchell's *Gone with the Wind* antebellum Atlanta, you won't find it, thanks to General Sherman, who burned it all down in 1864. However, it's worth the time and effort to drive northwest of the city's business district (five miles or so out Peachtree Street) to Peachtree Battle Avenue, then left to Habersham Drive, Northside Drive, West Paces Ferry Road (that's the **governor's mansion** at no. 391, by the way, and it's open from 10 to 11:45 a.m. Tuesday through Thursday at no charge), to Tuxedo Road. It's in a residential area that can, despite its more recent vintage, rival any antebellum section, with dogwoods, azaleas, magnolias, and some of the most beautiful private residences you could find anywhere in the country.

A short drive to the little community of **Roswell,** just north of Atlanta, will also take you back to pre–Civil War days. There are a number of homes of that vintage which have either been preserved through continuous residency or restored by enthusiastic and appreciative new owners. The childhood home of President Theodore Roosevelt's mother, Bulloch Hall, is in Roswell. There's a visitors center at 227 S. Atlanta St. (tel. 404/992-1665).

Right in the center of town, a four-block tract of Atlanta's history lies beneath newer city streets. Called **Underground Atlanta,** this was an empty catacomb that lay deserted and gathering dust for the better part of a century when railroad viaducts were built over its rococo buildings in post–Civil War days. Then a group of far-sighted and determined Atlanta businessmen decided to restore the crumbling area, and the result was an authentic, completely charming picture of Atlanta in the 1800s. Then, over the years, the historic "city beneath a city" became a little shabby, so much so that in 1977 a new renovation effort was mounted. For a time after that the Underground fairly sparkled with specialty shops, restaurants, and bars—even street entertainment. Then another decline set in and the Underground was closed.

In 1989, a massive redevelopment of the Underground was completed, and it opened with more than 200 establishments, including shops, restaurants, and nightspots. Dante's Down the Hatch is here, as is Ruby Red's Warehouse (a sing-along Dixieland jazz club and restaurant), both tenants before the decline set in; and scheduled for a 1990 opening is the Coca-Cola Pavilion, dedicated to the history and international appeal of this native drink. You really shouldn't leave Atlanta without at least one visit to the Underground—this is, after all, literally the point at which Atlanta was born, with the planting of Zero Milepost in 1837.

The **Martin Luther King National Historic District,** 449 Auburn Ave. (tel. 404/524-1956 or 331-3919), includes the major landmarks of the civil-rights leader's life. His white marble tomb, with an eternal flame symbolizing his dream of a brotherhood of mankind, is the heart of the Freedom Hall complex. You may also view a multimedia presentation on his life; tour Ebenezer Baptist Church, where he was pastor and from which he was buried; and walk one block east to the Victorian home where he was born on January 15, 1929. The two-square block area is included in the Martin Luther King, Jr. National Historic District. National Park Service rangers, headquartered across the street from Freedom Hall, lead half-hour walking tours of the neighborhood. The tomb and other outdoor areas may be visited without charge, but donations are requested at Ebenezer Church, the birthplace, and the film. Open daily.

Much of your Atlanta sightseeing will be concentrated in **Grant Park,** between Cherokee Avenue and Boulevard SE. There are miles and miles of walkways and roads through the park, some of them along the breastwork built for the city's defense in 1864. This is where you'll find **Zoo Atlanta,** 800 Cherokee Ave., Atlanta, GA 30315 (tel. 404/624-5600). As we were going to press, the zoo was undergoing a complete redevelopment, building natural habitats for all the animals which simulate their native environments. There will be an African rain forest with four resident gorilla families and a walk-through aviary; and an East African savanna, with lions, giraffes, rhinos, ostriches, and many others. Admission is $6.25 for adults, $3.25 for ages 3 through 11; and hours are 10 a.m. to 5 p.m. daily, till 6 p.m. on weekends between Memorial Day and Labor Day.

For a breathtaking view of the Battle of Atlanta, go by the neoclassical building that houses the **Cyclorama,** 800 Cherokee Ave. in Grant Park (tel. 404/624-1071), a 42-foot-high, 356-foot-circumference, 100-year-old painting with a 3-dimensional foreground and special lighting, music, and sound effects. It's impressive, and when you see the monumental work, you'll know why Sherman made that famous "War is hell" remark! This is one of only three cycloramas in the U.S., and it has recently been fully restored—it's an artistic and historical treasure not to be missed. There are 15 shows daily, from 9:30 a.m. to 4:30 p.m. Adults pay $3.50; senior citizens, $3; children 6 through 12, $2; and those under 6, free.

The **state capitol,** built in 1884, is on Capitol Square, and the gold-topped dome stands 237 feet above the city. Besides a **hall of fame** (with busts of famous Georgians), and a **hall of flags** (with U.S., state, and Confederate battle flags), it houses the **Georgia State Museum,** which is free and open from 8 a.m. to 5:30 p.m. Monday through Friday. In the museum, you'll find collections of Georgia minerals and Indian artifacts, dioramas of famous places in the state, and fish and wildlife exhibits.

Remember the "Uncle Remus" stories? Well, Joel Chandler Harris, who created the **Uncle Remus** character through whose voice he recorded Afro-American folk tales, lived at 1050 Gordon St. SW (tel. 404/753-8535), in the Wren's Nest (so named for the wrens who nested in his mailbox). The **Wren's Nest** is a national historic landmark and has the original family furnishings, photographs, and memorabilia. The beautiful Victorian house is currently undergoing restoration and is open for guided tours Tuesday through Saturday from 10 a.m. to 4 p.m., and Sundays from 2 to 4 p.m., closed Monday and major holidays. Tours are given on the hour and half hour. Admission is $3 for adults, $2 for seniors and teens, and $1 for ages 4 through 12. The Wren's Nest also sponsors special storytelling programs for the public.

The **SciTrek-Science and Technology Museum of Atlanta,** 395 Piedmont Ave. NE (tel. 404/522-5500), is in the downtown Atlanta Civic Center. It's a hands-on science museum where you participate in interactive exhibits that have you lifting an automobile engine with one hand, hearing a whisper across a room, and turning your body into a battery. It's open Tuesday through Sunday from 10 a.m. to 5 p.m., with admission of $5 for adults, $3 for ages 3 through 17.

In the Robert W. Woodruff Arts Center, 1280 Peachtree St. NE, the **High Museum of Art** (tel. 404/892-4444) houses impressive collections of Western art, African art, and first-rate traveling exhibitions. Hours are 10 a.m. to 5 p.m. Tuesday through Saturday (until 9 p.m. on Wednesday), from noon on Sunday, with a $4 admission charge for adults, $2 for seniors, $1 for ages 6 through 17; no charge on Thursday.

About 12 miles west of downtown, just off I-20 West, the **Six Flags Over Georgia** theme park, 7561 Six Flags Rd., is one of the best in the country. There are more than 100 rides (including the giant "Great American Scream Machine" roller coaster), a multitude of shows, and several restaurants. The $17.50 admission charge covers all rides and shows. Ages 55 and over and children 42 inches tall and under pay $10.95. It's open late May through Labor Day from 10 a.m. to 10 p.m., seven days a week (until midnight on Friday and Saturday); weekends only other times (call 404/948-9290 for specific information, or write P.O. Box 43187, Atlanta, GA 30378). The park is dedicated to Georgia's history under the flags of England, France, Spain, the Confederacy, Georgia, and the U.S. Hours and prices are subject to change, so call to check.

Off U.S. 78/Stone Mountain Freeway, 16 miles east of downtown, **Stone Mountain Park** (tel. 404/498-5600), in Stone Mountain, is one of the Southern Atlantic region's premier attractions. More than six million visitors, second only to Walt Disney World, flock to the 3,200-acre park each year to enjoy a wealth of attractions and recreation. Foremost, of course, is the world's largest granite monolith, which rises from a 5-mile circumference to 825 feet. Carved on its sheer north flank is the world's largest sculpture, a 90-by-190 foot carving of Confederate heroes Robert E. Lee, Thomas "Stonewall" Jackson, and President Jefferson Davis. You can take a Swiss skylift to the top, or hike up an easy trail on the other side. Elsewhere in the park you can play golf, swim from a sand beach, visit an authentic antebellum plantation, an antique auto and music museum, and ride around the mountain's base on a steam locomotive. There's also an ice skating rink, biking, fishing, and campgrounds, all done in extremely good taste. One-time admission to the park is $4 per car, $15 for an annual permit. The six major attractions—skylift, auto/music museum, railroad, riverboat, plantation, wildlife trails—are each $2.50 for adults, $1.50 for children ages 4 to 11. Golf greens fees are $15 for 18 holes Tuesday through Friday, $17 on Saturday and Sunday. RV sites in the campground are $8.50 for partial hookups and $9.50 for full hookups. Tent sites are $8 per night. You can also stay at the Stone Mountain Inn (see "Where to Stay," above). The park is open daily year around: in summer from 10 a.m. to 9 p.m., in other seasons from 10 a.m. to 5:30 p.m.

Tours

Gray Line, 3745 Zip Industrial Blvd. (tel. 404/767-0594), has a "Grand Circle" tour that can run from $15 to $20, depending on how "grand" you want your "circle" to be. They also have a *great* "Gone with the Wind" tour that lasts about 4½ hours and visits old plantations around Atlanta. Call for specific dates and times (it doesn't run every day).

P.S.

Speaking of *Gone with the Wind,* you can view the movie any day of the week at the CNN Cinema 6 Theater, CNN Center (tel. 404/827-2491). There are two showings daily (call for exact schedules). If you haven't seen it, don't miss this opportunity.

XVI

CENTRAL AND WESTERN GEORGIA

1. EXCURSIONS FROM ATLANTA
2. PINE MOUNTAIN
3. PLAINS AND OTHER AREA ATTRACTIONS

This inland section of Georgia is the land of Scarlett O'Hara, peach orchards, pecan groves, and Jimmy Carter. It is also a land of giant textile mills, pulp and paper plants, and manufacturing centers for automobiles, metal, chemicals, and furniture that bear the definite stamp of the New South. Which is not to say that Georgia, which suffered mightily under the heel of General Sherman during the Civil War, does not retain and value its Old South heritage. It does, and there are symbols of it everywhere. But primarily, this part of the state looks forward, not backward.

1. Excursions from Atlanta

Besides its own long list of attractions, Atlanta is a good jumping-off point for a multitude of sights and activities—both historical and modern, natural and man-made. I'll start with—

Antebellum Georgia
If you looked for antebellum Georgia around Atlanta, you were in the right church but the wrong pew. The state's pre–Civil War moonlight-and-magnolias romance lives on, 60 to 100 miles east of Atlanta in charming towns with patriotic names like Washington, Madison, Monticello, Milledgeville, Eatonton, and a host of others.

Madison, off I-20 an hour's drive from Atlanta, is most people's favorite. Late in 1864, with Atlanta in flames behind them, Gen. William T. Sherman's Union juggernaut reached Madison's outskirts. Happily for us, they were met by former U.S. Senator Joshua Hill, a secession opponent who'd known Sherman in Washington. Old ties prevailed, and the town was spared. Stop first at the **Madison-Morgan Cultural Center,** 434 S. Main St., which is U.S. 441 (tel. 404/342-4743). The red-brick schoolhouse, circa 1895, displays a delightful collection of vintage tools and furniture, Civil War artifacts and photos, and an early 1800s log house. Live programs range from Shakespeare and Gilbert & Sullivan, to gospel singing and clog dancing. It's open Monday through Friday from 10 a.m. to 4:30 p.m., on Saturday and Sunday from 2 to 5 p.m. Adults pay $2, students, $1 (free on Wednesday).

Pick up a self-guided walking-tour map and other information at the center and walk past the majestic Greek Revival, Federal, Georgian, neoclassical, and Victorian homes lining Main Street, Academy Street, Old Post Road, and the pretty courthouse square. You'll also find plenty of places to purchase antiques and handcrafts. When you're famished, stop by **Ye Old Colonial Restaurant,** on the square (tel. 404/342-2211), a Victorian bank building where you can "cash in" on excellent southern cooking at very modest prices Monday through Saturday.

East of Madison, **Washington** has even more antebellum homes. Landmarks include the **Washington-Wilkes Historical Museum,** 308 E. Robert Toombs Ave. (tel. 404/678-2105), open Tuesday through Saturday from 10 a.m. to 5 p.m. Adults pay $1, children, 50¢. Also, check out the **home of Robert Toombs,** the Confederacy's flamboyant secretary of state, at 216 Robert Toombs Ave. (tel. 404/678-2226), open Tuesday through Saturday from 9 a.m. to 5 p.m., and on Sunday from 2 to 5:30 p.m. Admission is $1 for adults, 50¢ for children. Head for lunch at **Another Thyme,** a delightful spot on the courthouse square (tel. 404/678-1672).

Just 20 miles southeast of Washington, **Liberty Hall,** at sleepy little Crawfordville, was the home of Confederate Vice-President Alexander Hamilton Stephens. The adjoining **Confederate Museum** (tel. 404/456-2221) has an extensive collection of Civil War memorabilia. It's open Tuesday through Saturday from 9 a.m. to 5 p.m., and on Sunday from 2 to 5:30 p.m. Adults are charged $1.50; children, 75¢. Don't leave Crawfordville without stopping by **Mrs. Bonner's Café** (tel. 404/456-2347), across from the red-brick courthouse. The delightful Mrs. "B" has served her legendary sweet-tater pie and other southern favorites for more than 50 years. You may camp out, swim, and fish at **Alexander Stephens State Park,** near Liberty Hall (tel. 404/456-2602).

South of Madison on U.S. 441, **Eatonton** was the birthplace of author Joel Chandler Harris. Look for the statue of Br'er Rabbit on the courthouse lawn. The **Uncle Remus Museum** has a wonderful collection of memorabilia about Br'er Rabbit, Br'er Fox, and Harris's other storybook critters. It's open Tuesday through Saturday from 9 a.m. to 5 p.m., on Sunday from 2 to 5:30 p.m. Adults pay $1; children, 50¢.

South of Eatonton, **Milledgeville** was Georgia's capital from 1803 to 1868. Like Madison, it was miraculously spared Sherman's wrath, and today is a treasure trove of antebellum architecture. Pick up a guided-tour map at the **Baldwin County Chamber of Commerce,** 130 S. Jefferson St., and walk back into history. The **Old Governors Mansion,** a pink-marble Palladian-style beauty at 120 S. Clark St. (tel. 912/453-4545), has been exquisitely restored and refurnished as the home of the president of Georgia College. You may tour the antique-rich public rooms Tuesday through Saturday from 9 a.m. to 5 p.m., and on Sunday from 2 to 5 p.m. Admission is $1 for adults, 50¢ for children. Fans of the late author Flannery O'Connor (*The Violent Bear It Away*, *A Good Man Is Hard to Find*) should see her memorial room in the library of **Georgia College.**

You can temper all this history with delicious relaxation at **Hard Labor Creek State Park** (tel. 404/557-2863), near Madison. *Golf* magazine rates the park's scenic 18-hole course as one of the finest public courses in America. You can also swim at a sand beach, fish for bass and catfish, and hike the 5,000 wooded acres. The park has 49 campsites with electricity, water, rest rooms, and showers for $7 a night; and 20 fully furnished cottages at $45 for two bedrooms, $55 for three bedrooms. Rates are slightly higher on weekends. For more information, call the number above or write: Superintendent, Hard Labor Creek State Park, Rutledge, GA 30663.

Hard Labor Creek is just one of scores of parks in Georgia's excellent system. From the mountains down to the coast, they're great places to break your trip for a day or so, or spend an entire vacation. For information, contact Georgia Natural Resources Department, Parks, Recreation & Historic Sites Division, 205 Butler St. SE, Atlanta, GA 30334 (tel. toll free 800/542-7275, 800/342-7275 in Georgia).

Northeast Georgia Mountains

For a metropolitan area of 2½ million, Atlanta is amazingly close to nature. Within 70 to 120 miles, or about a 1½- to 2½-hour drive, city dwellers can hike through national forests and test their mettle on the rugged Appalachian Trail, scale Georgia's highest peak, fish trout streams, and canoe and swim in mountain lakes. They may come up for a day and browse Tyrolean shops in an "Alpine village," and see the site of America's first gold rush. At dusk, they can return home, or stay over in a comfortable lodge, a country inn, or a fully furnished state-park cottage or campground.

About 70 miles north of Atlanta, the little town of **Dahlonega** is ideal as a one-day mini-adventure, or the start of a longer exploration. Back in 1828 a trapper named Benjamin Parks stubbed his toe on a rock and uncovered a vein of gold that quickly sent prospectors streaming into the hills, so the story goes. Dahlonega is a Cherokee Indian word, meaning "precious yellow," and until the Civil War, the precious substance flowed into a major U.S. Treasury mint. Although it's no longer a major industry, enough gold is still around to periodically releaf the dome of Georgia's state capitol, and intrigue visitors who pan for it at **Crisson's Mine,** outside town (tel. 404/864-6363).

True to its heritage, Dahlonega's public square sports a rustic yesteryear look. Old galleried brick buildings and stores have been turned into shops purveying gold-panning equipment, gold jewelry, mountain handcrafts, antiques, ice cream, and fudge. In the center of the square, the red-brick **Gold Museum** chronicles the history of the gold rush and the many mines that flourished in these parts. A 28-minute film is especially worthwhile. Operated by the Georgia Parks Department, the museum is open Tuesday through Saturday from 9 a.m. to 5 p.m., and on Sunday from 2 to 5:30 p.m. Adults pay $1.50; ages 6 to 12, 75¢.

Dahlonega's second-most-famous landmark is just off the square. The **Smith House,** 202 S. Chestatee St. (tel. 404/864-3566), is renowned for its monumental family-style southern buffets that include fried chicken, ham, roast beef, barbecue, a dozen or more vegetables, relishes, cornbread and biscuits, and dessert for about $12 per person. Breakfast is served on Saturday and Sunday only, from 7 to 10 a.m. Lunch is offered Tuesday through Friday from 11 a.m. to 3 p.m., and dinner Tuesday through Sunday from 5 to 8 p.m.

A block away, the **Worley Homestead,** 410 W. Main St., Dahlonega, GA 30533 (tel. 404/864-7002), is one of northern Georgia's most charming bed-and-breakfast inns. Seven guest rooms in the circa-1845 home are furnished with antiques. Rates of $50 to $60 double include a whopping southern breakfast.

From Dahlonega, U.S. 19 winds scenically north into the mountains, toward one of the state's prettiest parks. At Neel's Gap, take a break at the **Mountain Crossing/Walasi-Yi Center.** The stone-and-log building is a legacy of the depression-era Civilian Conservation Corps, and a landmark on the Appalachian Trail, which crosses here on its way to Maine. You can sip cider at the little snackbar, and purchase mountain crafts and guidebooks. Five miles farther north, about 20 miles from Dahlonega, **Vogel State Park,** Blairsville, GA 30512 (tel. 404/745-2628), invites you to hike around pretty Lake Trahlyta, fish for bass and bream, canoe, and in summer have a refreshing swim. Nestled in the vale of soft-green mountains, campsites have power and water hookups, hot showers, and laundries. Cottages are comfortably furnished, with wood-burning fireplaces. Lodging charges are standardized throughout the state park system: rates are $8 a night for tent and pop-up camping, $8 for RV hookups; cottages cost $35 to $45 a night for a one-bedroom, $45 to $55 for a two-bedroom, and $55 to $65 for a three-bedroom, November 1 to March 31; and $34, $42, and $48 respectively, April 1 to October 31.

From Vogel, drive north five miles on U.S. 19 and head east on Ga. 180. At the junction of Ga. 180 and Ga. 348, either continue east to **Brasstown Bald Mountain,** or head south on Ga. 348 and drive across the spectacular Richard Russell Scenic Highway. Or you can have your Bald and your scenic highway, too. Drive on to **Brasstown,** and take the paved road to within 930 yards of the summit of Georgia's highest mountain (4,784 feet). At the parking area, you'll find picnic tables, vending machines, and scenic overlooks. The most panoramic views are from the very top, reached by hiking a woodland trail, or in summer by riding a minibus. The glass-enclosed visitors center on top has displays of mountain flora and fauna, and on clear days you can see across northern Georgia, into Tennessee and the Carolinas.

After exploring Brasstown, backtrack on Ga. 180, and head south on the **Richard Russell Scenic Highway.** Along the two-lane road's 16-mile course, stop several times to gaze across mountains and valleys. The drive is especially awesome in fall, when hardwoods blaze with colors. At 3,500-foot Tesnatee Gap, the highway crosses the Appalachian Trail. Park by the roadside and take a 10-minute walk among the earnest backpackers. Follow Ga. 348 to its dead-end at Ga. 75-Alt. Turn left and drive 2.3 miles to a dead-end at Ga. 17/75. Go right .3 mile, then left on Ga. 356 and 1½ miles into Unicoi State Park.

Unicoi State Park, P.O. Box 256, Helen, GA 30545 (tel. 404/878-2824), is even more beautiful than Vogel. Around a pristine lake, in the midst of 1,000 acres of woodlands, the heart of the park is the Unicoi Lodge and Conference Center. Warm and wood-beamed, the lodge has an excellent cafeteria-style dining room, serving three meals a day at very modest prices. There's also a gift shop stocked with mountain arts and crafts. Furnished cottages and campsites are tucked into the wooded hillsides.

Anna Ruby Falls is the scenic masterpiece of a 1,600-acre **Chattahoochee National Forest** recreation area adjoining Unicoi. From a paved parking area, it's an easy and very beautiful half-mile walk through the woods, by a rushing white-water stream, to an observation platform at the base of 153- and 50-foot cascades.

From Unicoi, drive two miles south into **Alpine Helen.** Once a quiet Appalachian village, Helen has been turned into a bit of Bavaria in the Georgia hills. Main Street buildings wear red roofs, flower boxes, balconies, and murals. You can shop for sweaters, porcelains, cuckoo clocks, and Christmas ornaments; enjoy wurst and beer to oom-pah music at an outdoor biergarten; and in September and October join the revelry of Oktoberfest. Numerous alpine-style hotels have comfortable accommodations and restaurants. More Appalachian than alpine, **Betty's Country Store,** at the north end of town (tel. 404/878-2943), serves sandwiches and chili, and it is a fun place to browse for mountain produce and cookbooks.

Five miles east of Helen on Ga. 255, the **Stovall House,** Rte. 1, Box 103-A, Sautee, GA 30571 (tel. 404/878-3355), is one of the prettiest country inns you'll ever happen onto. Under the stewardship of affable Ham and Kathy Schwartz, the circa-1837 farmhouse has five lovely guest rooms, furnished with antiques and all the modern comforts. Amenities include a wide veranda for leisurely rocking, and a restaurant serving first-rate southern, American, and continental dishes at moderate prices. Rooms are $30 single, $55 double; children 12 and under stay free with their parents.

Another 20 miles farther east, the Lake Rabun Hotel is another mountain gem. The lake itself may remind you of *On Golden Pond*. Ringed by mountains and summer cottages, dotted with canoes and sailboats, it is pure tranquility. Built in 1922, the **Lake Rabun Hotel,** Lakemont, GA 30552 (tel. 404/782-4946), is a 16-room wood-and-stone time warp. Knotty-pine rooms are filled with handmade rhododendron furniture, vintage photos, and piles of parlor games. There's no TV or room phones. The hospitality of owners Dick and Barbara Gray is legendary. During the day, you may hike the surrounding woodlands, and fish and canoe on the lake, and look forward to rehashing your adventures with fellow guests around the fireplace. Rates are an amazingly low $45 double. The hotel is open from April 1 to October 31.

---

2. Pine Mountain

Over on Georgia's western edge, almost at the Alabama line, there's a resort that comes close to qualifying as a philanthropic enterprise and makes an ideal headquarters for exploring points west and south of Atlanta.

Callaway Gardens, on U.S. 27 at Pine Mountain, were begun back in the '30s, and—like Colonial Williamsburg—every cent of profit generated by the resort is plowed back into development. In other words, the Callaway family, which built this beautiful place, derives no private gain at all from its operation, with all monies administered by a nonprofit, state-chartered foundation.

The gardens themselves are a fantastically complete collection of native plants and flowers, to which experimental gardening adds an exotic note. Recreational facilities include swimming and boating, 63 holes of golf on courses that serve as the site of the PGA National Junior Championships and the PGA Club Professional Championships, 19 tennis courts, fishing, biking, horseback trail riding, quail hunting, and skeet and trap shooting. And all this on 2,500 acres of what used to be abandoned, worn-out farmland.

This lovely resort is the result of one man's dedicated efforts to restore the natural beauty of the region and create a restful, scenic recreational environment for Georgia residents. Cason Callaway, head of one of Georgia's most prosperous textile mills, once said, "What I'm trying to do here is hang the picture a little higher on the wall for the people of this region. Every child ought to see something beautiful before he's six years old. . . . All I've done is try to fix it so that anybody who came here would see something beautiful wherever he might look." So well did he succeed that people from all over the world visit Callaway Gardens each year.

By rebuilding the soil, nurturing the plant life already there and importing more, building a sand beach that is the largest man-made inland beach in the world, providing inn and cottage accommodations, and opening it all to people of modest means, Cason Callaway did indeed "hang his picture a little higher"; and by the time of his death in 1961 thousands were walking the nature trails and making full use of the facilities he'd provided in a breathtaking scenic setting. And it would have gladdened his heart to see the busloads of school children that roll into the gardens each academic year for free horticultural, botanical, and nature-study educational programs sponsored by the foundation.

WHERE TO STAY

The best possible place to stay is at the gardens themselves. However, because of their popularity, reservations must be made as far in advance as possible —at least a month, longer if you can.

There are 350 rooms in the **Callaway Gardens Inn,** Pine Mountain, GA 31822 (tel. 404/663-2281, or toll free 800/282-8181), all spacious with a brightly colored, homey decor that seems just right for this setting. Two pools and a wading pool, nature programs, bicycles, fishing, and access to beach facilities are part of the package when you stay at Callaway Gardens. There are fees, however, for fishing, tennis, horseback riding, hunting, and skeet and trap (see "Things to See and Do," below). Rates are seasonal, with doubles ranging from $70 to $125.

In addition to the inn, there are the lovely **Mountain Creek Villas,** with fireplaces, screened porches or patios, and fully equipped with all cooking utensils and dishes, linens, televisions, and outdoor grills. The one-bedroom size will accommodate four adults, or a family of up to six (or eight if you squeeze a little). These are beautifully situated on wooded sites and make a great stopover on an extended trip or an ideal "home away from home" on a "stay put" vacation in this area. The same free family facilities apply to the cottages as at the inn. Cottages are available on a per-day basis any time except the summer months, when they are reserved for families only, on a weekly basis. For cottage rates and reservations, you should write well in advance to Central Reservations, Dept. R,

Callaway Gardens, Pine Mountain, GA 31822, or call 404/663-2281, or toll free 800/282-8181.

Note: Both the inn and the cottages have golf and tennis package deals, and both offer courtesy cars for transportation throughout the gardens.

Other Choices in the Area

Very close to Callaway Gardens, the **White Columns Motel,** Pine Mountain, GA 31822 (tel. 404/663-2312), is within walking distance of two good, moderately priced restaurants and is in a comfortable, convenient location, with the beach entrance to Callaway Gardens just a hop, skip, and a jump away. Rooms are attractive and come with cable TV. Rates at the White Columns vary from $30 to $45, seasonally, and they accept pets.

And at the little town of Hamilton, just five miles away, the **Valley Inn Resort,** Hwy. 27, Hamilton, GA 31811 (tel. 404/628-4454), is also a small, well-run motel with accommodations that are comfortably furnished, some with kitchens, and a pool and restaurant. Rates (which include admission to the gardens) range from $45 to $85 over the course of the year.

DINING AT THE GARDENS

There are five places to eat in the gardens themselves, all very good, with quite moderate prices. The **Plantation Room,** in the inn itself, is tastefully decorated in a country-dining-room style, with flowered wallpaper, deep carpets, and comfortable oak chairs. There's an à la carte menu and children's plates (with baked ham, fried chicken, roast beef, and the like), but it really outdoes itself in the three buffets each day. For breakfast there's an array of bacon, sausage, ham (all homemade), eggs, french toast, their own speckled heart grits, fresh berries and fruits (according to season), the beverage of your choice, and almost anything you can imagine—really a feast, and one of the best meals of the day at the inn. The lunch buffet and the one at dinner not only offer the meats mentioned above, but sometimes throw in continental dishes like crêpes and quiche. And on Friday, the evening Captain's Galley seafood buffet can only be called sumptuous. As for vegetables, well, they're the freshest, especially during the summer, when they come to the table just one or two hours after being picked in Mr. Cason's Vegetable Garden—and I've always found the seasonings excellent, with the taste of "southern" but without the overcooking that so often goes with it. If you've never eaten corn just pulled from the stalk, for example, you'll find out here that it's quite different from the "store-bought" kind pulled days before.

For intimate, candlelit dinners, the **Georgia Room** provides just the right elegant setting, with a continental menu and soft piano music.

The English Tudor–style **Gardens Restaurant** also has a country air, and it overlooks Mountain Creek Lake and the Lake View Golf Course. No breakfast here, but lunch (from 11:30 a.m. to 2 p.m.) is sometimes a soup-and-salad buffet (salads are a real specialty in this room, with ingredients coming from the vegetable garden in the summer), and there's always a good variety of hot dishes. At dinner (6:30 to 9:30 p.m.), the star of the menu, I think, is the French onion soup—delicious! Entrees usually include baked ham, chicken in one form or another, and one or two other meats (veal, lamb, etc.).

The Veranda is the place for dinner in a setting of casual charm.

Up in the country store, the **Country Kitchen** has a cozy, old-fashioned atmosphere and serves breakfast and lunch only (hours are 8:30 a.m. to 5 p.m., and they'll fix breakfast any time of the day). The ham, bacon, and sausage are homemade and the speckled heart grits are a trademark of the gardens and the Country Kitchen. Also, don't miss trying the many varieties of muscadine sauces, jams, and jellies that you'll find on your table. These are grown and manufactured right in the gardens. The luncheon menu features generous salads, hamburgers (big, juicy, and good), and the prices are slightly higher than, say, Burger King (only to be expected, since "hamburger" here means much more than meat on a bun).

Golf and tennis pro shops both have snackshops, with hot dogs, hamburgers, soft drinks, etc., at budget prices.

THINGS TO SEE AND DO

Callaway Gardens—which includes floral and hiking trails, a greenhouse complex, Pioneer Log Cabin, the Ida Cason Callaway Memorial Chapel (a lovely native-fieldstone and log structure by a waterfall on a small lake), Mr. Cason's Vegetable Garden, and acres of picnic grounds—has an admission price of $4 for adults and $1 for children 6 to 11 (children under 6, free). Of course, if you're a guest at the inn or the cottages, there's no charge.

The best place to start any exploration of the gardens is the **Information Center**, where an eight-minute slide show lets you get your bearings as to what is here, as well as giving you the fascinating history of this place. Spring is especially lovely, with more than 600 varieties of azaleas, but it doesn't matter what season it is when you enter the 5-acre **John A. Sibley Horticulture Center**, an innovative indoor-outdoor complex. **Mr. Cason's Vegetable Garden** comprises 7½ acres planted with fruits and vegetables, and the 160-year-old **Pioneer Log Cabin**, with authentic furnishings, paints a vivid picture of early settler life. The nondenominational **Ida Cason Callaway Memorial Chapel** (named for Cason Callaway's mother) is simplicity itself, yet quite elegant, with stained-glass windows depicting the seasons at the gardens. Organ concerts are scheduled throughout the year, marriages take place within its walls with comparative frequency, and it's open for a moment of quiet meditation at all times.

One of my favorite spots in the garden is the **Country Store** (actually, it isn't in the gardens, but close by the entrance). In fact, for several years following my trek north, I ordered three-pound slabs of their marvelous country-cured bacon sent to me in New York each month, where my family pronounced it "real" bacon, as opposed to the thin-sliced, "chip" bacon available in supermarkets. The bacon and cured ham, preserves, grits, water-ground cornmeal, and hundreds of other items, both locally made and imported, keep me window-shopping long after I've met the upper limits of my shopping budget.

As for recreation, if you're a day visitor in the summer, the charge is $9 for adults, $4 for ages 6 to 11 (no charge for those under 6), for admission to the **Robin Lake Beach.** That one price entitles you to swim (the sand beach is a man-made creation that rivals the things nature does herself), play miniature golf, use paddleboats for the deep water, and ride a riverboat, train, or canoe; as well as enjoy a Water Ski Spectacular and a "Flying High Circus," performed by members of the Florida State University troupe. These facilities, like the gardens, are free to guests at the inn or cottages.

Golfers will find three 18-hole courses as well as one 9-hole executive (par 31) course, with two pro shops and fees that run as follows: $20 to $25 for daily greens fees, $22 for power cart for 18 holes. Tennis courts (including eight Rubico and nine all-weather) cost $12 and $10, respectively, per hour.

Fishing (with artificial lures only) is available at $12 per person for a half day (includes boat with electric trolling motor), $22 for two people, and $32 for three.

Hunters can go for quail on a large preserve that's open from October 1 to March 31 for $125 for a half day (which includes guides and dogs) if they have the required Georgia hunting license—and there's skeet and trap shooting every day at the hunting preserve for $3 per round, plus shells (no charge for guns). The ranges are lit for night shooting.

---

3. Plains and Other Area Attractions

This corner of Georgia has had special significance for two U.S. presidents. Franklin D. Roosevelt retreated to his "Little White House" at Warm Springs for spiritual and physical refreshment, and Jimmy Carter was born in Plains, a little town that often didn't even appear on state maps. Both are within easy sightseeing distance from Callaway Gardens, which I recommend as the overnight base. In addition, Columbus is just 30 miles away, with antebellum and Victorian homes, plus an opera house dating from the Civil War that was rescued from decay and destruction by city citizens. An infamous Civil War prison camp, Andersonville, is just a day trip away; you'll also find a restored 1850s village, Westville; and, in between, driving is made a pleasure by scenery that varies from mountains to rolling plains, from wooded areas to prosperous farms.

WARM SPRINGS

Just 17 miles from Callaway Gardens (take Ga. 190 and follow the signs) is the simple white wooden house that was FDR's **"Little White House."** He had discovered Warm Springs as far back as 1924, shortly after he contracted polio, when he went there for the beneficial effect of swimming in the warm spring water; then in 1926 he bought the springs, hotel, and some cottages and began developing facilities to help paralytic patients from all over the country through the Georgia Warm Springs Foundation, which he founded. Later, when he became president, this was the retreat he loved most, and the house you visit today is much as he left it when he suffered a massive cerebral hemorrhage in 1945 and died while sitting for a portrait in the Warm Springs cottage. The unfinished portrait (by artist Elizabeth Shoumatoff), his wheelchair, Fala's dog chain, ship models, sea paintings, and gifts from citizens of which he was particularly fond are preserved as he last saw them.

Next door on the historic site, the **Franklin D. Roosevelt Museum** (tel. 404/655-3511) holds more memorabilia and shows a 12-minute movie depicting his life when in Warm Springs. The Little White House is open daily from 9 a.m. to 5 p.m. (closed Thanksgiving and Christmas Days), and admission fees of $3 for adults, $1.50 for ages 6 to 12, cover both.

PLAINS

Jimmy Carter, 39th president of the U.S., was born 80 miles southeast of the Gardens (U.S. 27 south to Columbus, then Ga. 280 east). You'll know Plains by the little green-and-white train depot, the water tower brightly painted with the stars and stripes. Despite the fame of its most outstanding citizens, there is still a small-town charm that clings to both the town and the people. The early 1900s buildings are much like they were before the depression of the '30s forced their closing (most were used as warehouses until Jimmy Carter's campaign got under way and brought business back to town). Turner's Hardware and Walters Grocery Store are longtime establishments. The depot (built in 1888) now houses a visitors center and a gift and book shop, but its looks haven't changed a great deal. All in all, Plains can be proud of the common sense that has recognized the importance of preserving the surroundings from which a rural peanut grower went out and became president of the U.S.

Of course, you can almost stand in the middle of "downtown" and see the whole town, but for do-it-yourself walking or driving tours, go by the **Plains Visitor Center,** east of Plains on U.S. 280, where Sibyl McGlaun and her very friendly staff will furnish maps and brochures. If you'd like advance information, write them at P.O. Box 69, Plains, GA 31780. Two publications I particularly liked (and have had fun reading even after coming home) are "Plains, Carter Country U.S.A." and "Armchair Tour of Jimmy Carter Country," both of which I picked up at the depot.

The one-story, ranch-style brick house that is **Carter home,** home of our former chief executive, is on Woodland Drive, and when the Carters are in residence, there are Secret Service booths at both this entrance and the one on Paschal Street (you can get a pretty good look at it by walking or driving west on Church Street). Then there's the **Plains Methodist Church,** at the corner of Church and Thomas, where Jimmy asked Rosalynn for their first date. When he's in town, Jimmy teaches Sunday school at Maranatha Baptist Church. Visitors are invited—check the notice in the window of Hugh Carter's Antiques on Main Street. If you want to see an even *more* rural, now-historic site, take a 2½-mile drive out to **Archery,** where Jimmy Carter lived as a child when his father operated a country store. It's west of town on U.S. 280 (it's really *off* U.S. 280, but anybody in town can give you explicit directions).

In nearby **Americus,** on the grounds of Georgia Southwestern College, Wheatly and Glessner streets (tel. 912/928-1273), the **James Earl Carter Library** holds a permanent display of memorabilia of the Carter family, with the focus on the former president and his first lady.

The **Plains Bed and Breakfast,** P.O. Box 217, Plains, GA 31780 (tel. 912/824-7252), is the Victorian home where Jimmy Carter's parents spent their early married life. Now operated by affable Grace Jackson, the four guest rooms have private baths and turn-of-the-century furnishings; breakfast is included in the rates of $50 to $55.

ANDERSONVILLE

Twenty miles northeast of Plains (U.S. 280 to Americus, then Ga. 49 north) is a national historic site that marks the most infamous of Confederate prison camps. Conditions at Andersonville were unspeakably horrible, with severe overcrowding (it was built to hold 10,000, but had at one time a prisoner population of over 32,000), polluted water (from a creek), and starvation rations which led to nearly 15,000 deaths. The commander, Capt. Henry Wirtz, although powerless to prevent the fatalities and an absolute victim of circumstances he had no way of controlling, was tried and hanged after the Civil War on charges of having conspired to murder Union prisoners of war. Today you can visit a small museum, see slide shows on the camp's sad history, see the remains of wells and escape tunnels, and see Providence Springs, which legend says gushed up in answer to prayers of prisoners during the drought of 1864. The site is open daily, and there's no admission charge.

After visiting the historic site, browse the antique shops in the adjacent village of Andersonville. Stop by the **visitors center** in the old train depot and meet Peggy Sheppard, a gregarious transplanted New Yorker who spearheaded the village's rejuvenation. Also, see the fascinating Civil War artifacts at the **Little Drummer Boy Museum.**

The small town of **Montezuma,** 12 miles north of Andersonville, is the center of an 85-family Mennonite dairy-farming community. You may enjoy Pennsylvania Dutch–style roast beef and shoo-fly pie, and first-class southern cooking, at **Yoder's Dietsch Haus** on Ga. 26, 3 miles east of Montezuma (tel. 912/472-2024). This clean-as-a-whistle cafeteria is open for breakfast, lunch, and dinner Monday through Saturday, and also has a too-tempting bread and pastry shop.

WESTVILLE

An intriguing day trip from Callaway Gardens is the 50-mile drive south on U.S. 27 to Lumpkin and the little village of Westville, a restored 1850s town with unpaved streets, 19th-century buildings and homes, and craftsmen who demonstrate such oldtime skills as syrup-making, cotton-ginning, and blacksmithing. It's open every day except major holidays from 10 a.m. to 5 p.m. during the week, 1 to 5 p.m. on Sunday; and admission is $3.50 for adults, $1.50 for students, no charge for preschoolers.

COLUMBUS

This was the last frontier town of the original 13 colonies, and its wide streets (99 to 164 feet), shaded by marvelous old trees in grass plots, still reveal much of the original city plan of 1828. Situated on the Chattahoochee River at the foot of a series of falls, Columbus early utilized its water supply to become an important manufacturing center, supplying swords, pistols, cannon, gunboats, and other articles of war to the Confederate Army during the Civil War (it fell to Union forces in April of 1865 in one of the last battles of the war). Today there's a lovely riverside walkway, the **Columbus Chattahoochee Promenade,** with gazebos and historical displays, stretching from the Columbus Iron Works Trade and Convention Center to Oglethorpe Bridge, which is open from 10 a.m. to 5 p.m. Tuesday through Friday and 1 to 5 p.m. on Saturday and Sunday. The **Columbus Chamber of Commerce,** 901 Front Ave. (tel. 404/327-1566), and the **Georgia Welcome Center,** Victory Drive and Tenth Avenue (tel. 404/571-7455), can furnish detailed sightseeing information. **Heritage Tours** leave (from the Hilton Hotel) on Wednesday and Saturday at 10 a.m. for two-hour guided tours that visit the **Springer Opera House** (a restored 1871 theater in which Edwin Booth and other distinguished actors performed, and which was refurbished by Columbians to become a cultural center once again) and several other historic houses. The tour fee is $5 for adults, $2.50 for ages 6 through 12.

Fort Benning (tel. 404/545-2958) is five miles south of the city on U.S. 27, and there is an interesting **National Infantry Museum** reflecting the history of the foot soldier from Revolutionary days up to the present. It's free, and open weekdays except Monday from 10 a.m. to 4:30 p.m., from 12:30 p.m. on Saturday and Sunday.

If you're staying overnight, the **Columbus Hilton,** 800 Front Ave., Columbus, GA 31901 (tel. 404/324-1800), adjoins the Iron Works Convention Center. One wing of the 178-room hotel was part of the brick and wood-beamed Empire Mills complex. Doubles are $60 to $90. In the historic district, the **DeLoffre House,** 812 Broadway, Columbus, GA 31901 (tel. 404/324-1144), is a cozy inn with four antique-filled guest rooms, fireplaces, and all the modern amenities. Doubles are $55 to $65.

INDEX

NOW, SAVE MONEY ON ALL YOUR TRAVELS!
Join Frommer's™ Dollarwise® Travel Club

Saving money while traveling is never a simple matter, which is why, over 29 years ago, the **Dollarwise Travel Club** was formed. Actually, the idea came from readers of the Frommer publications who felt that such an organization could bring financial benefits, continuing travel information, and a sense of community to value-conscious travelers all over the world.

In keeping with the money-saving concept, the annual membership fee is low—$18 (U.S. residents) or $20 U.S. (Canadian, Mexican, and other foreign residents)—and is immediately exceeded by the value of your benefits which include:

1. The latest edition of any TWO of the books listed on the following pages.
2. A copy of any one Frommer City Guide.
3. An annual subscription to an 8-page quarterly newspaper, *The Dollarwise Traveler*, which keeps you up-to-date on fast-breaking developments in good-value travel in all parts of the world—bringing you the kind of information you'd have to pay over $35 a year to obtain elsewhere. This consumer-conscious publication also includes the following columns:
   Hospitality Exchange—members all over the world who are willing to provide hospitality to other members as they pass through their home cities.
   Share-a-Trip—requests from members for travel companions who can share costs and help avoid the burdensome single supplement.
   Readers Ask . . . Readers Reply—travel questions from members to which other members reply with authentic firsthand information.
4. Your personal membership card, which entitles you to purchase through the club all Frommer publications for a third to a half off their regular retail prices during the term of your membership.

So why not join this hardy band of international Dollarwise travelers now and participate in its exchange of information and hospitality? Simply send $18 (U.S. residents) or $20 U.S. (Canadian, Mexican, and other foreign residents) along with your name and address to: Frommer's Dollarwise Travel Club, Inc., 15 Columbus Circle, New York, NY 10023. Remember to specify which *two* of the books in section (1) and which *one* in section (2) above you wish to receive in your initial package of member's benefits. Or tear out the next page, check off your choices, and send the page to us with your membership fee.

FROMMER BOOKS
PRENTICE HALL TRAVEL
15 COLUMBUS CIRCLE
NEW YORK, NY 10023

Date_____

Friends:
Please send me the books checked below:

FROMMER™ GUIDES

(Guides to sightseeing and tourist accommodations and facilities from budget to deluxe, with emphasis on the medium-priced.)

☐ Alaska	$14.95	☐ Japan & Hong Kong	$13.95
☐ Australia	$14.95	☐ Mid-Atlantic States	$14.95
☐ Austria & Hungary	$14.95	☐ New England	$14.95
☐ Belgium, Holland & Luxembourg	$14.95	☐ New York State	$14.95
☐ Bermuda & The Bahamas	$14.95	☐ Northwest	$14.95
☐ Brazil	$14.95	☐ Portugal, Madeira & the Azores	$13.95
☐ Canada	$14.95	☐ Skiing Europe	$14.95
☐ Caribbean	$14.95	☐ Skiing USA—East	$13.95
☐ Cruises (incl. Alaska, Carib, Mex, Hawaii, Panama, Canada & US)	$14.95	☐ Skiing USA—West	$13.95
		☐ South Pacific	$14.95
☐ California & Las Vegas	$14.95	☐ Southeast Asia	$14.95
☐ England & Scotland	$14.95	☐ Southern Atlantic States	$14.95
☐ Egypt	$13.95	☐ Southwest	$14.95
☐ Florida	$14.95	☐ Switzerland & Liechtenstein	$14.95
☐ France	$14.95	☐ Texas	$13.95
☐ Germany	$14.95	☐ USA	$15.95
☐ Italy	$14.95		

FROMMER $-A-DAY® GUIDES

(In-depth guides to sightseeing and low-cost tourist accommodations and facilities.)

☐ Europe on $40 a Day	$15.95	☐ New York on $60 a Day	$13.95
☐ Australia on $30 a Day	$12.95	☐ New Zealand on $40 a Day	$13.95
☐ Eastern Europe on $25 a Day	$13.95	☐ Scandinavia on $60 a Day	$13.95
☐ England on $50 a Day	$13.95	☐ Scotland & Wales on $40 a Day	$13.95
☐ Greece on $30 a Day	$13.95	☐ South America on $35 a Day	$13.95
☐ Hawaii on $60 a Day	$13.95	☐ Spain & Morocco on $40 a Day	$13.95
☐ India on $25 a Day	$12.95	☐ Turkey on $30 a Day	$13.95
☐ Ireland on $35 a Day	$13.95	☐ Washington, D.C. & Historic Va. on	
☐ Israel on $40 a Day	$13.95	$40 a Day	$13.95
☐ Mexico on $35 a Day	$13.95		

FROMMER TOURING GUIDES

(Color illustrated guides that include walking tours, cultural & historic sites, and other vital travel information.)

☐ Australia	$9.95	☐ Paris	$8.95
☐ Egypt	$8.95	☐ Scotland	$9.95
☐ Florence	$8.95	☐ Thailand	$9.95
☐ London	$8.95	☐ Venice	$8.95

TURN PAGE FOR ADDITONAL BOOKS AND ORDER FORM.

A

FROMMER CITY GUIDES

(Pocket-size guides to sightseeing and tourist accommodations and facilities in all price ranges.)

☐ Amsterdam/Holland	$5.95	☐ Minneapolis/St. Paul	$5.95
☐ Athens	$5.95	☐ Montréal/Québec City	$5.95
☐ Atlantic City/Cape May	$5.95	☐ New Orleans	$5.95
☐ Belgium	$5.95	☐ New York	$5.95
☐ Boston	$5.95	☐ Orlando/Disney World/EPCOT	$5.95
☐ Cancún/Cozumel/Yucatán	$5.95	☐ Paris	$5.95
☐ Chicago	$5.95	☐ Philadelphia	$5.95
☐ Dublin/Ireland	$5.95	☐ Rio	$5.95
☐ Hawaii	$5.95	☐ Rome	$5.95
☐ Las Vegas	$5.95	☐ San Francisco	$5.95
☐ Lisbon/Madrid/Costa del Sol	$5.95	☐ Santa Fe/Taos/Albuquerque	$5.95
☐ London	$5.95	☐ Sydney	$5.95
☐ Los Angeles	$5.95	☐ Washington, D.C.	$5.95
☐ Mexico City/Acapulco	$5.95		

SPECIAL EDITIONS

☐ A Shopper's Guide to the Caribbean	$12.95	☐ Manhattan's Outdoor Sculpture	$15.95
☐ Beat the High Cost of Travel	$6.95	☐ Motorist's Phrase Book (Fr/Ger/Sp)	$4.95
☐ Bed & Breakfast—N. America	$11.95	☐ Paris Rendez-Vous	$10.95
☐ California with Kids	$14.95	☐ Swap and Go (Home Exchanging)	$10.95
☐ Caribbean Hideaways	$14.95	☐ The Candy Apple (NY with Kids)	$12.95
☐ Guide to Honeymoon Destinations		☐ Travel Diary and Record Book	$5.95
(US, Canada, Mexico & Carib.)	$12.95		

☐ Where to Stay USA (Lodging from $3 to $30 a night) $10.95

☐ Marilyn Wood's Wonderful Weekends (NY, Conn, Mass, RI, Vt, NH, NJ, Del,Pa) $11.95

☐ The New World of Travel (Annual sourcebook by Arthur Frommer previewing: new travel trends, new modes of travel, and the latest cost-cutting strategies for savvy travelers.) $14.95

SERIOUS SHOPPER'S GUIDES

(Illustrated guides listing hundreds of stores, conveniently organized alphabetically by category.)

☐ Italy	$15.95	☐ Los Angeles	$14.95
☐ London	$15.95	☐ Paris	$15.95

GAULT MILLAU

(The only guides that distinguish the truly superlative from the merely overrated.)

☐ The Best of Chicago	$15.95	☐ The Best of Los Angeles	$14.95
☐ The Best of France	$16.95	☐ The Best of New England	$15.95
☐ The Best of Hong Kong	$16.95	☐ The Best of New York	$14.95
☐ The Best of Italy	$16.95	☐ The Best of San Francisco	$14.95

☐ The Best of Washington, D.C. $14.95

ORDER NOW!

In U.S. include $2 shipping UPS for 1st book; $1 ea. add'l book. Outside U.S. $3 and $1, respectively.

Allow four to six weeks for delivery in U.S., longer outside U.S.

Enclosed is my check or money order for $_____

NAME_____

ADDRESS_____

CITY_____ STATE_____ ZIP_____

A